1 MONTH OF
FREE
READING

at

www.ForgottenBooks.com

By purchasing this book you are eligible for one month membership to ForgottenBooks.com, giving you unlimited access to our entire collection of over 1,000,000 titles via our web site and mobile apps.

To claim your free month visit:

www.forgottenbooks.com/free922343

ISBN 978-0-260-01501-3
PIBN 10922343

PORTA
LINGUARUM ORIENTALIUM

INCHOAVIT

J. H. PETERMANN

CONTINUAVIT

HERM. L. STRACK.

ELEMENTA LINGUARUM

**HEBRAICAE, PHOENICIAE, BIBLICO-ARAMAICAE, TARGUMICAE,
SAMARITANAE, SYRIACAE, ARABICAE, AETHIOPICAE,
ASSYRIACAE, AEGYPTIACAE, COPTICAE, ARMENIACAE,
PERSICAE, TURCICAE,**

ALIARUM

STUDIIS ACADEMICIS ACCOMMODAVERUNT

**J. H. PETERMANN, H. L. STRACK, E. NESTLE, A. SOCIN,
F. PRAETORIUS, AD. MERX, AUG. MUELLER, FRIEDR.
DELITZSCH, C. SALEMAN, W. SHUKOWSKI,
G. JACOB, ALII.**

PARS V.
GRAMMATICA SYRIACA

EDITIO ALTERA AUCTA ET EMENDATA

SCRIPSIT

DR. EBERARDUS NESTLE.

BERLIN,
H. REUTHER'S VERLAGSBUCHHANDLUNG.

LONDON,	NEW YORK,	PARIS,
WILLIAMS & NORGATE	**B. WESTERMANN & Co.**	**MAISONNEUVE**
14, HENRIETTA STREET	838, BROADWAY.	**& CH. LECLERC**
COVENT GARDEN.		25, QUAI VOLTAIRE.

1889.

SYRIAC GRAMMAR

WITH

BIBLIOGRAPHY, CHRESTOMATHY AND GLOSSARY

BY

Dr. EBERHARD NESTLE.

SECOND ENLARGED AND IMPROVED EDITION

OF THE

BREVIS LINGUÆ SYRIACÆ GRAMMATICA.

TRANSLATED FROM THE GERMAN

BY

ARCHD. R. S. KENNEDY, B. D.,

PROF. OF ORIENTAL LANGUAGES, UNIV. OF ABERDEEN.

BERLIN,
H. REUTHER'S VERLAGSBUCHHANDLUNG.

LONDON,   NEW YORK,   PARIS,
WILLIAMS & NORGATE   B. WESTERMANN & Co.   MAISONNEUVE
14, HENRIETTA STREET,   838, BROADWAY.   & CH. LECLERC
COVENT GARDEN.   25, QUAI VOLTAIRE.

1889.

PREFACE TO THE GERMAN EDITION.

Had I alone been concerned, I should not have undertaken a new edition of the Syriac Porta. For what we need for Syriac, as for most other Semitic languages, is the investigation of *special* questions, linguistic, historic and other, similar to those which de Lagarde has given us on the figtree and Astarte or Wellhausen on the remains of Arabic heathendom, and not fresh presentations of what everybody knows. Moreover, since the appearance of the first edition (1881), I have ceased to have occasion to lecture on Syriac. On the other hand, the speedy sale of my book showed me that it really supplied a want, and accordingly I have done what I could for the new edition. Like other parts of the Porta, the Syriac grammar no longer appears in Latin but in German and English—which explains the arrangement of the second half of the book. The part comprising the *Grammar*, notwithstanding the addition of a few observations on the Syntax, occupies less space than in the first edition. As regards the *Bibliography,* I thought

first of omitting almost entirely sections I and II
(pp. 3—30), retaining only such books as are still of
importance; finally, however, I resolved to make the
bibliography in these and the other divisions as complete as possible. Somewhere, it seems to me, one
ought to find such a record of the labours of our
predecessors. Up to p. 30, books which I have not seen
myself are indicated as before by an asterisk. The diffi-
culties with which I had to contend, in having to work
at a distance from a library, can only be understood
by those who are similarly situated; even Klatt's Bibliography was not accessible. On the other hand I
have here to thank a number of friends, particularly
abroad, most of them personally unknown to me, who
have helped me by sending me their publications, a
number of which will be found in the "appendicula";
I would specially thank Prof. I. H. Hall of New York
for the aid he has rendered me in the Bibliography.
This section of the book, large enough as it is, I
could easily have increased in one direction at least,
for I have made a practice of noting down all the
reviews with which I have become acquainted; of
these, however, I have only occasionally cited one or
two, it being still worth while to see, for example,
what a scholar like de Sacy had to say to the elder
Hoffmann in 11 pages of the Journal des Savants.
From A. Müller's new Oriental Bibliography (I, 1—3)
I might have added a few more titles; I mention the

following as having been overlooked: Baethgen, F.,
Siebenzehn makkabäische Psalmen nach Theodor von
Mopsuestia ZfdatW. 87, 1—60; Cardahi, Gabriel,
Al-Lobab. Dictionnaire syriaque-arabe. Vol. 1 [Con-
tient les onze premières lettres.] Beyrouth, impr.
catholique 1887. fr. 30. — Wright, W., Notulae
Syriacae [Cambridge] Christmas 1887. "Only 150
copies printed for private circulation." 15 pages.

In the *Chrestomathy* I have retained the first
four chapters of Genesis, notwithstanding the ob-
jections raised by Socin; such translations are ex-
ceptionally well adapted for a comparative study both
of the vocabulary and of the grammar (with the exception of the Syntax), in the same way as the four
versions of the Psalter so conveniently arranged by
de Lagarde for Arabic. A systematic comparison of
the versions of the bible would give us more and fuller
information concerning the relation of the Semitic
idioms, as regards their respective vocabularies, than
the stray observations and notes on which we have
hitherto had to rely. — The extract from the N. T.
occupies more space with the Leipzig types, than I
could calculate from the American impression from
which it is taken; still an extract pointed in this
way was needed to familiarise the student with the
Nestorian punctuation, particularly the distinction
between ܲ and ܸ, é.

In this edition I have given the *Vitæ Prophetarum*

in full, notwithstanding their somewhat unattractive contents. With regard to these fragments it has quite recently been suggested that the Syriac texts are the original, the Greek texts only a translation. The latter, in different recensions as in Syriac, will be found—not reckoning the editions of Epiphanius (*e. g.* Migne vol. 43, not in Dindorf's edition)—in Tischendorf's Anecdota 110, in the Journ. of the Exeget. Society 1887, 1 ff. by Hall; best, however, in the cod. vat. 2125 (Marchalianus!).

Of the legends of the *finding of the Cross* I give two new recensions with appendix, for which I am indebted to the kindness of Wright, Martin and Bickell. I still hope to fulfil the promise I made in the preface to the first edition, to publish a collection of the various fragments. I have left the text precisely as it is given in the manuscripts; *e. g.* in 113, 12. 116, 57. 117, 78. 124, 222. 131, 76. The extracts· in the first edition from Jacob of Edessa (Severus) and Daniel of Salach, I have here omitted as being too difficult; all the words of the first edition, however, have been retained in the glossary, which has in consequence become more comprehensive, and has unfortunately, I cannot doubt, brought with it many of the mistakes of the earlier edition.

There will also, no doubt, be things in the grammar which need change or correction [*v.* below]. In § 3 I regret not to have done Jacob of Edessa the honour to adduce his mnemonic sentence عَتَشـه يِـشـه أَمَّ ادّمي (BH Gr. 1, 194/5); for the Nestorian cf. de Lagarde, Mittheilungen 2, 27. 183 . . . . Nestorian 'Abdīšō' (p. 25, n. 1) appears to stand under Arabic influence. § 25, 3 b cf. de Lagarde, Agathangelus 133, n. 2, where, however, the influence of *r* seems to be overlooked . . . I hope also, that the printing, which, towards the close, had to be done very hastily, will be found pretty correct.

Ulm a. D., 18. April 1888.

————

The English edition of the Syriac Grammar has had the benefit of a revision of the proofs by Prof. G. Hoffmann of Kiel. Some of his remarks have already been inserted in the text, others I am allowed to put together here:

§ 2. The name Estrangela H. explains on the ground of Fihrist 1, 12, 11 اسطرنجيلا = στρογγύλη (χειρ) *i. e.* the oldest bookwriting as opposed to still older forms of writing *e. g.* the כְּתָב מְרֻבָּע of the stone-inscriptions. The passages of Bar Ali and Bar Bahlul (Payne Smith) go all back to Išo'bar Nun of the 9th cent., who already combined Estrang(e)lāyā with "Evangelium", but wrongly, because he did not under-

stand the word. ܣܛܝܐ meaning "Linear- oder Kritzel-
schrift" has nothing to do with it. Paule (sic) bar
'Anqa of Edessa (عَنْقَاء the Arabic name of the bird
Phoenix), perhaps a brother of the Petros bar 'Anqa,
who is known as a copyist of MSS. in the 6ᵗʰ and 7ᵗʰ
centuries (Wright, Catal. 474) seems to have written
in the ܟܣܢܐ ܩܦܘܕܝܐ, propably a cloister of the Cap-
padocians (of Armenia, *v.* de Lagarde, Abhandlungen
254), from which this mode of writing has also the name
ܩܦܘܕܝܐ (de Lagarde, Praetermissa 96). Regarding
the dissemination of Syriac in Armenia *v.* Hoffmann,
Kirchenversammlung in Ephesus 12, 40 (the Armenians
had a school in Edessa) [and Agathangelus ed. de
Lagarde 77, 5].

For كارشونى (Arabic ܣ = ܢ = ܓ) we find in
Wright Catal. 3, 1302 ܓܪܣܘܢ; elsewhere (Land, Anecd.
1, 11) *gerisoni;* cf. also Assomani in P. Smith 790.
The Syrians called themselves as exiles in a strange
land Gersonides after Moses among the Midianites.

§ 3. The chief point as to the Nestorian vocalization is this, that the Nestorians, besides short $e =$
ε, had also long $e = \eta$, ⸗ or ⸗; BH understands by
⸗ the *e* which according to later and West-Syrian
pronunciation had become *i*. Many examples of long
ē, in Mss. and in the writings of BH, but not as yet
noticed with sufficient accuracy.

§ 11. With the modern Nestorians when reading the Pešiṭtâ, the stress-accent of an isolated word keeps its proper place; but the accentuation of the sentence displaces it as in Neo-Syriac. In both cases very often the ultimate is accentuated, *e. g.* in nouns and verbs *ūn, ān, īn, ēn, īt^h* (adv.): *ainaihún, qiṭlil^h, heidín* &c.

§ 15. Syriac verse proves the contrary; even the ancient Syrians certainly pronounced two consonants at the beginning sans gêne, *mlēk^h* &c.; ܐܣܝܪ *ḥrēn*; cf. also foreign words like ܡܕܠܩ, ܟܘܡܣܗܐ, ܦܪܘܣܝܡܝܢ.

p. 29, n. 1. ܡܡܘܢ, Μαμμων seems to be a foreign word from the Phoenician מנם *"money"*; compare the inscription of Ešmûnazar (Corp. Inscrr. Scm. n. 3, p. 14, 5) and that of תבנת (*"Tabnit"*, Rev. Arch. 1887, p. 2) וכל מנם *"and (or) any money"*; מנם perhaps — νομι(σ)μα.

§ 40 a that the verbs ܦ have passed into ܩ is the old view; mine is, that ܩ is older and ܘ in the Anlaut in Syriac and Arabic a later formation.

Thus far G. Hoffmann; of others of his remarks I may perhaps make use on another occasion.

In the Bibliography add to p. 20, 37 c cf. Bensly, The missing fragment of the Latin translation of the fourth book of Ezra (Cambridge 1875) p. 3 n.

p. 23 (cf. 64) Bagster's Syriac N. T. appeared first 1828. 568 pp.; then frequently without date.

For other omissions *v.* The Independent (New-York) July 19. 1888. p. 17; for new books A. Müller, Orientalische Bibliographie, Berlin, Reuther.

It would be ungracious of me not to express, in conclusion, my indebtedness to Prof. Kennedy for the pains he has taken with the translation and for his assistance in correcting the proofs.

Ulm a. D., 15. Oct. 1888.

E. Nestle.

Table of Contents.

Grammar.

Litteratura Syriaca.

Chrestomathia.

Glossarium.

Syriac, *i. e.* the language of the Christian Ara- 1
maeans, who had their headquarters in Edessa in [a]
northern Mesopotamia, is, in the first place, *histor-*
ically important, since it was through the medium of
Syriac literature that christian and philosophic learning
passed to the Arabs and Persians, and even to India
and China. In the second place, as a member of the
North-Semitic group of languages, Syriac has a certain
linguistic importance, which would only be enhanced,
if what holds good in the department of Teutonic philology, viz: that the Low, as opposed to the High,
German represents an earlier linguistic development,
should be proved to hold good also in Semitic philology. Such, at all events, appears to be the relation of
Aramaic to Hebrew and Phœnician.

Cf. Ταῦρος—the name of a mountain in Asia Minor—
with Aramaic טור, Hebr. (Phœn.) צור; Lagarde, Mitteilungen
I, 60.

Moreover, although Syriac as a national language [b]
has been supplanted by the speech of the Arab in-
vaders, it is still spoken—in a much altered form,
it is true—in certain localities, *c. g.* on the shores

of Lake Urumiyah, on the Tur'abdin (mountain of the monks) and here and there in the Lebanon district. Consequently it affords, even more than Hebrew, material for the investigations of the linguistic historian.

Regarding Neo-Syriac *v.* especially Th. Nöldeke, Grammatik der neusyrischen Sprache am Urmiasee und in Kurdistan. Leipz. 1868. A. Socin und E. Prym, Der neu-aramäische Dialekt des Turabdin. Göttingen 1881. A. Socin, Die neu-aramäischen Dialekte von Urmia bis Mosul. Texte und Übersetzungen. Tüb. 1882. *11*, 224 S. 4⁰. ZDMG. 21, 183.

c   Although a few traces of different dialects may still be found, the distinction between the eastern or Nestorian and the western or Jacobite tradition is rather that of different schools, as in Hebrew, than of real dialects.

I. ORTHOGRAPHY AND PHONOLOGY.
(§§ 2—18.)

A. ORTHOGRAPHY. (§§ 2—13.)

2
a   The Jacobite character, now most frequently employed in Syriac printed books, is rather a cursive character, while the Nestorians have more faithfully preserved the old uncial forms of the so-called Estran-

ge l o. The 22 letters of the Syriac alphabet[1] are read and written from right to left, and assume somewhat different forms according as they are joined to the letter preceding, or to the letter following, or to both. It was at one time usual in some cases to write from the top downwards by turning the page to the left through an angle of 90°.

The names, forms, sounds and numerical value of the Syriac letters are given in the accompanying table.

The names of the letters (ܚܶܬ̈ܟ, ܐܳܠܰܦ) are almost *b* the same as in Hebrew (cf. esp. Hebr. *Rēš* not *Rōš*, Nöldeke ZDMG. 32, 592); for ܐܳܠܰܦ *âlaf* we find also ܐܠܶܦ *alef*, ܕܳܠܰܕ *dâlad* alongside of ܕܳܠܰܬ *dâlat*. Ligatures are scarcely to be found; we note here only ܦ *l + âlaf*, ܠ *âlaf + l*, and X *l* at the end of a word joined to the initial *âlaf* of the next.

The earliest traces of this special Syriac character, *c* which has a common origin with that of Palmyra, are apparently to be met with on coins of Edessa dating from the first Christian century. In the manuscripts that are still extant, the oldest of which, now in the British Museum, is dated Edessa 411 A.D., we find two, and even three, forms of the Syriac character:

---

[1] Elias of Tirhan gives the number as 30, obtained by adding the 6 aspirated letters b g d k p t and the Gk. γ and π.

Aa

Name	Form				Value	
	not joined	joined			phonetic	nume-rical
		to letter pre-ceding	to pre-ceding a. follg.	to letter follewg.		
ܐܠܦ *Álaf*	۱ ܐ	۱ ܐ	—	—	' spiritus lenis	1
ܒܝܬ *Bēth*	ܒ ܒ	ܒ ܒ	ܒ ܒ	ܒ ܒ	b, β	2
ܓܡܠ *Gâmal*	ܓ ܓ	ܓ ܓ	ܓ ܓ	ܓ ܓ	g, γ	3
ܕܠܬ *Dâlath*	? ܕ	? ܕ	—	—	d, δ	4
ܗܐ *He*	ܗ ܗ	ܗ ܗ	—	—	h	5
ܘܘ *Vav*	ܘ ܘ	ܘ ܘ	—	—	v, w'	6
ܙܐ *Zain*	۱ ܙ	۱ ܙ	—	—	z in zero	7
ܚܬ *Cheth*	ܚ ܚ	ܚ ܚ	ܚ ܚ	ܚ ܚ	ch, ḥ	8
ܛܬ *Ṭeth*	ܛ ܛ	ܛ ܛ	ܛ ܛ	ܛ ܛ	ṭ	9
ܝܘܕ *Yud*	ܝ ܝ	ܝ ܝ	ܝ ܝ	ܝ ܝ	y	10
ܟܦ *Kâf*	ܟ ܟ	ܟ ܟ	ܟ ܟ	ܟ ܟ	k, χ	20
ܠܡܕ *Lâmadh*	ܠ ܠ	ܠ ܠ	ܠ ܠ	ܠ ܠ	l	30
ܡܝܡ *Mīm*	ܡ ܡ	ܡ ܡ	ܡ ܡ	ܡ ܡ	m	40
ܢܘܢ *Nūn*	ܢ ܢ	ܢ ܢ	ܢ ܢ	ܢ ܢ	n	50
ܣܡܟܬ *Semkath*	ܣ ܣ	ܣ ܣ	ܣ ܣ	ܣ ܣ	s	60
ܥܐ *'E*	ܥ ܥ	ܥ ܥ	ܥ ܥ	ܥ ܥ	' guttural sound	70
ܦܐ *Pē*	ܦ ܦ	ܦ ܦ	ܦ ܦ	ܦ ܦ	p, f	80
ܨܕܐ *Ṣâde*	ܨ ܨ	ܨ ܨ	—	—	ṣ emphatic	90
ܩܘܦ *Qūf*	ܩ ܩ	ܩ ܩ	ܩ ܩ	ܩ ܩ	q	100
ܪܝܫ *Rīsh*	? ܪ	? ܪ	—	—	r	200
ܫܝܢ *Shīn*	ܫ ܫ	ܫ ܫ	ܫ ܫ	ܫ ܫ	sh, š	300
ܬܘ *Tau*	ܬ ܬ	ܬ ܬ	—	—	t, ϑ	400

1) the oldest Majuscle, known as Estrangelo, Gospel-character (ܠܟܬ̈ܝ܊ܐ = ܚܟܬ̈ܝ̣ܠܐ ܐܘ̇ܠ ܫܘܪܒܐ, J. D. Michaelis, not from στρογγυλος Assemani N,[1] or στραγγαλια), said to have been invènted by Paul bar ܚܨܒܐ of Edessa, and to have been re-introduced by the brothers Emmanuel and Nache, and Johannes of Kartemin about 988.[2] From it was developed the character of the **Nestorians**, still in use among the Syrians of Lake Urumiyah. 2) A smaller character, Semiminuscle, adopted by the **Jacobites**. 3) The character of the **Malkites**, which, according to Land, is an imitation of the Greek, according to Duval and others has more faithfully preserved the oldest forms. It is used only for Palestinian Syriac.

Arabic and Malayalim in Syriac characters is called **Garshuni** ܓ݁ܪܫܘܢܝ [cf. Gerson, Ex. 2, 22.]; on the cryptography of Bardesanes *v.* D § 13.

The indication of the **vowels** in MSS. and printed [3] books likewise follows a twofold system.

---

[1] N in the sequel = Nöldeke (kurzgefasste syrische Grammatik, Leipzig 1880), D = Duval (Traité de Grammaire Syriaque, Paris 1881), H = G. Hoffmann, ZDMG = Zeitschrift der deutschen morgenländischen Gesellschaft.

[2] BO [= Bibliotheca Orientalis *v.* Litt.] 2, 352. 3, 2, 378. Lagarde, Praetermissa 95, 73, BH [= Bar Hebraeus *v.* Litt.], chron. eccl. 1, 417. G. Hoffmann, LCBl 79, 1708. Khajjath, Syri orientales 143. Lagarde, Mitteilungen 2, 257.

1) The Jacobite with the help of Greek vowels;
2) the Nestorian, which has arisen from the more
ancient employment of a single diacritical point.

Barhebræus[1] gives the following table:

Sign	Example			Name	
	Particle	Verb	Noun	East Syrians	West Syrians
ܰ	ܐܦ	ܨܐܪ	ܟܠܡܬܐ	—	ܐܡܩܐ
ܳ	ܐܒܪ	ܢܙܒܢ	ܨܡܕܐ	—	ܥܕܣܐ
ܶ	ܐܪܐ	ܐܦܠ	ܡܕܠܐ	ܐܩܡܐ ܘܢܩܨܨ	ܨܘܢܐ
ܶ	ܐܦܐ	ܟܐܨܦ	ܐܗܠ	" ܘܢܩܐ	ܨܘܢܐ
ܺ	ܒܥܕ	ܒܡܩܕܡܐ	ܡܒܡ	ܐܩܡܐ ܫܕܘ ܣܩܒܝܟܐ	ܐܩܡܐ
ܺ	ܒܠ	ܒܐܓܠ	ܟܩܡܐ	" ܡܟܫܫܡܕܐ	ܨܘܢܐ
ܽ	ܦܘܣ	ܝܘܚܝ	ܫܘܨܐ	ܐܩܡܐ ܘܐܦ ܟܓܡܝܟܐ	ܐܩܡܐ
ܽ	ܚܦܙ	ܝܡܙܦܝ	ܐܘܩܐ	" ܘܐܦ ܘܨܡܣܐ	ܨܘܢܐ

According to the above, the Jacobites distinguish
only the five vowels a^v, o^o, $e^{\cdot}$, $i^{\cdot}$, $u^{\wedge}$, contained in the
mnemonic word ܨܘܡܙܒܡܩܕ or ܨܘܡ ܡܩܐ ܟܠ; the
Nestorians seven, in some cases six or even eight, by
giving a double sound to e, i and u. Mnemonic sentence:
ܒܓܪܝܡܚܢ ܐܣܠ ܝܡ ܕܒܡܒܕܟܐ (on *à* v. § 6 c).

— is only another form of —, although later Nest. grammarians make — equivalent to ܪܨܘܢܐ, — to ܣܨܘܢܐ; see the list
of BH and 6 c.

----

[1] The last and most important national grammarian († 1286)
v. infra.

The pronunciation of the various consonants 4 is widely different according to time, place, and their position in the word.

ا between two vowels is pronounced almost as *y* (ܝ), which is not unfrequently written instead.

ܘ was in later times no longer audible after *u*: ܣܘܚܐ = *šūḥā*.

For the six consonants ܒܓܕܟܦܬ *v*. § 8.

ܘ serves, like ܝ in the middle and ا at the end of words, as mater lectionis. As consonants ܘ and ܝ approach the English *w* and *y* respectively.

ا before smooth consonants is pronounced as a smooth (*tenuis*); *vice versā* ܒ before medials is pronounced as a medial (*media*), before ܕ as ܓ, *e. g.* ܢܒܩܘܠܝ, ܦܬܟܪ, ܐܒܢܐ; ܫܡܦܐ (shame), ܬܒܨܪܘ etc.; ܓ before medials as ا; ܒ before medials as ܘ, before *t* as ܝ, and by the Palestinian Syrians almost as ا.

For ܥ we find a pronunciation indicated sometimes like ܚ, sometimes like ا —the latter especially before ܢ.

ܓ often like Arab. ج, Engl. *j* (D p. 29 n. 3); aspirated ܟ almost as *f*, *e. g.* ܐܦܪܐ *'afrā*, cf. Theodore —Feodore.

The Syrian grammarians divide the consonants 5 1) according to the organs of speech by which they are produced (ܒܡܦܩܢܐ, ܐܬܘܬܐ) into gutturals (ܚܢܓܪܝܐ, ܫܪܫܢܝܐ) ܥ ܚ ܗ ا; palatals (ܚܟܝܐ) ܨ ܓ ܩ;

*dentals (ܡܥܫܬܐ) or sibilants (ܚܫܘܡܥܫܬܐ) ܣ ܙ ܐ ܫ ܨ;
**linguals ܬ ܕ ܛ; ***labials ܣ ܡ ܒ ܦ.

* with open mouth ܦ ܒ; with the middle of the tongue and upper part of the palate ܓ.

** with the point of the tongue and upper and lower teeth ܕ.

*** with the point of the tongue and upper teeth ܛ.
So Elias of Soba; others only slightly different.

2) According as they accord with each other in the root, or not, into friendly ܢܫܡܬܐ and hostile ܣܢܐܬܐ e. g. ܒ ܦ, ܬ ܕ, ܪ ܘ, ܐ ܠ, ܣ ܙ.

3) According to their signification into radical ܡܬܡܢܝܬܐ or ܐܣܛܘܟܣܐ᾿ and servile ܡܫܚܠܦܬܐ, ܡܫܡܗܢܝܬܐ, ܡܫܡܫܢܝܬܐ.

⁶ₐ The vowels were, in the earliest period, only partially indicated by ܘ ܝ ܐ; afterwards words written with the same consonants but having a different pronunciation were distinguished by a diacritical point (ܢܘܩܙܐ ܡܦܪܫܢܐ), which is already employed in Palmyrene to distinguish ܪ (r) and ܕ (d). The point *over* the word served to indicate the stronger and more obscure pronunciation, *under* the word, the lighter and clearer. ܡܢ *man*, ܡܢ *men*; ܒܗ *bâh*, ܒܗ *beh*; ܡܠܟܐ *malkâ*, ܡܠܟܐ *melkâ*; ܗܘ *hau*, ܗܘ *hu*; ܗܝ *hâi*, ܗܝ *hî*; ܗܢܘܢ *hânon*, ܗܢܘܢ *henon*; ܕܝܢܐ *dinâ*, ܕܝܢܐ *dayyânâ*; ܚܕܐ *'aulâ*, ܚܕܐ *'avvâlâ*; ܒܝܫܐ *bîšâ*, ܒܐܝܫܐ *bây⁰šâ*. This or a similar system is usually adopted in the oldest existing MSS.

from the beginning of the fifth century, and also employed in printed books, partly alongside of the system
that was afterwards elaborated.

About the end of the seventh or beginning of the [b]
eighth century, when translations from the Greek were
being made in great numbers, it would seem that Jacob of Edessa († 708) hit upon the idea of using the
Greek vowel-letters A E H O OY to indicate the pronunciation of the Syriac.[1] Hence arose the Jacobite
vowel-signs given above. Their present recumbent position is owing to the fact that in those days one still
wrote from top to bottom.

The introduction of these signs has also been ascribed to
Theophilus of Antioch († 785/6), who is said to have translated the two books of the poet Homer on the capture of Ilion
into Syriac; thus still D § 73. Latest authority for Jacob, Wright
Syr. Lit. 840, n. 20—24. (Encyclop. Brit. vol. 22.)

Regarding the pronunciation of the vowels, the [c]
following may be noted:

$\mathfrak{f}$ $\mathfrak{i}$ *P^ethāḥā* is with all Syrians a clear, short *a*.

$\mathfrak{f}$ $\mathfrak{i}$ (also $\mathfrak{j}$) *Z^eqāfā* is pronounced by the western
Syrians as an obscure *o*, like Qameṣ by the Polish
Jews; by the eastern Syrians as a long *a, e. g.* ‍ܡܝܢܐ

---

[1] Before this, or perhaps at the same time, Jacob made an
unsuccessful attempt in the same direction, in which the Mandæan
system, according to Wright, the Greek, according to D, served
as his model.

Peshiṭṭo or *-ṭā*; the latter pronunciation has been proved on historical and philological grounds to be the older (μαρανaθα, ταλιθα). The representation of the long vowel by the short Greek o (μικρον) on the part of the western Syrians is explained, like ָ in Hebrew, by the fact that in the choice of signs the quality and not the quantity of the sounds was the determining factor.

For ī the eastern Syrians have sometimes ܐ (= *ĕ*, ε, ֶ), sometimes ܐ, in later times also ܐ (both = *ē*, η, ֵ), without any clearly marked distinction.

Besides the names given above we find also ܦ݁ܬ݂ܳܚܳܐ or ܦ݁ܬ݂ܳܚܳܐ ܪܰܘܝܚܳܐ for ܐ, as distinguished from ܪܒ݂ܝܨܐ ܙܥܘܪܐ = ܐ; also ܐܰܣܳܩܳܐ for ܪܘܳܨܝ and ܪܒ݂ܝܨܐ ܙܥܘܪܐ together.

In correct MSS. and prints ܐ (*ĕ*) accompanies the preformative of the verb ܢܶܩܛܘܠ, ܐܶܬ݂ܩܛܶܠ; but 1 p. impf. sometimes ܐܶܩܛܘܠ, ܐܶܩܛܘܠ: also in the form ܡܶܠܟ݁ܬ݂ܳܐ, ܐܶܢܳܫܳܐ; but part. regularly ܩܳܛܶܠ and ending of 1 pf. ܩܶܛܠܶܬ݂. On the other hand with the passive part. and the derived stems of verbs ṗ we find ܐ e. g. ܩܛܝܠܐ, ܨܒ݂ܝܐ, ܡܚܘܕܬ݂ܐ; elsewhere ܐ in shut and sharpened syllables. On the contrary ܐ is found before every quiescent ܐ or ܘ, especially in the prefixes of verbs ܟ̇ܐ: ܐܶܚܰܕ pf.; ܒ݁ܐܡܪܝܢ, ܐܶܚܘܕ impf.; also for western ʽ e. g. ܪܚܶܡ, ܐܪܙܐ, ܩܳܐܶܡ, ܪܶܓ݂ܙܳܐ, ܙܥܳܡ, ܐܣܬܡܟ݂ܐ, ܪܳܚܶܡ.

To the western ܘܳ corresponds the eastern ܘܳ *u* or ܘܳ *ō*, the former also named ܥܨܳܨܳܐ ܪܘܝܚܐ or ܪܒ݂ܝܨܳܐ, the latter also ܪܘܳܨܳܐ or ܐܰܣܳܩܳܐ.

o not *u* appears *e. g.* in the impf. Peal ܢܩܘܡܘܢ, in the pron. and suff. of 2 and 3 pers. ܗܘ, ܚܕ &c.; *u* on the other hand in the termination ܢܩܛܠܘܢ of the impf. whereas from ܗܝ, on account of the contraction, ܢܩܘܡ; *o* in the nomen agentis ܩܛܘܠܐ, near a guttural, &c.

NOTE 1. Regarding the transcription of Greek words see the Lexicon. The representation of Gk. ε by Syr. ܗ (*h*)*e* admits of a simpler explanation than that given by D p. 47 n. 1. A closer examination of these transcribed words throws much light on the pronunciation both of Syriac and of Greek.

NOTE 2. The Syriac names of the vowels imply nothing regarding the quantity of the Syr. vowels (in our sense of the word). The majority (ܐ and ܐ being the minority) whether with or without matres lectionis, give no clue to their quantity; whether *e. g.* the ˆ in ܩܘܪܒܐ, ܬܩܝܠܝܢ, ܩܘܡܗ be long or short can only be determined by the laws of Inflexion.

As diphthongs may be noted:

1) *au* ܘ, for which the E. Syrians always write ܘ[1], ܡܘܬܐ *mautâ*, not till a later period pronounced *mo-*, hence *t* always with Q. (*v.* § 8).

2) *ai* ܝ, ܝ, ܒܝܬܐ *baitâ* also with Q.; to be distinguished from ܒܝܬ *bēt*; solitary exception ܐܝܟ, pronounced *'āχ*, „how".

---

[1] Also before consonantal ܘ with a vowel, and even before ܘ doubled, the Nestorians always write ˆ for *a e. g.* ܩܘܝ, ܩܘܘܠ, ܩܘܝܐ; the only exceptions acc. to BH are the pass. parts. ܩܝܡ, ܗܘܡ &c.

3) *ai* ܐܝ, ܝ—; specially frequent in the terminations of adjectives.

4) With suffixes we find additional combinations
of vowels, ܘܗܝ—, ܝܗܘ—, ܝܗܘ— and, particularly in
Greek words, ܐܘ *eu* or *ew*. Cf. also in the N. T. words
such as ܡܣܟܠܢܐ, ܟܘܢܐ, ܡܘܪܒܐ, ܣܬܠܝܐ, ܟܘܨܦܝܐ.

c   For the Hebr. Śewa, whether mobile or quiescent,
as well as for the d o u b l i n g there is no special sign
in Syriac any more than in Ethiopic (Gram. Æthiop.
§§ 7. 9). The want of a sign corresponding to Dag.
forte is all the more comprehensible since the doubling
ceased to be audible among the Western Syrians at a
tolerably early period.

7   A d d i t i o n a l s i g n s. Several of these are clearly
a extensions of the simple diacritical point. First, the
p l u r a l p o i n t s (ܢܩܙ̈ܐ ܣܓܝ̈ܐ̈ܢ)[1], employed equally
by E. and W. Syrians, particularly with the n o u n,
when the singular and the plural have the same consonants: ܡܠܟܐ *malkä*, ܡܠܟ̈ܐ *malkē* (with ܝ : ܚܨ̈ܝ̈ܐ), ܡܠܟܬܐ
malk°t^ă, ܡܠܟ̈ܬܐ *malkāt^ă*; also with collectives ܥܢ̈ܐ *°ănă*
sheep, ܪܟ̈ܫܐ *rak^šă* horses. They are likewise used with
the v e r b *e. g.* 3 f. pl. pf. ܟܬ̈ܒ *k°t^db^*, especially with
verbs ܠ, where ܓܠܝ *g°lay* 3 f. pl. pf. might be confounded with ܓܠܝ *g°lăy* imp. sg.

_____

[1] The name Ribbui ܪܒܘܝ was first given to these points
by later Maronite grammarians from the Hebrew.

A further extension is the diacritical point *b* with the Verb. We have already seen (§ 6 *a*) how a point *over* the word was used to distinguish the more fully vocalised forms, such as the part. act. Peal and the Ethpaal from the perf. Peal and the Ethpeel accompanied by a point *under* the form (ܟܬܒ, ܐܡܪ, ܓܠܐ, *kât͟eb͟*, *'âmar*, *gâlē* from ܟܬܒ, ܐܡܪ, ܓܠܐ, *k͑et͟ab͟*, *'emar*, *g͑lâ*, ܐܬܩܛܠ *et͟qattal* from ܐܬܩܛܠ *et͟q͑tel*). We have now to add that two points (often called ܡܚܘܝܢܐ or ܩܘܫܝܐ) rendered it possible to distinguish a third form with the same consonants, *e. g.* the passive part. of ܓܠܐ *g͑lē* (in addition to *gâlē* and *g͑lâ* above) or in the sing. perf. ܩܛܠܬ 1 m., ܩܛܠܬ 2 m., ܩܛܠܬ 3 f. (last form written by the Nestorians with two points under ܩܛܠܬ). This system was of course still inadequate inasmuch as ܩܛܠܬ may equally well represent three forms of the Pael. Similarly ܐܫܘܕ is 1 p. impf. Peal, ܐܫܘܕ perf. Afel, ܡܫܘܕ part. Pael, ܡܫܘܕ part. Afel. Cf. D 67.

1) Much more important is the sign for the harder and softer pronunciations of the 6 ܟܓܕܦܬ, corresponding to the Hebr. Dagesh lene and Rafe. It consists of a small point, generally coloured red by the Nestorians, placed *over* — Qušŝåy(å) ܩܘܫܝܐ hardening — or *under* — Rukkåk͟(å) ܪܘܟܟܐ softening — these consonants.

Jacob of Edessa seems to have been the first both to introduce the ܡܰܟ݂ܣ and to distinguish the harder pronunciation (by a point).

2) The rules for the pronunciation of the Begadkephath are not so constant as in Hebrew but the following hold good in the main: Q. stands

a) at the beginning of a word after a vowelless consonant ܨܶܒ ܟ݂ܡܝܐ; hence after *h mappicatum* of the 3 pers. pron. ܗ݁ and ܗ݂;

b) likewise in the middle of a word ܡܰܠܟܕ݂, ܟܶܬ݂ܒܶܬ݂ *mal-kå*, *ketʰ-betʰ*, particularly after diphthongs and

c) when a consonant is doubled ܣܰܒܒܰܪ *sabbar*, ܐܶܦܩ *appeq*, except at the end of a word ܐܶܢܶܬ݂ *'achel(b).

3) R., on the other hand, is found

a) at the beginning of a word after a vowel ܢܗܘܐ ܡܙܒܢ;

b) likewise in the middle of a word, even after the slightest vowel sound, hence, in particular, after a doubled consonant and when preformatives have been added, *e. g.* ܨܡܚ and ܢܨܡܚ;

c) always with the suffixes of the 2 pl. ܟ݂ܘܢ and ܟ݂ܝܢ, except after the diphthong ܝ݁ of the plural.

NOTE 1. Thus far the Syriac usage is the same as the Hebrew; an important distinction, however, appears in the fact that in Syriac even unaccented syllables with a long vowel may be shut, *i. e.* may be followed by Q., *e. g. stat. emph.* and fem. of the part. ܨܡܚ, ܡܨܒܛܐ, ܟܬ݂ܒܝܢ (Exceptions § 38 *g*); while, on

the other·hand, the feminine ‍ may be aspirated after syllables
with a short vowel.

2. By 2 b and 3 b is explained the difference between ܪܚܡܐ
and ܪܚܡܐ (ܦܥܠ and ܦܥܠ), ܡܚܙܝܐ and ܡܚܙܝܐ (cf. ܡܲܠܟܹܐ and
from ܡܠܟܝܢ).

3. After a the fem. ‍ has mostly R.: ܚܨܝܕ݂ܐ, ܡܚܙܦܨܡܐ
(Exception ܡܚܙܒܓ݂ܬܐ); in exceptional cases after â, e. g. ܠܨܡܐ; R.
always with ‍ of the adjectival termination ܠܢܝ; Q. always with
‍ in the fem. of adjs. in ܢܝ, ܡܢܐ—.

4. An additional helping-vowel does not affect the earlier
pronunciation, thus ܢܡܨܡܐ and ܢܡܨܡܐ, ܫܓܡܡܐ and ܣܚܡܡܐ,
ܢܪܨܡ and ܢܪܨܡ (in poetry).

5. For the distinction between ܚܨܝܡܝ and ܝܨܕܡܝ, ܐܦܚܡܕܝ
and ܐܦܚܡܕܝ v. §§ 39. 47c; for the hardening of the first radical
in the 1 impf. Pael § 38, of the vowelless prefix of the impf. after
ܘ and ܕ § 49.

6. Of ܝ and ܦ we find a third and even a fourth pronunciation current. While aspirated ܦ corresponds to the modern
Gk. φ, the Gk. π is harder than ܦ with Q, and in accurate MSS. is
indicated sometimes by a point in the ܦ, sometimes, among the
Nestorians, by two points under it, and, finally, in Palestinian
Syriac by an inverted ܦ (so also with γ), while the Nestorians
indicate by ܦ the almost vocalic ܦ in such words as ܢܦܡܐ,
ܠܦܕܚܟ, ܣܡܡܝ, ܙܦܡܐ Mt. 3, 12 etc. cf. ZDMG 32, 746.

The signs ܡܚܪܘܙܢܝ and ܡܚܢܢܝ, chiefly used in
poetry, indicate respectively the shorter or more hurried,
and the longer or fuller pronunciation of a word or of

a consonant without or with vowels. The former is a
horizontal or (Nestor.) sloping stroke *over* the consonant, e. g.: ܟܣ݂ܩܐ *'es-qᵉtʰā*, not *'e-seq-tʰā*; the latter
the same stroke *under* the consonant: ܕܢܝܟܚ *de-chel-tʰā̊*,
not *dech-lᵉtʰā* or *dechltʰā*, ܡܪܚܣ *chamerhon*, not
chamrhon. Both strokes are in frequent use to distinguish the Ethpeel from the Ethpaal.

b   The so-called lineola occultans, an extension
of ܡܙܥܗܠ, is placed by some authors over, by others
under a silent consonant; it is especially frequent with
ܗ of the enclitic auxiliary verb ܐܘ݅ܗ, with ܝ of the
pron. of the 1 and 2 pers., with ܗ of the 3 pers., with
ܐܢܬ, ܐܢܝܣܐ, ܣܥ݂ܣ, ܣ݂ܙ &c.

c   In accurate MSS. other signs are found, such as a hyphen
between two words, corresponding to the Hebr. Makkeph: also
a line above the end of a word ܐ݈ܙ݂ܩ, meant to draw the tone
to the following word; another under, ܡܚܦܥ݂ܢܐ meant to retain
the tone on the first, e. g. ܡܩ݂ ܡܩ݂ܕܚ݂ܡ and ܡܚܕܚܡ݂ ܘ ܡܩ݂ܐ
(*malkta dšabba* and *malktat šabbā*) &c.

d   Not unfrequent is the sign of abbreviation 'ܡܝܣܐ
= ܐܣܘܡܣܡ|, 'ܣܐ = ܣܣܡܝ, 'ܐܣ = ܣܐܝܡܐ, 'ܙ = ܝܣܡ.

10   Of the so-called puncta extraordinaria the
follg. may be named:

1. a point is placed, as in Gk. and Heb. MSS., over
every letter that is to be deleted;

2. words requiring to be transposed are indicated

either by three points placed under them, or by the letters ܨ ܐ;

3. for quotations there are special marks », which, in theological MSS., vary according as the quotation is taken from an orthodox or an heretical author.

The ancient grammarians are silent as to the posi- **11** tion of the tone. We may however regard it as a rule that in general the penult is accented, never the ante-penult; the ultimate only where the preceding syllable has only a half-vowel or a helping-vowel, e. g. in the noun, ܢܙܰܠ like ܡܶܠܟܳܐ, in the verb ܡܶܠܟܝ, ܢܩܶܨ, ܢܶܩܨܽܘ. There is no doubt, however, that originally the tone lay on long terminations like ܡܶܠܟܝܶܢ, ܡܶܠܟܝܽ, ܡܶܠܟܬܳܡ.

We find rhetorical accents mentioned as early **12** as the 5th century; at a later period, i. e. from about 600 A. D. onwards, there existed a very elaborate accentual system with as many as 30 to 40 accents and marks of interpunction. The four principal are ܡܶܩܨܳܐ, closing the apodosis or second half (ܩܘܕܟܢܐ), and ܡܫܰܠܝܐ, closing the protasis or first half of the sentence (ܣܘܦܪܐ); ܟܘܟܒܐ dividing the former, ܡܩܦܐ[1] or ܐܘܠܝ dividing the latter into several members, as re-presented in the following scheme.

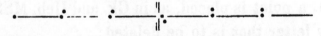

---

[1] Name and form correspond to the Hebrew Šewa.

In some printed books ⟨ is found at the end of an interrogative sentence. For details Phillips, Martin, D. pp. 137—161 may be consulted.

13   The numbers were in early times represented by the letters of the alphabet, the numerical values of which have been given in the table. For 500 it was customary to write ܣܢ, for 600 ܣܢ, for 900 ܣܢܢ. The stroke over the respective groups serves to distinguish them from vocables having the same letters. In recent times dates are written in the Arabic manner ܐܘܡܐ 1888. Special numerical signs and ciphers, the so-called Arabic ciphers, are found at a tolerably early date in ancient inscriptions and in certain manuscripts. Cf. ZDMG. 16, 577. Land, Anecd. I, Tab. 25. Wright's Catalogue.

B. PHONOLOGY. (§§ 14—18.)

14   The relation of the Syriac consonants to those of
a   Arabic and Hebrew is represented in the following table, which is confined to the sibilants and the dentals.[1]

	6		5		4		3	2		1	
	a	b	a	b	a	b	o	a	b	a	b
Arab.	ظ	ط	ض	ص	ش	س	ز	ذ	د	ث	ت
Hebr.	צ(ט)	ט	צ	צ	שׂ(ס)	שׁ	ס	ז	ר	ד	תׁ	ת
Syr.	ܛ	ܛ	ܨ		ܣ	ܣ	ܙ	ܙ	?	?	ܕ	ܬ

----

[1] Cf. § 1 and the remarks of G. Hoffmann LCBl 87, 18, 606 on Nöldeke's "Semitic Languages".

The student should look up illustrations in Gen.
1—4.

It is to be noted that when, in a root, ض = ‏ ـ ‏ ‏ـ‏ ‏ـ‏ *b*
comes into contact with another ‏ـ‏, the first ‏ـ‏ becomes
‏ا‏; cf. Lagarde, Semitica I, 22, N. ZDMG. 32, 405.
ضلع = ‏צֶלַע‏ = ‏ܬܟ‏; صفلع, ‏צָפַרְדֵּעַ‏, ‏أَوِّلُكَ‏.

Every syllable begins with a consonant and with *15*
one only. Apparent exceptions, such as ‏ܫܡܳܐ‏ (Q.), have *a*
frequently a helping vowel prefixed, in this case *e*
‏ܐܫܡܳܐ‏, ‏ܠܫܡܝ‏; ‏ܐܫܘܝܝ‏; elsewhere *a*, as often in ‏أَقْصِكا‏ =
‏רְקִיעַ‏, ‏ـܐܙܝ‏. ‏ܝܬܡ‏ and similar forms are pronounced
as if written—as they frequently are—‏ܐܝܬܡ‏ &c.

Syriac differs from Hebrew in the following points: *b*
1) Short vowels remaining in the tone-syllable are
not confined to the Verb ‏ܩܛܠ‏ (Heb. ‏קָטַל‏) *e. g.* ‏ܕܗܒ‏ =
‏זָהָב‏.

2) Short vowels before the tone are not lengthened
but dropped ‏ܩܛܠ‏ = ‏קָטַל‏, ‏ܕܗܒ‏ = ‏זָהָב‏.

3) A long vowel may stand in a shut syllable
‏ܩܘܕܫܐ‏, ‏ܡܥܕܗ‏ (H. ‏קָמְתֶּם‏).

As in Hebrew, a syllable cannot end in more than *c*
one consonant, except in such forms as ‏ܡܫܟܬ‏, ‏ܐܢܬ‏.

Consonantal Changes. As in the other Semitic *16*
languages the ‏ܬ‏ of the reflexive, when the first radical *a*
is a sibilant, takes the place of the latter and assumes

Bb

the same degree of hardness: ܐܬܟܫܦ, ܐܬܟܪܟ, ܐܬܪܕܦ, ܐܬܪܟܒ from ܟܫܦ, ܟܪܟ, ܪܕܦ, ܪܟܒ; but see verbs ܛܕ.

b In many other cases a consonant is assimilated to a following one in pronunciation; *v.* § 4.

c Vowelless ܢ is assimilated to the following consonant, which is thereby doubled: ܐܦܩ for *an-pek*, ܓܒ for *genb*, ܫܢܬܐ *šattā*, ܫܬܐ; *vice versâ* a doubling is sometimes dissolved by ܢ (or ܪ); ܓܢܒܪܐ, H. גִּבּוֹר, ܟܘܪܣܝܐ, H. כִּסֵּא.

d The following are not pronounced: 1) ܐ in the beginning of words like ܐܢܫ, ܐܢܬ; so ܐܢܐ when standing without accent after or instead of a verb; 2) ܗ of the unemphatic pronouns ܗܘ, ܗܝ, in the suff. of the 3. pers. ܐܝܕܘܗܝ *'īdʰau*, ܩܪܝܗܝ *qᵉrāi*, in the auxiliary verb ܗܘܐ in the irregular ܝܗܒ (*v.* § 48); 3) ܝ in ܫܠܝ (*v.* § 19); 4) ܠ in ܐܙܠ (*v.* § 48) and ܪ in ܡܪܬ (§ 32) and ܗܪܟܐ (§ 48 *g*).

e By aphæresis ܐ, ܝ, and ܢ disappear in the imper. of the corresponding verbs (*v.* § 41 ff.), as also in certain nominal forms ܥܕܬܐ, ܫܢܬܐ (H. עֵדָה, שֵׁנָה); by contraction very frequently ܐ after preformatives ܢܐܠܦ = *nᵉallef*, ܡܐܠܦܢܘܬܐ, ܐܟܘܠ I eat; [one of the double consonants in stems ܓܙ, ܙܓ = *zᵉgag*, ܨܥܕܬܐ; ܟܪ, ܩܝ;] the fem. ܬ in ܚܕܬ new, f. ܚܕܬܐ *ḥᵉdʰattā*. Apocope is chiefly found in the 3 pl., where ܩܛܠܘ is frequently written for ܩܛܠܘܢ or ܩܛܠܝܢ. The Hebr. feminine ending

ܡ appears in the stat. abs. only as ܿܢ, ܡܟܚܩ, ܐܡܿܟܩܐ; similarly in a few cases ܬ for ܡ—.

ܐ may be prefixed to foreign words beginning f with two consonants, and to verbs ܩܐ, and is frequently inserted as a mater lectionis: ܐܠܝ̈ܟܟܐܠ *dallitâni*, ܚܛܟܟ part. Finally we note the addition of a paragogic ܠ to certain parts of the verb, *e.g.* 1 p. pl. ܟܚܟܚܡ for ܡܟܚܡ; 3, in imper. 2 pl. ܡܟܚܟ, ܟܚܟܚܡ for ܐܡܟܚܡ, ܡܟܚܐܩ.

The **gutturals** do not affect the vocalization to the same extent as in Hebrew; they even seem to have been originally capable of being doubled. They prefer *a* to *e*, *e. g.* in the part. Peal ܐܟܚ̇ܡ for ܟܚܟܡ, in the Pael, Afel ܐ̇ܩܙܐ for *adʰneḥ*; *o* (*u*) is frequently retained in the impf.; the E. Syrians often write *a* for *e*, even when there is no guttural, ܐܕܟܐ, ܐܙܚܩܕ, ܐܕܐܣܒܕܢܐ[1].

The **quiescent** consonants are pretty much as in Hebrew.

1. ܐ, like the Hebr. ה, stands for *â* and *ē* at the end of words ܟܚܚܡ, ܟܚܟܚܐ — *malkâ, malkē*.

2. In the beginning of words, where it has always a helping-vowel, it surrenders its vowel to vowelless prefixes ܠܐܚܟ̇ܿ *valâhâ*, ܐܙܝܩ *lâdʰâm*; the Nestorians however, *vᵉ'alâhâ*, *lᵉ'âdʰâm*; but when two prefixes come together they also wrote ܟܚܚܟܐܠ ܐܩܙܚܐܩ *lᵉ'elfâ vᵉlabʰûhôn*.

[1] List in Martin, Syriens Orientaux et Occidentaux (1872) Tables 1—8.

3. Without a vowel ‍‍ܐ, in the middle of a word, quiesces not only in *a*, ܡܟܰܣܝܳܢ (for *mᵉassᵉyânâ*), but also in *e*, ܡܟܰܐܬܡܳ, and *ī*, ܡܐܡܪ݂ (but Nest. *mēmrā*).

4. In Afel it becomes ܘ, more rarely ܝ: ܐܘܦܶܠ, ܐܝܬܶܒ; for ‍ܐ between two vowels *v.* § 4.

5. For ܘ in the beginning of words *v.* § 44 *a*, for ܘ in the middle and for the changes it undergoes § 46 *b*; for ܝ § 46 *a*. Except ܚܝܐ to live and perhaps ܣܝܒ to set, there are no verbs mediæ ܝ, but very many tertiæ ܝ; on the other hand there are no verbs tertiæ ܘ.

18   Since the Quantity (long or short) of the vowels like the doubling of the consonants, is in most cases no longer recognisable by outward and visible signs, no unfailing rule can be given regarding their permanence and disappearance; vowels in sharpened syllables are of course equally unchangeable with those naturally long. Noteworthy, however, is the case with which the characteristic vowel of a form may change its position, *e. g.* in the segolate forms ܡܶܨ, ܢܶܫܝ, ܡܪܶܡ, alongside of ܡܶܨ݂ܐ, ܢܶܫ݂ܐ, ܡܪܶܡ݂; and in the feminines ܡܶܨܬܳ, ܢܶܫܟܬ, ܡܪܶܡܬ alongside of ܡܶܟܠܬ, ܢܶܟܣܬ, ܡܪܶܡܬ; in the imper. ܡܪܶܡܘ, ܢܶܟܣܘ.

II. MORPHOLOGY. (§§ 19—49.)

A. PRONOUN. (§§ 19—23.)

(ܣܟܦ ܡܠܬܐ, ܡܥܒܕܐ ܫܡܗܝܬܐ).

The Personal Pronoun (ܡܬܘܡܝܐ, ܩܕ̈ܡ) used 19 independently:

I	ܐܢܐ		we	ܐܢܚܢ, ܚܢܢ
thou	ܐܢܬ,	f. ܐܢܬܝ	you	ܐܢܬܘܢ, f. ܐܢܬܝܢ
he	ܗܘ,	she ܗܝ	they	ܗܢܘܢ, f. ܗܢܝܢ

After the participle, and more rarely after the adjective, *a* the pronouns are used enclitically with shortened forms. This usage is most frequent with the pronouns of the first person, least so with those of the third. Exx. ܐܡܪ ܐܢܐ, ܐܡܪܢܐ I say, so almost always even in the oldest translation of the Gospels (Curetonian) which, instead of the elsewhere usual ܐܡܪܝܢܚܢ, or ¹ܐܡܪܝܢ ܚܢܢ (both = 'ām°rînan), still frequently writes ܐܡܪ ܐ, but can hardly have any longer read *anachnan* or *enachnan*; ܡܚܟܡܐ = ܚܟܝܡ ܐܢܐ; ܡܚܟܡܐ Lk. 1, 28 = ܚܟܝܡ ܐܢܬܝ, but here = ܚܟܝܡ ܐܢܬ; ܐܚܟܡ = ܐܚܟܡ ܐܢܬܘܢ = ܐܚܟܡܬܘܢ; ܚܟܝܡ ܐܢܬܝܢ; before enclitic ܗܘ and ܗܝ *â* becomes *a*, ܗܘ ܐܢܐ 'enau, it is I, among the Nestorians.

The 3 pl. has special enclitic forms ܐܢܘܢ, f. ܐܢܝܢ, which are also used, instead of suffixes, to express the object.

The personal pronouns in Syriac are employed much more *b* frequently than *e. g.* in Hebrew to express the copula: ܐܢܐ ܐܢܐ and ܗܘ ܐܢܐ, ܗܘ ܗܘ for ܗܘ ܗܘ.

For the suffixes of the noun (ܡܩܦܬܐ, ܫܡܗܢ̈ܝܬܐ) *c*

---

¹ See Jacob of Edessa ed. Phillips 7, 13, Elias of Sobha c. 3.

affixa relationis) *v.* § 31, for those of the verb (ܡܩܛܠܗ
ܡܬܩܛܠ) *v.* § 39.

20 Demonstrative pronoun (ܐܚܘܝܢ̈ܝ):
a) this ܗܿܢ, ܗܿܢܐ f. (ܗܿܐ) ܗܿܐܐ pl. c. ܗܿܠܝܢ
b) that ܗܿܘ f. ܗܿܝ   pl. m. ܗܿܢܘܢ, f. ܗܿܢܝܢ.
Very rare ܗܿܠܡ and ܗܿܠܗܘܢ.

21 The interrogative pronoun (ܡܫܐܘܠܢ̈ܝ) is ܡܿܢ
who? and ܡܿܐ (also written ܡܿܢ *môn*) ܡܿܢܐ what?; interrogative adverb ܡܿܐ how? and adjective ܐܝܢܐ, f. ܐܝܕܐ,
pl. ܐܝܠܝܢ, which (man &c.)?

22 All the functions of the relative pronoun are
discharged by ܕ, ܕܿ (H. ܙֶה), generally alone, though
frequently preceded by ܗܿܢܐ, ܗܿܘ, ܐܝܢܐ; ܡܿܢ ܕ every one that.

23 A set of possessive pronouns much used in later
translations is compounded of ܕܝ, an older form of ܕ,
the dative particle ܠ, and the suffixes: ܕܝܠܝ; ܕܝܠܟ,
ܕܝܠܗ, ܕܝܠܟܝ; ܕܝܠܟ̄; ܕܝܠܗܿ, ܕܝܠܢ, ܕܝܠܟܘܢ; ܕܝܠܟܝܢ
ܕܝܠܗܝܢ.

B. NOUN. (§§ 24—33.)

24 Substantive and Adjective. Nouns (ܡܿܢܬܐ)
are partly primitive (ܐܣܘܦܢ̈ܝ, ܟܡܠܐ, ܒܟܕܗܐ, ܡܚܨܡܢ̈ܝ),
partly derivative (ܟܡܠܬܢ̈ܝ, ܒܟܕܦܢ̈ܝ, ܒܟܨܨܡܢ̈ܝ). The
latter class may be derived from verbs or from other
substantives, and that in various ways. They may be
composed simply of the consonants of the root with

one or more vowels, long or short, or may be formed
by the doubling of a radical or by prefixing, inserting,
or affixing one or more consonants.

Certain formations are employed as adjectives and
participles or in particular significations.

The following list, in which the forms from strong 25
stems are followed by those from weak stems, and the
masculine by the feminine forms, does not profess to
give more than the most frequently occurring nominal
forms in Syriac.

1. With a short vowel:

a) qaṭl, qeṭl, quṭl, or qṭal, qṭel, qṭul[1]: ܡܠܟ,
ܡܚܠܟܐ; ܬܡܗ, ܠܒܐ; ܡܪܩܣ, ܩܘܪܒܐ; a in abs. and constr.
states almost entirely confined to final gutturals and r:
ܐܣܐ (acc. to Nestorian
pronunciation reš, acc. to the Jacobite riš), ܙܪܐ; rarely
with a ܚܠܡܐ, ܫܘܡܐ; ܫܘܡܐ, ܚܬܐ; but from ܚܡܬܐ st.
cstr. ܚܡ; ܬܚܕ, ܬܚܠܡܐ; ܫܘܕܐ, ܟܬܒܐ, ܟܬܒܐ; ܬܚܠܡܐ.

The feminines of the strong form take the vowel
with the first or the second radical as may most con-
duce to ease of pronunciation: ܡܚܫܚܬܐ, ܡܙܚܬܐ as well
as ܡܨܪܐ, ܬܣܠܕܐ alongside of ܬܚܠܬܐ, ܡܙܠܬܐ (Q. because
originally ܡܙܠܬ which was also in use), ܡܣܬܡܐ and

---

1 Cf. Heb. גֶּבֶר and גְּבַר etc., בְּאֵר and בּוֹר, שֵׁבֶט and שׁוֹט; Nest.
ܟܨܪܝܡܦܐ, alongside usual ܟܨܪܬܦܘܢ.

ܚܙܘܩܐ, ܐܙܘܩܐ; ܡܥܩܐ, ܬܣܚܩܐ; ܟܘܕܩܐ, ܙܘܠܩܐ; ܟܘܪܩܐ; ܩܘܚܦܩܐ;
ܩܘܚܬܩܐ.

b) With these, as a rule, coincide the forms with (originally) two short vowels (Hebr. Gr. § 25), since traces of the second vowel can only be detected here and there, where the second radical has *a* or the third R.; ܩܪܐ, ܙܘܩܐ; ܐܟܠ, ܐܩܠܐ; but ܚܣܩ, ܩܘܩܐ; adjective ܣܪܝܒ, ܣܒܝܩܐ (pronounced *ḥaṭâ*).

Feminines: ܬܡܩܐ, ܩܠܚܩܐ; ܚܠܕܐ, ܬܩܪܐ, ܪܘܡܩܐ, ܬܡܩܐ; ܬܡܩܐ, ܟܩܩܐ (from ܟܣܩܐ).

2. With a long vowel:

a) after the first consonant:

α) qâṭal ܟܟܪܡ, ܟܚܩܐ; rare in Syriac.

β) qâṭel, the usual form of the active participle of the Qal, ܢܚܩ, ܩܩܐ; ܟܠܐ; ܩܐܡ; ܐܚܪ, ܩܘܩܐ; ܢܚܪ.

γ) qâṭôl, nomina agentis ܟܩܩܐ, ܥܙܘܡܐ.

b) after the second consonant:

α) qeṭâl: ܚܢܢܐ; ܣܐܦܐ; ܩܩܐ, ܐܣܩܐ, ܐܡܩܐ; ܚܡܩܐ, ܩܩܐ; ܚܨܩܐ.

β) qaṭîl: the usual passive participle of the Qal: ܚܟܡܐ; subst. ܩܣܥܩܐ; ܡܩܩܐ, ܐܚܝܩ, ܒܚܝܡ, ܡܡܪ, ܚܟܡܐ.

γ) qaṭûl, the IIeb. passive part., rare in Syriac; ܪܘܡܩܐ, ܚܩܩܘܩܐ, ܐܣܘܩܐ.

3. With the middle radical doubled:

a) qaṭṭâl, qeṭṭâl intensive adjectives and nomina opificum: ܩܠܩܐ, ܐܩܩܐ; ܙܢܩܐ, ܩܩܐ; ܢܩܩܐ, ܐܩܩܐ.

b) quṭṭâl, nomina actionis II ܪ̈ܘܚܳܡܳܐ, ܥܴܡܳܠܳܐ, and colour names ܐܘܟܴܡܳܐ.

c) qaṭṭîl, very many adjectives ܗ̇ܝܺܡ, ܟ̈ܐܻܡܐ, ܥ̣ܩܻܡ, ܥܟ̣ܨܪ, and part. perf. ܐܟܺܝ̣, ܣܻܝܡ.

d) qaṭṭul ܟ̣ܫ̣ܕܪܐ, ܐܫ̣ܘܚܐ, ܢܟ̣ܡܘܐ.

4. With formative additions:

a) with preformatives:

1) with *m*:

α) the infinitives,

β) the participles of the derived stems,

γ) many substantives ܡܚ̈ܥܨ, ܡܚ̈ܐܨܐ; ܡܚ̈ܨ̇ܟܐ, ܡܚ̈ܨܟܐ; ܡܨ̣ܪܟܐ; ܡܚ̈ܡܢܐ, ܡ̣ܕܠܐ, ܡܨ̣ܡܕܐ; with long vowel in the stem ܡܨ̣ܫܘܟܐ, ܡ̣ܣ̣ܡܐܠ, ܡ̣ܬܟܒ, ܡܚ̣ܨ̇ܬ̇ܨ; with long vowel in the preformative ܡ̣ܚ̈ܨ̣ܟ̣ܠܐ[1], cf. ܡ̣ܚܨ̇ܐܐ, H. מָקוֹר.

2) with *t*, derived from III and V ܟ̣ܚ̈ܨ̣ܪܐܐ, ܡ̈ܚ̣ܨܡܪܐ, ܡ̣ܨ̈ܨܡܐ; very many feminines ܡ̈ܚ̣ܨܡܕܐܐ, ܡ̈ܚ̣ܨܣܐܐ, ܡ̈ܚ̣ܟܡܐܐ[2].

b) With afformatives:

1) with *ān* for substantives: ܐܨ̣ܪܢܐ, ܫ̣ܚܟܢܐ, ܩ̣ܨܡ̣ܪܢܐ, especially from stems ܦ: ܐܚ̣ܟܢܐ, it is also the favourite

---

[1] Acc. to Lagarde GGA. 1884, 278 because = ܡܚ̈ܐܨܘ for ܡ̈ܚܨܟܘ, from a stem corresponding to the Arabic ضمس.

[2] With *y* a few (foreign?) names of animals and plants (N. 127,2); with *n* ܢ̣ܘܨ̣ܐ, a few biblical proper names commencing in Hebrew with *y* ܣ̣ܥܕܠ, ܠܨ̣ܡ; on Nimrod *v.* Lag. Arm. St. p. 112.

termination for the formation of nomina agentis from the derived participles and from adjectives, in which a fem. *ṭ* has often been preserved or, in cases, inserted ܬܡܨ̈ܐ, ܢܡܨ, ܣܡܟ̈ܐ, ܐܣܥܕܐ¹.

NOTE. Besides *ān* also *ōn*: ܬܡܨ̈ܢܐ, ܚܢܘܢܐ (Loan-words?) see Lagarde GGN. 1882, 400/404; Rahlfs, BH zu den salomonischen Schriften Leipz. 1887, N LOBl. 87, 25, 851.

ōn is the usual diminutive ending ܡܚܟܬܢܐ, more rarely *os* ܨܨܕܐ; or both combined.

2) *āy* for derived adjectives, ܡܚܟܬܝ f. ܡܚܟܬܝܐ, pl. ܡܚܟܬܝܐ.

1) and 2) may be combined *ānāy*, ܐܡܣܢܝ, ܐܚܟܢܝ.

3) *ī*, f. *īth*; ܪܥܝܐ, ܡܚܟܡܝܐ. Masculine abstract substantives with *y* (ܝ) are also formed from verbs ܣܢܥܕܐ, ܣܢܡܨ, ܢܡܝܐ, of which a st. abs. apparently does not occur.

4) Feminine abstract nouns in *uth* ܘ, st. cstr. ܘܬ, st. emph. ܘܬܐ ܡܚܟܬܘ, specially frequent in scientific terminology.

Forms with more than three radicals are not unfrequent, but they are too irregular to be properly classified. A few rare examples of compound words are to be met with, as ܬܣܐܣܐ foundation, ܣܩܕܚܣܐ enemy; one or two with ܚܟܠ, ܐܟܣ, ܨܣܝ, none with ܐܟ and ܐܣ;

---

¹ GH., ZDMG. 82, 755.

Greek words and proper names have found their way
into Syriac in great numbers.

c) On the vocalisation of the feminines see § 18
and GH., ZDMG. 32, 750.

As regards the two genders, the usage is essenti- 26
ally the same as in Hebrew. A considerable number
are common gender (D. 269, N. 87). Among feminines
without the feminine termination are the names of
members of the body occurring in pairs, names of
places and materials (D. 268, N. 84), and the numbers
from 3—10; *e. g.* نقم, أُلُ, صم, تُدَ.

The dual has left a trace of itself only in حزَ 2, 27
مَخاتِ 200 and مَيوَّ.

The plural has two terminations, m. ـٍ, f. ـُ; 28
نِمِ, نَوَمِ; مَحَمِلا, مَحَمِتِ. Masculines from ّ stems [a]
ending in the sing. in *e* take ـِ, feminines in مُ and
ـِ take مُ and ـٌ; نَلا, مَحَسِ; مَحَتِمِ, مَحَتِمُ;
مَحَسَقِ.

Many nouns with a masculine form in the singular [b]
take the feminine termination in the plural; حزِم bed,
pl. حزَمِ; أزَلا place, أزَّمِ, أمَا physician, أمَمِ; *vice*
versâ many feminines take the masculine plural, *e. g.*
مَلا, مَحْمَا word; pl. مَلِيِ *mellin*; مَضَا, مَضَبَا week,
مَضَمِ; أمَا cubit, أمَسِ; مَحَزَا, مَحَزَبَ cave, مَحَمِ.
A few have both forms in the plural: أُفَ father, *v.*
§ 32, مَنِ horn, مَتَسِ and مَتَنِ; مِ hand, أمَوِ and

ܐܽܪܳܡܳܐ; ܝܰܘܡ day, ܩܽܘܫܬܳܐ and ܩܽܘܫ; ܚܰܝܠ strength,
ܚܰܝܠܳܐ, st. emph. (*v. infr.*) ܠܶܒܳܐ, hence ܠܶܒܰܘܳܬ̈ܳܐ, ܠܶܒ
heart, ܠܶܒܳܘ̈ܳܬ and ܠܶܒ̈ܰܘܳܬ.

c   A few substantives are used only in the singular
ܚܛܺܝܬܳܐ sin, ܩܽܘܫܬܳܐ and ܩܽܘܫܬܳܐ truth, ܗܰܝܡܳܢܽܘܬܳܐ faith;
others only in the plural ܚܰܝ̈ܶܐ life, ܡܰܝ̈ܳܐ water (*v.*
§ 32), ܪ̈ܰܚܡܶܐ mercy; ܫܡܰܝ̈ܳܐ heaven is construed both
as sing. and as plural.

29   There are no c a s e - e n d i n g s in Syriac any more
a than in Hebrew. The various cases (ܦܬ̈ܘܳܚܶܐ, *v.* G o t t -
heil, Elias of Sobha u. 32 ff.) are expressed by means
of prepositions, the dative and often the accusative by
ܠ, the genitive by ܕ. The genitive relation, moreover,
was still expressed by the shortened form of the Noun
in the so-called construct state. This, the usual method
in Hebrew, was called ܪܽܟܳܢ ܫܡܳܐ ܕܰܣܡܺܝܟܽܘܬܳܐ (a m -
p u t a t i o n o f t h e n o u n i n a n n e x i o n). The short
independent form of the noun was known as the absolute
state.

b   In addition to these, we have in Aramaic a t h i r d
form, the so-called e m p h a t i c s t a t e which supplies
the place of the prefixed definite (determining) article
(wanting in Aramaic) and which is formed by affixing
the termination *â* ܳܐ to the noun. The masculine
plural ends in *e* ܶܐ (st. cstr. + *â* GH. in LCBl. 87, 18,
607), from ܝ stems *aiyâ* (*ayya*) ܰܝܳܐ. This form, we

may add, has become so common that it frequently
stands where determination is not implied, and in many
cases is the only form in use.

The following table gives a summary of the various *c*
classes of nouns and their inflexion:

		Sing.		Plur.	
	st. abs. and cstr.	st. emph.	st. abs.	st. cstr.	st. emph.
I a	ܡܰܠܟ king	ܡܰܠܟܳܐ	ܡܰܠܟܶܐ	ܡܰܠܟܰܝ	ܡܰܠܟܶܐ
b	ܪܶܓܶܠ foot	ܪܶܓܠܳܐ	ܪܶܓܠܶܐ	ܪܶܓܠܰܝ	ܪܶܓܠܶܐ
c	ܡܰܩܕܫ sanctuary	ܩܘܕܫܳܐ	ܩܘܕܫܶܐ	ܩܘܕܫܰܝ	ܩܘܕܫܳܐ
d	ܛܰܠܝ child	ܛܰܠܝܳܐ	ܛܠܳܝܶܐ	ܛܠܳܝܰܝ	ܛܠܳܝܶܐ
e	ܝܘܡ day	ܝܘܡܳܐ	ܝܘܡܶܐ	ܝܘܡܰܝ	ܝܘܡܳܐ
f	ܥܰܝܢ eye	ܥܰܝܢܳܐ	ܥܰܝܢܶܐ	ܥܰܝܢܰܝ	ܥܰܝܢܳܐ
g	ܝܰܡ sea	ܝܰܡܳܐ	ܝܰܡܡܶܐ	ܝܰܡܡܰܝ	ܝܰܡܡܳܐ
h	ܢܝܳܚ rest	ܢܝܳܚܳܐ	ܢܝܳܚܶܐ	ܢܝܳܚܰܝ	ܢܝܳܚܳܐ
II a	ܥܳܠܰܡ eternity	ܥܳܠܡܳܐ	ܥܳܠܡܶܐ	ܥܳܠܡܰܝ	ܥܳܠܡܳܐ
b	ܣܳܗܶܕ witness	ܣܳܗܕܳܐ	ܣܳܗܕܶܐ	ܣܳܗܕܰܝ	ܣܳܗܕܳܐ
III a	ܡܰܫܬܝ banquet	ܡܰܫܬܝܳܐ	ܡܰܫܬܝܶܐ	ܡܰܫܬܝܰܝ	ܡܰܫܬܝܳܐ
b	ܚܶܙܘܳܐ vision	ܚܶܙܘܳܐ	ܚܶܙܘܶܐ	ܚܶܙܘܰܝ	ܚܶܙܘܳܐ

There is little to add by way of detail:

a) Class I comprises the nouns with one short
vowel, from which those with (originally) two short
vowels (§ 25 1 *b*) can no longer be distinguished. From
c and *a* of the shorter form, it is impossible to infer
the vowel of the longer form: ܪܶܓܠܳܐ ܪܶܓܶܠ; ܡܰܠܟܳܐ ܡܰܠܟ;
ܩܘܕܫܳܐ ܩܘܕܫ.

b) Like ܥܰܡ is inflected the diminutive ܥܠܰܝܡܳܐ st. cstr. ܥܠܰܝܡܳܝ; ܥܰܡܡܳܐ takes ܥܰܡܡ; from ܗܰܘܢܳܐ reason and ܓܰܘܢܳܐ colour the W. Syrians form ܗܶܘܢ̈ܶܐ and ܓܶܘܢ̈ܶܐ.

c) Nouns from ܥܥ stems repeat the consonant only in the plur. of ܥܰܡ̈ܡܳܐ people and ܝܰܡ̈ܡܳܐ sea.

d) The part. of verbs ܠܝ deserves special attention The active is ܓܳܠܶܐ, ܓܳܠܝܳܐ, ܓܳܠܝܺܢ; the passive ܓܠܶܐ, ܓܠܶܝܳܐ, ܓܠܶܝ̈ܢ, ܓܠܶܝܳܬܳܐ.

d Peculiar are certain masculine plurals with *ân* inserted, with which Phœnician and Assyrian may be compared, such as ܫܰܠܺܝܛ ruler ܫܰܠܺܝܛܳܢ̈ܶܐ, ܪܰܒ great, with reduplication ܪܰܘܪ̈ܒܳܢܶܐ; see the list in N. 74.

30 *a* The Feminine. The rarely occurring stat. abs. ends in the sing. in *ā*, like the emph. state of the masc., the constr. in —*t* ܬ, the emph. in *t* + *ā* ܬܳܐ.

	Sing. st. abs.		cstr.	emph.	Plur. abs.	cstr.	emph.
I	ܡܕܺܝܢܳܐ	city	ܡܕܺܝܢܰܬ	ܡܕܺܝܢ̄ܬܳܐ	ܡܕܺܝܢ̈ܳܢ	ܡܕܺܝܢ̈ܳܬ	ܡܕܺܝܢ̈ܳܬܳܐ
II	ܐܰܪܡܠܳܐ	widow	ܐܰܪܡܠܰܬ	ܐܰܪܡܰܠܬܳܐ	ܐܰܪ̈ܡܠܳܢ	ܐܰܪ̈ܡܠܳܬ	ܐܰܪ̈ܡܠܳܬܳܐ
III a	ܣܥܳܪܳܐ	companion (f.)	—	ܣܥܰܪܬܳܐ	ܣܥܳܪ̈ܢ	—	—
b	ܥܶܓܠܳܐ	calf	—	ܥܶܓܠܬܳܐ	ܥܶܓ̈ܠܳܢ	—	—
c	ܝܺܕܥܳܐ	knowledge	—	ܝܺܕܰܥܬܳܐ	ܝܺܕ̈ܥܳܢ	—	—
d	ܛܠܺܝܳܐ	maiden	—	ܛܠܺܝܬܳܐ	ܛܠܺܝ̈ܳܢ	—	—
e	ܚܕܳܘܳܐ	joy	—	ܚܕܽܘܬܳܐ	ܚܕ̈ܘܳܢ	—	—
IV	ܡܰܠܟܘ	kingdom	ܡܰܠܟܘܬ	ܡܰܠܟܘܬܳܐ	ܡܰܠܟ̈ܘܳܢ	—	—

		Sing. st. abs.		cstr.	emph.	Plur. abs.	cstr.	emph.
V	a	ܕܡܘ	image	ܕܡܘܬ	ܕܡܘܬܐ	ܕܡܘ̈ܢ	—	ܕܡܘ̈ܬܐ
	b	ܒܥܘ	request	—	ܒܥܘܬܐ	ܒ̈ܥܘܢ	—	—
	c	ܒܪܝ	creation	ܒܪܝܬ	ܒܪܝܬܐ	ܒܪ̈ܝܢ	—	—
VI		ܡܢܬ	part	ܡܢܬ	ܡܢܬܐ	ܡ̈ܢܘܢ	ܡ̈ܢܘܬ	ܡ̈ܢܘܬܐ

NOTE 1. Class I suffers no change because the last syllable begins with a consonant.

2. Class II, on account of the two consonants, requires sometimes *a* as ܐܪ̈ܡܠܬܐ, sometimes *e* as ܫܐܠܬܐ, ܫܐ̈ܠܬܐ request—in this respect, however, the eastern pronunciation is often at variance with the western—sometimes *u* as in ܫܘܥܝܬܐ (does it occur?) ܫܘ̈ܥܝܬܐ. For the uncertainty as regards Q. and R. of the ܬ, see above.

3. Class III comprises the segolate feminines with the change in the position of the vowel mentioned in § 18. To this class belong also the forms under V and VI from ܠܐ stems, which must not be confounded with those of class IV.

4. For the double plural of certain substantives *v.* § 28 *b*; to these add ܐܬܘ̈ܬܐ, ܡܠܘ̈ܬܐ, ܦܘܡܐ and ܦܘ̈ܡܬܐ. ܐܬܐ sign, ܐܬܘ̈ܬܐ; ܫܢܐ, ܫ̈ܢܘܬܐ; ܡܐܐ hundred ܡܐܘ̈ܬܐ have only the feminine form. ܐܪ̈ܥܬܐ takes ܐܪ̈ܥܬܐ.

5. Adjectives in ܝ form the feminine in ܝܬܐ: ܪܘܚܢܝ, ܪܘܚܢܝܬܐ, pl. ܪܘܚܢ̈ܝܬܐ; those in ܝ, ܝܐ, on the other hand, take ܝܬܐ, pl. ܝ̈ܬܐ: ܪܘܚܢܝܐ, ܪܘܚܢܝܬܐ, ܪܘܚܢ̈ܝܬܐ.

---

[1] On ܬܐ ܣܐ s. Philippi, ZDMG. 40, 650; de Lagarde, Mitt. 2, 358 f., χασύτας = ܟܣܘܬܐ.

31 The appending of the suffixes presents little diffi-
a culty. The singular forms given in §23 (with ܝ̱) when
joined to the plural of nouns become ܬܳܟ݂; ܪܝܼܡ, ܡܥܶܒ݂;
ܩܶܐܘ, ܐܶܢܶܬ; ܝܼܡ; ܩܶܬ݂ܰܡ, ܡܶܬܰܡ; ܐܳܐܡ, ܡܰܐܡ.

b With the suffixes the noun generally assumes the
form of the st. emph., dropping the terminations *â* and
ē; no change occurs except where ease of pronunciation
demands the insertion or restoration of a vowel, or a
change in its position, especially before the vowelless
and consonantal suffixes ܙ; ܡܶܡ, ܡܶܡ; ܡܥ, ܡܥ. In the
case of the masculines, in the above paradigms *e. g.*,
the position of the vowel is shifted only in ܢܶܟ݂ܓ݂ܝ
compared with ܡܟ݂ܕ݂ܓ݂ܝ. Insertion in ܡܶܡܕ݂ܡܥ, ܡܕ݂ܘ݂ܗܳܬ݂;
similarly in ܐܶܬ݂ܝ, ܐܶܬ݂ܝ݂ܘܥ alongside of ܐܶܬܝ, ܐܶܬ݂ܝ݂ܘܥ; in
ܐܶܫܶܢ and ܡܨܨܟ݂ܡ my burden from ܐܡܶܩܟ݂ܡ, ܡܶܐܓ݂ܚܙ,
ܡܨܨܕ݂ܡ etc.

c Nouns from ܝ stems form with the suffix of the
first person ܐܶܚܕ݂ܚ, ܡܨܚ݂ܪ, ܡܨܕ݂ܪ, ܡܟ݂ܚ݂ܚ, which the
Jacobites pronounce ܡܨ̄ܚܚ *gabī, šelī*, the Nestorians
gab[h], šel; with ܡܥ and ܡܡ: ܡܟ݂ܚ݂ܚ, ܐ̄ܢܕ݂ܡܥ, ܡܗܚ݂ܨ݂ܡܥ;
so also ܡܟ݂ܪ݂ܨ݂ܡܥ, but Nest. ܡܟ݂ܝ݂ܪ݂ܨ݂ܡܥ, because in the st.
abs. ܡܟ݂ܪ݂ܙ, which is, at the same time, the form with
the suffix of the 1 pers.; in the same way ܡܶܐܘܨ݂ܣ݂ܚ.

In the **plural** of these words the radical *y* is sometimes dropped and sometimes retained, ܝܟ݂ܚ and ܡܶܚ݂ܚ,
ܝܟ݂ܚ݂ܩܥ and ܝܟ݂ܚ݂ܩܥ; ܡܥܕ݂ܡܘ and ܡܥܕ݂ܡܘ; with sub-

stantives, as distinguished from adjectives and participles, it seems to be more frequently dropped: ܡܰܠܟ̈ܰܝ, ܡܰܠܟ̈ܰܝܟܘܢ.

Of the feminines those ending in *ūt*, *īt*, *āt* always remain unchanged, as do the rest always before the vocalic suffixes, frequently also before ܝ, while they generally insert a helping-vowel before the 2 and 3 plur.; in this case they assume the same form as in the st. constr. Thus we find alongside of each other ܡܰܠܟܽܘܬ݂ܝ, ܫܒܺܝܬ݂ܝ, ܥܽܘܕܪܳܢܽܘܬ݂ܝ, and ܬܶܫܒܽܘܚܬ݂ܝ, ܣܰܗܪܬ݂ܝ, ܐ̱ܩܰܡܬ݂ܝ; so ܪܗܘܬ݂ܝ, ܡܢܳܬ݂ܝ, ܢܰܦܫܝ alongside of ܢܰܦܫܳܬ݂ܝ, ܡܰܠܟܰܬ݂ܝ, ܫܰܦܚܰܬ݂ܝ, ܢܶܚܒܰܬ݂ܝ; ܡܕܺܝܢܬ݂ܝ, ܡܕܺܝܢ̱ܬܗܘܢ alongside of ܡܕ̈ܝܢܳܬ݂ܗܘܢ. Cf. also ܐܰܡܬ݂ܝ my maid, but ܒܪܰܬ݂ܝ my daughter. d

More or less irregular in their formation are a number of substantives, of which the following are the most important. 32

ܐܰܒ݂ܳܐ father, wanting (acc. to BH) in abs. and const., with suff. 1 p. ܐܰܒ݂ܝ, before the others ܐܰܒ݂ܘ, thus ܐܰܒ݂ܘܟ݂, ܐܰܒ݂ܘܗ̄ܝ, ܐܰܒ݂ܘܢ; in the pl. ܐܰܒ݂ܳܗ̈ܶܝܢ, ܐܰܒ݂ܳܗ̈ܶܐ and, metaphorically, ܐܰܒ̈ܗܶܝܢ, ܐܰܒ̈ܗܳܬ݂ܳܐ, then pronounced *abbā*.

ܐܰܚܳܐ brother, with suff. like ܐܰܒ݂ܳܐ, pl. ܐܰܚ̈ܶܝܢ; in the same way ܚܡܳ, ܚܡܳܐ father-in-law, with suff. of 1 p. ܚܡܝ, before other suff. ܚܡܘܗܝ, pl. ܚܡ̈ܗܶܐ.

ܚܳܬ݂ܳܐ sister, pl. ܐܰܚ̈ܘܳܢ, ܐܰܚ̈ܘܳܬ݂ܳܐ.

ܐ̱ܚܪܺܢܳܐ another, f. ܐ̱ܚܪܺܬ݂ܳܐ, pl. ܐ̱ܚܪ̈ܳܢܶܐ, f. ܐ̱ܚܪ̈ܳܢܝܳܬ݂ܳܐ.

ܐܶܡܳܐ mother, ܐܶܡܝ, ܐܶܡܶܗ, pl. ܐܶܡܗ̈ܳܬܳܐ.

ܐܰܡ݈ܬܳܐ maid, pl. ܐܰܡܗ̈ܳܬܳܐ.

ܐܰܢ̱ܬܬ݂ܳܐ or ܐܰܢ̱ܬܬܳܐ[1] (pronounce *'att^e t^h ā, atā*) woman, cstr. ܐܰܢ̱ܬܰܬ, pl. ܢܶܫ̈ܝܢ, ܢܶܫ̈ܶܐ.

ܒܰܝܬܳܐ house, ܒܶܝܬ, contracted ܒܶܝ, pl. ܒܳܬ̈ܝܢ, ܒܳܬ̈ܶܐ (note Q.).

ܒܰܪ son, ܒܪܳܐ, ܒܶܪܝ, ܒܪܶܗ, ܒܪܳܗ, ܒܶܪܗܽܘܢ, pl. ܒܢ̈ܝܢ, ܒܢ̈ܰܝ, ܒܢ̈ܰܝܳܐ.

ܒܪܰܬܳܐ daughter, cstr. ܒܰܪܰܬ, ܒܰܪܬܶܗ, but ܒܪܰܬܝ, pl. ܒܢ̈ܳܬ, ܒܢ̈ܳܬܳܐ.

ܡܳܪܝܳܐ lord, cstr. ܡܳܪܳܐ; ܝ discarded before suff., thus ܡܳܪܝ, ܡܳܪܶܗ, ܡܳܪܰܢ (1 Cor. 16, 21), pl. ܡܳܪ̈ܰܘܳܬܳܐ and ܡܳܪ̈ܶܐ, ܡܳܪ̈ܰܝ or ܡܳܪ̈ܰܘܳܬܳܐ, fem ܡܳܪܬܳܐ (Μαρθα, Q.).

ܡܰܝ̈ܳܐ water, ܡܰܝ̈ܢ, ܡܰܝ̈, bef. suffixes with or without ܝ, ܡܰܘ̈ܗܝ or ܡܰܝ̈ܰܘܗܝ.

ܡܕܺܝܢ݈ܬܳܐ city, abs. ܡܕܺܝܢܳܐ, cstr. ܡܕܺܝܢܰܬ; pl. ܡܕ̈ܺܝܢܳܬܳܐ, ܡܕ̈ܺܝܢܳܢ.

33 a **The Numerals.** The cardinals (ܦܫܺܝܛܳܐ simple) from 1 to 10 have separate forms for both genders, and, as in the other Semitic languages, in the case of the numbers 3 to 10, the feminine forms are used with masculine substantives and *vice versâ*. They are placed in apposition sometimes before — the more usual position — sometimes after the object numbered.

---

[1] In inscriptions also ܐܢܬܬܗ ZDMG. 36, 147.

masc.	1	ܚܰܕ	2	ܬܪܶܝܢ	3	ܬܠܳܬܳܐ	4	ܐܰܪܒܥܳܐ	5	ܚܰܡܫܳܐ
fem.		ܚܕܳܐ		ܬܰܪܬܶܝܢ		ܬܠܳܬ		ܐܰܪܒܰܥ		ܚܰܡܶܫ

masc.	6	ܫܬܳܐ	7	ܫܰܒܥܳܐ	8	ܬܡܳܢܝܳܐ	9	ܬܶܫܥܳܐ	10	ܥܶܣܪܳܐ
fem.		ܫܶܬ		ܫܒܰܥ		ܬܡܳܢܶܐ		ܬܫܰܥ		ܥܣܰܪ

To form the numbers from 11 to 19 ܥܣܰܪ is added *b* for the masculine, ܥܶܣܪܶܐ for the feminine, to a shortened form of the units.

masc.	11	ܚܕܰܥܣܰܪ	12	ܬܪܶܥܣܰܪ	13	ܬܠܳܬܰܥܣܰܪ
fem.		ܚܕܰܥܶܣܪܶܐ		ܬܰܪܬܰܥܶܣܪܶܐ		ܬܠܳܬܰܥܶܣܪܶܐ

masc.	14	ܐܰܪܒܰܥܣܰܪ	15	ܚܰܡܫܰܥܣܰܪ	16	ܫܬܰܥܣܰܪ
fem.		ܐܰܪܒܰܥܶܣܪܶܐ		ܚܰܡܫܰܥܶܣܪܶܐ		ܫܬܰܥܶܣܪܶܐ

masc.	17	ܫܒܰܥܣܰܪ	18	ܬܡܳܢܰܥܣܰܪ	19	ܬܫܰܥܣܰܪ
fem.		ܫܒܰܥܶܣܪܶܐ		ܬܡܳܢܰܥܶܣܪܶܐ		ܬܫܰܥܶܣܪܶܐ

Several variations are found in the orthography, especially of the feminine; *e. g.* ˆ is often wanting over ܣ of ܥܶܣܪܶܐ.

The tens are the plural forms of the units, (in- *c* cluding ܥܣܰܪ) and are of the common gender. ܥܶܣܪܺܝܢ 20, ܬܠܳܬܺܝܢ 30, ܐܰܪܒܥܺܝܢ 40, ܚܰܡܫܺܝܢ 50, ܫܬܺܝܢ 60, ܫܰܒܥܺܝܢ 70, ܬܡܳܢܺܝܢ, also written ܬܡܳܢܺܝܢ 80, ܬܶܫܥܺܝܢ 90.

They are joined to the units in such a way that the larger number is placed first, followed by the

smaller, which shows the gender and is always accompanied by ܘ, *e. g.* ܚܡܫܬ ܡܐܐ and ܚܡܫܬ ܡܐܝ. The object
numbered is generally placed after in the absolute
plural.

d   The remaining cardinal numbers are used as proper
substantives.

ܡܐܐ 100, in st. emph. ܡܐܬܐ=Fr. *une centaine* (pl.
ܡܐܘܬܐ (ܡ̈ܐܘܢ) (dual!) 200, ܬܠܬܡܐܐ 300, ܐܪܒܥܡܐܐ 400,
ܚܡܫܡܐܐ 500 &c.; ܐܠܦ, emph. ܐܠܦܐ 1000, ܬܪܝܢ ܐܠܦܝܢ
2000, ܬܠܬܐ ܐܠܦܝܢ 3000, ܐܪܒܥܐ ܐܠܦܝܢ 4000 &c.; (ܪܒܘܬܐ
10000; ܚܡܫܝܢ ܪܒܘܢ 50000).

e   The numbers from 2 to 10 receive the determination by means of suffixes, which occasion certain
changes in the form: ܬܪܝܟܘܢ you two, ܬܪܝܗܘܢ they
two, ܬܪܝܗܝܢ; ܬܠܬܝܗܘܢ (with anomalous Q.) &c.

f   The ordinal numbers (ܡܢܝܢܐ, ܡܢܝܢܬܐ) are formed
by the ending ܝ.

	masc.	fem.		masc.	fem.
1.	ܩܕܡܝܐ	ܩܕܡܝܬܐ	6.	ܫܬܝܬܝܐ	ܫܬܝܬܝܬܐ
2.	ܬܪܝܢܐ [1]	ܬܪܝܢܝܬܐ	7.	ܫܒܝܥܝܐ	ܫܒܝܥܝܬܐ
3.	ܬܠܝܬܝܐ	ܬܠܝܬܝܬܐ	8.	ܬܡܝܢܝܐ	ܬܡܝܢܝܬܐ
4.	ܪܒܝܥܝܐ	ܪܒܝܥܝܬܐ	9.	ܬܫܝܥܝܐ	ܬܫܝܥܝܬܐ
5.	ܚܡܝܫܝܐ	ܚܡܝܫܝܬܐ	10.	ܥܣܝܪܝܐ	ܥܣܝܪܝܬܐ

---

[1] Barely ܬܪܝܢܝܐ

Note. In 4, 6, 7 the Nestorians pronounced the second consonant hard.

Further formations of this kind are preferably avoided, and even for those given above ܕܬܪܬܝܢ ܗܘ, ܗܝ ܕܬܠܬܐ &c. were often used.

The cardinal numbers also serve to indicate the day of the month ܒܚܕ, ܒܬܪܝܢ or ܒܬܪܝܢܐ, ܒܚܡܫܐ, ܒܬܠܬܥܣܪܐ (Esth. 3, 12) &c.

The distributives are expressed by repetition of the numeral: ܚܕ ܚܕ, ܚܕܐ ܚܕܐ (pl. ܚܕܚܕܢܐ, f. ܚܕܚܕܢܝܬܐ some), more rarely by ܟܠ, ܟܠ ܚܕ each. g

A few fractional numbers are found as in Hebrew: ܬܘܠܬܐ, ܪܘܒܥܐ (with silent ܒ § 6) ܚܘܡܫܐ; once and twice ܙܒܢܬܐ ܘܬܪܬܝܢ;—fold is expressed by ܚܕ with ܒ *e. g.* sevenfold ܚܕ ܒܫܒܥܐ, hundredfold ܚܕ ܒܡܐܐ.

For the names of the days and months see the Glossary.

C. VERB (ܡܠܬܐ) (§§ 34—48).

In addition to the two verbal forms of the perfect and imperfect, Syriac employed, more than did the other Semitic languages, the participle with or without the auxiliary verb *to be* to express the present, in this respect approaching the Indo-Germanic family. The Syriac grammarians under Greek influence even went the length of regarding the above con- 34

struction as a third tense, which they named اصَل مُلُ؟
(present, in addition to اصَل أَحَصُ past and اَعَل أَحمِس
future).

35   The Syriac conjugations or stems may be most
conveniently arranged in three groups of two, in all
six conjugations. These are: the simple stem, the
intensive stem, and the causative stem, each with
its corresponding reflexive or passive, as represented
in the usual paradigm:

    1. Peal   ܩܛܠ and Ethpeel   ܐܬܩܛܠ
    2. Pael   ܩܛܠ and Ethpaal   ܐܬܩܛܠ
    3. Aphel   ܐܩܛܠ and Ettafal   ܐܬܩܛܠ

To these we must add a few other formations, *e. g.*
a second causative form, the Šaphel and its reflexive,
Eštaphal (Aethiop. Gram. § 43), in some cases a Paiel
or Pauel (Aeth. Gr. § 40) and other quadriliteral forms.

36   The inflectional endings are:

    a) in the perfect:

	1	2 f.	2 m.	3 f.	3 m.
Sing.	ܬ	ܬܝ	ܬ	ܬ	—
Plur.	(ܢ)ܢ	ܬܝܢ	ܬܘܢ	(ܝ)ܝ	(ܘ)ܘ

    b) in the imperfect:

	1	2 f.	2 m.	3 f.	3 m.
Sing.	ܐ	ܬܝ	ܬ	ܬ	ܢ
Plur.	ܢ	ܬܘܢ	ܬܘܢ	ܢ	ܢܘܢ

c) in the imperative:

	Plur.			Sing.	
	f.	m.		f.	m.
	‍(ـَـ)ـ—‍	(ـٝـ)ه—		‍ـ—‍	—

NOTE. Where longer and shorter endings are found side by
side, the former are to be regarded as secondary or derived.[1]

The Syrians distinguish two moods (ܐ‍ܠܡ‍ or ‍ܐ‍ܖܡ‍, 37
also ‍ܡ‍ܙ‍ܐ), the indicative (ܩ‍ܛܠ) and imperative[a]
(ܩ‍ܛ‍ܘ‍ܠ). The jussive[2], and the apocopated and emphatic
forms of Arabic are wanting; the infinitive and the
participle (ܩ‍ܛܠ‍ ܬ‍ܟܬ‍, ‍ܡ‍ܩܛܠ) belong rather to the
Noun.

The strong verbs are called by the Syrians ‍ܡ‍ܫ‍ܟܠ‍ܐ, b
the weak ‍ܡ‍ܥܠ‍ܐ.

Verbs of the simple stem are either transitive 38
(‍ܡ‍ܥܠܬ‍ܐ), or intransitive (‍ܩ‍ܨܡܬ‍ܐ); the latter have[a]
generally e in the perfect ‍ܕ‍ܚ‍ܠ‍ fear, ‍ܒ‍ܛܢ‍ be pregnant;
in some cases the vowel varies according to the signification: ‍ܚ‍ܪܒ‍ lay waste, ‍ܚܪܒ‍ be waste; in other
cases there is no change: ‍ܗ‍ܦܟ‍ vertere and se vertere,
‍ܦ‍ܪܫ‍ part and go apart.

There is no reflexive with n, corresponding to the b
Hebr. Niphal. The significations of the derived stems

---

[1] GH, ZDMG. 32, 757.

[2] Are traces of it to be found Jer. 10, 11 and in the inscription of Teima 11 (ܝ—not ܢ)? Berl. Sitz. Ber. 84,817. 87,448.

present the same variety as in Hebrew; thus the Pael
is frequentative, intensive, causative &c., while the
reflexive takes the place of the passive, which is wanting.

c   Forms with more than three radicals are derived
to a large extent from nouns; even words like ܐ݇ܟ݂ܨܡܝܢ,
ܐ݇ܟܦܪܢ, ܐ݇ܟܡܕܢܟ݂ܡ are invented by the theologians
and cited by the grammarians.

For Paradigm see following page.

NOTES a) ܩܛܠ is more suitable for a model than ܣܠܩ or
ܩܠܝ on account of R. and Q.

b) In the MSS. the silent endings o and ܘ—the latter especially—in the plural of the perfect and in the imperative are frequently
omitted. For proofs that they were once audible see note to § 16 e
and compare Mk. 5, 41. ταλιθα κουμι (cod. AD), with κουμ (א BO).
On the longer forms in ܘ—, ܘ—, and ܢ of the 1 pers. v.
§ 36 note.

c) Intransitive verbs with e retain their vowel (so in Arab.
but not in Hebr. 54ᵇ and Aeth. 56). ܣܚܦ Job 7, 5. 30, 30 is cited
by the grammarians as solitary example of an intrans. perfect
med. o; acc. to N also ܐܚܦܠ (but Q., v. I) p. 225 n. 1).

d) In the impf. and imper. the intransitive have usually a,
which is treated quite as the u of the paradigm ܢܫܐ?, ܢܬܡܫ;
but ܡܛܡܗ, ܢܡܛܘܗ, ܡܛܗ, ܢܡܛܘܗ; not many have e as: ܐܙܒ
sell and ܢܚܡ make, ܢܡܫ and ܢܚܡ, with a few ܢܗ v. § 42.

e) The eastern Syrians write ȯ i. e. o not ܘ in the pf. ܩܩܕܘܡ,
impf. and imp. ܢܚܩܕܗ, ܩܩܕܗ; ܘ u, on the other hand, in
ܢܡܚܩܗ, ܢܡܩܩܗ (v. II and p. 10); the prefix of the impf. they
point with — (ĕ, later ĭ).

Strong Verb.

Perfect.

	Plural.					Singular.				
	1 c.	2 f.	2 m.	3 f.	3 m.	1 c.	2 f.	2 m.	3 f.	3 m.
Peal										
Pael										
Aphel										

Imperfect.

	Plural.					Singular.				
Peal										
Pael										
Aphel										

Imperative.

	Plural.		Singular.	
	f.	m.	f.	m.
Peal				
Pael				
Aphel				

Infinitive.   Participle.

	Infinitive.	active.	passive.
Peal			
Pael			
Aphel			

Strong Verb with Suffixes.

Perfect.

Peal.	1 pers.	2 m.	2 f.	3 m.	3 f.	1 plur.	2 m.
3 m.	ܩܰܛܠܰܢܝ	ܩܰܛܠܳܟ	ܩܰܛܠܶܟܝ	ܩܰܛܠܶܗ	ܩܰܛܠܳܗ	ܩܰܛܠܰܢ	ܩܰܛܠܟܽܘܢ
3 f.	ܩܛܰܠܬܰܢܝ	ܩܛܰܠܬܳܟ	ܩܛܰܠܬܶܟܝ	ܩܛܰܠܬܶܗ	ܩܛܰܠܬܳܗ	ܩܛܰܠܬܰܢ	ܩܛܰܠܬܟܽܘܢ
2 m.	ܩܛܰܠܬܳܢܝ	—	—	ܩܛܰܠܬܳܝܗܝ	ܩܛܰܠܬܳܗ	ܩܛܰܠܬܳܢ	—
2 f.	ܩܛܰܠܬܺܝܢܝ	—	—	ܩܛܰܠܬܺܝܘܗܝ	ܩܛܰܠܬܺܝܗ	—	—
1	—	ܩܛܰܠܬܳܟ	ܩܛܰܠܬܶܟܝ	ܩܛܰܠܬܶܗ	ܩܛܰܠܬܳܗ		ܩܛܰܠܬܟܽܘܢ
Plur.							
3 m.	ܩܛܰܠܽܘܢܝ	ܩܛܰܠܽܘܟ	ܩܛܰܠܽܘܟܝ	ܩܛܰܠܽܘܗܝ	ܩܛܰܠܽܘܗ	ܩܛܰܠܽܘܢ	ܩܛܰܠܽܘܟܽܘܢ
3 f.	ܩܛܰܠܳܢܝ	—	—	ܩܛܰܠܳܝܗܝ	ܩܛܰܠܳܗ	ܩܛܰܠܳܢ	ܩܛܰܠܶܝܟܽܘܢ
2 m.	ܩܛܰܠܬܽܘܢܝ	—	—	ܩܛܰܠܬܽܘܗܝ	ܩܛܰܠܬܽܘܗ	ܩܛܰܠܬܽܘܢ	—
2 f.	ܩܛܰܠܬܶܝܢܝ	—	—	ܩܛܰܠܬܶܝܘܗܝ	ܩܛܰܠܬܶܝܗ	—	—
1	—	ܩܛܰܠܢܳܟ	ܩܛܰܠܢܶܟܝ	ܩܛܰܠܢܳܝܗܝ	ܩܛܰܠܢܳܗ	—	ܩܛܰܠܢܳܟܽܘܢ

Imperfect.

Sing.						
3 m.	ܬܩܛܠܝܘܗܝ	ܬܩܛܠܗ	ܬܩܛܠܢܢ	ܬܩܛܠܢܝ	ܬܩܛܠܟܝ	ܬܩܛܠܟ
2 f.	ܬܩܛܠܝܢܝ	—	—	ܬܩܛܠܝܢܢ	ܬܩܛܠܝܢܝ	—
Plur.						
3 m.	ܬܩܛܠܘܢܝ	ܬܩܛܠܘܢ	ܬܩܛܠܘܢܢ	ܬܩܛܠܘܢܝ	ܬܩܛܠܘܢܟܝ	ܬܩܛܠܘܢܟܘܢ
3 f.	ܬܩܛܠܢܝ	ܬܩܛܠܢ	ܬܩܛܠܢܢ	ܬܩܛܠܢܝ	ܬܩܛܠܟܝ	ܬܩܛܠܟܝܢ

Imperative.

Sg.						
m.	ܩܛܘܠܝܢܝ	—	—	ܩܛܘܠܝܢܢ	ܩܛܘܠܝܢܝ	ܩܛܘܠܝܢܝ	—
f.	ܩܛܘܠܝܢܝ	—	—	ܩܛܘܠܝܢܢ	ܩܛܘܠܝܢܝ	ܩܛܘܠܝܢܝ	—
	ܩܛܘܠܝܢܝ	—	—			ܩܛܠܝܢܝ	
Pl. m.	ܩܛܠܘܢܝ	—	—	ܩܛܠܘܢܢ	ܩܛܠܘܢܝ	ܩܛܠܘܢܝ	
	ܩܛܠܘܢܝ	—	—	ܩܛܠܘܢܢ	ܩܛܠܘܢܝ	ܩܛܠܘܢܝ	—
	ܩܛܘܠܘܢܝ	—	—	ܩܛܘܠܘܢ	—	—	
	ܩܛܘܠܢܝ	—	—	ܩܛܘܠܢܢ	ܩܛܘܠܢܝ	ܩܛܘܠܢܝ	
f.	ܩܛܘܠܝܢܝ	—	—	ܩܛܘܠܝܢܢ	ܩܛܘܠܝܢܝ	ܩܛܘܠܝܢܝ	—

f) The formation of 3 m. sg. impf. by *n* instead of *y* (hence always=1 pl.) distinguishes the Syriac of Edessa together with the Mandaean not only from Hebr., Arab., Ethiop. and Phœn., but also from the western dialects of Palmyr., Aramaic-Palest., Samarit., Nabat. Whether there is any analogy between it and the forms of the impf. with ‫ܠ‬ in biblical Aramaic and in Talmudic is doubtful (cf. D § 181, Kautzsch, Bibl. Aram. § 47).

g) For Q. of the first radical in the 1 impf. Pael, and of the third in the part. *v.* § 8 A.5. As exceptions to the latter we find cited ‫ܡܟܲܣܸܐ‬, ‫ܡܟܲܪܸܟ‬, ‫ܡܟܲܣܸܐ‬. It is to be observed, further, that when the tone is thrown forward the passive participles of Pael and Aphel are not to be distinguished from the participles active. On the union of the participle with the pronoun and the ensuing contractions, see § 19 *a*.

h) Pael and Aphel present no difficulty. ‫ܐܫܟܚ‬ find may be regarded as Peal with prosthetic ‫ܐ‬ or as Afel with *e* for *a*, cf. ‫ܗܘܐ‬ and ‫ܐܗܘܐ‬, *m* in ‫ܬܚܦܟ‬ and ‫הַשְׁכַּח‬ in Daniel.

i) No confusion can arise between the **reflexive** or **passive** forms of the simple stem and those of the intensive, that is, between Ethpeel (‫ܐܬܟܬܒ‬, with the diacritical point ‫ܐܬܟܲܬܒ‬) and Ethpaal (‫ܐܬܟܲܬܒ‬, ‫ܐܬܟܬܒ‬) if the second or third radical is one of the ‫ܒܓܕܟܦܬ‬. In other cases, the 3 f. and 1 sg. of the perf., the 2 f. sg. and the 3 and 2 pl. of the imperf. and generally the imperative are written alike, so that ‫ܐܬܩܲܬܠܬ‬, ‫ܐܬܩܲܬܠܬ‬ may be read either as *eth qatlath*, *eth qatleth* of the simple stem, or as *eth qatt°lath*, *eth qatt°leth* of the intensive. When the vowel of the imper. is thrown back, however, we can distinguish between ‫ܐܬܩܲܬܒ‬ of the simple, and ‫ܐܬܩܲܬܒ‬ of the intensive stem. The Eastern Syrians give the latter form a second vowel on account of the doubling and consequently do not distinguish it from the perfect. The W. Syrians do the same in cases like ܐܣܰ̈ܪ݂ܐ. In printed texts the diacritical point developed into a diacritical line o v e r (Ethpaal) and u n d e r (Ethpeel) the middle radical.

k) The Ethpeel often takes the place of the Ettaphal (ܐܶܬ݂ܒܰܥ); in the 3 f. and 2 m. and f. impf. of the latter only two *t*'s are written ܬ݂ܶܬ݂ܒܰܥ; it is, however, like the Estaphal, comparatively rare.

The strong verb with suffixes.   39

Notes on the paradigm (pp. 44—45).

a) One or two of the forms are found only in the works of Syrian grammarians; the suff. 2 f. pl. is omitted, since it is treated exactly like the masc.; ܐܶܢܶܝܢ and ܐܶܢܘܢ serve as suffixes of the 3 pl.

b) In the perfect the 3 f. sg. is distinguished from the 1 sg. with suffixes of the 2 and 3 pers. only by the R. of the ܵ; from the 2 m. with 1 pers. by R. and the difference of vowel.

In the 3 pl. suffixes are also appended to the lengthened forms ܩܰܛܠܽܘܢܳܟ, ܩܰܛܠܽܘܢܶܟ &c., which others point as ܩܰܛܠܽܘܢܳܟ; cf. in the imperative ܩܽܘܛܠܽܘܢܳܝ alongside of ܩܽܘܛܠܽܘܢܳܟ.

d) When the impf. represents the imper., it takes the suffixes of the latter, hence the 2 impf. often in ordinary cases ܬܶܩܛܠܽܘܢܳܝ.

e) For ܝܗܝ and ܝܗܘ we find, especially in the dialect of the Peshittā, ܗ—, ܠܰܡܕܳܗ, ܠܰܡܕܽܘܗܝ; the form (—ܝܗܘ) is also found in some instances with the inf., which, with the exception of the suff. of the 1 pers., is otherwise treated like a noun (ܠܡܶܩܛܠܶܗ).

f) Pael, Aphel and the derived stems append their suffixes after the analogy of the Peal. In the m. sg. and in the lengthened plural forms, the imper. Pael frequently retains the vowel of the

second radical ܡܶܬܚܰܫܰܠ; so sometimes the impf. Peal; cf.
ܡܶܬܚܰܫ̈ܟܰܢ KvD. ed. Wright [v. litter. p. 57] 166 n. 3; 172 n. 2.

40 Verbs with gutturals are not to be reckoned in
_a_ Syriac among the **weak** verbs since those _primæ gutt._
and in most cases those _mediæ gutt._ present no deviation
from the inflexion of the strong verb. Even those _tertiæ_
gutt. differ from the above only in respect that they
take _a_ 1) for _e_ (part. act. Peal, Ethpeel, Pael, Aphel)
and 2) often for _o_ (impf. and imp.)—the latter especially in verbs ending in ܥ. In some cases we find both
_o_ and _a_ (ܬܶܫܡܰܥ and ܢܶܫܟܰܚ), in one or two _o_ alone.
It is not always possible to say with certainty whether
a given form is an example of 1) or of 2); _e. g._ in ܐܙܥܶܩ,
ܢܶܙܥܰܩ, the former may represent an original z"_eq_, or the
latter may be for _nez'oq_; but cf. Hebr. צָעַק, יִצְעַק.

_b_ In a few verbs ܐ appears as third radical: ܒܰܝܰܐ
comfort, ܛܰܡܶܐ defile (both Pael), and gives up its
vowel to the second radical when the latter is vowelless:
ܒܰܝܰܐܬ (3 f.) ܒܰܝܶܐܬ (2 m.); in the pl. ܒܰܝܰܐܘ, acc. to the
Syrian grammarians, the ܘ is still audible, perhaps
bayya'ü. (In the same category we would place the
subst. ܣܳܢܶܐܐ hater, cf. § 30 _c, d_). ܣܬܺܝܬܐ (as original part.)
is found alongside of the later ܣܬܺܝܬ, ܣܬܺܝܬܐ, ܣܬܶܝ.

41 In verbs ܠܐ, the ܐ at the beginning of the word
_a_ takes a full vowel instead of a Šewa, viz: in the part.
pass. of the Peal (ܐܰܚܶܕ) and in the imper. with ܘ, ܐܶܦܰܠ,

ܐܗܕܙ, and *e* in the perf. Peal and in Ethpeel, ܐܬܟ, ܐܬܐܡܕ, ܟܠܐ, ܐܬܐܠܙܐ &c.; in a few perfects *a* is written by the E. Syrians for *e*, as ܟܟ for ܬܟܝ &c.

The E. Syrians further distinguish the perfect ܐܡܕܝ from the imperative ܐܡܕܝ.

After the preformative, ܐ quiesces in *e* when the ᵇ vowel of the second radical is *o*, in *i* when it is *a*: ܐܬܟ, ܬܐܡܕ, ܐܡܕܙ; ܬܐܟܬܐ; the follg. have *o*: ܐܬܟ, ܐܡܠܙ, ܐܡܣ, ܐܡܡ, ܐܡܗܙ, ܬܟܝ, ܬܟܡܕ, ܐܕܟ; the follg. *a*: ܐܐܠ, ܐܡܕܝ, ܐܡܕ, ܐܡܣ, ܐܟܦ. Only one ܐ is written in the first pers. of the imperf. ܐܡܕܝ, so in the Pael ܠܟܝ.

In the Pael ܐ in Western Syriac gives up its ᶜ vowel to the preformative, according to §§ 16. 17, and is thereafter frequently dropped, especially in ܟܟܡ; ܬܡܟܚ, ܟܦܐܬ, ܦܐܠܟ; so in the Ethpeel and Ethpaal: ܬܟܐܦܬ, ܬܦܐܬܟ; ܐܬܐܠܟ, ܐܬܐܦܟ, in which, however, it is now and then assimilated to the ᴢ: ܬܡܙܟܟܐ, ܬܡܙܟܟ; ܐܟܣܬܣܗܟܡ, ܣܟܬܟܕܡ. (H-Julian [vid. Litt. p.57] 8, 1, 5 &c.).

Aphel and Šaphel with their reflexives follow the ᵈ analogy of verbs ܦܦ: ܐܬܟܘܐ, ܐܬܟܦܘܐ, ܐܡܣ, ܣܡܦܣ, ܐܬܟܘܦܟܐ.

For ܐܙܐ, ܐܡܟܣ and ܐܐܝܠ *v.* § 48. The first consonant of *e* ܐܡܦܗ, from ܐܡܟܣ, points to a Hebrew origin.

Verbs ܦ.   42

The first consonant is apocopated in the imper. *a* Peal, and assimilated to the second when it would otherwise stand without a vowel in the close of a syllable; hence there is no irregularity in the perf. and part. Peal, in the Pael, Ethpeel and Ethpaal.

b Assimilation does not take place in a considerable number of verbs, especially those with ܗ for the middle radical: ܢܗܰܡ, ܢܗܰܪ; the same applies to the apocope in the imper. (thus ܢܚܽܘܪ notwithstanding impf. ܢܶܚܽܘܪ), especially with such verbs as are also tertiae ܝ.

c The vowel of the imper. follows that of the impf.; *a* is often found even where the perf. has *a*; *e. g.* ܢܣܰܒ take, ܣܰܒ, ܬܶܣܰܒ; ܢܛܰܪ keep, ܛܰܪ, ܬܶܛܰܪ and ܛܽܘܪ, ܬܶܛܽܘܪ; ܦܽܘܩ, ܬܶܦܽܘܩ; ܫܽܘܬ, ܬܶܫܽܘܬ; with *e* ܗܶܒ, ܬܶܬܶܠ; ܦܶܠ, ܬܶܦܶܠ. Doubly weak are *e. g.* ܢܚܳܐ, ܢܶܓܳܐ, ܢܚܳܐ.

Peal. Imp. of ܢܦܰܩ: ܦܽܘܩ, ܦܽܘܩܝ, ܦܽܘܩܘ, ܦܽܘܩܶܝܢ.

of ܝܗܰܒ: ܗܰܒ, of ܢܛܰܪ: ܛܰܪ.

Impf. ܐܶܦܽܘܩ, ܬܶܦܽܘܩ, ܬܶܦܩܽܘܢ, ܬܶܦܽܘܩܝܢ, ܢܶܦܽܘܩ

ܢܶܦܩܽܘܢ, ܬܶܦܩܳܢ, ܬܶܦܩܽܘܢ, ܢܶܦܩܳܢ, ܢܶܦܩܽܘܢ.

Inf. ܡܶܦܰܩ.

Aphel. Perf. ܐܰܦܶܩ, ܐܰܦܩܰܬ, ܐܰܦܩܶܬ, ܐܰܦܩܶܬ, ܐܰܦܶܩ

ܐܰܦܶܩܘ, ܐܰܦܩܶܝܢ, ܐܰܦܩܬܽܘܢ, ܐܰܦܩܬܶܝܢ, ܐܰܦܶܩܢ.

Imp. ܐܰܦܶܩ, ܐܰܦܶܩܝ, ܐܰܦܶܩܘ, ܐܰܦܶܩܶܝܢ.

Impf. ܐܰܦܶܩ, ܬܰܦܶܩ, ܬܰܦܩܝܢ, ܬܰܦܶܩ, ܢܰܦܶܩ

ܢܰܦܶܩ, ܬܰܦܩܽܘܢ, ܬܰܦܩܳܢ, ܢܰܦܩܽܘܢ, ܢܰܦܩܳܢ.

Inf. ܡܰܦܳܩܽܘ; Part. act. ܡܰܦܶܩ, pass. ܡܰܦܰܩ.

Ettaphal. Perf. ܐܶܬܛܲܟ݁ܰܣ, Impf. ܢܶܬܛܲܟ݁ܰܣ, Imp. ܐܶܬܛܲܟ݁ܰܣ.

Verbs ܟܢ.   43

In the part. pass. Peal, in the Ethpeel, Pael, and *a*
Ethpaal—instead of the two last often Palpel and
Ethpalpal—verbs of this class present no irregularity,
except that in such Ethpeel forms as ܐܶܬܚܲܠ݁ܰܠܘ, ܐܶܬܚܲܢ݁ܰܢܝ
the double radical is written only once, ܐܶܬܚܲܢ݁ܰܢܘ.

Elsewhere the identical consonants are fused into *b*
one, and the vowel thrown back on the first radical.
The latter after preformatives is pronounced hard, which
is the case with the other radical in the perf. and part.
only when it was originally followed by a vowel. Thus
ܬܚܘܣ, ܐܶܩܦ, cf. Hebr. יָסַד; ܩܲܦܶܐ, ܩܲܦܗ, ܩܲܦܗ but ܩܲܦܡܗ and ܩܲܦܡ,
ܩܕܘܦܝ; on the other hand again ܩܲܦܣ.

Imper. and impf. have *a*; *o* appears in ܬܬܠ, ܟܘܠ; *c*
for *e* is cited only ܩܡ, ܬܩܡ, ܬܩܝܘܡ, imp. ܩܡ, ܩܝܘܡ, forms
which D § 185 assigns to a root ܢܩܡ (but cf. ܩܘܘܪ, ܥܒܕ).

The uninflected part. act. Peal is formed like that *d*
of verbs ܟܗ: ܩܐܡ, but ܩܲܦܐ, ܩܲܦܣ; still we find, especially with ܟܠ, also ܟܐܠܟܡ. In the Aphel, too, there
frequently appears a similar ١: ܢܐܬܣ, ܡܐܠܬܣ.

Perf.	Peal.	Aphel.	Ettaphal.	Part. Peal
Sing. 3 m.	ܩܦ	·ܐܩܦ	ܐܬܩܦ	act.
3 f.	ܩܦܬ	ܐܩܦܬ	ܐܬܩܦܬ	sg. m. ܩܦ
2 m.	ܩܦܬ	ܐܩܦܬ	ܐܬܩܦܬ	f. ܩܦܐ
2 f.	ܩܦܬܝ	ܐܩܦܬܝ	ܐܬܩܦܬܝ	pl. m. ܩܦܝܢ
1	ܩܦܬ	ܐܩܦܬ	ܐܬܩܦܬ	f. ܩܦܢ
Plur. 3 m.	ܩܦܘ	ܐܩܦܘ	ܐܬܩܦܘ	pass.
3 f.	ܩܦܬ	ܐܩܦܬ	ܐܬܩܦܬ	ܩܦܝܦ
2 m.	ܩܦܬܘܢ	ܐܩܦܬܘܢ	ܐܬܩܦܬܘܢ	
2 f.	ܩܦܬܝܢ	ܐܩܦܬܝܢ	ܐܬܩܦܬܝܢ	Part. Aph.
1	ܩܦܢ	ܐܩܦܢ	ܐܬܩܦܢ	act. ܡܩܦ
Impf.				pass. ܡܩܦ
Sing. 3 m.	ܢܩܦ	ܢܩܦ	ܢܬܩܦ	
2 f.	ܬܩܦܝܢ	ܬܩܦܝܢ	ܬܬܩܦܝܢ	Part. Ett.
Plur. 3 m.	ܢܩܦܘܢ	ܢܩܦܘܢ	ܢܬܩܦܘܢ	ܡܬܩܦ
3 f.	ܢܩܦܢ	ܢܩܦܢ	ܢܬܩܦܢ	Inf.
Imp.				Peal. ܡܩܦ
Sing. m.	ܩܦ	ܐܩܦ	ܐܬܩܦ	Aph. ܡܩܦܘ
Plur. m.	ܩܦܘ, ܩܦܝ	ܐܩܦܘ	ܐܬܩܦܘ	Ett. ܡܬܩܦܘ

44   Verbs ܥܥ and ܥ.

a   There remain but two ܥܥ verbs in Syriac, the defective participle ܗܘܐ it is becoming, and the Pael ܟܢܫ assemble with its passive. As in Hebrew, verbs ܥܥ have passed into the class ܥ, from which they are scarcely to be distinguished except in the Aphel.

The first radical, where it should have Šewa, takes *b* an *i*, which passes over to the vowelless consonant of the preformative, ܢ݁ܪܬ *ireᵗʰ* not *yireᵗʰ*, also frequently written ܐܪܬ, Ethpeel ܐܬܝܟܡ (Nest. ܐܬܝܕܥ). In the perf. Peal non-gutturals take *e*, in the impf. accordingly *a*, ١ being written in place of ܝ: ܬܐܟܡ, so inf. ܡܐܟܠ.

In the Aphel ܐܡܬܝ *ʾ* and ܐܝܟܠ *ʾ* alone show the *c* original *y*, *v* appearing in all the others: ܐܘܟܡ, ܐܘܕܥ &c.

ܢܣܒ and ܢܬܠ apocopate the ܝ in the imper. Peal, *d* while after preformatives it is assimilated to the following consonant: ܢ݁ܒ, ܝܕܥ; ܬܬܠ, ܬܚܬ; ܢܬܠ, ܢܚܬ, ܢܦܩ. In other respects they follow the usual inflexion of the class.

For ܣܠܩ *v.* § 48, *g* 5.

Verbs ܚܙ̈. 45

These transfer (with the Jacobites) the vowel of the ١ to the preceding vowelless consonant, and have usually *e* in the perf. ܚܙܐ, ܢܚܬ, ܓܠܐ; ١ between two vowels is pronounced as *y*, and in some cases the latter consonant is written instead, *e. g.* Pael ܚܨܨ.

Imp. ܚܨܐ, impf. ܬܚܨܐ; part. act. ܚܨܐ, ܚܨܡ, pass. ܚܨܝ. In the Aphel, in many cases either the ١ is dropped or it is placed before the first radical ܐܚܨܬ (cf. § 43 *d*); similarly the Ethpeel of ܚܨܐ is not unfrequently written ܐܬܚܨ; so ܐܟܪܝ it displeases for ܟܪܝܠ

46 Verbs ܩܡ.

a   A verb med. *y* is perhaps to be seen in ܣܡ set (*v.* § 17,5), for its imper. is ܣܝܡ and its impf. ܢܣܝܡ; in the perf., inf. and part. it is not to be distinguished from the other verbs of this class.[1]

b   When the first radical is vowelless, ܘ unites with the following *a* to form *a*; with *e* and *i* it becomes *ī*, with *u* and *o*, it becomes *ū*; when it would be doubled in Pael and Ethpaal it usually becomes ܘ, as also in the part. act. Peal before inflectional additions. The preformative of the Ethpeel is usually written with two ܬ's, so as to reach the same weight with the strong verb.

Perfect.	Peal.	Ethpeel.	Pael.	Aphel.
Sing. 3 m.	ܩܡ	ܐܬܬܩܝܡ	ܩܝܡ	ܐܩܝܡ
3 f.	ܩܡܬ	ܐܬܬܩܝܡܬ	ܩܝܡܬ	ܐܩܝܡܬ
2 m.	ܩܡܬ	ܐܬܬܩܝܡܬ	ܩܝܡܬ	ܐܩܝܡܬ
2 f.	ܩܡܬܝ	ܐܬܬܩܝܡܬܝ	ܩܝܡܬܝ	ܐܩܝܡܬܝ
1	ܩܡܬ	ܐܬܬܩܡܬ	ܩܝܡܬ	ܐܩܝܡܬ
Plur. 3 m.	ܩܡܘ	ܐܬܬܩܝܡܘ	ܩܝܡܘ	ܐܩܝܡܘ
3 f.	ܩܡܝ	ܐܬܬܩܝܡܝ	ܩܝܡܝ	ܐܩܝܡܝ
2 m.	ܩܡܬܘܢ	ܐܬܬܩܝܡܬܘܢ	ܩܝܡܬܘܢ	ܐܩܝܡܬܘܢ
2 f.	ܩܡܬܝܢ	ܐܬܬܩܝܡܬܝܢ	ܩܝܡܬܝܢ	ܐܩܝܡܬܝܢ
1	ܩܡܢ	ܐܬܬܩܝܡܢ	ܩܝܡܢ	ܐܩܝܡܢ

---

[1] On these verbs *v.* A. Müller, ZDMG. 33, 698, Nöldeke, ib. 37, 525; Hebr. Gr. §§ 71, 72.

	Peal.	Ethpeel.	Pael.	Aphel.
Imp. Sing.	ܩܘܡ	ܐܬܩܡ	ܩܡ	ܐܩܡ
Plur.	ܩܘܡܘ	ܐܬܩܡܘ	ܩܡܘ	ܐܩܡܘ
Impf.				
Sing. 3 m.	ܢܩܘܡ	ܢܬܩܡ	ܢܩܡ	ܢܩܡ
2 f.	ܬܩܘܡܝܢ	ܬܬܩܡܝܢ	ܬܩܡܝܢ	ܬܩܡܝܢ
1	ܐܩܘܡ	ܐܬܩܡ	ܐܩܡ	ܐܩܡ
Plur. 3 m.	ܢܩܘܡܘܢ	ܢܬܩܡܘܢ	ܢܩܡܘܢ	ܢܩܡܘܢ
Inf.	ܡܩܡ	ܡܬܩܡܘ	ܡܩܡܘ	ܡܩܡܘ
Part. act.	ܩܐܡ, ܩܝܡ	ܡܬܩܡ	ܡܩܡ	ܡܩܡ
pass.	ܩܝܡ	—	ܡܩܡ	ܡܩܡ

NOTE 1. The verb ܡܝܬ die has alone retained in the perf. Peal a trace of the intransitive pronunciation ܡܝܬ, ܡܝܬܬ, ܡܝܬܘ, ܡܝܬܝܢ &c., elsewhere quite as ܩܡ.

2. ܙܝ attend forms its Aphel like verbs ܐܙܠ ܥܥ, and similarly the first radical must be pronounced hard after the preform. in ܐܟܝܠ measure and ܐܬܩܢ make ready, while otherwise the preforms. are vowelless; only in poetry do we find here and there ܢܩܘܡ &c.

3. The inf. Peal is sometimes written with an ܘ to which it has no claim: ܡܩܘܡ, ܡܙܘܥ.

4. Instead of the doubled ܢ (Hebr. Gr. 71, b), ܘ appears in ܗܘܢ, ܐܘܢ, ܢܩܘܦ; ܟܘܐ means dazzle, ܟܝܪ wake.

5. ܘ remains in verbs whose third radical is ܝ, a guttural or ܐ: ܗܘܐ be, ܚܘܐ show, ܬܘܗ, ܬܘܗ be astonished, ܕܘܨ rejoice (but ܚܕܝ), ܚܘܪ be white (but ܚܙܐ see). According to N. these

are mostly denominatives, and by no mean traces of a formation
older than that of ordinary med. ܘ verbs.

6. A Palpel and an Ethpalpal are formed *e. g.* from ܪܡ
be high, ܪܡܪܡ raise, ܐܬܪܡܪܡ; from ܙܘܥ, ܙܥܙܥ shake,
ܐܬܙܥܙܥ.

7. In the Ethpeel frequently but one ܠ is written, and in-
version and assimilation are dispensed with in the case of sibilants,
thus ܐܬܩܛܠ, ܐܬܐܠ, ܚܫܡ; but in Ethpaal ܐܬܙܒܢ, ܐܬܩܕܡ.

47　　Verbs ܐܬܐ.[1]

a　This class comprises the two classes of Hebrew
verbs, ה״ל (originally ל״י, ܘ no longer appears in Syriac
as third radical) and ל״א, which are treated in all
respects like verbs ה״ל. On the few that retain ܝ see
§ 39 *b*.

b　The paradigm shows in the intransitives
'*y*' as a consonant in the 3 f. sg. perf., but in all
the other forms it has become fused with the
preceding *i* to form ܝ‍ـ; in the transitives it becomes *å*, *åt* in the 3 sing., disappears entirely in the
3 pl., and forms a diphthong with the preceding *a* in
the other persons. According to the traditional teach-
ing of the grammarians, the termination ܘ in ܣܓܝܘ and
ܓܠܘ is still audible, thus: *s⁹gʰīu, g⁹ldu*.

c　Note Q. in ܓܠܝܬ=2 sg. to distinguish it from
ܓܠܝܬ with R.=1 sg., following the analogy of the strong
verb.

The imper. of ܠܐ one expects to end in *ay*, which, *d* however, is now found only in ܝܡܰܝ swear and ܐܫܰܝ drink. In the Ethpeel, the E. Syrians, following the analogy of the strong verb, pronounce *et^hgal*, which they usually write ܐܬܓܠܝ, in place of ܐܬܓܠܝ. The W. Syrians do the same in certain words *e. g.* ܐܬܥܩܕ or ܐܬܥܩܝ ψ 6, 5. The lengthened form is frequently found in the plural of the imper., and is usually written with Aleph: ܥܡܘ and ܡܢܥܘ, ܙܢܝܐ; in the fem. the lengthened form alone occurs ܩܝܡܝܢ.

The vocalisation of the impf. is in all verbs the *e* same. The plural differs from the corresponding Hebrew in showing a trace of the last radical, namely in the ending of 3 m., which is pronounced (by the East Syrians) *on* (ܘܢ) not *un* (ܘܢ). The *e* ܐ of the passive forms (also in the part. pass. Peal) is written by the E. Syrians — not —; so here and there in other forms. The *i* of the 1 p. s. pf. they write — ܣܝܕ.

	Peal.		Ethpeel.	Pael.	Aphel.
Perfect.					
Sing. 3 m.	ܩܛܠ	ܩܛܠ	ܐܬܩܛܠ	ܩܛܠ	ܐܩܛܠ
3 f.	ܩܛܠܬ	ܩܛܠܬ	ܐܬܩܛܠܬ	ܩܛܠܬ	ܐܩܛܠܬ
2 m.	ܩܛܠܬ	ܩܛܠܬ	ܐܬܩܛܠܬ	ܩܛܠܬ	ܐܩܛܠܬ
2 f.	ܩܛܠܬܝ	ܩܛܠܬܝ	ܐܬܩܛܠܬܝ	ܩܛܠܬܝ	ܐܩܛܠܬܝ
1	ܩܛܠܬ	ܩܛܠܬ	ܐܬܩܛܠܬ	ܩܛܠܬ	ܐܩܛܠܬ

		Peal.		Ethpeel.	Pael.	Aphel.
Plur.	3 m.	ܓܠܘ	ܚܕܝܘ	ܐܬܓܠܝܘ	ܓܠܝܘ	ܐܓܠܝܘ
	3 f.	ܓܠܝ̈	ܚܕܝ̈	ܐܬܓܠܝ̈	ܓܠܝ̈	ܐܓܠܝ̈
	2 m.	ܓܠܝܬܘܢ	ܚܕܝܬܘܢ	ܐܬܓܠܝܬܘܢ	ܓܠܝܬܘܢ	ܐܓܠܝܬܘܢ
	2 f.	ܓܠܝܬܝܢ	ܚܕܝܬܝܢ	ܐܬܓܠܝܬܝܢ	ܓܠܝܬܝܢ	ܐܓܠܝܬܝܢ
	1	ܓܠܝܢ	ܚܕܝܢ	ܐܬܓܠܝܢ	ܓܠܝܢ	ܐܓܠܝܢ
Imp.		ܓܠܝ		ܐܬܓܠܝ	ܓܠܐ	ܐܓܠܐ
		ܓܠܝ		ܐܬܓܠܝ	ܓܠܝ	ܐܓܠܝ
		ܓܠܘ		ܐܬܓܠܘ	ܓܠܘ	ܐܓܠܘ
		ܓܠܝ̈ܝܢ		ܐܬܓܠܝ̈ܝܢ	ܓܠܝ̈ܝܢ	ܐܓܠܝ̈ܝܢ
Impf.						
Sing.	3 m.	ܢܓܠܐ		ܢܬܓܠܐ	ܢܓܠܐ	ܢܓܠܐ
	2 f.	ܬܓܠܝܢ		ܬܬܓܠܝܢ	ܬܓܠܝܢ	ܬܓܠܝܢ
	1	ܐܓܠܐ		ܐܬܓܠܐ	ܐܓܠܐ	ܐܓܠܐ
Plur.	3 m.	ܢܓܠܘܢ		ܢܬܓܠܘܢ	ܢܓܠܘܢ	ܢܓܠܘܢ
	3 f.	ܢܓܠܝ̈ܢ		ܢܬܓܠܝ̈ܢ	ܢܓܠܝ̈ܢ	ܢܓܠܝ̈ܢ
Part.	act.	ܓܠܐ		ܡܬܓܠܐ	ܡܓܠܐ	ܡܓܠܐ
	pass.	ܓܠܐ		—	ܡܓܠܝ	ܡܓܠܝ
Inf.		ܡܓܠܐ		ܡܬܓܠܝܘ	ܡܓܠܝܘ	ܡܓܠܝܘ

f How the suffixes are appended is shown by the table on pp. 60—61.

NOTE 1. In the inf. Peal, in the Pael and Aphel (3 m. and f. sg. and pl. of perf.) the *y* retains its power as a consonant, except before ܩ and ܝܝ, thus: ܠܠ‍ܙ‍ܡ‍ܠ, ܩܡ‍ܙ‍ܢ, ܩ‍ܡ‍ܙ‍ܢ‍ܝ, ܝ‍ܚ‍ܡ‍ܠ; ܝ‍ܚ‍ܡ‍ܬ‍ܐ, ܩ‍ܝ‍ܚ‍ܬ‍ܐ.

2. The ܠ of the 2 s. perf. is hard.

3. The decomposed diphthong *au* (3 m. pl. perf. and pl. imper.) is written ܘܐ or ܘܘ—, or even ܘܘܐ.

4. Barhebræus does not admit the l e n g t h e n e d forms of the 3 m. pl. perf. with suffixes of the 2 and 3 pers., ܝ‍ܟ‍ܘܢ, nor yet the s h o r t forms of the fem. pl. imper. ܝ‍ܟ‍ܠ‍ܠ, ܝ‍ܟ‍ܝܢ and others.

5. ܩ‍ܡ usually forms ܩ‍ܡ‍ܠ‍ܬ, ܩ‍ܡ‍ܝ, ܩ‍ܡ‍ܐ‍ܘܠ‍ܬ, but also ܩ‍ܡ‍ܐ‍ܘܗ, ܩ‍ܡ‍ܐ‍ܘܠ‍ܬ.

Doubly weak and defective Verbs.   48

When, in a verb, two weak consonants immediately *a* follow each other, the first of the two is not treated as a weak letter (see, however, § *f*); cf. ܩ and ܟ‍ܟ, ܠ‍ܡ, ܩ and ܟ‍ܟ, ܠ‍ܘܗܣ, ܢ‍ܣ; so ܟ‍ܟ and ܟ‍ܟ ܝ‍ܗ‍ܡ; we need only discuss ܗܘܐ be and ܚ‍ܝ‍ܐ live.

ܗܘܐ is, as a rule, regular, except that in the perf. *b* the ܗ is not pronounced when the verb is used enclitically. The ܘ is sometimes dropped in the impf., especially in the jussive and in poetry: ܢ‍ܗ‍ܐ, ܠ‍ܗ‍ܐ, ܢ‍ܗ‍ܝ, ܠ‍ܗ‍ܡ‍ܐ. Besides the active participle we find the passive ܗܘܐ, ܗ‍ܘܐ c r e a t e d, and (acc. to N 183) the verbal adjective ܗܘ‍ܝ, ܗ‍ܘܐ b e e n.

Perfect.

	1 Sing.	2 m.	2 f.	3 m.	3 f.	1 Plur.	2 m.
Perf.							
3 m.	ܩܪܢܝ	ܩܪܟ	ܩܪܟܝ	ܩܪܝܗܝ	ܩܪܗ	ܩܪܢ	ܩܪܟܘܢ
3 f.	ܩܪܬܢܝ	ܩܪܬܟ	ܩܪܬܟܝ	ܩܪܬܗ	ܩܪܬܗ	ܩܪܬܢ	ܩܪܬܟܘܢ
2 m.	ܩܪܝܬܢܝ	—	—	ܩܪܝܬܝܗܝ	ܩܪܝܬܗ	ܩܪܝܬܢ	—
2 f.	ܩܪܝܬܝܢܝ	—	—	ܩܪܝܬܝܗܝ	ܩܪܝܬܝܗ	ܩܪܝܬܝܢ	—
1	—	ܩܪܝܬܟ	ܩܪܝܬܟܝ	ܩܪܝܬܗ	ܩܪܝܬܗ	—	ܩܪܝܬܟܘܢ
Plur.							
3 m.	ܩܪܘܢܝ	ܩܪܘܟ	ܩܪܘܟܝ	ܩܪܘܗܝ	ܩܪܘܗ	ܩܪܘܢ	ܩܪܘܟܘܢ
3 f.	ܩܪܝܢܝ	ܩܪܝܟ	ܩܪܝܟܝ	ܩܪܝܢܝܗܝ	ܩܪܝܢܗ	ܩܪܝܢ	[ܩܪܝܟܘܢ]
2 m.	ܩܪܝܬܘܢܢܝ	—	—	ܩܪܝܬܘܢܝܗܝ	ܩܪܝܬܘܢܗ	ܩܪܝܬܘܢܢ	—
2 f.	ܩܪܝܬܝܢܢܝ	—	—	ܩܪܝܬܝܢܝܗܝ	ܩܪܝܬܝܢܗ	ܩܪܝܬܝܢܢ	—
1	—	ܩܪܝܢܟ	ܩܪܝܢܟܝ	ܩܪܝܢܝܗܝ	ܩܪܝܢܗ	—	ܩܪܝܢܟܘܢ

Imperfect.

Sing. 3 m.	2 f.	Plur. 3 m.	3 f.

Imperative.

Sing. m.	f.	Plur. m.	f.

c ܚܝܳܐ is regular in the perf. and imper., but the imperf. is formed as if from a verb ܦܥ or ܥܥ (cf. Hebr. Gr. § 76*c*) and is written ܢܺܐܚܶܐ, ܢܚܶܐ or ܢܚܚܶܐ (E. Syr. ܢܚܶܐ), ܬܚܶܐ, ܐܶܚܶܐ; inf. ܡܶܚܳܐ. Aphel ܐܰܚܺܝ, ܐܰܚܝܶܬ; impf. ܢܰܚܶܐ, ܐܰܚܶܐ; part. ܡܰܚܶܐ; imp. ܐܰܚܳܐ; inf. ܡܰܚܳܝܽܘ.

d Verbs which are at the same time ܦܢ and ܠܐ, ܦܐ and ܠܐ, ܦܢ and ܠܐ share the peculiarities of the two classes to which they respectively belong.

1. ܢܟܳܐ injure, ܢܰܣܺܝ (Pael) tempt, ܢܨܳܐ quarrel, ܢܫܳܐ forget; impf. ܢܶܟܶܐ, ܢܶܨܶܐ, ܬܶܨܽܘܢ. Aphel ܐܰܟܺܝ, ܐܰܫܺܝ, part. ܡܰܟܶܐ.

2. ܐܶܬܳܐ come, ܐܦܳܐ bake, ܐܠܳܐ bewail.

ܐܶܬܳܐ, ܐܶܬܳܬ (E. Syr. ܐܶܬܳܬ), ܐܶܬܰܝܬ, 1 ܐܶܬܺܝܬ; ܐܶܬܰܘ, ܐܶܬܝܳ; imp. ܬܳܐ, ܬܳܝ, ܬܰܘ, ܬܰܝܶܝܢ (ܬܳܐܝܶܝܢ); impf. ܢܺܐܬܶܐ; inf. ܡܺܐܬܳܐ. Aphel ܐܰܝܬܺܝ, ܢܰܝܬܶܐ, imp. ܐܰܝܬܳܐ, inf. ܡܰܝܬܳܝܽܘ; Ettaf. ܐܶܬܬܰܝܬܺܝ.

ܐܦܳܐ, ܢܺܐܦܶܐ, ܐܦܳܐ (Lev. 26, 26 by some ܢܺܐܦܽܘܢ); Ethpe. ܐܶܬܐܦܺܝܬ, ܡܶܬܐܦܶܐ, ܡܶܬܐܦܝܳܢ.

ܐܠܳܐ, pl. f. ܐܠܰܝ̈ܢ, 1 ܐܠܰܝܢ; impf. ܢܺܐܠܶܐ; imp. ܐܠܺܝ, ܐܠܳܝ.

ܐܳܣܺܝ Pael, heal; impf. ܢܐܰܣܶܐ, ܐܰܣܶܐ; imp. ܐܰܣܳܐ, Ethpa. ܐܶܬܐܰܣܺܝ.

e ܝܺܡܳܐ swear, ܝܥܳܐ (H. יָצָא) bud; pf. pl. ܝܰܡܘ and ܝܡܰܘ; impf. ܢܺܐܡܶܐ, ܢܺܐܥܶܐ; inf. ܡܺܐܡܳܐ, ܡܺܐܥܳܐ; imp. ܝܡܺܝ (*v*. § 47 *d*), f. ܝܡܳܝ; Aph. ܐܰܘܡܺܝ, ܐܰܘܥܺܝ; so also ܐܰܘܕܺܝ.

f ܥܥ and ܠܐ: ܥܳܐ scold, ܠܐܺܝ be weary; perf. ܥܳܘ; impf. ܢܶܥܶܐ; imp. ܥܺܝ, inf. ܡܶܥܳܐ, part. ܥܳܐ; Ethpe. ܐܶܬܥܺܝ; Pa. ܥܰܝ; 3 f. ܠܐܶܝܬ, 2 m., 1 ܠܐܺܝܬ; pl. ܠܐܰܘ, ܠܐܰܝܢ; impf. ܢܶܠܐܶܐ;

Aph. أَزّ. اِزاَل, أَزِّلَت; ـأَزِّيْب, أَزّيْت are found only in the participle; so with ﻫﻮﻩ be becoming, أَزِّه, أَزِّوُا be convenient.

The following are irregular: 1) أَزِل go, in which ل *g* is silent, whenever اِ can receive its vowel أَزِكا *ázà*, أَزِكِيْ *ázīn*; pf. أَزِكدَه *'ezat*; impf. نِزِكِلن *nīzūn* (Nest. ه); imp. زِل. 2) سَكِّ go up with assimilation of *l* wherever س can take its vowel, thus impf. تِسَّق, and consequently تِسَّقِم; imp. سَّق, سَّمِب; Aphel أَسِّق. 3) أَسَّكِب find, impf. تِسَّكِب (*v.* § 38 *h*). 4) أَسَّكِد drink, part. أَسِّق, impf. تِسَّق; imp. أَسَّكِد (§ 47 *d*); Aph. أَسَّقِد. 5) يَهِّب give, in poetry also يَهِّب, without impf. and inf., يَهِّه only as inf. absol., يَهِّه, يَهِّه; imp. يَه, يَهِّب, يَهِّه, يَهِّب, with ه: يَهِّه, with suff. يَهِّه, يَهِّه, acc. to others يَهِّه, يَهِّه. Alongside of the above we have 6) نِتِّل give, only impf. and inf. نِتِّل. 7) يَهِّب run forms its imper. by omitting the *r*, which however is written after the initial ه, thus يَهِّه, يَهِّه *haṭ*.

D. THE PARTICLES § 49.

The lexicon must be consulted for the list of 49 particles (أَسِّه); we give here only those that undergo ^a grammatical change.

The inseparable prepositions ܒ, ܕ, ܠ, with the ^b copula ه, comprised in the mnemonic نِهِّه, before a

vowelless consonant receive *a*, rarely *e* (the latter
e. g. before ܐܕܐ (§ 15 *a*) six). Of *ī* with ܂ there is still
a trace in ܒܝ, § 23. With suffixes ܥܡ, ܥܡܚ; ܨܪ, ܨܡ;
ܨܗ; ܕܝ, ܕܝܦ, ܡܩܝ; ܡܩܡ; similarly with ܠ.

c   On Q. with the ܠ of the impf. after ܘ and ܂ *v.* §38*g*;
on words beginning with ܐ § 17*b*2.

d   ܝܬ has been introduced from the Palestine Targum
into the Syriac O. T. in 15 passages as sign of the definite
accusative (Gen. 1, 1. 1 Chr. 4, 41, the rest in Eccles.
and Cant.); also ܝܬܐ being, nature used reflexively;
ܡܢ ܝܬܗ of one's own accord.

e   ܡܢ is not joined to the following word except in
a few expressions such as ܡܢܫܠܝ instantly (seldom
ܡܢ ܫܠܝܐ), ܡܟܐ from here, ܐܝܡܟܐ whence? ܡܟܝܠ or
ܡܟܝܠ thus, ܡܕܡ something.

f   ܡܛܠ on account of, before suffixes ܡܛܠܬܟ, *e.g.*
ܡܛܠܬܗ, ܡܛܠܬܟܝ, ܡܛܠܬܟܘܢ.

g   ܠܘܩܒܠ (st. cstr., also ܂ ܠܘܩܒܠܐ) over against,
ܠܘܩܒܠܟ, ܠܘܩܒܠܗ, ܠܘܩܒܠܝܟܘܢ, but ܠܘܩܒܠܟ, ܠܘܩܒܠܡܟ.

h   The following also take the suffixes of the singular:
ܡܢ from, ܥܡ with, ܠܘܬ to, towards, ܐܝܟ like,
ܒܬܪ, ܒܣܬܪ behind, after (with *a* retained before 1 sg.,
2 and 3 pl.); with the plural suffixes ܥܠ over, ܚܠܦ
instead of, ܚܕܪ around, ܒܬܪ after, ܣܛܪ except,
ܒܠܚܘܕ only, ܩܕܡ before, ܬܚܝܬ (ܬܚܬ) under.

III. NOTES ON THE SYNTAX (§§ 50—56).

Syriac resembles Ethiopic in the greater freedom 50 it enjoys in regard to the arrangement of the different members of the sentence as compared with Arabic and Hebrew. In later writers, however, imitation of the Greek sentence construction resulted in a style so clumsy—and that not alone in translations from Greek authors—as to give rise to complaints among the Syrians themselves.

The pronoun is more extensively employed than 51 in Hebrew, *e. g.* for the subject comprised in the [a] verb: اَحَد رِب هو; for the article, especially in translations from Greek (cf. Ethiop., French [il]le, Ital. il[la]) we find (هو and) هو. Again, the pronoun is used to anticipate a Genetive حكحنا هرصو, or the object of the verb with or without ل; also to accompany independent prepositions with ر, or with repetition of the preposition with or without emphasis هو عموما احنا on that (very) day. Finally we note the employment of the pronoun to express the so-called Ethic Dative اتي لكم, and its reflexive use in expressions like حكحت اشموه Simeon of his pillar=Simeon the Stylite.

The position of the demonstrative pronoun is *b* sometimes before, sometimes after the substantive.

c　In the case of a genetive with its no m en r e g e n s, the suffix is always appended to the second substantive when the first is in the construct state, ܡܣܟܢܘܬ ܗܝܡܢܘܬܗܘܢ their want of faith; in most cases, also, when ܕ is used, ܠܚܡܐ ܕܣܘܢܩܢܢ our necessary bread.

d　The following are used to express emphasis: ܢܩܦ (Hebr.), ܕܪܫ; ܩܢܘܡܐ, ܡܬܘܡܐ, but especially ܟܝܢ, nature. Is ipse ܗܘ ܗܘ ܗܘ.

e　One, τις ܐܝܢܐ, nobody ܠܐ ܐܢܫ and ܐܢܫ ܠܐ, even ܐܢܫ ܐܢܕܝܢ a certain woman, ܡܕܡ something (N. Mand. Gram. § 150). For the reciprocal pronoun we find ܚܒܪ and ܚܒܪܐ "companion", not confined to persons; ܟܠܝܘܡ every day, ܟܠܗ ܝܘܡܐ the whole day.

52　The Verb.

a　The impersonal finite verb stands generally in the feminine, ܓܕܫܬ and ܓܕܫ accidit, the participle (and adjective) more frequently in the masculine (§ 48 *f.*); these verbs also show a fondness for the passive: ܐܬܐܡܪ ܠܝ, ܐܫܬܡܥ ܠܢ, ܐܬܒܥܝ, dixi, audivimus, quaesiverunt; more rare are expressions like ܗܘ ܕܒܥܐ ܢܬܬܣܝܡ, Lagarde, Psalt. Hier. p. 156.

b　The perfect has the force of a future-perfect in the protasis of a conditional sentence, but it is seldom found in the apodosis; the perfect of emphatic assurance is rare, except in the Old Testament.

Our present is scarcely ever expressed by the *c* imperfect; on the other hand, after verbs requiring another verb to complete their meaning (such as will, begin, &c.) the imperfect is regularly found, with and without ؟ or ܘ. Either both verbs stand in the same mood, with or without ܘ, or the second appears in the imperf., with or without ؟; the participle and the infinitive with ܠ are less frequent in this construction. ؟ frequently serves to introduce direct speech.

The proper form for the present is the participle, *d* which completely supplanted the imperfect in later Syriac. It also stands in dependent clauses, even after an imperative ܡܣܡܝ ܐܨܚ ܘܢܪܒܘܢ let both grow. To express a condition or state, it is usually preceded by ܟܕ. The passive participle differs from the active in frequently expressing the past—ܡܝܬ dying, ܡܝܬ dead—or the gerundive.

The infinitive absolute is found as in Hebr. *e* both before and (rarely) after the finite verb; when depending on another verb, the infin. is always preceded by ܠ. It stands frequently after ܗܘܐ, ܐܝܬ, ܡܟܐ it is or is not (possible); after a preposition it requires ܠ, *e. g.* Gen. 4, 13 ܡܢ ܕܢܫܬܒܩ.

ܗܘܐ is employed as auxiliary verb: **53**

a) quite pleonastically to strengthen the negative ܠܐ: ܗܘܐ ܠܐ, also ܬܘܒ — ܗܘܐ ܠܐ not only.

ⵀ*

b) for the imperative, joined to an adjective or participle, ܫܠܡ ܗܘܳܐ ἔρρωσο.

c) The perfect ܗܘܳܐ expresses:

α) with another perfect, the pluperfect (Matt. 14, 3) or the simple perfect;

δ) with an imperfect, the conjunctive of the present;

γ) with a participle, the imperfect of the indicative, in conditional sentences the conjunctive.

d) The imperfect with participles and adjectives denotes the subjunctive.

e) For be ܐܝܬ with suffixes is more usual than ܗܘܳܐ, ܐܝܬܘܗܝ he is; ܗܘܳܐ ܐܝܬ (he) it was.

54   The object, especially when definite, but often also when not definite (undetermined), is introduced by ܠ; instead of the suffix of the object we find as frequently ܠ.

55   The Noun.

a   Adjectives and participles in the predicate still appear in the absolute state, although no longer without exception; the same applies to the substantive in adverbial expressions, especially after ܦ, to numbers, and to the names of the months; (infinitive).

b   The construct, which may stand, as in Hebr. before a preposition (ܡܦܩ ܒܪܘܚܐ ἀπολογία), is supplanted in Syriac, more and more, by the emphatic state

followed by ?: ܗܳܘ̣ܟ݁ ܙܽܣܟܕܗ, ܗܳܘ̣ܟ; ܙܽܣܕܗܳ, or ܗܳܘ̣ܟ; ܣܗܳܟܽܣ;.
In this construction, a great variety of small words—
especially the copula (pron.)—may stand between the
two substantives, and the genetive may even, as in
Greek, precede its *nomen regens* (cf. Aeth. Gr. § 132).

The position of the attributive adjective is generally *c*
after its substantive, as often before it, however, when
expressing an honourable title or quality. The adjective
usually agrees in state with the substantive, but, in
exceptional cases, both the other possible variations
occur, least frequently the emph. st. of the adjective
with the absolute of the noun.

Miscellaneous. **56**

Instead of ܡ̣ܶ in the comparative, we often find, *a*
as a result of Greek influence, ܐܘ̣, ἥ Matt. 11, 22. 24.

In addition to the simple negative ܠܐ there is the *b*
more emphatic form ܠܳܘܣ ܠܐ (ܠܐܘ — ܠܐ neither—nor),
ܕܠܐ; ܠܐܶ *ne* serves as subjective negative, and is employed in questions implying a doubt (μήτι), and in
ܙܕܠܐܽܣ, ܘ̣ܝ in clauses expressing fear or purpose.

To introduce impossible conditional clauses we find *c*
ܕܠܐ and ܠܐ ܕܠܐ, also ? ܠܐ ܕܠܐ.

The relative ? is very seldom omitted. *d*

READING EXERCISE. Matt. 6, 10—13.

ܐܒܘܢ ܕܒܫܡܝܐ ܢܬܩܕܫ ܫܡܟ. ܬܐܬܐ ܡܠܟܘܬܟ. ܢܗܘܐ
ܨܒܝܢܟ. ܐܝܟܢܐ ܕܒܫܡܝܐ ܐܦ ܒܐܪܥܐ. ܗܒ ܠܢ ܠܚܡܐ
ܕܣܘܢܩܢܢ ܝܘܡܢܐ. ܘܫܒܘܩ ܠܢ ܚܘܒܝܢ ܐܝܟܢܐ ܕܐܦ ܚܢܢ
ܫܒܩܢ ܠܚܝܒܝܢ. ܘܠܐ ܬܥܠܢ ܠܢܣܝܘܢܐ. ܐܠܐ ܦܨܢ ܡܢ ܒܝܫܐ.
ܡܛܠ ܕܕܝܠܟ ܗܝ ܡܠܟܘܬܐ ܘܚܝܠܐ ܘܬܫܒܘܚܬܐ ܠܥܠܡ
ܥܠܡܝܢ ܐܡܝܢ.

Aβûn dᵉβašmáyâ, neϑqáddaš šᵉmáχ. tíϑē malkuϑáχ; nehveh ṣeβyànáχ, aikánnâ δᵉβašmáyâ áϕ b'ár'â. hàβ-lan laḥmâ δᵉsunqā́nan yaumānâ; vašᵉβóq-lan ḥaubain aikánnâ δ'áϕ ḥnan šᵉβaqn lᵉḥayyàβain. vᵉlā́ ϑa'lan lᵉnesyṓnâ, éllâ ϕáṣṣán men bîšâ; meṭṭul dᵉδîláχ-hī malkúϑâ vᵉḥáilâ vᵉϑešbóḥtâ lᵉ'ālam 'àlᵉmîn, amén.

AIDS TO TRANSLATION.

ܐܒܘܢ § 32.—ܕܒܫܡܝܐ, ܕ = § 22 + ܒ § 49*b* + ܫܡܝܐ, **heaven**, which though always plural in form is also construed as singular (§ 28*c*); st. abs. ܫܡܝܢ, cstr. ܫܡܝ.—ܢܬܩܕܫ 3 m. sg. impf. Ethpaal from denominative verb ܩܕܫ (Pael); indicative and jussive are not distinguished.—ܫܡܟ from ܫܡ **name**, with suff. 2 m. sg., emph. ܫܡܐ, with suff. ܫܡܗ, ܫܡܗܘܢ, in the plural, with inserted ܗ, ܫܡܗܝܢ, ܫܡܗܐ, cf. ܐܒܐ, ܐܒܗܐ § 32.—ܬܐܬܐ, E.

Syr. ܬܐܬܐ, 3 f. sg. impf. Peal from ܐܬܐ come, § 48 *d*, 2.—ܡܠܟܘܬܟ, abstract feminine ܡܠܟܘܬ § 30 IV + suff. 2 sg. m.; note Q. of the ܟ as distinguished from Hebr. מַלְכוּתְךָ.—ܢܗܘܐ 3 m. sg. impf. of ܗܘܐ §§ 47, 48 *b*.—ܨܒܝܢܟ, m. subst. in ܝܢ, ܝܢܐ from ܨܒܐ wish, will, with suff., § 25, 4, *b*, 1.—ܐܝܟܢܐ how? interrogative adverb used relatively with following ܕ, cf. §§ 21. 22.—ܐܦ also, cf. Hebr. and Aram. אַף.—ܒܐܪܥܐ (E. Syr. ܒܐܪܥܐ).=ܐܪܥܐ emph. from ܐܪܥ=Hebr. אֶרֶץ, Aram. אֲרַע, אַרְעָא, Arab. أرض (§ 14 *a*; 26 fem.)+prep. ܒ § 17 *b* 2.

ܗܒ § 48 *g* 5—ܠܢ § 49 *b*; in later Syriac written as one word ܗܒܠܢ.—ܠܚܡܐ, st. emph. from abs. ܠܚܡ, H. לֶחֶם—ܕܣܘܢܩܢܢ=ܕ to express the genetive (§ 55*b*)+ ܣܘܢܩܢ, ܣܘܢܩܢܐ m. subst., need, necessity, from the stem ܣܢܩ need—of Peal only part. pass. in use+ suffix, which in such a combination is almost always appended to the second member, although belonging strictly to the first or to the whole expression (§ 51 *c*).—ܝܘܡܢܐ, adj. acc. to § 25, 4 *b* 1 from ܝܘܡ, ܝܘܡܐ § 29, I, *e*.

ܘܫܒܘܩ imp. sg. m. of ܫܒܘܩ pardon; for ܘ *v.* § 6 *c*; 38 *c*, *e*; the prefixing of ܘ does not produce a firmly closed syllable, hence ܒ with R.—ܠܢ *v. supra.*—ܚܘܒܝܢ, our debts, from ܚܘܒܐ, st. cstr. and abs. ܚܘܒ § 30, I *e*, pl. ܚܘܒܝܢ, ܚܘܒܐ+suff. 1 p. pl.; the E. Syrians write ܚܘܒܝܢ acc. to § 6 *d* 1, so ܝܘܡܢܐ above.—ܕ ܐܝܟܢܐ and ܐܦ *v. sup.*—ܚܢܢ § 19—ܫܒܩܢ shorter

form of the 1 pl. perf., § 36 a.—ܚܘܼܬܵܒܲܝܢ our debtors;
dative partic. ܠ + plur. of intensive noun ܚܵܝܒ § 25, 3 a
from a root med. ‍o, the ‍o passing into ‍ܝ § 46 b.

ܘܠܵܐ and not, ܠܵܐ=non and ne—ܬܲܥܸܠ lead us
2 m. sg. impf. Aphel (ܐܲܥܸܠ) from the root ܥܠܠ with
suff. of 1 per. pl., § 43. As in Hebr., the imper. cannot
stand with the negation.—ܠܢܸܣܝܘܿܢܵܐ, prepos. ܠ, which
also denotes motion and direction + ܢܸܣܝܘܿܢܵܐ—H. נִסָּיוֹן
§ 25, 4 b, 1 note, from the root ܢܣܐ, only in Pael.—ܐܸܠܵܐ
but, doubtless contracted from ܐܸܢ if and ܠܵܐ not.—ܦܲܨܵܢ
deliver us, m. sg. imp. Pael of ܦܨܐ with suff. 1 p. pl.,
§ 47.—ܡܸܢ ܒܝܼܫܵܐ from the evil (one); preposition
ܡܸܢ § 49 c; ܒܝܼܫܵܐ st. abs. msc. of ܒܝܼܫ (cf. Aram. בִּאְשָׁא);
if to be rendered "from evil" (neutr.), we should
expect ܒܝܼܫܬܵܐ (§ 26).—ܡܸܛܠ prep., (from ܡܵܛܠ, ܡܵܛܘܿܠ
with ܠ, √ܛܠܠ) on account of (§ 49 f); with follg.
ܕ becomes a conjunction.—ܕܡܸܟܒܲܪ § 23.—ܗ݈ܘ the fem.
pron. (§ 19), as copula more correctly written as
enclitic ܗܘ. — ܐܲܠܵܗܵܐ § 28 b; 29, I, f.—ܬܸܫܒܘܿܚܬܵܐ (acc. to
others ܐ with R.) § 30 A. 2, plur. ܬܸܫܒܚܬܵܐ of Pael ܫܲܒܲܚ
praise.—ܠܥܲܠܡܝܼܢ st. constr., which still appears, especially in a connexion like the present (§ 29, II a).—ܐܡܝܼܢ
we prefer to derive from the Gk. ἀμήν, rather than
from the Hebr. אָמֵן in spite of Jer. 28, 6.

LITTERATURA SYRIACA.

***Hebediesu** [† 1318], tractatus continens catalogum librorum chal-
daeorum, tam ecclesiasticorum quam profanorum, ed. Abraham
Ecchellensis. Rom, 653. 12⁰.   sh. 5. M. 7. 50.

Index of Biblical and Ecclesiastical Writings, Drawn up by *Mar
Abd Yeshua*, Metropolitan of Nisibis and Armenia, A. D. 1298.
Appendix A. in *G. P. Badger*, the Nestorians and their Rituals.
1852. *2*, p. 361—379.

Joseph Simonius Assemanus Syrus Maronita [† 1768], Bibliotheca
orientalis clementino-vaticana, in qua manuscriptos codices syriacos
recensuit . . . Rom, fol. I, 719 de scriptoribus syris orthodoxis II,
721 de scriptoribus syris monophysitis III, 1, 725 de scriptoribus
Nestorianis cont. Catalogum Ebediesu.   III, 2, 728 de Syris
Nestorianis. Vol. I. M. 15.   M. 200. 400. 425.

J. S. Assemanns orientalische bibliothek oder nachrichten von syrischen schriftstellern. in einen auszug gebracht von *Aug. Friedr.
Pfeiffer*. Erlangen, 776, 2 ps. [8 + 16] 594 S.
                             M. 1. 50. 2. 4. 4. 50.

Bibliothecae apostolicae vaticanae codicum manuscriptorum *catalogus*
in tres partes distributus. *Steph. Evodius Assemanus* archiepi-
scopus Apameensis et *Jos. Sim. Ass.* Rom, fol. Partis I tomus II,
758 et Partis I tomus III, 759 complectens codices chaldaicos sive
syriacos.

[*Angelo Mai* († 1854)], scriptorum veterum nova collectio e vaticanis
codicibus edita. Tom. V. Rom, 831. 4⁰. Codices chaldaici
sive syriaci vaticani assomaniani, p. 1*—82*.

    Indices alphabetici auctorum et operum codicibus syriacis,
hebraicis, et copticis comprehensorum. T. V. p. 243/51.

    Summa codicum orientalium vaticanorum in Tomo IV et V de-
scriptorum, additis etiam hebraicis et syriacis, quos Assemanus
tribus tonus impressis descripsit . . . Syriaci 459. T. X(2) 874.

---

*) De asterisco vide praefationem.

Nestle.

Bibliothecae *Mediceae Laurentianae* et *Palatinae* codicum mss. orientalium *catalogus* ... Steph. Evod. Assemanus archiep. Apameae recensuit ... Antonio Francisco Gorio curante. Flor. 742 fol. cum tabb. M. 25.

Catalogus codicum manuscriptorum orientalium qui in *Museo Britannico* asservantur. Pars prima codices syriacos et carshunicos amplectens [ed. Rosen et Forshall]. Lond. 38 fol. sh. 12.

Catalogue of the syriac manuscripts in the *British Museum* acquired since the year 1838. By *W. Wright.* [Lond.] 3 ps. 70. 71. 72. 4⁰. (70 sh.) M. 50. 70. vol. 2. M. 15.

*T. J. Lamy, les manuscrits syriaques du Musée britannique. Bulletin Acad. d'arch. belgique. 49ᵉ année, 2ᵉ Série, 1880.

Catalogi codicum manuscriptorum bibliothecae *Bodleianae* pars sexta, codices syriacos, carshunicos, mandaeos complectens. Confecit *R.. Payne Smith.* Oxon. 64. 4⁰. [sh. 21.] M. 16.

Manuscrits orientaux. Catalogues des manuscrits syriaques et sabéens (mandaites) de la bibliothèque nationale [ed. *H. Zotenberg*]. Paris 74. 4⁰. 8. 246. [2]. M. 10.

Königliche Bibliothek, Berlin. Kurzes Verzeichnis der Sachau'schen Sammlung syrischer Handschriften von *E. Sachau.* Nebst Übersicht des alten Bestandes. Berlin, 85. 28. 35. M. 1. 50.

*E. Rödiger, Üb. d. oriental. Handschriften aus Etienne Quatremère's Nachlass in München. 8⁰, br. Extr. (Brill). fl. —. 50.

B. Dorn, Über 4 von der kaiserlichen öffentl. Bibliothek zu St. Petersburg im Jahr 1852 erworbene syr. Handschriften. St. Petersburg 1854. A. 16 pag. M. — 60.

De codice palimpsesto graeco-lat.-syriaco cf. Cozza, Sacr. Bibl. Vet. fragm. 1867; de codice evangeliorum Gerhardino: *Irmischer,* Handschriften-Katalog der Königlichen Universitäts-Bibliothek zu Erlangen n 19.

J. Fr. Gaab, Über die Litteratur der christlichen Syrer. Paulus, Neues Repertorium. 3 (1791) 358 ff.

Andr. Theoph. Hoffmann, kurze geschichte der syrischen literatur vide *Berthold,* Journal XIV (22) 225/91.

C. v. Lengerke, de studio litterarum Syriacarum theologis quam maxime commendando comment. 1. 2. 2 part. Regim. 1836. M. —. 50. 1.

Gust. Bickell, conspectus rei Syrorum literariae additis notis bibliographicis et excerptis anecdotis. Monast. 71. 112. M. 2. 40. (Pars I, p. 1—58 separatim prodiit.)

Neve, F., de la renaissance des études syriaques. Paris 1854.

La littérature syriaque. Rép. franç. 1876, Jan. 7.

L'abbé *P. Martin,* Rapport sur les progrès des études Araméennes. Compte rendu de la 1ᵉʳᵉ Sess. du congrès d. Orient. 1873. t II.

— Pierre Dowaï et la poësie sacrée chez les Maronites ibid.

P. Pick, Syriac Litterature. Mac Clinstock & Strong's Cyclop. Vol. 10. (1881).

Frothingham, A. L., Historical Sketch of Syriac Literature and Culture I. Amer. Journ. of Philol. V, 2, 200—220.

W. Wright, Syriac Literature. Encyclopedia Britannica. vol. 22. p. 824—856. [opus plenissimum, 1237 notae marginales.]

I. GRAMMATICAE, CHRESTOMATHIAE ET LEXICA.

*1 1539 *Ambrosius, Theseus,* . . . introductio in chaldaicam linguam, syriacam atque armenicam et decem alias linguas. [Papiae] fol. (Weigel 15 R.) M. 18. 22. 50. 25. 50.

2 1554 *Angelus Caninius*, institutiones linguae syriacae, assyriacae atque thalmudicae, unà cum aethiopicac atque arabicae collatione. Paris, Stephanus. 4⁰. M. 2.

3 1556 [*Joh. Alb. Widmanstadtius*] Syriacae linguae . . . prima elementa. quibus adjectae sunt christianae religionis solennes quotidianaeque precationes. Viennae Austriacae. 4⁰. [56 pp.] M. 2. 50. 4. 50. 6. 10. 11. 30.

*4 1560 *Joh. Mercerus*, tabulae in grammaticen linguae chaldaeae, quae et syriaca dicitur. Paris, Morelli. 4⁰.

5 1569 Grammatica chaldaea et syra Immanuelis Tremellij [Genevae], Stephanus [in appendice Nⁱ Tˡ et seorsim]. M. 2. 10. 4. 80.

6 1571 *Syrorum peculium.* hoc est vocabula apud syros scriptores passim usurpata: targumistis vero aut prorsus incognita: aut in ipsorum vocabulariis adhuc non satis explicata. *Andr. Masius* [Du Mas † 1573] sibi suae memoriae juvandae caussa colligebat. Antverp., Plantin. fol. (in Bibl. Polygl. T. VI).

6 1571 Grammatica linguae syriacae inventore atque auctore *Andrea Masio*: opus novum, & à nostris hominibus adhuc non tractatum . . . Antverp., Plantin. fol. (in Bibl. Polygl. T. VI).

7 1572 Dictionarium syro-chaldaicum *Guidone Fabricio Boderiano* [Fevre de la Boderie] collectore et auctore. Antverp., Plantin. fol. [in Bibl. Polygl. T. VI]. [de autographis Fabri et Masii cf. Serapeum 45. 16. 272.] [4 ff.] 23 pp. M. 10.

8 1572 [*Joh. Alb. Widmanstadt* et *Guido Fevre de la Boderie*] Syriacae linguae prima elementa. Antverp., Plantin. 4⁰. cf. n. 3.

9 1574 *Bonavent. Cornel. Bertramus*, צלם comparatio grammaticae hebraicae & aramicae, atque adeo dialectorum aramicarum inter se: concinnata ex hebraicis Antonii Cevallerij praeceptionibus, aramicisque doctorum aliorum observationibus. [Genevae,] Vignon. 4⁰. M. 4. 20. 4. 50.

A*

*10 1579 *Joh. Mercerius*, tabulae in grammaticon linguae chaldaicae, quae et syriaca dicitur. Vitebergae. 8⁰. cf. 4.

11 1594 Institutio linguae syrae ex optimis quibusque apud Syros scriptoribus, in primis Andrea Masio collecta a *Casparo Wasero* Tigurino. Lugd. Bat. 4⁰.

*12 1594 *Victorius Petrus* paradigmata de quatuor linguis orientalibus praecipuis arabica, armena syra aethiopica. Paris. 4⁰. M. 12.

13 1596 Grammatica syriaca sive chaldaica Georgii Michaelis *Amirae* Edenensis e Libano. Romae. 4⁰.

*14 1602 Grammatica chaldaica descripta ex tabulis *Merceri* ... ita mutata ... ut plane nova grammatica dici possit (opera *Drusii*.) Franeqer.

15 1606 L'harmonie etymologique des langues hebraïque, chaldaïque, syriaque, grecque, latine, françoise, italienne, espagnole, allemande, flamende, angloise etc. par *M. Estienne Guichard*. Paris.
                                                    M. 10.

16 1611 Gymnasium syriacum ... ex novo testamento syro et aliis rerum syriacarum scriptoribus collecta novis & genuinis characteribus adornata a *M. Christoph. Crinesio*, Schlaccowaldo-Bohemo Wittebergae. 4⁰.   M. 2.

*17 1612 = 9. Amstelodami. 4⁰.

18 1612 Lexicon pentaglotton, hebraicum, chaldaicum, syriacum, talmudico-rabbinicum et arabicum ... ex testamento novo syriaco ... concinnatum a ... Valentino *Schindlero* Oederano ... opus novum nunc post authoris obitum ex ipso autographo fidelissime descriptum. Hanoviae. fol.   sh. 10. M. 7.75.

*19 1612 = 18. Francofurti. fol.   M. 7.75.

20 1612 Lexicon syriacum, e novo testamento et rituali Severi patriarchae quondam Alexandrini syro collectum ... atque ... tredecim disputationibus propositum, auctore et praeside *M. Christoph. Crinesio*. Wittebergae. 4⁰.

21 1615 *Joh. Buxtorfi* [filii] grammaticae chaldaicae et syriacae libri III. Basileae.   M. 2.

22 1616 *Joh. Gasbar Myricaeus*, prima elementa linguae syriacae ... quibus adjecta sunt exercitia etc. Colon. Allobrog.

*23 1617 Grammatica aramaea h. e. chaldaicae et syriacae elementa. Bremae.

*24 1619 = 22. Genevae. 4⁰. (Grammaticae syro-chaldaeae libri duo.)   M. 2. 4.

*25 1619 = 11. *C. Waser*, grammatica Syra. Leidae. 4⁰.
                                                    sh. 7. 6 d.

*26 1619 *Henr. Opitius*, Syriasmus restitutus et hebraismo chaldaismoque harmonicus Lips. 4⁰.   M. 3.

27 1622 Lexicon chaldaicum et syriacum; quo voces omnes ...

quotquot . . . in novi testamenti translatione syriaca reperiuntur . . . a *M. Joh. Buxtorfio* jun. Basileae. 4⁰. M. 4. 4. 50. 10.

28 1622 *Joh. Bapt. Ferrari*, Nomenclator syriacus Romae. 4⁰.

29 1623 *Mart. Trost*, lexicon syriacum ex inductione omnium exemplorum novi testamenti syriaci adornatum. Cothenis Anhaltinorum. 4⁰. M. 2. 3. 4. 10.

30 1627 *Hieron. Avianus*, clavis poeseos sacrae, trium principalium linguarum orientalium, hebraeae, chaldaeae ac syrae rhythmos exhibens. Lips.

*31 1627 *Herm. Nicolai*, idea linguarum aramaearum per comparationem . . . Copenh.

32 1628 *Abrahami* Ecchellensis collegii Maronitarum alumni linguae syriacae sivè chaldaicae perbrevis institutio ad eiusdem nationis studiosos adolescentes. Rom. 12⁰. M. 3.

*33 1628 *Ludovici de Dieu* grammatica linguarum oriental., Hebraeorum, Chaldaeor. et Syror. inter se collatarum. Lugd. Bat.

*34 1628 *M. Thomae Erpenii* grammatica chaldaea ac syra opera et cura *Constantini l'Empereur de Oppijk S. S. T. D. et L. H.* ac C. P. in Acad. Lugduno Batav. in lucem edita.

35 1635 *Harb. Thorndyke*, epitome lexici hebraici, syriaci, rabinici et arabici unà cum observationibus circa linguam hebraeam et graecam. Londin. fol.

36 1635 *Schindleri* lexicon pentaglotton . . . in epitomen redactum à G. A. [Gulielmus Alabaster]. Lond. fol.

37 1636 *Thomas à Novaria* Obicinus, thesaurus arabico-syro-latinus. Romae:

Index alphabeticus ad formam dictionarii pro thesauro . . . a P. F. Marco Bonelio Lucensi editus ib. eod.

38 1636 *Isaac* Scindrensis, Maronita e Libano, archiepisc. Tripolis Syriae, grammatica linguae syriacae. Rom.

39 1637 *Eclogae sacrae* novi testamenti syriacae graecae latinae cum observationibus. quibus praemittuntur rudimenta grammaticae syriacae opera *Joh. Mich. Dilherri*. Jenae. 12⁰.

40 1638 Eclogae sacrae novi testamenti, syriacae, graecae latinae. cum notis et observationibus ita explicatae ut . . . adhibitis grammaticae syriacae rudimentis antehac excusis attentus lector linguam syriacam proprio marte possit addiscere. Adduntur indices locupletissimi et manuale lexici syriaci. Jenae. 12⁰.

*40ᵇ 1643 *Senertus, A.*, Trosti grammatica ebraea eademq. univers. hypotyposis harmonica linguarum Orient. Chaldaeae, Syrae, Arabicaeque c. matre Ebraea. 4⁰. M. 2.

41 1646 Circulus conjugationum perfectarum orientalium, ebraeae, chaldaeae, syrae, arabicae, aethiopicae juxta methodum Schickardi. Jenae. 4⁰.

42 1647 *Schickard*, institutiones linguae ebraeae noviter recognitae

et auctae. acc. harmonia perpetua aliarum linguarum orientalium, chaldaeae, syrae, arabicae, aethiopicae opera *Joh. Ern. Gerhardi.* Jenae. 4⁰.

48 1647 *Josephus Acurensis,* grammatica linguae syriacae. Rom.

*44 1647 *Christ. Ravis,* discourse on the original tongues, viz. Ebrew, Samaritan, Calde, Syriac, Arabic and Aethiopic, together with a general Grammar of the said tongues. Lond. 12⁰.

*45 1649 = 18. Hanoviae. fol.

46 1649 [*Joh. Ern. Gerhard*] Σκιαγραφια linguae syro-chaldaicae cum analyseos syriacae specimine. Hallis Saxon. 4.

*46ᵇ 1649 = 42. (Witteberg[?]).   M. 1. 80.

47 1650 *Joh. Buxtorfi* grammaticae chaldaicae et syriacae libri III.... editio secunda auctior et emendatior. Basileae. M. 1. 1. 20. 2.

48 1651 *Andr. Sennert,* grammatica chaldaica et syra. Wittenberg. 4⁰.

49 1652 *Joh. Henr. Hottinger,* Tigurinus, grammaticae chaldaeo-syriacae libri duo; cum triplici appendice chaldaea, syra et rabbinica. Tiguri.

*50 1653 *Briani Waltoni* introductio ad lectionem linguar. orient. Hebr. Chald. Samaritan. Syriac. Arabic. Persic. Armenic. Copticae. Londin. 12⁰.

51 1653 = 18 etc. Francof. fol.   M. 5. 7. 20.

52 1658 *Eclogae sacrae* novi testamenti syriacae graecae latinae cum observationibus. quibus praemittuntur rudimenta grammaticae syriacae opera *Joh. Mich. Dilherri.* Jenae. 12⁰. [ed. 3ª] 26. 250. (4) pp.

53 1658 *Joh. Leusden,* scholae syriacae libri tres. unâ cum dissertatione de literis et lingua Samaritanorum. Ultrajecti.   M. 1. 1. 75. 3.

54 1658 *Gulielm. Beveridgius,* grammatica syriaca tribus libris tradita . . ut menstruo spatio . . ipsa linguae medulla exugatur . . in usum bibliorum πολυγλωττατων Waltoniensium. | Accedit eiusdem: de linguarum orientalium praesertim hebr., chald., syr., arab. et samar. praestantia necessitate et utilitate.| London.   M. 3.

55 1658 *Joh. Henr. Hottinger,* grammatica quatuor linguarum hebraicae, chaldaicae, syriacae et arabicae harmonica . . . accedit technologia linguae arabicae theologico-historica. Heidelbergae. 4⁰.

*55ᵇ 1659 *Th. Erpenius,* grammatica hebraea generalis ed. III, cui accessit Grammaticae syrae et chaldaeae eiusd. auctoris ed. II. L. Bat. [sec. Brill.]   fl. 1. 25.

56 1661 *Joh. Henr. Hottinger,* etymologicum orientale; sive lexicon harmonicum ἑπταγλωττον, quo . . et chaldaicae syriacae . . . dialectorum . . . voces juxta seriem radicum hebraicarum exhibentur . . . accessit brevis apologia contra Abrahamum Ecchellensem Maronitam. Francofurti. 4⁰.

57 1662 Eclogae sacrae novi testamenti, syriacae, graecae latinae.

cum notis et observationibus ita explicatae ut . . . adhibitis grammaticae syriacae rudimentis antehac excusis attentus lector linguam syriacam proprio marte possit addiscere. Adduntur indices locupletissimi et manuale lexici syriaci opera *J. M. Dilherri* . . . qui novam addidit Praefationem. Jenae. 12⁰.

*58 1664 = 56 *Hottinger*, Etymologicum orientale. Turic. 4⁰.

*59 1664 *Andr. Sennert*, scrutinium linguarum orientalium ebraeo-chaldaeo-syro-arabico-persico-aethiopicae. Vitebergae. 4⁰.

60 1665 *M. Dav. Grafunder*, grammatica syriaca cum Syntaxi. Wittebergae. M. 1. 50.

*61 1666 *Andr. Sennert*, Grammatica orientalis eademque harmonica etc. seu (ab altera tituli parte) Ebraismus, Chaldaismus, Syriasmus, Arabismus etc. Wittenberg. 4⁰. M. 3.

62 1667 *Aegid. Gutbir*, lexicon syriacum continens omnes N. T. syriaci dictiones et particulas . . . Hamburgi. M. 2. 30.

63 1669 *Edm. Castle*, lexicon heptaglotton, hebraicum, chaldaicum, syriacum, samaritanum. aethiopicum, arabicum conjunctim, et persicum separatim . . . cui accessit brevis et harmonica . . . grammaticae omnium praecedentium linguarum delineatio. Authore Edmundo Castello, S. T. D. . . . Londini, Roycroft fol. (Appendix Bibl. Polygl. Walt.) M. 75. £ 2. 16. 4. 4.

64 1670 *Joh. Friedr. Nicolai*, Hodegeticum orientale harmonicum quod complectitur I Lexicon linguarum ebraicae, chaldaicae, syriacae, arabicae, aethiopicae et persicae harmonicum II grammaticam linguarum earundem . . . III dicta biblica . . . Jenae. 4⁰.
M. 4.

65 1672 *Joh. Leusden*, schola syriaca una cum synopsi chaldaica et dissertatione de literis et lingua Samaritanorum. Editio secunda. Ultrajecti. M. —. 50. 1. 20. 2. 50.

*66 1676 *Jac. Alting*, synopsis institutionum chaldaearum et syrarum. Francofurti.

*67 1677 *Christoph Cellarius*, porta Syriae. Cizae. 4⁰.

68 1678 *Henr. Opitius*, syriasmus facilitati et integritati suae restitutus simulque hebraismo et chaldaismo harmonicus, regulis iisdem quinquaginta absolutus. . . . cura M. Daniel. Hasenmulleri φιλανατολικογλώττου. Lipsiae. 4⁰. M. 3.

69 1679 *Joh. Wilh. Hilliger*, summarium linguae aramaeae i. e. chaldaeo-syro-samaritanae. Wittebergae. 4⁰. M. 1. 50.

70 1682 *Christoph. Cellarius*, porta Syriae patentior sive grammaticae novae . . . editio secunda. Cizae. 4".
M. —. 80. 1. 20. 1. 25. 1. 50. 2. 20.

71 1683 *Christoph. Cellarius*, glossarium syro-latinum, nuper vulgatis utriusque testamenti excerptis accommodatum. Cizae. 4⁰.
M. —. 75.

72 1683 *Ludov. de Dieu* . . . grammatica linguarum orientalium
Hebraeorum, Chaldaeorum et Syrorum inter se collatarum. ex
recensione *David Clodii.* Francofurti. 4⁰.

73 1686 *Edmund Castle*, lexicon heptaglotton . . . Londini impr.
Th. Roycroft, sumptibus Roberti Scott. fol. = 63 cum novo titulo.

*74 1686 *J. Nicolai*, Hodegetici Orientalis pars II. editio 2. inscripta:
critica sacra. Francof. et Hamburg.

75 1686 *Caroli Schaaf* opus aramaeum complectens grammaticam
chaldaico-syriacam: selecta targumim . . . lexicon chaldaicum . . .
Ludg. Bat.   sh. 7.   M. 3.   4. 50.   6.   7. 50.

*76 1689 *Joh. Aug. Danz*, aditus Syriae reclusus. Jenae.   M. —. 70.

77 1691 *Henr. Opitius*, syriasmus etc. [= 26] secunda vice multis
in locis auctior editus. Lipsiae.   M. 1.   1. 50.   2. 10.

*78 1694 *Herm. von der Hardt*, syriacae linguae fundamenta. Helmst.

79 1695 *Valent. Schindler*, Lexicon Pentaglotton. Francofurti. fol.

80 1695 *Andr. Müller*, opuscula nonnulla orientalia uno volumine
comprehensa. Francof. ad O. 4⁰. [cf. ZDMG. 35, XV. N. 19].

81 1696 Brevis institutio linguae syriacae, J. H. Maji hebraicae atque
chaldaicae nuper emissis harmonica ad collegiorum usum conscripta
a M. G. O. B. Francofurti. 4⁰.

*82 1699 *Christ. Ludovicus*, hebraismus, chaldaismus, targumico-
talmud.-rabbinism. et syriasm. harmon. etc. Lips. s. a. (1699?)
(? = Wittebergae 1699. 4⁰. *Ludovici, Chr.* Syriasmus ex Opitio
in compendium redactus. 4⁰. M. 1).   M. 1. 50.

83 1700 *Joh. Aug. Danz*, Aditus Syriae reclusus . . . editio secunda.
Jenae.

84 1701 *Jac. Alting*, synopsis institutionum chaldaearum et syrarum.
Francofurti. in: Fundamenta etc. ed. sexta.

85 1702 *Geo. Otho*, palaestra linguarum orientalium, h. e. quatuor
primorum capitum Geneseos I textus originalis II targumim
I chaldaicae . . II syriaca . . . ex bibliis polyglottis anglicanis
Francofurti 4⁰ [acc.] glossarium linguarum orientalium octuplex.
                                                          M. 2.   2. 40.

86 1706 *Sim. Ockleij*, introductio ad linguas orientales. Cantabrig.

*87 1707 *Joh. Phil. Hartmanni* hebraicae, chald. syr. et samaritanae
linguarum institutio harmonica. Francofurti. 4⁰.

88 1709 *Carol. Schaaf*, lexicon syriacum concordantiale . . . (cum
novo testamento). Lugd. Bat. 4⁰.   M. 10.   12.   15.

*88ᵇ 1714 Element. lingg. syr. sam. aeth. Patav. 12⁰.

*89 1715 *Joh. Aug. Danz*, aditus Syriae reclusus editio 3. Jenae.

90 1717 *Carol. Schaaf*, lexicon syriacum concordantiale . . . editio
secunda, priori emendatior et auctior. Lugd. Bat. 4⁰.
                                                          M. 22.   40.

91 1717 *Jac. Alting*, synopsis institutionum chaldaearum et syrarum.
Francofurti.   M. 1. 50.

92 1722 *J. A. Dans,* Aditus Syriae reclusus. editio quarta Jenae.
M. 1. 75.

93 1725 *Sam. Fridr. Bucher,* thesaurus orientis s. compendiosa et
facilis methodus linguarum hebraeae, chaldaeo-targumicae, talmu-
dico-rabbinicao, syriae, samaritanae, arabicae, persicae. Francofurti
et Lipsiae. 4⁰.

94 1730 *Jac. Alling,* synopsis etc. in: Fundamenta editio octava.

*94^b 1731 *F. Masclef,* grammatica hebr. . . . 2 voll. Ed. II. Acc.
grammat. chald. syr. et samaritana. Paris. M. 3. 50. 6.

95 1741 *Christ. Bened. Michaelis,* syriasmus id est grammatica linguae
syriacae. Halae Magdeburgicae. 4⁰.
M. 1. 1. 20. 1. 25. 1. 40. 1. 50.

96 1742 *Ant. Zanolini,* grammatica syriaca. Pataviae. 4⁰. M. 1. 50.

97 1742 *Ant. Zanolini,* lexicon syriacum. ibid. M. 4.

98 1746 *Jac. Alling,* synopsis etc. in: Fundamenta editio nona
Francofurti.

99 1747 *Jac. Alting,* id. M. 3.

100 1751 *J. A. Danz,* Aditus Syriae reclusus. editio novissima. innu-
meris. in locis correctior et emendatior reddita a *M. Joh. Christoph.
Mylio.* Francofurti.

*101 1754 *Jac. Scherking,* Nyckelen til de fyra Oriental Spraken,
Hebraik, Chaldaik, Syriak, och Arabisk. Skara.

*102 1758 *J. G. Kals,* Grammatica Hebraeo-harmonica cum Arab.
et Aramaea. Amstel.

103 1759 *Ign. Weitenauer,* hierolexicon linguarum orientalium hebraicae, chaldaicae et syriacae . . . et cujusque harum linguarum
grammatica. August. Vind.

104 1759 *Ign. Weitenauer,* trifolium syriacum, sive nova grammaticae methodus qua intra aliquot horas explicare canonem bibliorum syriacum possis ibid.

*105 1762 *Ign. Weitenauer,* S. J., Hexaglotton geminum intra bre-
vissimum tempus docens linguas Gallic. Ital. Hispan. Graec. Hebr.
Chald. Anglic. German. Belgic. Latin. Lusit. Syriacam etc.
August. Vind. et Frib. Brisg. 4⁰. 2 voll. M. 4.

106 et 107 1768 *Joh. Dav. Michaelis,* abhandlung von der syrischen
sprache, und ihrem gebrauch: nebst dem ersten theil einer syrischen chrestomathie. Göttingen, Barmeier 768.
M. 1. —. 75. 1. 50.

107^b 1791 *J. Fr. Gaab,* Conjecturen über einige Stellen in der syr.
Chrestomathie von Michaelis. Paulus, Neues Repert. 3 (1791)
366 ff.

108 1772 *Joh. Dav. Michaelis,* id. Göttingen, Vandenhoeck [novus
titulus].

109 1773 *Joh. Lor. Isenbiehl,* beobachtungen von dem gebrauche
des syrischen puncti diacritici bei den verbis. Göttingen. 4⁰.

110 1783 *Joh. Dav. Michaelis*, syrische chrestomathie, erster theil.
zweito unveränderte auflage. Göttingen.
111 1784 *Joh. Dav. Michaelis*, grammatica syriaca. Halae. 4⁰.
M. 1. 1. 20. 1. 50. 2.
112 1784 *Jac. Ge. Christ. Adler*, brevis linguae syriacae institutio
in usum tironum edita. Altonae.   M. 1.
113 1786 *Joh. Dav. Michaelis*, abhandlung von der syrischen sprache
. . . zweite auflage mit zusätzen. Göttingen. 124. 118 pp.
M. 2. 50 [pretium reductum M. 1].
*114 1787 et 1789 *Innoc. Fessleri*, Institutiones linguar. orient. Hebr.
Chald. Syr. et Arab. Vratisl. Halis et Jen.
115 1788 *Edm. Castelli* lexicon syriacum ex eius lexico heptaglotto
seorsim typis describi curavit atque sua adnotata adjecit *Joann.
Dav. Michaelis*. Gottingae. 4⁰. pars I. pp. VIII. 1—476.
pars II. pp. 477—980. (P. 1. M. 6. 8.)
M. 25. 30. 45. 50. 53. 54. 58. 60. 70. 75.
fr. 45. sh. 32. 42.
115ᵇ *J. Fr. Gaab*, Wünsche bei Castellus syrischem Lexikon nach
Michaelis Ausgabe. Paulus Memorabilien. 1 (1791) 82 ff.
115ᶜ *G. W. Lorsbach*, Archiv: Über die Mängel des syrischen Wörter-
buches von Castellus. 100 pp.   M. 4.
116 1788 *Joan. Godofr. Hasse*, lectiones syro-arabico-samaritano-
aethiopicae. Regiomonti et Lipsiae.   M. 1. 1. 50.
117 1788 *Wilh. Friedr. Hezel*, syrische sprachlehre, durchaus nach
seiner hebräischen eingerichtet. Lemgo. 4⁰. M. 1. 1. 50.
118 1789 *Geo. Guil. Kirsch*, chrestomathia syriaca maximam partem
historici argumenti cum lexico syriaco. Hofae.
M. 1. 1. 50. 1. 80.
119 1789 *Jos. Ant. Schneller*, flores philologici ex linguis hebraica,
syriaca, chaldaica et graeca . . collecti. Dillingae.
*119ᵇ 1789 *J. A. Fessler*, institutt. linguar. oriental. hebr., chald., syr.
et arabic. 2 partes. Vratislav. = 114.   M. 1. 80.
120 1791 *Joh. Gottfr. Hasse*, praktisches handbuch der aramäischen
oder syrisch-chaldäisch-samaritanischen sprache. des praktischen
unterrichts der gesammten orientalischen Sprachen dritter theil.
Jena. (8) 203 (4).   M. 1. 20. 1. 50.
121 1793 *Olai Gerh. Tychsen* elementale syriacum sistens grammaticam chrestomathiam et glossarium, subiunctis novem tabulis
aere expressis Rostochii.   M. 1. 20. 1. 25. 1. 50.
122 1793 *Joh. Jahn*, aramäische oder chaldäische und syrische sprachlehre für anfänger. Wien.   M. 1. 1. 50.
123 1795 *Heinr. Adolf Grimm*, neue syrische chrestomathie mit
glossarium. Lemgo.   M. 1. 50. 2.
124 1802 *Friedr. Theod. Rink* und *Joh. Sever. Vater*, arabisches,
syrisches und chaldäisches lesebuch . . . mit verweisungen auf

die grammatik und mit erklärenden wortregistern. Leipzig. Pars chald. et syr. pp. 1—72. M. 1. 50.

125 1807 *Gust. Knös*, chrestomathia syriaca maximam partem e codicibus manu scriptis collecta. Gotting. M. 3 pret. reduct. 1.

*126 1816 *C. M. Agrelli*, Otiola Syriaca (de particulis ling. Syr., de ratione, qua Syri verba aliorum referunt etc.) Lund. 4°. M. 1.50.

127 1817 *Joh. Sev. Vater*, handbuch der hebräischen, syrischen, chaldäischen und arabischen grammatik. zweite ausgabe. Leipzig (pars syr. et chald. p. 99—246). M. 4. 50.

*128 1819 *Thomas Yates*, Syriac Grammar principally adapted to the new Testament in that language. Lond. M. 3. 50.

129 1820 *Joannis Jahn*, . . . elementa aramaicae seu chaldaeo-syriacae linguae latine reddita et nonnullis accessionibus aucta ab Andrea Oberleitner. Viennae. (M. 8.)
M. 1. 1.20. 1. 50. 1.75. 2. 3. 4. Lire 4.

*130 1824 *Hampus Tullberg*, Elementale Syr. P. I et II. Lond.

131 1825 *Aug. Hahn* et *Friedr. Lud. Sieffert*, chrestomathia syriaca sive S. Ephraemi carmina selecta ediderunt notis . . et glossario locupletissimo illustraverunt. Lipsiae. (M. 4.)
M. 1. 1. 50. 1.75. 2. 2.25. fr. 2. 50.

132 1826 *Paul Ewald*, Lehrbuch der syrischen Sprache. Erlangen. M. 1. 20.

133 1826/7 *Andr. Oberleitner*, chrestomathia syriaca una cum glossario syriaco-latino huic chrestomathiae accommodato. Viennae. Pars prior, chrestomathiam cont. 26. posterior pars, glossarium cont. 27 (M. 21). vol. 1. M. 2. M. 5. 6. 7. 75. 8. 9.

134 1827 *Andr. Theoph. Hoffmann*, grammaticae syriacae libri III. cum tribus tabulis varia scripturae aramaicae genera exhibentibus. Halae. 4°. 16. 418 pp. M. 8. 9. 10. 11.
Leipz. Lit. Ztg. 1829, 1538 ff., de Sacy, Journal des Savants 1829, 579/90.

*135 1829 *Christ. Bened. Michaelis*, grammatica Syriaca Romae [= 94]. fr. 2. 50.

136 1829 *Joh. Dav. Michaelis*, chrestomathia syriaca. editio tertia glossario adnotationibusque instructa a *J. C. C. Doepke*. Göttingae.
Joh. Christ. Carol. Doepke, glossarium chrestomathiae syriacae J. D. Mich. accommodatum. ib. 4. 192 pp.
M. 2. 50 pret. reduct. 1.
H[offmann] Jen. Lit. Ztg. 1830. 12.

137 1829 *Friedr. Uhlemann*, elementarlehre der syrischen sprache, mit vollständigen paradigmen, syrischen lesestücken und dem dazu gehörenden wörterbuche für akademische vorlesungen bearbeitet. Berlin. (M. 6.) 26. 254. 23. 19 pp. M. 1. 50. 1 80. 2. 2. 50.

*137[b] 1831 *A. Brunton*, Extracts from the Old Test. with outlines of hebrew, chaldee and syriac grammar. 3d edit. Edinb. M. 9.
               M. 1. 80.

138 1832 *Geo. Heinr. Aug. Ewald*, Abhandlungen zur orientalischen und biblischen literatur. Erster [einziger] theil. Göttingen. „III. Ueber das syrische punktationssystem nach syrischen handschriften." p. 55—129.   M. —. 75. 2.

139 1832/6 *Ge. Guil. Kirschii*, chrestomathia syriaca cum lexico denuo edidit *Ge. Henr. Bernstein*. Lipsiae. pars prior. chrestomathia ex codicibus manuscriptis emendata et aucta 1832. pars posterior. lexicon penitus novatum. 1836. 8. 582. 226. *12* pp.
          M. 5. 50. 6. 50. 7. 7. 50. 8. 10.

140 1833 ܥܡܪ ܐܘܚܕ ܕܚܨܐ. [liber abecedarius] lithogr. Malta 1833.
             M. 1. 50.

141 1834/38 *Caroli Magni Agrellii*, supplementa syntaxeos syriacae praefatus est *Joann. Godofr. Ludov. Kosegarten*. Gryphiswaldiae. appendicula ad supplementa sua ibid. 1836. appendicula posterior ibid. 1838.   M. 4.

*142 1836/7 *H. K. Tullberg*, initia linguae syriacae. 3 partes Lund.
           M. 3. 50. 4. 50.

*143 1837 *George Phillips* [† 1886]', elements of syriac grammar. Cambridge.   (sh. 5.) M. 2. 5. 6.

144 1838 *Aemil. Roediger*, chrestomathia syriaca edita et glossario explanata ab Ae. R. annexae sunt tabulae grammaticae. Halis Saxon.   M. 1. 50. 2. 2. 50. 3. 4.

145 1839 *C. M. Agrellii*, supplementa ad lexicon syriacum castellianum ed. Lindgren. Fasc. I. Ups. 4⁰.   M. 2.

146 1843 *Gregorii Barhebraei* qui et Abulfarag' grammatica linguae syriacae in metro Ephraemeo. textum e cod. bibl. Gottingensis edidit vertit, annotatione instruxit Ern. Bertheau. Gottingae. *16.* 135.   M. 2. 75 pret. reduct. 1. 20.

147 1843/5 *Henr. Andr. Chr. Haevernick*, supplementorum ad lexica syriaca particula prima Regiomonti Borussorum 43; particula secunda ib. 45. 4⁰. [programmata universitatis.] I. M. —. 40.
            M. 1. 30. 2. 50.

*148 1845 *Ge. Phillips*, elements of syriac grammar. second edition. Cambridge.   sh. 7. 6.

*149 1845/6 *J. C. Swyghuisen-Groenewoud*, institutio ad grammaticam aramaeam (cum append. specimina vers. syr. Peschito). 2 voll. Traj. ad Rhen. (M. 12.)   M. 6. 9.

150 1847 [*Lagarde, Paulus de*], horae aramaicae: scripsit Paulus Boetticher. Berolini.
     II explicatio vocabulorum CX e linguis jafetiticis in dialectos aramaicas transsumptorum p. 16—46.   M. 1. 1. 75.

151 1848 [*Lagarde, Paulus de*], rudimenta mythologiae semiticae, supplementa lexici aramaici scripsit P. B. Berolini.

M. 1. 1. 50.

*152 1854 *Uhlemann's* syriac grammar, translated from the german by *Enoch Hutchinson*, with a course of exercises in syriac grammar, and a chrestomathy and brief lexicon prepared by the translator. New-York & Edinburgh. sh. 14.

153 1857 *Friedr. Uhlemann*, grammatik der syrischen sprache mit vollständigen paradigmen, chrestomathie und wörterbuch für akademische vorlesungen und zum selbststudium bearbeitet. zweite überarbeitete und vermehrte ausgabe. Berlin. 12. 276. 64. 63. pp. M. 7. 50. 10. fr. 12. 50.

154 1857 Lexicon linguae syriacae collegit digessit edidit *Geo. Henr. Bernstein*. Volumen primum Fasciculus I [et II, 1, 240 coll.] Berolini. fol. sh. 7. M. 2. 2. 50. 3. 8. 60. 5.

*155 1858 *B. Harris Cowper*, syriac grammar translated and abridged from Hoffmann. London. sh. 7. 6.

1860 *C. M. Agrelli*, supplementa. Berolini.

156 1860 *Jos. Guriel*, elementa linguae chaldaicae, quibus accedit series patriarcharum Chaldaeorum a J. G. exarata. Rom. 256 pp.

M. 4. 50.

157 1866 *Joann. Bapt. Wenig*, S. J., schola syriaca complectens chrestomathiam cum apparatu grammatico et lexicon chrestomathiae accommodatum. pars prior. chrestomathia cum apparatu grammatico. Oeniponte. M. 5. 7. 50.

158 1866 [Abecedarium cum precibus nonnullis et psalmis] titulo caret. Alep imprimerie Maronite.

*158^b 1866 *Phillips* [= 143 8] 3d edit. revised and enlarged. M. 6.

159 1867/70 *Adalb. Merx*, grammatica syriaca, quam post opus Hoffmanni refecit A. M. Halis. particula prima 67. part. secunda 70. 8. 387 pp. M. 10. 11. 15.

160 1868 Chrestomathia syriaca quam glossario et tabulis grammaticis explanavit *Aem. Roediger*, editio altera aucta et emendata. Halis. (M. 7. 50.) M. 4. 25. 5.

*160^b 1869 ܡܬ̈ܡ ܕܡܟܬ̈ܠܐ ܘܫ̈ܝܐ (Éléments de lecture . . .) [grammatica syriaca per Abdyesum Khaiath] Mossoul impr. des Chaldéons.

161 1870 *Herm. Zschokke*, institutiones fundamentales linguae aramaicae seu dialectorum chaldaicae ac syriacae in usum juventutis academicae editae. Vindobonae. (lire 6. 25.) lire 4. M. 3. 50. 5.

*162 [1871] Fragments of ܣܘܪ̈ܝܐ ܡܟܬ̈ܒܘ ܙܘܡܐ or syriac grammar of *Jacob of Edessa*, edited from mss. in the British Museum and the Bodleian library by *W. Wright*, LLD. Only fifty copies printed for private circulation. [London.] 4°. M. 3.

168 1871/3 Chrestomathia syriaca edita a *P. Pio Zingerle*. Romae. 71.
Lexicon syriacum in usum chrestomathiae suae elaboratum a
P. P. Z. Romae. 73. (M. 14.)
M. 12. I Lire 6. 50. sh. 9. II sh. 3. 6.

164 1872 Oeuvres grammaticales d'Abou 'lfaradj dit Bar Hebreus édi-
tées par M. l'abbé *Martin* Tome I contenant le k'tovo d'tsem'he.
61. 271. Tome II contenant la petite grammaire en vers de
sept syllabes et le traité „de vocibus aequivocis“ texte et com-
mentaire. Paris [authograph.] 16. 127 pp.
M. 20. 22. sh. 27.
cf. Th. Nöldeke ZDMG. 26. 828/35.

165 1873[74] *Abbé P. Martin,* syro-chaldaicae institutiones seu introductio practica ad studium linguae aramaeae. Parisiis 73. [alius
titulus: grammatica chrestomathia et glossarium linguae syriacae
a P. M. Paris 74.] 7. 102 pp.

166 1874 Syrisch-arabische glossen. erster band autographie einer
gothaischen handschrift, enthaltend *Bar Ali's* lexicon von alaf
bis mim herausgegeben von *Georg Hoffmann*. Kiel. 4⁰. (M. 20.)
[cum novo titulo 1886. M. 10]. 8. 284 pp.

167 1876 Livre de lecture syrien. Mossoul, imp. des pères Dominicains (Paris, Challamel).

168 1876 *Frid. Field,* Otium Norvicense pars altera tentamen de
quibusdam vocabulis syro-graecis in R. Payne Smith S. T. P.
Thesauri Syriaci fasciculis I—III reconditis. Oxonii [non
prostat]. 4⁰. 4. 28 pp.

169 18[68—]79 *Thesaurus Syriacus* collegerunt *Stephanus M. Quatre-
mere Georgius Henricus Bernstein G. W. Lorsbach Albertus
Jac. Arnoldi Carolus M. Agrell F. Field Aemilius Roediger*
auxit digessit exposuit edidit *R. Payne Smith*, S. T. P. Tomus

1. ‏ܠܡ‎. Oxonii. (M. 105.) col. 1—1866. M. 82. 85.

fasc. 6 (1883) col. 1867—2256 ‏ܠܒܬ‎ 7 (1886) —2700. ‏ܡܘ‎

Ad fasc. 2 vide de Lagarde GGA. 71. 28. 1081—1114 = Symmicta (I) 78—99. ad fasc. 6 J. Loew, ZDMG. 37. (83) 469/76;
ad fasc. 7. 41. 359—364. 1—7. M. 125.

170 1879 Eliae Nisibeni interpres. vide *P. de Lagarde*, praetermissorum libri duo. Gottingae. pp. 1—96.

*170ᵇ 1879 Grammaire de la langue Araméenne selon les deux dia-
lectes syriaque et chaldaique comp. avec l'arabe, l'hébreu et le
babylonien par sa Grandeur Mgr. David Archevêque Syrien de
Damas. Mossoul, impr. des Pères Dominicains. [arabico.] M. 6.

171 1880 ‏ܡܬܚܟܡ̈ܠܐ ܕܣܘܪ ܝܐ‎ ‏ܟܬܒܐ‎ oder syrische grammatik des *Mar
Elias* von Tirhan. herausgegeben und übersetzt von *Friedrich
Baethgen.* Leipzig. 81. 47 pp. M. 7. 10.

172 *Alb. Schultens*, institutiones aramaeae. p. 1—282 [s. l. et a. inter annos 1745 et 49]. 4⁰.

173 ܖܡܚܠܟܬܚܡܡܙ ܣܘܖܡܕܐܐ: ܗܢ ܚܟܡܝ ܡܠܐ ܘܡܚܕܦܐ ܡܚܗ ܡܠܩܕܠ

ܘܣܘܕܝܐ ܙ ܡܚܠܐ ܚܟܡܕܐ. [Grammatica syriaca in dialecto neo-syriaca. Urmia 96 pp. 4⁰. perfect?]

174 A syriac lexicon to the new testament by *E. Henderson*. London, Bagster ca. 1865. sh. 1. 6. (sh. 2. 6.) M. 2. 75.

• 175 [c. 1851] Syriac Reading Lessons: consisting of copious Extracts from the Peshito version of the Old and New Testaments; and the Crusade of Richard I from the Chronicles of Bar Hebraeus, grammatically analysed and translated: with the Elements of Syriac Grammar. By B. Davidson. London, Bagster. sh. 5. sh. 3. 6. 1. 6.

176 1880 | الإحكام | في صرف السريانيّة ونحوها وشعرها

تأليف القس جبرئيل القرداحيّ اللبنانيّ معلّم العربيّة

والسريانيّة في المدرسة الأربانيّة برومة الكبرى | مُعفى

عنهُ | Al 'Yhkam seu linguae et artis metricae Syrorum institutiones auctore *P. Gabriele Cardahi* Libanensi linguarum arabicae et syriacae in Collegio Urbano de Propaganda Fide professore. Romae ex typographia polyglotta S. C. de Propaganda Fide MDCCCLXXX. 82 + 1. 8. Löscher. M. 3. 75. 5. 6.

177 1880 *Th. Nöldeke*, Kurzgefasste syrische Grammatik. Mit einer Schreibtafel von Julius Euting. Leipzig, Weigel. *32*. 279 (2). GGA. 1880, 51. P. Martin, Bullet. crit. 81, 7. H. Strack, ThLBl. 82, 5. G. Hoffmann, LCBl. 82, 10. M. 9. 12.

178 1881 *Eb. Nestle*, Brevis linguae syriacae grammatica, litteratura, chrestomathia cum glossario. In usum praelectionum et studiorum privatorum scripsit. Carolsruhae et Leipzig. Reuther. *6*. 78. 128. — Porta linguarum orientalium. Pars V. M. 4. 5. 40. Bull. crit. 81, 7. 132/4; Fr. Baethgen, DLZ. 81, 9; Athenaeum 2783, 296; H. Strack, ThLBl. 82, 5; V. Ryssel, ThLZ. 82, 5; LCBl. 83, 11. prior editio praesentis operis.

179 1881 Traité de Grammaire Syriaque par *Rubens Duval*. Paris, Vieweg. *40*, 447. M. 20. H. Derenbourg, Rev. Crit. 81. 49. 433—447; E. Drouin, Rev. de Ling. 15 Janv. 82.

180 *C. R. Brown*, an Aramaic method Ps. 2. Elements of grammar. Chicago, Am. Publ. Soc. of Hebrew. 96 p. 12⁰. cloth 1 D.

180b 1884 Outlines of Syriac Grammar. For the use of Classes in Hamilton Theological Seminary. By *S. Burnham*. Hamilton,

N. Y., Van Slyck, printer Republican Office. 8⁰. 34 pp. cum appendice.

Cetera Grammaticorum indigenarum opera e. gr. Ilusaini Hertheni Eliae Sobhensis vide sub IV.

APPENDIX.

181 *J. C. Wakii*, kurze Anzeigung, wie nemlich die uralte teutsche Sprache meistentheils ihren Ursprung a. d. Coltisch- od. Chaldäischen habe, u. das Bayerische vom Syrischen herkomme. Reg. 1718. Hpgt.   M. 3.

182 *Alb. Homoet*, Encomium linguae Aramaeae. Messopoli Zelandorum 1726. 4⁰.

183 *J. H. Lysius*, De usu linguae syriacae. Regiom 1726. 4⁰.   M. —. 60.

184 *M. J. G. Hasse*, de dialectis linguae syriacae diss. 4⁰. Regiom. 1787.   M. —. 75.

185 *E. Quatremère*, Journal Asiatique Janvier-Mars 1835.

186 Dr. *F. Larsow*, Societatis Asiaticae Parisiensis sodalis, De Dialectorum linguae Syriacae reliquiis. Formis expressum academiae regiae Berolinensis 1841. 1—28. 4⁰.
Einladung des Gymnasiums zum grauen Kloster.   M. —. 75. 1. 1. 50. 2.

187 *Tornberg*, de linguae aramaeae dialectis. Upsala 1842. 4⁰.   M. 1. 50.

188 *P. de Lagarde*, Beiträge zur baktrischen Lexikographie (1868) p. 79 sq.

189 De linguae Syriacae recentissimae indole et structura cum antiquiore comparatis. Scripsit *Otto Fraatz* Clausthaliensis. Commentatio Gottingae, 1843. VI. 41. 4⁰.

190 *Th. Nöldeke*, Beiträge zur Kenntniss der aramäischen Dialecte. ZDMG. 21 (67) 183—200. 22 (68) 443—527. 3. Ueber Orthographie und Sprache der Palmyrener 24 (70) 85—109.

191 *M. l'abbé Martin*, Syriens orientaux et occidentaux. Essai sur les deux principaux dialectes Araméens. Paris 72. 183. 20 tabb. Journal Asiatique extrait no. 4. Avril-Mai 305—488.

192 *M. l'abbé Martin*, Tradition Karkaphienne, ou la Massore chez les Syriens. Paris 70. 135. 19. 7 tabb. Journal Asiatique extrait no. 13. (1869.) Oct. Nov. VI Sér. tom. XIV. 245—379.

193 *M. l'abbé Martin*, Histoire de la Ponctuation ou de la Massore chez les Syriens. Paris 75. 128. VI. Journal Asiatique extrait no. 3. Février-mars-avril 75.

194 Zur geschichte der syrischen punctation. von dr. Eberhard Nestle. ZDMG. *30*. (76) 525—33.

195 *Caroli M. Agrell*, S. Th. Doct. Commentatio de varietate generis
et numeri in ll. oo. Hebraea, Arabica et Syriaca. P. I. VI.
1—82. Lundae MDCCCXV. Litteris Berlingianis. Pars posterior
ibid. eod. 83—146. (1).
196 *Conradus Kessler*, de formatione quorundam nominum syriacorum.
Marpurgi ad Lognnam 75. 58. 8⁰.   M. 1. 50.
cf. Th. Nöldeke ZDMG. 29. (75) 646—54.
197 *Siegmund Fränkel*, die Aramäischen Fremdwörter im Arabischen.
(Eine von „het Provinciaal Utrechtsch Genootschap van Kunsten
en Wetenschappen" gekrönte Preisschrift.) Leiden, Brill.
         fl. 5. 25.
198 *J. A. Corcoran*, Syriac Grammars Am. Cath. Quart. Rev. Oct.
1877.

II. BIBLIA.

I. *versio simplex, Peschittho.*

a. *tota biblia.*

1 Biblia polyglotta Parisiensia Michaelis le Yay.   Lutetiae, Vitré
1645. fol. Syriace.
     Pentateuchus T. VI. 632.   Josue-Paralipomena T. VII. 642.
Esdras-Sirach T. VIII. 635.   Isaia-Macchab. T. IX. [645]. Nov.
Test. T. V, 1 Evv. 630.   V, 2. Act. Epp. Apoc. 633.
                       T. VI.   M. 10.
2 Biblia sacra polyglotta Londinensia Briani *Walton* Londinii, Roycroft. 657.
     T. I Pentateuchus 654.   T. II 655, III 656 ceteri libri cano-
nici T. IV 657 libri deuterocanonici T. V Nov. Test. T. VI appendix. [T. VII et VIII Castelli Lexicon Heptaglotton].
     £ 24. 42. M. 500. 510. — T. V M. 48. T. VI M. 45.
3 Londini 823/6. 4⁰. [sic] ܚܕܥܠ ܨܪܡܚܐ ܘܘܢܕܡܚܐ ܚܕܚܚܐ ܛ ܚܕܚܠ
ܐܚܙܡܘ. vide 7.   M. 7.

b. *partes bibliorum.*

4 *Epitome bibliorum* continens insigniora veteris ac novi testamenti
dicta hebraice chaldaice syriace graece latine et germanice in usum
scholarum collecta . . . a *M. Valentino Schind[e]lero* Oederensi.
Viteberga 578.
Nestle

*5 Geneseos capita V. priora cum aliis dictis Biblicis [Dt. 6, 3. Mt.
    4, 10] hebraice, chaldaice, syriace, arabice, aethiopice et persice
    per *Joh. Frider. Krebsium.* Jenae 692.
*6 *Valentinus Friderici,* dicta sacrae scripturae, hebraea, chaldaea ac
    syra secundum articulorum theologicorum seriem intra privatos
    parietes, Deo adjuvante resolvet, eadem non minus philologice
    quam theologice illustraturus. Lipsiae, s. a. pp. 32.

c. vetus testamentum.

7 Vetus Testamentum syriacè eos tantum libros sistens, qui in
    canone hebraico habentur, ordine vero quoad fieri potuit, apud
    Syros usitato dispositos. In usum ecclesiae Syrorum Malabaren-
    sium jussu societatis biblicae recognovit et ad fidem codicum
    mss. emendavit, edidit *S. Lee.* Londini 24. 4⁰. [alia exx. 1823]
    705 pp.   M. 20. 28. fl. 5.
       [saepe cum novo testamento colligatum cf. n. 3.]

8 ܚܠ ܟܐܚܩ ܝܘܠܝܐܘ ܝܘ܆ .ܠܩ�ܩܘܟ ܚܩܠܠܝܝ ܘ : ܠ�ܩܚ ܝܘܚ ܟܚܠܩ
    ܠ�ܩ܆ܩ. [Vetus testamentum syriace et neosyriace. Urmiae 52. 4⁰.]

9 Translatio syra Poscitto veteris testamenti ex codice Ambrosiano
    sec. fere VI photolithographice edita curante et adnotante Sac.
    Obl. Antonio Maria *Ceriani.* Mediolani. fol.
       Pars I. 76, II. 77, III. 79, IV. 83. 330 ff. à M. 40, in charta
    grandiore à M. 60.

d. partes veteris testamenti.

10 Excerpta veteris testamenti syriaci cum latina interpretatione nova
    et adnotationibus Christ. *Cellarii.*   *Cizae* 682. 4⁰.
                                 M. 1. 20.   1. 50.   2. 20.   4.
11 Pentateuchus syriace ex polyglottis anglicanis summa fide edidit
    M. Geo. Guil. Kirsch. Hofae . . . Lipsiae 787. 4⁰. M. 3. 4.
12 *Geo. Otho,* palaestra linguarum orientalium Francofurti 702. 4⁰.
    vide I, 85.
*13 [tit. syr. Psalterium syriacum et carshunicum. typis monasterii
    St. Antonii de Kozchaya montis Libani 1585.] fol.
*14 [tit. syr. idem. ibidem 1610.] fol.
15 [tit. syr. Liber psalmorum syro-latinorum, edidit *Gabriel Sionita*
    Edenensis.] Parisiis mense martio 624. 4⁰. [Rosenthal 35, 330.
    1625. 275 ff. 4⁰. M. 18.]
16 Psalmi Davidis regis et prophetae lingua syriaca nunc primum
    ex antiquissimis codicibus manuscriptis in lucem editi a *Thoma
    Erpenio* qui et versionem latinam adjecit. Lugd. Bat. 625. 4⁰.
    (8) 346 pp.   M. 3.

17 Liber psalmorum Davidis idiomate syro verbo divino salvatori
nostro dicatus (por *Thomam Evam*). Romae 737. 4⁰.

M. 1. 1. 50. 1. 80.

18 Psalterium syriacum recensuit et latine vertit Thomas Erpenius
notas philologicas et criticas addidit *Joan. Aug. Dathe.* Halae 768.
40. 324. (*2*). M. 1. 1. 50. 1. 80.

19 Psalterium Syriacè. Londini, Soc. Bibl. 822. [pp. 251 cum
ps. 151.]

20 Psalterium Syriacè. Londini, Soc. Bibl. 825. [pp. 249.]

M. 2. 3.

21 [tit. syr. Liber psalmorum beati David regis et prophetae. Urmiae
1841. 4⁰. (cum canonibus.)]

*21ᵇ Psalterium Chaldaicum Romae 42 vide inter libros eccle-
siasticos.

*22 [Liber Psalmorum Constantinopoli editus a Mar Jacob ante 860.]

*23 [Liber Psalmorum Mausili 866 (cum canonibus)]. 12⁰.

23ᵇ ܟܬܒܐ ܕܡܙܡܘܪ̈ܐ ܘܣܡ ܡܥܡܕ̈ܐ ܡܢ ܚܙܝܐ܂ ܠܡܢܘ.
ܟܬܒ̈ܐ ܕܡܟܣܝܐ ܩܘܕܝ̈ܫܐ ܕܗܘ̈ ܩܠܕܬܐ 1868. 143. 8⁰. [neo-syr.]

23ᶜ : ܟܬܒܐ ܕܡܙܡܘܪ̈ܐ ܘܣܡ ܡܥܡܕ̈ܐ ܩܘܕܫ̈ܐ ܘܠܡܢܘ: ܟܬܒܐ:
ܐܬܟܡ ܚܡܕ̈ܐ [1874] *151* pp.

nova impressio 1878, revisa 1886.

24 Psalterium syriacum ad fidem plurium optimorum codicum habita
ratione potissimum hebraici textus nunc accuratissimo exactum a
Josepho David chorepiscopo Syro Mausiliensi cui accedunt X
cantica sacra Mausili 77. *56*. 376 pp. M. 5. 9.

25 Psalterium syriacum e codice Ambrosiano seculi fere sexti in usus
academicos imprimendum curavit *Eberardus Nestle.* Lugduni
Batavorum, Tubingae. 79. 4⁰. M. 3. 50.

*26 Psalmus VI octoglottos, et quidem gallice, arabice, graece,
hebraice, latine, chaldaice, anglice et syriace [ed. Jac. Gerscho-
vius]. Gryphiswaldinae 636. 4".

*27 Psalterii Davidici hexaglotti et decastyli decas prima, cum hexa-
glottarum et ogdostylarum concordantiarum Centuriis quinque . . .
[ed.] Jacobus Laurentii F. Michaelis N. *Gerschovius.* Gryphiswaldiae. 640 fol.

*28 Septem psalmi poenitentiales. Romae 584.
*29 iidem ibidem 1642.

30 Psalmi poenitentiales syriaci cum versione latina v. cl. Thomae
Erpenii et punctis vocalibus atque latina interlineari expressione
in usum facilioris et accuratioris lectionis instructi a M. D.
H[asenmüller]. [Lipsiae et Francofurti 678]. 4⁰.

31 Psalmus CXIX hebraice, chaldaice syriace arabice cum commen-

tariis hebraicis Sal. Jarchi et Aben Ezrae ... opera *Balthasaris Scheid.* Argentorati 700. 4⁰. [aliis 1665]. 　　　　M. 1. 20.
81ᵇ — 89.

*81ᶜ *Viccars* decapla in psalmos: sive comment. ex X linguis; (hebr., arab., syriac., chald., rabbin., graec., rom., ital., hispan. et gallic.) Una c. specim. ling. copticae, persic. et anglic. Fol. London 1655. 　　　　　　　　　　　　　　　　　　M. 7. 75.

82 Specimen philologicum, quo *Obadias* propheta hebraice chaldaice syriace et arabice cum commentariis rabbinorum Jarchi, Kimchi et Aben Esrae ... exhibetur a *Iudovico Michaele Crocio.* Bremae 673. 4".

*83 *Jonae & Obadia* oracula syriace. Notas philologicas et criticas addidit *H. A. Grimm.* Duisburg 805.

*84 The book of *Jonah* in four oriental versions; namely chaldee, syriac, aethiopic and arabic with corresponding glossaries edited by *W. Wright.* London 57. (sh. 7. 6.) sh. 4. M. 3. 50. 5.

*84ᵇ Die 5 Megilloth nebst dem syr. Targum gen. „Peschito" z. erst. Male in hebr. Quadratschrift mit Interpunctation edirt etc. Prag 1866. 8⁰. 　　　　　　　　　　　　　　　　　M. 8.

e. *libri apocryphi veteris testamenti.*

85 Libri veteris testamenti apocryphi syriace e recognitione *Pauli Antonii de Lagarde.* Lipsiae et Londinii 61. *39.* 278 pp.
　　　　　　　　　　　　　　　　(M. 20.) M. 14.

*85ᵃ Das Buch Sirach mit aramäischer Übersetzung und Erklärung. Breslau 1798. 　　　　　　　　　　　　　　　M. 2.

*85ᵇ Josua ben Sirach hebräisch deutsch und aramäisch übersetzt von Ben Sew. 2. verb. und vermehrte Auflage. Wien 1807.

*86 The first *epistle of Baruch* translated from the syriac with an introduction by the Rev. Dr. *Jolowics.* London 55 (Syro-Egyptian Society).

87 Monumenta sacra et profana ex codicibus praesertim Bibliothecae Ambrosianae Mediolani. 4. tom. V. fasc. 2 (71?) Liber IV Esdrae Syriace p. 41—111, Apocalypsis Baruch syriace 113—180. ed. M. A. Ceriani.

87ᵇ *Parva Genesis*: Monumenta *2*, 1. p. *9.*

87ᶜ *Jul. Caes. Scaliger.* Librorum *Esrae* admirabile ac divinum Compendium apud me est, *Syra* conscriptum lingua. Exerc. 308.

87ᵈ Some apocryphal Psalms in Syriac. By Professor *Wright.*
　　　Reprinted from the „Proceed. of the Soc. of Bibl. Arch.," June, 1887. 11 pp.

f. *novum testamentum.*

cf. *Jac. Geo. Christian Adler*, Novi Testamenti Versiones Syriacae Simplex, Philoxeniana et Hierosolymitana. Denuo exa-

minatae et ad fidem codicum manu scriptorum Bibliothecarum
Vaticanae, Angelicae, Assemanianae, Mediceae, Regiae aliarum-
que novis observationibus atque tabulis aere incisis illustratae.
Hafniae 1789. (8) 206. (4) 8 tabb. 4⁰. M. 1. 80.

38 Liber sacrosancti evangelii de Jesu Christo domino et deo nostro
. . . div. Ferdinandi Rom. imperatoris designati jussu & libera-
litate characteribus et lingua syra . . . scriptorio prelo diligenter
expressa [ab Jo. Alb. Widmanstadt et Moses Mardinensis] Viennae
Austriae 555. 4⁰ Ed. Pr.

[alia exemplaria a tergo primi folii „Viennae Austriae excudebat
Michael Zymmermann . . . Anno 1562". Quae f. 2ᵛ sub V. VII
citantur „dedicationes" in omnibus desunt exemplaribus, quae
sub III, in multis. Pauli epistolae XIIII locum variant.]
sh. 7. 6. 14. M. 10. 45. 50. 54.

39 η καινη διαθηκη testamentum novum דייתיקא חודתא auctore Imman.
Tremellio. excudebat Henr. Stephanus. anno 569. fol. M. 7.

¹40 eadem editio. Lugduni in bibliopolio Salamandrae 571. fol.

41 της καινης διαθηκης απαντα. ܐܘܢܓܠܝܘܢ ܩܕܝܫܐ؟ novum Jesu Christi
D. N. testamentum. sacrorum bibliorum tomus quintus. Antverpiae, Plantinus 571 Kal. Febr. fol. [editor Guido Fevre de
la Boderie].

42 דייתיקא חדתא typis hebr. titulo caret. [Antverp., Plantin. c. 573].

43 דייתיקא חדתא novum domini nostri Jesu Christi testamentum
syriace. Antverpiae, Plantin. 575. 16⁰. (lit. hebr., in fine: variae
lectiones ex N¹ T¹ syrici manuscripto codice Coloniensi nuper a
Franc. Raph[elengio] collectae. M. 2. 4. 50. 6.

44 דייתיקא חדתא η καινη διαθηκη novum Jesu Christi D. N. testamentum ex editione Guidonis Fabricii Boderiani. Parisiis apud
Jo. Benenatum. Excud. Steph. Prevosteau. 584. 4⁰. alia exx.:
ap. Hil. Le Bouc et Jo. Gueffier. 1586. 4⁰. Fl. 3. 75.

45 Novum testamentum dni nri Jesu Christi syriace, ebraice, graece,
latine, germanice, bohemice, italice, hispanice, gallice, anglice,
danice, polonice studio et labore Eliae Hutteri Germani. Noribergae 599. fol. 2 voll. M. 21. 24.

46 Novum domini nostri Jesu Christi testamentum syriace cum versione latina, ex diversis editionibus diligentissime recensitum.
accesserunt in fine notationes variantis lectionis ex quinque impressis editionibus diligenter collectae a Martino Trostio. Cothenis
Anhaltinorum 621. 4⁰. M. 2. 50 3.

47 — ut 46, in fine operis eodem die „26 Sept." sed „1622". M. 3.

48 a) Novum domini nostri Jesu Christi testamentum syriace, cum

punctis vocalibus & versione latina Matthaei . . . pleno et emen-
dato editum, accurante *Aegidio Gutbirio*, 88. Th. D. & Prof.
P. Clavis operis, lexicon, grammaticam syr. & notas complexa,
seorsum prodit. Hamburgi 664. pp. „606"; praecedit alius titulus
aere incisus „anno M. DC. LXIII."

b) alia exemplaria pp. 604. M. 2. 2. 50. 3. 3. 80. 4. 4. 50.

Nescio quot impressiones exstant anni „1664"; magnopere inter se
differunt exemplaria:

a. quoad titulum 1) Gutbirio 88. Th. D. et Prof. P 2) D. et Gymn. Hamb.
Prof. P. 3) D. Log. Metaph. et linguarum orient. Prof P.
b. quoad praefationem: 1) prima plaga desinit: *hujus formulae* et arabica
aethiopicaque verba paginae 17 hebraicis scribuntur literis 2) prima
plaga desinit *auspiciis alicujus* et pag. 17 arabici aethiopicique charac-
teres inveniuntur. 3) ut 2) sed prima plaga minutioribus literis expressa est.
c. quoad zifros marginales Evangelii Matthaei 1) sunt minutissimi. 2) sunt
majores, iidem qui in reliquis libris.
d. quoad paginationem 1) a 523 ad 526 usque 606 pergit. 2) paginae recte
numeratae sunt 523 usque 604.
e. quoad textum: 1) Apoc. 21, 24 in ima pagina 604 (d, 1) una linea omissa,
deinde extra formam paginae addita est. 2) hac linea in sequentem
paginam transposita omnes lineae usque ad finem libri suo loco motae sunt.
f quoad colophonem syriacum 1) quatuor lineis (21 verbis) constat. 2) quinque verbis constat.

49 אדרח דירתיקא novum domini nostri Jesu Christi testamentum
syriace. Sulzbaci, ex officina Joh. Holst 1684, prostat Norimbergae apud Wolfg. Endterum. 12⁰. 192 pp. lit. hebr.
M. —. 60. 1. 50.

*50 = 48 novo titulo. Hamburgi 694.

51 Novum Jesu Christi testamentum juxta editionem polyglottam etc.
Londini, ap. Smith et Walford 698. fol. [= 2 tom. V. novo titulo.]

52 Sacrosancta Jesu Christi evangelia jussu sacrae congregationis de
propaganda fide ad usum ecclesiae nationis Maronitarum edita.
Romae 703. fol. (syriace et carshunice.) (34) 341. (14) pp.
M. 39.

pars 2, acta apostolorum epistolae catholicae et divi Pauli cum
apocalypsi d. Joannis ibid. eod. (16) 519 [ ] (6) pp.

53 = 48. Hamburgi 706. novo titulo. M. 3.

54 Novum domini nostri Jesu Christi testamentum syriacum cum
versione latina cura et studio *Johannis Leusden* et *Caroli Schaaf*
editum. Ad omnes editiones diligenter recensitum et variis lectionibus magno labore collectis adornatum. Lugd. Bat. 709. 4⁰.
Acc. Schaaf, C., Lexicon syriacum concordantiale *ibid. eod.*
5 fl. M. 10. 50. 12. 30.

55 Biblia sacra quadrilinguia novi testamenti graeci cum versionibus
syriaca, graeca vulgari latina et germanica . . . syriacis ex polyglottis anglicanis et ed. Schaafii petitis . . . accurante *M. Chri-
stiano Reineccio.* Lipsiae 713. fol. M. 6. 6. 60.

56 = 49, novo titulo Norimbergae, sumptibus Wolfg. Maur. Endteri
715. 12⁰. M. 1.
57 = 54 novo titulo: secunda editio a mendis purgata. Lugd. Bat.
717. 4⁰. [10] 799 pp. 7 fl. M. 15.
58 = 48 novo titulo. Francofurti 731. M. 2. 50. 3. 80. 4.
59 = 55 novo titulo. Lipsiae 747. 21. 968 pp.
60 = 48 novo titulo. Hamburgi 749. 604 pp.
61 Novum testamentum syriace denuo recognitum atque ad fidem
codicum manuscriptorum emendatum. Londini, (soc. bibl.) Watts.
816. 4⁰. 552 (1) pp. M. 4. 5. 6. 8. 50
   (titulus latinus in multis exx. deest; item notitia „Brevi prodi-
bunt codicum mss. collationes ad quorum fidem emendata est
haec editio“; „denuo“ respicit ad Nr. 71. cf. The Syriac New
Testament of the British Foreign and Bible Society. Reprinted
from the „Quarterly Record,“ Nr. 55, of the Trinitarian Bible
Society for January, 1874. 8 pp.)

62 ܟܬܒܐ ܩܘܡܟܐ ܕܕܝܬܩܐ ܚܕܬܐ ܚܟܡܬܐ ܫܘܕܝܢܐ ܘܐܬܚܐ ܐܣܪ

ܚܡܐ ܕܟܪܐ ܕܡܬܩܕܠܐ ܀ ܐܪܣܐܪ ܟܚܐܢܣ ܥܪܝܣܠܐ ܘܩܐ

ܣܡܠܐ ܟܐܬܥܡ ܟܚܡܣܢܐܐ ܀ ܬܚܩܝܠܐ ܟܬܒܐ ܙܪܥܠܐ ܡܩ;

pp. [N. T. syr. et carsh. cur. Silv. de Sacy Paris 1824. 4⁰.]
M. 14. 20. 24. 40.
63 [tit. syr. Novum testamentum syriace. Londini, soc. bibl. 26.
360 pp. 4⁰.]

63ᵇ דיתקא חרתא | דמשיחא: | = | אתחתם חדהאיה | בלבדן מדינתא: |
בשנת משמיצ שלום לפ'ק דמשיחא: 12⁰. foll. קץ N. T. syr.
litteris hebraicis (Macintosh [1]836).
64 Syriac New testament. London, Bagster [40?]. 4⁰. sh. 2.
65 [tit. syr. Novum testamentum syriace et neosyriace. Urmiae 46.]
4⁰. 829 pp. M. 10.

65ᵇ ܟܬܒܐ ܕܕܝܬܩܐ ܚܕܬܐ ܕܡܪܢ ܝܫܘܥ ܡܫܝܚܐ. ܩܕܡܬܐ ܡܢ ܐܘܪܫܠܐ

ܗܘ ܕܝܗܒܐ ܡܙܡܐ ܩܕܡܝܬܐ: ܡܩܕܝܚܡܐ ܚܠ ܝܗܘ ܕܝܠܢܐ: ܕܗܡܐ

ܡܙܡܐ ܡܢܨܚܠܐ. ܠܕܡܢܝ ܚܡܡܢܠܐ ܕܝܫܐ ܚܟܚܕܠܝܕܐ ܘܐܥܢܙܐ.

1868. Nov. Test. syr. New York 621. 8⁰. [neo-syr.]

65ᶜ ܟܬܒܐ | ܕܕܝܬܩܐ ܚܕܬܐ | ܕܝܫܘܥ ܡܩܘܝ ܡܚܡܣܐ. | — |

ܐܪܣܐܪ ܚܩܝܡܠܐ ܕܠܕܡܢܝ: ܘܐܥܢܙܐ ܀: | ܣܡܠܐ ܚܩܝܡܐ |

| ܐܚܪ܀: N. T. syriace. New York 1874. 637. [accedunt Psalmi].
— altera impressio 1878, tertia revisa 1886.

66 The syriac new testament with an english translation. in parallel columns. London, Bagster [?]. 4⁰. 1876.

g. partes novi testamenti.

67 Eclogae sacrae novi testamenti syriacae graecae latinae. cum notis et observationibus ita explicatae ut . . . adhibitis grammaticae syriacae rudimentis antehac excusis attentus lector linguam syriacam proprio marte possit addiscere. Adduntur indices locupletissimi et manuale lexici syriaci. Opera *Joh. Mich. Dilherri.* Jenae 638. 12⁰.

(editio anni 646, Halae et typis Oelschlegelianis grammaticam [et manuale] sistit, eclogas omittit.)

*68 — Jenae 658.

69 — Jenae 662. *(36)* 503 [=523] (111) pp.

70 Excerpta novi testamenti syriaci cum latina interpretatione auctore *Christoph. Cellario.* Cizae 682. M. 1.

71 Evangelia sancta, nec non Acta Apostolorum syriace, cum interpretatione latina, Broxbourne, Soc. Bibl. (Watts). 815. 4. 519 pp.
[curavit Buchanan]. M. 5. 8. 15.

*72 Novum testamentum triglottum graece syriace et latine (vulg. ed.). Acc. subsidia critica. Evangelia. Londini 28. 4⁰.
[curavit Groenfield; Evv. tantum]. M. 7.50.

72 [tit. syr. Quatuor evangelia syriace characteribus nestorianis exarata.] Londini, soc. bibl. 29. 4. sec. codicem ms. Jos. Wolf ed. T. Pell Platt. 284 pp.

*73ᵇ *B. Schults,* Ho Emreh daloho (Verba dei ad peccatores ex 4 evangelistis collecta). Syriace. Halae. 8⁰. M. 1.50.

*73ᶜ Clavis·Syriaca: a Key to the Ancient Syriac Version, Called „Peshito", of the Four Holy Gospels. By the Rev. Henry F. Whish, M. A., Corpus Christi College, Cambridge. London: George Bell and Sons. Cambridge: Deighton, Bell and Co. 1883. 12⁰.

74 Sanctus Matthaeus syriace graece latine germanice bohemice italice hispanice gallice anglice danice polonice ex dispositione et adornatione *Eliae Hutteri* Germani. Noribergae 599. 4⁰.

*75 S. Matthaeus syriace et latine. Cothenis Anhaltinorum 621. 4⁰.

76 Evangelium s. Matthaei syriacum una cum punctis vocalibus . . . editum accurante *Aegidio Gutbirio.* olim impressum Hamburgi typis et impensis autoris anno 663 nunc invenitur Longosalissae Thuring. apud haeredes Gutbirianos, ubi totum quoque novum testamentum syriacum prostat.

77 Sanctus Marcus syriace graece latine . . . [ut 74]. Noribergae 600. 4⁰.

78 S. Marci evangelistae evangelium syriace. literis et punctis hebraicis apposita e regione versione latina. in gratiam linguarum orien-

talium tyronum seorsim excusum. Cothenis Anhaltinorum 622. 4⁰.
56 pp. M. 6.

79 Postilla sacramentalis ab amicis dicta polyglotta, herfürgegeben
von *Gothofrido Kiliani*, pastorn in Glückstadt. Glückstadt, in
verlegung des autoris, druckts Melchior Koch. 668. 4⁰.

*80 a) Passio domini nostri Jesu Christi syriace, juxta quatuor evan-
gelistas. Parisiis Anton Vitré. 635. 12.

b) — idem. ibidem ab eodem 672. 12.

81 Historia passionis et mortis Jesu Christi ejusque resurrectionis et
ascensionis in coelum ex lingua lusitanica in syriacam transcripta
et secundum quatuor evangelistas collecta opera et studia B[en-
jamin] S[chultz]. Halae Magdeburgicae 755. M. 1.

+81ᵇ Historia Passionis Domini nostri Jesu Christi. Ex textu syriaco
desumta. Cum elementis linguarum syriacae, samariticae et aethiopicae. Patav. 1714. 12⁰. M. 2.

82 Acta apostolorum syriace. seorsum recudi curavit *D. Joh. Henr.
Callenbergius*. Halae 747. (lit. hebr.)

83 Epistola S. Pauli ad Romanos lingua syriaca . . . ex testam. syr.
Viennensi desumpta inque gratiam φιλαρογλωττων publici juris
facta . . . studio *M. Christoph. Crinesi*. Wittebergae impensis
Lach. Schurer, typis Gormannianis (alia exemplaria: typis et
sumptibus Johannis Gormanni) 612. 4⁰. M. 2.

+84 *Ludovici de Dieu* animadversiones in Pauli epistolam ad Romanos
cum versionibus Syri, Arabis. Lugd. Bat. 646. 4⁰. fr. 12.

85 Epistola S. Pauli ad Romanos syriace. seorsim recudi curavit
D. J. H. Callenbergius. Halae 747. (lit. hebr.)

86 Pauli Apostoli prior epistola ad Corinthios syriace. seorsum recudi
curavit D. J. H. Callenbergius. Halae 747. (lit. hebr.)
Acced. epistola secunda sine titulo latino ib. 747.

+87ᵃ⁻ᵉ Epistola D. Pauli ad Galatas, syriace litteris hebraicis cum
versione latina *Antonii Cevallerii;* vide ejusdem Rudimenta hebr.
linguae [Genevae] 560. 4⁰. ib. 567. 4⁰. (M. 2.) Wittebergae
574. 4⁰. Lugd. 575 fol. Genevae 590 [91. 92.] 4⁰.
(M. 2. 50.)

+88 Epistola s. Pauli ad Galatas, syriace et latine studio Tremellii.
Genevae, Perrin 570. 4⁰.

89 Dyodecas aureorum psalmorum Davidicorum, eorum qui sunt
praecipue prophetici de Jesu Christo . . . nempe 2. 8. 16. 22.
40. 45. 68. 69. 72. 97. 110. 118 hebr. chald. cum latina versione,
et graece ex LXX interpretibus. Item epistola S. Pauli ad *Galatas*
graece, syriace, latine et germanice, seorsim nunc edita pro
studiosis earum linguarum. Bremae 614.

90 Epistola S. Pauli ad Colossenses syra in gratiam auditorum suorum
cum vocibus tam primitivis tam derivativis separatim edita a

J[oh.] C[hristoph.] W[ichmannshausen]. (mendose aliis W[agen-
seil]). Vitembergae 702. 4⁰.   M. 2.

91 Epistola s. Pauli ad Titum lingua syriaca cum interpretatione
latina a Christophoro Crinesio s. l. [Vittembergae] e typographeo
Joh. Gormanni 618. 4⁰.

*92 Epistola s. Pauli ad Titum. syriace. Hafniae 626.

93 Epistola d. Pauli ad Titum et Philemonem syriace adjunctis
versione latina litteris vocalibus et ligaturis Syrorum in usum
philo-syrorum tyronum excusa, edi curante Balthas. Scheidio.
Argentorati. 668. 4⁰. 12 pp.

94 — eaodem. Argent. 700. 4⁰.

*94ᵇ S. Pauli ep. ad Philemonem spec. loco ed. J. H. Petermann.
Berol. 1844. [Sachau, Catal. p. VI. n].

95 Divi Johannis apostoli et evangelistae epistola catholica prima
syriace adjuncto e regione charactere hebraeo et versione latina
. . . praemittitur alphabetum syriacum velut manuductio quaedam
ad eius linguae lectionem faciliorem, opera et studio Mart. Trosti.
Cothenis Anhaltinorum 621. 4⁰. (4) 22 pp.   M. 5.

*96 Epistola I S. Johannis, syriace et latine. Lips 632. 4⁰.

97 Epistola d. Johannis apostoli et evangelistae catholica prima
syriace juxta exemplar Cotheniense . . . adjuncto e regione
charactere ebraeo itemque versione latina . . . editore Andrea
Sennerto. (Wittebergae) 652. 4⁰. 21 pp.   M. 3.

98 Epistolae quatuor, Petri secunda, Johannis secunda et tertia, &
Judae fratris Jacobi una. ex celeberrimae bibliothecae Bodleianae
Oxoniensis ms. exemplari nunc primum depromptae et charactere
hebraeo, versione latina, notisque quibusdam insignitae, opera &
studio Edwardi Pococke, Angli-Oxoniensis. Lugd. Bat. 630. 4⁰.
[10] 66 pp.

98ᵇ Williams Manuscript ‖ The Syrian Antilegomena Epistles 2 Peter.
2 and 3 John, and Jude Written A. D. 1471 by Suleimàn of
Husn Keifa ‖ Edited by Isaac H. Hall Baltimore, Maryland
Publication Agency of the John Hopkins University 1886, fol.
[8 ff. letterpress, 17 ff. photogr.]   M. 15.

99 Epistola II Johannis syriace cum interpretatione latina Edw.
Pocockii vide Cellarius Porta, Cizae 677. 4⁰.   M. —. 50.

100 Apocalypsis s. Johannis ex manuscripto exemplari e bibliotheca
clariss. viri Josephi Scaligeri deprompto, edita charactere syro et
ebraeo, cum versione latina et notis, opera & studio Ludovici de
Dieu. Lugd. Bat., Elzevir. 627. 4⁰. 20. 211 pp. M. 2. 2.40.

*101 Revelatio quae facta est super Johannem evangelistam a Deo in
Pathamun insula, in quam ejectus fuit a Nerone Caesare. vide
Ludov. de Dieu criticae sacrae p. 763/861. (Amstelaedami)
693. fol.

102 Sylloge canticorum novi testamenti syriace et latine a Sebastiano
Schrottero edita. Erfurti 650.*)
appendix:
103 Remains of a very ancient recension of the four *gospels* in syriac
hitherto unknown in Europe; discovered, edited and translated by
William Cureton. London 58. 4⁰. *95.* 87. 160 pp.
(M. 24.) M. 15. 16. 17.
cf. Ewald, Jahrb. 9, 69/87. GGA. 58. 1712/6. Edinburgh
Rev. 59. 168/90.
*104 Fragments of the *Curetonian Gospels* edited by W. Wright.
[London 72.] 4⁰. 4ff.
„Only one hundred copies printed for private circulation."
M. 2. 75. 3. 50.
*104ᵇ primus edidit *Roediger* in: Monatsberichte der Berliner Akademie 1872. Juli 557.
104ᶜ Evangelienfragmente. Der griechische Text des Cureton'schen
Syrers wiederhergestellt von *Friedrich Baethgen.* Leipzig 1885.
96 92 pp. M. 10.

h. *libri apocryphi novi testamenti.*

*105 Contributions to the apocryphal literature of the new testament,
collected and edited from syriac manuscripts in the british
museum with an english translation and notes by *W. Wright.*
London 65. cf. Bickell, Theol. Quart. Schr. 1866. 468/79.
(sh. 7. 6.) M. 3. 50 5. 50. 7. 50.
†105ᵇ *B. H. Cowper,* the Apocryphal Gospels. 1867.
106 *Apocryphal Acts of the Apostles,* edited from syriac manuscripts
in the british museum and other libraries by *W. Wright.* London 71.
Vol *1.* the syriac text. *17.* 333 vol. *2.* the english translation. 298. - M. 12.
cf. Nöldeke, ZDMG. 25, 670/9; Geiger, ibid. 26, 798/804.
106ᵇ Syrische Lieder gnostischen Ursprungs. Eine Studie über die
apokryphen syrischen Thomas-Acten. Von *Karl Macke.* ThQS.
74. 1—70.
107 The departure of my lady Mary from this life edited and translated by *W. Wright.*
Journal of sacred literature and biblical record, 4ᵗʰ series,
vol. *6* & *7.* Jan. & Apr. 65. London.
108 Fragments du livre gnostique intitulé *Apocalypse d'Adam,* ou
Pénitence, ou Testament d'Adam, publiés d'après deux versions
syriaques, par *M. Ernest Renan.* Journal Asiatique. Sér. *5.*
Tom. *2.* 417/71. Nov. Dec 1853. Paris.

*) Omisi alphabeta cum appendicibus, orationes dominicas, similia.

*108[b] Apocalypsis Pauli germanice a *P. Zingerle* in: Heidenheim, Vierteljahrsschrift 4, 139; cf. Perkins, Journ. Amer. Or. Soc. 8, 182 — J. f. Sacr. Litt. Jan. 65, 872.

II *Versio Thomae Heracleensis, Philoxeniana.*

109 Syriace fragmenta *Esaiae* versionis ex graeco probabiliter *Philoxenianae* et recensionis Jacobi Edesseni etc.

Monumenta sacra et profana T. V. fasc. 1, 1—40 2. Mediol. 73. 4[0]. Lire 18.

110 Sacrorum *Evangeliorum* versio syriaca *Philoxeniana* ex codd. mss. Ridleianis in bibl. coll. Nov. Oxon. repositis nunc primum edita: cum interpretatione et annotationibus *Josephi White*. Oxon. 778. 4[0]. 2 voll. T. 33. 652 pp.

cf. Doederlein, Theol. Bibl. 1, 163, Michaelis, Orient. Bibl. 16, 167. M. 15 (110 et 113 M. 28).

111 | Actorum Apostolorum & epistolarum versio Philoxeniana ex domestica typographia *Jos. White* Oxoniensis, sine titulo: extant non nisi 6 exemplaria, impressa post ann. 790 et ante 798.| 190 pp. 4[0].

112 Prolegomena in versionem syriacam Philoxenianam novi testamenti edidit J. White. Oxon. 798.

[Acc.] versionis Philoxenianae specimen cum adnot.

113 *Actuum Apostolorum* et *Epistolarum* tam catholicarum quam paulinarum, versio syriaca Philoxeniana ex codice ms. Ridleiano nunc primum edita: cum interpretatione et annotationibus *Josephi White*. Oxonii 4[0]. M. 12. 60.

tom. *1*. actus apost. et epist. cathol. complectens. 799. 275. 52 pp. cf. de t. *1*. GGA. 1802. 35/6. tom. *2*. epistolas paulinas compl. 803. *19*. 399 pp.

114 Das heilige *Evangelium des Johannes*. syrisch in harklensischer übersetzung mit vocalen und den punkten kuschoi und rucoch nach einer vaticanischen handschrift nebst kritischen anmerkungen von *Geo. Heinr. Bernstein*. Leipzig 53. (M. 8.) 5. fr. 6.

cf. ZDMG. 10, 628.

114[b] Syriac Manuscript | Gospels of a Pre-Harklensian Version ‖ Acts and Epistles of the Peshitto Version ‖ Written (probably) between 700 and 900 AD. By the Monk John—Presented to the Syrian Protestant College by 'Abd ul-Messiah of Mardin.

[Letterpress 4 ff. 3 photogr. ed. *I. H. Hall*, Philadelphia.]

III *versio hexaplaris Pauli Tellensis* (a. 616/7).

115 Josua imperatoris historia illustrata atque explicata ab *Andrea Masio*. Antverpiae, Plantin. 574 fol. 154. 350 (29). [c. nov. tit.(?) Amst. 1609.]

116 Specimen ineditae et hexaplaris bibliorum versionis syro-csthran-ghelae cum Simplici atque utriusque fontibus graeco et hebraeo collatae, cum duplici lat. vers. ac notis. edidit ac diatribam de rarissimo codice Ambrosiano unde illud haustum est, praemisit *Johannes Bern. de Rossi*. Parmae 778. 4⁰. (ps. *1.*) 16 pp.
M. 1. 50. 1. 75.

de cod. Ambr. cf. epistolam J. J. Björnståhl (Mediol. 2 Märt. 1773) Samlaren 8. 126 p. 234, aliam eiusdem ad White cum epistola *Brancae* ad Bruns Rep. 3. (78), von einem syrisch-hexaplarischen Manuscripte in der Ambrosianischen Bibliothek zu Mayland. 166/187; ibid. de *Rossi* 187/212 von der syrisch-hexaplarischen Handschrift zu Mayland, nebst einem Vorbericht von *Joh. Gottfr. Eichhorn*.

117 — repetivit *Eichhorn*, Repertorium *3* (78) 209.

118 *Libri* IV *regum* syro-hexaplaris specimen. e manuscripto parisiensi syriace edidit *J. G. Hasse*. Jenae 782. M. 1. 20. 1. 75.

119 *Codex syriaco-hexaplaris* ambrosianus-mediolanensis editus et latine versus a *Matth. Norberg*. Londini Goth. 787. 4⁰. *[22]* 501 pp. M. 4. 5. 6. 10.

120 *Daniel* secundum editionem LXX. interpretum ex tetraplis desump-tam. ex codice syro-esthrangelo bibliothecae ambrosianae syriace edidit, latine vertit, praefatione notisque criticis illustravit *Caie-tanus Bugatus*. Mediolani 788. 4⁰. *[10] 32.* 168.
M. 3. 4. fr. 7.

121 |Psalmi sec. ed. LXX interpretum, quos ex cod. syr. estrangh. bibl. Ambrosianae syriace imprimendos curavit C. Bugatus sine titulo l. & a. Mediolani 820]. 4⁰. [aliis 1798.]

Petrus Cighera, de vita et scriptis Gaietani Bugati . . . com-mentarius additus praefationis loco ejusdem versioni psalmorum nunc primum in lucem prodeunti. ib. eod. M. 7. 9. fr. 10.

122 Codex syriaco-hexaplaris. liber quartus regum e codice parisiensi, Jesaias, duodecim prophetae minores, proverbia, Jobus, canticum, threni, ecclesiastes e codice mediolanensi edidit et commentariis illustravit, *Henricus Middeldorpf*. Berolini 35. 4⁰. Pars *1* textus syriacus. pp. *12.* 400. pars *2* commentari. pp. 401/658.
(M. 24.) 5. 6. 7.50. 8.

123 Libri *Judicum et Ruth* secundum versionem syriaco-hexaplarem ex codice musei britannici nunc primum editi graece translati notisque illustrati . . . ed. Thomas Skat Rørdam. Havniae 59/61. 4⁰. *8* 93 (2). M. 1. 25. 6.

124 Monumenta sacra et profana ex codicibus praesertim bibliothecae
ambrosianae. Mediolani. 4⁰.

a. Tom. *1*, fasc. 1 . . . . Baruch, Threni et Epistola Jeremiae versionis syriacae Pauli Telensis cum notis et initio prolegomenôn
in integram eiusdem versionis editionem. edidit S. O. Antonio
Maria Ceriani. 61. *8.* 1—72.

b. T. *2*, fasc. 1 − 4. Pentateuchi syro-hexaplaris quae supersunt
cum notis. accedunt nonnulla alia fragmenta syriaca. edidit S.
O. A. M. Ceriani. 63. *24.* 344 pp.   L. 46.

c. T. *7.* Codex Syro-hexaplaris ambrosianus photolithographice
editus curante et adnotante Sac. Obl. Ant. Maria Ceriani. Mediolani 74. fol. 140. 2. 193 ff.   M. 105. 115. 160.

125 Mittheilungen aus der syrischen hexapla-handschrift der psalmen
im brit. museum. [add. 14,434 ps. 56 (h. 57)] von Dr. *M.
Heidenheim.*

Deutsche vierteljahrsschrift für englisch theologische forschung
und kritik. Gotha. *1.* 275/8.

126 *Veteris testamenti ab Origene* recensiti fragmenta apud Syros
servata quinque. praemittitur Epiphanii de mensuris et ponderi-
bus liber nunc primum integer et ipse syriacus. *Paulus de Lagarde* edidit. Gottingae 80. *4.* 356. [Ex. Nu. Jos. Regn.
3. 4.]   M. 20.

IV *versio palaestinensis.*

127 Evangeliarium hierosolymitanum ex codice vaticano palaestino
deprompsit, edidit, latine vertit, prolegomenis ac glossario ador-
navit comes Franciscus Miniscalchi Erizzo. Veronae. 4⁰. tom. *1*
61. *3.* 580 (1) tabb. 2. t. *2* 64. *51.* 89. 1.   M. 60. 64. 80.
cf. Zahn, Forschungen 1, 329/50.

128 Fragmenta syro-palaestina [bibliorum tam veteris quam novi
testamenti etc.] vide Land, Anecdota T. *4.* Lugd. Bat. 75. 4⁰.
pp. 177/233. 103/224.

128[b] *J. P. N. Land*, de zoogenaamde hierosolymitaansche of christe-
lijk-palestynsche Bijbelvertaling.   M. —. 80.

Verslagen en Mededeelingen der k. Acad. d. Wetensch. Afd.
Letterk. Tweede Reeks, Deel 5, bl 196/208.

128[c] Th, Nöldeke, Ueber den christlich-palästinischen Dialect.
ZDMG. 22. 443/527.

[Haeredes comitis Fr. M. Erizzo typos Evangeliarii Academiae dei Lincei dono dederunt (Atti 1884/5 Rendiconti, 1. 6. 15
Febr. 85. p. 169), Paulo de Lagarde permissionem reimpressionis.]

III. LIBRI ECCLESIASTICI (LITURGICI, RITUALES).*)

Missale chaldaicum ex decreto s. congreg. de propaganda fide editum. Rom. 767. fol. 616 pp. M. 30. 90. 100. fr. 250.

Ordo chaldaicus missae beatorum apostolorum iuxta ritum ecclesiae malabaricae. Rom. 774.

acc. Ordo chaldaicus rituum et lectionum iuxta morem ecclesiae malabaricae. Rom. 775.

ܛܘܟܣܐ ܘܦܘܪܫܢܐ ܕܣܝܡܬܐ ܘܡܫܡܫܢܘܬܐ ܐܝܟ ܛܟܣܐ ܟܠܕܝܐ ܕܡܠܒܪ. Rom 844.

Missale syriacum iuxta ritum ecclesiae antioch. Syrorum. fol. Rom 843. M. 16. 25. 30.

Missale chaldaico-malabaricum. Romae 1857. 4°. M. 30.

Missale chaldaicum iuxta ritum eccl. nationis Maronitarum. Rom 1592/94 (*2* ff.) 288 pp. fol. M. 300.

alia editio + 4 ff. praef. arabice et latine. R. 1604. M. 300.

Missale syriacum iuxta ritum eccl. antiochenae nationis Maronitarum. Rom 716. fol. M. 45.

ܟܬܒܐ ܕܩܘܪܒܢܐ ܐܝܟ ܥܝܕܐ ܕܥܕܬܐ ܐܢܛܝܘܟܝܬܐ ܕܡܪ̈ܘܢܝܐ. Kozchayae 816.

idem. ibid. 838.

ܛܟܣܐ ܕܩܘܪܒܢܐ ܐܝܟ ܥܝܕܐ ܕܥܕܬܐ ܐܢܛܝܘܟܝܬܐ ܕܡܪ̈ܘܢܝܐ. ibid. 855.

Liber ministri missae iuxta ritum ecclesiae nationis Maronitarum. Rom 596. 4°. £ 2. 10.

Diaconale syriacum iuxta ritum ecclesiae antiochenae nationis Maronitarum. Rom 736.

idem. Romae 715.

ܟܬܒܐ ܕܡܫܡܫܢܘܬܐ ܐܝܟ ܥܝܕܐ ܕܥܕܬܐ ܣܘܪܝܝܬܐ ܕܫܡܫ̈ܐ ܡܪ̈ܘܢܝܐ. editio 7. Kozchayae 854.

The liturgy of S. Celestine ed. W. Wright in: Journal of sacred literature. April 867. p. 332. London. M. 1. 25.

Codex liturgicus ecclesiae universae in XV libros distributus . . . *Joseph Aloysius Assemanus* . . . castigavit, recensuit. Romae 4. 749/66.

Syriaca *1*, p. 174/276. *2*, 211/350. *3* (750) 136/237. *4*, 2 = t. *5* (752) 131/226. *6*, 4 = t. *7* (754) 91/108. *8*, 2. (756) 1/228. *8*, 3 = t. *9* (758) 1/119. *8*, 6 = t. *12* (766) 1/224. vol. 1—12. M. 460.

D. Severi alexandrini quondam patriarchae de ritibus baptismi et

*) see. *Bickell*, conspectus sect. 7 - 10.

sacrae synaxis apud Syros christianos receptis liber, nunc primum in lucem editus: *Guidone Fabricio Boderiano* exscriptore et interprete. Antverpiae, Plantin. 572. 4⁰. M. 10. £ 2. 2.

Ordo chaldaicus ministerii sacramentorum ss., quae perficiuntur a sacerdotibus iuxta morem ecclesiae malabaricae [versio syriaca ritualis romani]. Rom 845.

Ritus administrandi nonnulla sacramenta ad usum ecclesiae antiochenae Maronitarum. Rom 840.

Sacerdotale ecclesiae antiochenae nationis Maronitarum. Rom 752. M. 8.

Rituale aliaeque piae precationes ad usum ecclesiae Maronitarum. Rom 839.

Ordo baptismi adultorum [catechumenorum] iuxta ritum ecclesiae malabaricae Ohaldaeorum. Rom 859.

> [versio ordinis baptismi romani a Josepho Guriel edita.]

Officium defunctorum ad usum Maronitarum Gregorii XIII. impensa chaldaicis characteribus impressum. Rom 585.

91 ff. 4⁰ [ex. defect. M. 45] M. 100.

Psalterium chaldaicum in usum nationis chald. editum. [= seq. breviarium]. Rom 842.

Breviarium chaldaicum in usum nationis chald. a Josepho Guriel secundo editum. Rom 865. 16⁰.

ܟܣܘܠܐܟ ܘܐܡܘ؟ ܐܣܩܩܐ ܐܐܣܘܐ؟ ܐܐܕܟ ܟ؟ ܐܐܣܩܐ؟ ܐܩܚ

؟ܐܗܩܘܘ ܣܐܡܘ؟ ܐܩܐܗ. (opera Ebedjesu Chayat.) Mossul 866.

Breviarium feriale syriacum ss. *Ephraemi* et *Jacobi* Syrorum iuxta ritum eiusdem nationis, quod incipit a feria II usque ad sabbatum inclusive, additis variis hymnis ac benedictionibus, ab *Athan. Saphar* episcopo Mardinen. Rom 696.

Breviarium feriale syriacum ss. Ephrem et Jacob Syrorum iuxta ritum eiusdem nationis a feria II usque ad sabbatum iuxta exemplum editum anno 1696 . . . nunc accedit officium dominicale. Rom 787. 4⁰.

Officium feriale iuxta ritum ecclesiae Syrorum. Rom 851.

Liturgiae syriacae septimanae passionis dom. n. Jesu Christi excerptum e cod. ms. bibl. Lipsiensis ed. ac notis illustr. *J. Ch. Clodius.* Lips. 720.
42 pp. 4⁰. M. 1. 20. 1. 50. 2.

Officia sanctorum iuxta ritum ecclesiae Maronitarum. pars hiemalis [cura Fausti Nairon]. Rom 656. fol. [inde a dominica dedicationis ecclesiae usque ad purificationem B. M. V.]

> Vol. II. Breviarii chaldaici aestiva pars. [incip. a festo s. Nuhrae martyris]. Rom 666.

Officium simplex septem dierum hebdomadae ad usum ecclesiae Maronitarum. Rom 624.

altera editio Innocentii X. ibid. 717.

tertia editio e revisione Stephani Evodii patriarchae. ib. 731.

Officium feriale iuxta ritum ecclesiae Syrorum Maronitarum, Innocentii X Pont. Max. iussu editum, denuo typis excusum regnante
Pio VIII. P. O. M. ed. 3. Rom 830.

[ed 4ⁿ?] Rom 835.   M. 6.

Breviarium syriacum, officium feriale iuxta ritum ecclesiae Syrorum
Maronitarum, Innocentii X. P. M. iussu editum, denuo typis
excusum, ed. 5. Rom 863.

[acc. officium defunctorum.]

ܡܣܡܚܕܐ| ܐܡܪ ܚܡܪ| ܘܚܝܪ| ܘܚܬܪܘܚܡܪ. Kozchayae 855.

Carmina ecclesiae syriacae curavit *Ludovicus Spieth* in: *H. A. Daniel*,
thesaurus hymnologicus. tom. *3.*

Ein beitrag zur kunde der syrischen hymnologie. von prof. dr. *Pius
Zingerle* in: Heidenhoim, deutsche vierteljahrsschrift für englisch-
theologische forschung und kritik. Gotha *2,* 336/45.

Offices en l'honnour des Saints-Pierre ot Paul. 1⁰ Office Nestorien
67 pp. [autogr.] in: Saint Pierre et saint Paul dans l'église
nestorienne par *M. l'abbé Martin* . . . extrait de la revue des
sciences ecclésiastiques. Amiens 75.

Officium feriale (Schehime). Prima impressio in monasterio Sajidet
Tāmish in Kesrawan (Libanon) facta 1872. 591 pp. M. 12.

— denuo reimpressum Beryti ex typographia P. P. Soc. Jesu. 1876.
12⁰ [in duabis certe formis].

Service de la messe privée selon le rite syrien خدمة القداس
الاشعيمى بحسب الكنيسة السريانيّة بلجازة ذى
الغبطة السيّد بطريرك السريان الانطاكى Mossul, Dominic.
1868. 239. 12⁰ (approbatio, praefatio, titulus, rubricae arabice,
verba administrantis syriace).

„Die Wasserweihe nach dem Ritus der Syrier." In „Liturgie zum
Tauf-Fest der aethiopischen Kirche" etc., von Carl von Arnhard,
München, 1886. Textus Syriacus editus a Richard J. H. Gottheil. 4⁰.

Aus einer handschriftlichen Taufliturgie in: Vater (1802) 33/9.

    e codice Orphanotrophei Halensis, de quo vide: *La Croze*,
Histoire du Christianisme des Indes 3, 230; J. D. Michaelis,
Einleitung N. T. Th. 1. § 11; Marsch, Anmerkungen und Zu-
sätze (übersetzt von E. F. K. Rosenmüller 1, 162).

    versio litteralis huius fragmenti in: *Wagnits*, Journal für
Liturgie 2, 1.

Zingerle, P., Das syrische Festbrevier oder Festkränze aus Libanon's
Gärten. Aus dem Syrischen. 2 Theile. Villingen 1846. 8.

— Proben syrischer Hymnologie, aus dem Urtext übersetzt. ThQS.
1873. 462/509.

Nestle.

Analecta Syriaca. Hymnen, Proclamationen und Martyrergesänge
des Nestorianischen Breviers. Aus dem Syrischen übersetzt.
Mit Einleitung und Erläuterungen von D. J. M. Schönfelder.
ThQS. *48* (1866), 179/200.

Duval, R., Lettre sur le bréviaire nestorien. Journ. asiat. 1884.
janv. 106/8.

    cf. *Swainson*, C. A., *The greec Liturgies.* Cambridge 1884. 4⁰.
(15 sh.)

Morinus, de sacris Ecclesiae ordinationibus. Paris 1653. fol.

IV. LITTERATURA SYRORUM GENERALIS.

Hall, I. H., Syriac version of Epistle of King *Abgar* to Jesus.
(Hebr. 1885. Apr. p. 232/5.)

— Caspari, C. P., Jesu apokryfiske Brev til den edessenske Konge
Abgarus i udvidet middelalderlig Skikkelse bestemt til at tjene
som Amulet. Theol. Tidsskrift . . . i Norge *3* Raekke 1, 3 (1886)
427/8.

— *Lipsius*, R. A., Die Edessenische Abgarsage kritisch untersucht.
Braunschweig 1880. 92 pp.

— *Matthes*, K. C. A., Die Edessenische Abgarsage auf ihre Fort-
bildung untersucht. Leipzig 1882. 77 S.

Abraham Bethrabbanensis cf. Breviarium Mossulense p. 57.

Abraham Oascarensis regulae monachorum Ebedjesu, Nomocanon
tract. 7.

Abulfaragius vide *Gregorius.*

Acta sanctorum martyrum orientalium et occidentalium in duas partes
distributa adcedunt acta s. Simeonis stylitae omnia nunc primum
. . . e bibliotheca apostolica vaticana prodeunt *Stephanus Evodius
Assemanus* archiopiscopus apamoensis chaldaicum textum recensuit
. . . latine vertit admonitionibus, perpetuisque adnotationibus illustravit. Romae 748. fol. 2 voll.   M. 120.

ܐܟܬ̈ܐ ܕܡܪܝ ܘܩܕܝܫ ܐܬܘܪ Acta Sancti Maris, Assyriae,

. Babyloniae ac Persidis Seculo 1 Apostoli, Syriace sive Aramaice.
Juxta Manuscriptum Alqoschianum adjectis aliorum Codicum
lectionibus variantibus, Versione Latina et Annotationibus illu-
strata. Edidit nunc primum J.-B. *Abbeloos*, S. T. D., Domus
Pontificalis Praesul, Archiepiscopi Mechlinensis Vicarius generalis.
Bruxelles, Société Belge de Libraire, 12 Rue des Paroissiens, 12.
Leipzig, F. A. Brockhaus, 1885. 8⁰.

    cf. Th. Nöldeke, Östr. Monatsschr. f. d. Or. 11, 10.

Hoffmann, Georg. Auszüge aus syrischen Akten persischer Märtyrer, übersetzt und durch Untersuchungen zur historischen Topographie erläutert. Leipzig, 1880. Abhandlungen für die Kunde des Morgenlandes 7, 3. 325 pp. M. 10. 14.

Echte Akten heil. Märtyrer des Morgenlandes. Aus dem Syrischen übersetzt von P. Pius Zingerle. 2 Theile. 8. Insbr. 1836. 24 Bog. fl. 1. 6 ö. W.

Acta Sti Mar Abaln'l Masich. Aramaico et lat., ed. nunc prim. ex cod. Londin. et illustr. J. Corluy. Bruxell. 1886 (S. A.) M. 2.

Acta S. Pelagiae syriace edidit Joannes Gildemeister. Bonn, Marcus 79. 4⁰. 15, 12 pp. ThLZ. 79, 14, LCBl. 79, 46. M. 2. 3.

Acta S. Silvestri: Anecd. 3, 46/76.

Acta synodi Carthaginiensis anni 256: LR.*) 62/88.

The doctrine of Addai, the apostle, now first edited in a complete form in the original syriac, with an english translation and notes. by George Phillips, DD. London, Trübner 76. 15. 52. 53 pp. cf. Zahn, Forschungen 1, 350/82. sh. 7. 6. M. 5.

Alexandri magni ad Aristotelem litterae fictitiae: Roediger[2] 112/20. ad Pseudo-Callisthenem conf. Theod. D. Woolsey JAm. Or. Soc. 1854, 357/428 B. H. C[owper] the Acts of Addi. Journ. of. S. Lit. & Bibl. Rec. July 1858; Rimheld, Beiträge zur Geschichte und Kritik der Alexandersage. Hersfeld, Progr. 1873. 4⁰. Dr. H. Christensen, Beiträge zur Alexandersage; Hamburg, Willh. Gymn. 1b. 1883. 4⁰.

Notice of a Life of Alexander the Great translated from the Syriac by Rev. Dr. Justin Perkins, with Extract from the same, by Theodore D. Woolsey. cf. Zingerle ZDMG. 8 835/7. 9. 780/4.

Ein altes syrisches Alexanderlied. Übersetzt von P. Zingerle. Brünn 1882. (S.-A.) M. 1. 20.

Sancti Alexandri Alexandrini quae syriace supersunt fragmenta. Pitra 4, 196/200; lat. 430/4.

Alexandri episcopi Alexandriae sermo de anima et corpore deque passione domini in: Novae patrum bibliothecae tomus secundus [ed. A. Mai]. Romae 44. 4⁰. 531/9. 539/40.

Ambrosius, hypomnemata [= Pseudo-Justinus oratio ad Graecos]. Curet. Spic. 38/42.

Analecta Nicaena. Fragments relating to the council of Nice. the syriac text from an ancient ms. in the british museum, with a translation, notes etc. by B. Harris Cowper. Lond. 57. 4⁰. M. 6.

Analecta sacra Spicilegio Solesmensi parata edidit Joannes Baptista Card. Pitra Tom. 4 Patres Antenicaeni [orientales addidit titulus exterior] Parisiis ex publico Galliarum typographeo 1883 [tit.

---

*) LR. = Lagarde, reliquiae juris ecclesiastici syriace.

extr. A. Roger et F. Chernoviz, bibliopolis] *84.* 518 [non 158] pp.
ed. P. Martin, p. 1—257 text., 261 ff. versiones, citatur: Pitra 4.

Syriac Miscellanies or Extracts relating to the first and second general
Councils, and various other Quotations, Theological, Historical
and Classical. Translated into English from MSS. in the British
Museum and imperial Library of Paris. With Notes. By *B. H.
Cowper.* Will. & Norg. London 861. 112 pp. cf. Heidenheim:
Vierteljahrsschrift *1.* 465/9.   M. 3.

P. Lagardii *Analecta Syriaca.* [Lips.] Lond. 58. exemplaria facta
sunt 115.   M. 21. 20. — 12. 16.

Anonymi hymnus ad tonum hymnorum Ephraemi de paradiso in:
S. Ephr. Syri . . . opera selecta. ed. J. J. Overbeck. Ox. 1865.
351/55.

Antonius rhetor [7 s.], carminis contra calumniatores scripti exordium.
Roed. [2] 110/1. [cf. de Lagarde, Mitth. 1, 56 sq.]

The homilies of Aphraates, the persian sage. edited from syriac manuscripts of the fifth and sixth centuries in the british museum,
with an english translation by *W. Wright.* Lond. 69. 4°. Vol.
1 the syriac text.   (M. 41.)   25. 35. 36.

cf. Th. Nöldeke GGA. 1869. 39. 1521/32; Bickell, in Bibliothek
der Kirchenväter Kempten 1874. 102/3, Schönfelder ThQS. 1878.
195/256, C. Fr. Sasse [† 3. Juli 1880] Prolegomena in Aphraatis
sapientis Persae sermones homileticos. Lips. 1878.   40(1) pp.
M. —. 80. 1. 20; *Forget, Jac.,* de vita et scriptis Aphraatis Sapientis Persae, Lovanii 1882. 377 S. M. 5. Ryssel, St. & Kr.
1883. 2. 306/36.

De *hermeneuticis apud Syros Aristotelis Jo. Georgius Ern. Hoffmann* scripsit adiectis textibus et glossario. Lips. 69.
                                   M. 3.   7. 13.

— editio secunda immutata. Leipz. 73. 7. 218 pp. M. 4.

[Pseudo-]*Aristoteles* περι κοσμου προσ Αλεξανδρον: LA.*) 134/58.

The festal letters of Athanasius, discovered in an ancient syriac version and edited by *William Cureton.* Lond. 48. sh. 18. (Introductio sep. M. 2.)   M. 6. 5. 3. 50. 3. 2. 50.
etiam apud Mai, NPB. *6,* 1/160.

Das *Athanasius* dem grossen zugeschriebene glaubensbekenntniss
περι της σαρκωσεως του θεου λογου in syrischer übersetzung aus
einer nitrischen handschrift des britisch museum: analecta Nic.
p. 37. *Caspari,* Quellen zur ältesten Geschichte des taufsymbols.
1. 66. 143/60.

Babai (senior) ex Beth-Aināthā carmina cf. Breviarium Mossul. p. 39.
42. 47; de eo Thomas Margensis apud BO. 3, 1, 88/92.

Babai bar Nesibinaye duo carmina: Brev. Moss. p. 41. 42.

---

*) LA. = Lagardii Analecta.

Baethgen s. Fragmente, Philoxenus, Sindban.

Balaeus chorepiscopus (c. 430), carmina: *Ephraemi*, Balaei aliorumque opera selecta ed. Overbeck. Oxf. 65 p. 249/336 et: *Wenig*, Schola syriaca (66), 160/2. Thalhofer, Bibliothek *41, 67 et 44*.

Bardesanes (11. Juli 154/222) [discipulus ejus *Philippus*] de fato ܐܝ̈ܠܕ ܕܨܒ̇ܢ ܘܢܩܨ̇ ܐ̈ܙܠܘ Spic. 1—21.

cf. *Wright*, Apocryphal Acts p. 274 *Lipsius*, die apokryphen Apostelgeschichten *1*, 292; *Nöldeke*, qui acta Thomae e lingua Syriaca in Graecam, non e Graeca in Syriacam translata esse censet.

— *Hahn, Aug.*, *Bardesanes* gnosticus Syrorum primus hymnologus. Lips. 1819. (M. 1. 20.) —. 75.

cf. *Clark's* Ante Nicene Christian Library vol. 22, 25, *Merx*. Bardesanes (1863) 25.

Barhebraeus vide Gregorius.

Barsaumas Nisibonus cf. Brov. Moss. p. 58.

Barsuma, frater Gregorii Barhebraei vid. Greg. B. H.

[*Bar Zuʿbi*] *traité sur l'accentuation* chez les Syriens orientaux par *M. l'abbé Martin*. Paris 77. 6 30. 21 autogr. pp. Fr. 3. 3. 50.
[Actes de la société philologique, tome *7*, n° 1.]

Anaphora divi *Basilii* episcopi Caesareae Cappadociae ex vetustissimo codice Syrica lingua, & charactere scripto traducta per *Andream Masium*.

cf. Mosis Bar Cephae de Paradiso p. 235/54.

ibid.: 254/6 Precatio Divi *Basilii*, qua solet operatus sacris uti apud Deum, tralata ex Syrico per eundem *Andream Masium* Bruxellanum.
[iam ante Masium tralatio a Mose Mardinensi facta impressa est, ubi? quando?]

The tradition of the syriac church of Antioch, concerning the primacy and the prerogatives of S. Peter and of his successors the roman pontiffs. by the most rev. *Cyril Benham Benni*, syriac archbishop of Mossul (Niniveh). translated, under the direction of the author, by the rev. Joseph Gagliardi. London, Burns 71.
M. 7.

Bezold, die Schatzhöhle. 1883.

Die Schatshöhle nach dem syrischen Texte der Handschriften zu Berlin, London und Rom nebst einer arabischen Version nach den Handschriften zu Rom, Paris und Oxford, hrsg. von Carl Bezold. Leipzig 1888. *20*. 273. ThN. LCBl. 88, 8. M. 20.

Etiam sub titulo: Die Schatzhöhle syrisch und deutsch. 2. Teil. Pars I (versio germanica) prodiit 1883.

Liber thesauri de arte poetica Syrorum noc non de eorum poetarum

vitis et carminibus per *P. D. Gabrielem Cardahi* [القرداحي]
Maronitam è Libano. Rom, Prop. 75. 201 (3) pp. ⎯ M. 13.

فصل في شهور الروم Calendarium Syriacum Auctore Cazuinio.
Arabice Latineque edidit et notis instruxit Gulielmus Volck. Lipsiae 1859. 8.

Calendarium syrum in: *Genebrardus*, Psalmi Davidis. ed. V. Antv. 1592.

On a Syriac Table for finding Easter in years of the Seleucid Era by Prof. *Hall*. Proc. A. Or. Soc. for. Oct. 1885 (extr.) p. 4/10.

I. H. Hall, On a Modern Nestorian MS. Ecclesiastical Calendar. Am. Or. Soc. Proceed. Oct. 1886. Journ. *13*, 140/4.

Carolus Magnus die ante mortem suum evangelia quatuor cum Graecis *et Syris* optime correxisse dicitur a *Thegano* in vita Ludovici.

Chronicon Edessenum: BO. *1*, 388/417, Michaelis, Chrest. 46/74.
   translat. angl. in: Journ. of Sacr. Lit. 1864. *5* (n. 3.) 28.

Clementis Alexandrini quae syriace et armenice supersunt fragmenta. Pitra 4, 35; lat. 305.

Clementis romani recognitiones syriace. *Paulus Antonius de Lagarde* edidit. Lips. [et] Lond. 61.
   (M. 20.) 7. 50. 8. 10. 11. 12. 14.

Epistola prior [et posterior] Beati *Clementis* discipuli Petri Apostoli [de Virginibus]. .
   in: N. T. Graec. J. J. Wetstenii. Tom. *1* (1751) Proleg., syriace et latine, p. 1—14. 14—26. Colophon: „Ex Typographia Eliae Luzac. 1752.“

— *Funk*, die syrische Uebersetzung der Clemensbriefe.
   ThQS. 59, 3.

— *Hilgenfeld*, A., die Briefe des römischen Clemens und ihre syrische Uebersetzung. Zfw. Th. 20, 4.

Sancti patris nostri *Clementis romani* epistolae binae de virginitate syriace ... edidit *Joannes Theodorus Beelen*. Accedunt fragmenta nonnulla exegetici argumenti ... nunc primum edita. Lovanii 56.
   M. 5. 6. 7. 50. 8. 9. 10. 12.

— Sancti *Clementis Romani* quae syriace et armenice supersunt fragmenta. Pitra 4, 1. 2, lat. 276.

— Syrische Bijdragen tot de Patristik (door *J. P. N. Land*) I. Clemens Romanus de virginitate. II. Bardesanes de fato. (Overdruk uit de Godgeleerde Bijdragen voor 1856/7). 8⁰.

Codicum syriacorum specimina, quae ad illustrandam dogmatis de coena sacra nec non scripturae syriacae historiam facerent, e museo britannico elegit, explicuit, tabulisque sex lapidi incidi curavit *Franciscus Dietrich*. Marburgi 55. 4⁰. [progr. acad.]
   M. —. 80. 1. 50.

Commentarius anonymus in Canticum canticorum (ex codice anni 861): Mo*) 2, 9/31.   M. 4.

Ancyrae concilii canones.   Pitra 4, 215/21; lat. 444/9.

Neocesareae concilii canones.   Pitra 4, 221/3; lat. 449/51.

Concilii *Nicaeni* quae syriace supersunt.   Pitra 4, 224/37; lat. 451/62.

Concilium Seleuciae et Ctesiphonti habitum anno 410.   textum syria-cum edidit, latino vertit notisque instruxit. T. J. Lamy. Lovan. 68. 4⁰.

Constitutiones apostolicae vide LR. 2—32. 44—60.

Cosmas presbyter, [c. 474] epistola ad Symeonem [stylitam]: BO. 1, 237/9. Act. S. Mart. 2, 394.

Cureton vide Ignatius, Spicilegium.

Cyprianus ad Quintum et chorepiscopum epistolae; LR. 88/93. ad

ܣܘܒܠܐ 93 seqq.

Sancti *Cypriani* quae supersunt syriace.   Pitra 4, 72/9; lat. 338/44.

S. Cyrilli Alexandrini archiepiscopi commentarii in *Lucae* evangelium quae supersunt syriace e mstis apud museum britannicum edidit *Rob. Payne Smith*. Oxon. 58. 4⁰.   M. 16. 18. 22.

Fragments of the homilies of Cyril of Alexandria on the gospel of S. Luke, edited from a nitrian ms. by *W. Wright*. Lond. [74]. 4⁰. "only one hundred copies printed for private circulation."
                                                                    M. 3. 2. 50.

A Commentary upon the Gospel according to Luke, by S. Cyril, Patriarch of Alexandria. Now first translated into English from an ancient Syriac Version. By R. Payne Smith, M. A.   Oxford 1859. 2 partes. 8⁰.

Cyrilli Alexandrini librorum contra Julianum fragmenta Syriaca ed. *E. Nestle* in: Juliani imperatoris librorum contra Christianos quae supersunt Coll. . . . *C. J. Neumann* Lips. 1880 p. 42—63.

Die Gedichte des *Cyrillonas* (a. 396) nebst einigen anderen syri-schen ineditis. mitgetheilt von Dr. *G. Bickell*: ZDMG. 27(73) 566/625. — *Bickell, G.*, Berichtigungen zu Cyrillonas. ZDMG. 35 (1881) 531 f., cf. Thalhofer, Bibliothek 41, 9/63. Overbeck 379/81 ubi Isaco tribuuntur, quae sec. Bickell p. 57 Cyrillonae runt.

Dadjesu regulae, vid. Ebedjesu, Nomocanon tract. 7.

Damasus episc. Romae († 384) fragmenta duo: Mo 2, 5/7.

Daniel, H. A., Thesaurus hymnologicus. vol. 3.

Jos. David [chorepiscopus Mossulensis], Antiqua Ecclesiae Syro-Chal-daicae traditio de principatu Petri. Rom 1870.

H *Danielis Salachensis* explicatione verborum selectorum Davidis Prophetae. Nestle, Gramm. Syr. 86/90.

Debs, Jos., sacerdos maronita, confutationes contra assertiones sac.

---

*) Mo = Monumenta syriaca.

Jos. David, syr. ed., lat. vertit *H. N. Dahduh.* Beryti. 1871.
352 pp.   M. 3.
Didascalia apostolorum syriace [ed. *P. de Lagarde*]. Lips. 54.
L'ouvrage n'a été tiré qu'à cent exemplaires. (M. 12.) 6. 12.
Diocles [Peparethius, historiae romanae fragmentum] ܟܣܐܒܐ
ܟܣܢܝܐ ܕܣܦܪܐ‎??: LA. 201/5.
Diodorus Tarsensis († c. 394), excerpta: LA. 91/100.
[Anaphora *Diodori* Tarsensis] text. syr. ed. Bickell ZDMG. 27 (1873)
608/13 transl. Consp. p. 71 f.; cf. ZDMG. 35, 1881, 532 et apud
C. S. Hammond, the ancient liturgy of Antioch and other litur-
gical fragments. Oxf. 1879.
Sancti *Dionysii* episcopi Alexandrini quae syriace supersunt frag-
menta. Pitra 4, 169/75; lat. 413/17.
Epistola beati *Dionysii* ad Timotheum de morte apostolorum Petri
et Pauli, syriace. Pitra 4, 241/9; lat. 261/71.
Dionysius Barsalibi [† 1171 aliis „1172", „non ante 1207"], excerpta:
BO. *2,* 157 sqq. commentarii, ordo de poenitentibus, tractatus de
unione corporis Christi etc.
Dionysii Tellmahrensis [† 22. Aug. 845] chronici liber primus. e
cod. syr. vatic. ed. illustr. *O. F. Tullberg.* Ups. 50. 4º.
                                             M. 13. 50.   15.
    excerpta BO. *1,* 359/86 = Michaelis 16/46 BO. *2,* 72/7.
Berättelse om Alexander den Store, öfversättning från syriskan meed
anmärkningar. [ex Dionysii Tellm. chronico]. academisk afhand-
ling . . . af *Carl Axel Hedenskog.* Lund. 68.
    cf. *Bezold, Dormienti, Eusebius.*
    cf. Schönfelder, ThQS. 1865, 699/704.
Dionysii Thracis Ars grammatica . . . Edidit *Gustavus Uhlig.* Prae-
missa sunt praeter Prolegomena: *Adalberti Merxii* de versione
Armeniaca disputatio atque *Syri interpretis* lectione. Leipzig
1883(—84). Toubner *100.* 224. p. 57/73.
Dioscorides, cf. Löw, Aram. Pflanzennamen p. 13.
Doctrina Addaei (cf. *Addai*) LR. 32/44.
Doctrina Apostolorum = Doc. 24/35.
Doctrina Petri: LR. 99/116.
Ancient syriac *Documents* relative to the earliest establishment of
christianity in Edessa and the neighbouring countries, from the
year after Our Lord's ascension to the beginning of the fourth
century; discovered, edited, translated and annotated by the late
W. Cureton. with a preface by *W. Wright.* London 64. 4º. *14,*
196. 112 pp.   M. 24. 28. 30. 31. 50.
Ebediesu metropolita Sobae et Armeniac († 1318) catalogus librorum
cf. p. 1 et BO. *3,* 1. 3/362.
— *collectio canonum* ex chaldaicis bibliothecae vaticanae codicibus

sumpta et in latinam linguam translata ab *Aloysio Assemano.*
praecedit Epitome canonum apostolicorum auctore eodem Ebediesu: A. M[ai], scriptorum veterum nova collectio. Romae. 4⁰.
tom *10*, 41. p. 1/22. 23/168. syr. 169/90. 191/331.
— cf. de Lagarde, Praetermissa 90/3.

Ebediesu liber *Margaritae* de veritate christianae religionis. ibid. (2)
317/41. lat. 342/66.
— A translation of *The Jewel*, Written by *Mar Abd Yeshua*, Nestorian Metropolitan of Nisibis and Armenia, A. D. 1298. Appendix
B. in: Badger, G. P., The Nestorians & their Rituals. London
1852. *2*, p. 380/422.
— *Paradisus Eden* cf. P. *Zingerle* in: ZDMG. 29 (75) 496/555.

Ebedjesu. Ein Bild aus der Märtyrer-Zeit der persischen Kirche des
4. Jahrhunderts. Von M. v. Z. Mit Einleitung von W. K. Reischl.
Regensburg 1871.   M. 1. 60.

Elias (Darensis?) vid. Johannes Tellensis (Kleyn).

Elias, III, patriarcha 1176—90. Preces inter Psalmodiam 291/4.

Elias bar Schindya, episcopus nisibenus [975 † 7. Mai 1049].
— *annales* in: *Baethgen*, Fragmente syrischer und arabischer Historiker. Leipzig 1883.
— *grammatica:* ܡܩܕܡܝܬܐ ܐܡܝܪܐ ܘ A treatise on syriac grammar
by Mâr(i) *Eliâ* of Ṣôbʰâ edited and translated from the manuscripts in the Berlin Royal Library by *Richard J. H. Gottheil*.
A dissertation . . . Leipzig 1886. 32. 20. 15 pp. [Introductio
et capp. 1—4.]   M. 1. 75.
— *hymni:* in *Cardahi* 83/4.
— decisiones ecclesiasticae, vide Ebediesu, collectio, imprimis sect. 3.
— des Metropoliten E. v. N. Buch vom Beweis der Wahrheit des
Glaubens [aus dem Arab.] übersetzt und eingeleitet von *L. Horst*.
Colmar 1886. *28.* 127 pp.
— *interpres* vide *1*, 37 et 170 excerpta: Aphraates 38/9.
— *epistolae:* BO. *3*, 1. 272/4.
— *Sauvaire, H.,* A treatise on weights and measures by Eliya, Archbishop of Nisibin.
     Journ. Roy. As. Soc. Lond. N. S. 12, 1. Suppl. to vol. 9 pp.
291/313 Written in French.

Elias Tirhanensis, grammatica cf. *1*, 171.

Elias patriarcha (1615) epistola ad Fratres Minores in Alepo, BO.
3, 1. 600/1, ad Paulum 5. ib. 602.

Elxai cf. Hitzig ZDMG. 12, 318; *M. A. Levy* ib. 712 sec. Ign. Stern,
בן חנינה (Szegedin 1858); de Lagarde, Mitteilungen 2, 363.

Ephraem Syrus († 373).
— *opera omnia* quae exstant graece syriace latine in sex tomos

distributa . . . nunc primum . . . e bibliotheca vaticana prodeunt
syriacum textum recensuit *Petrus Benedictus S. J.* Romae. fol.
   Tom. *1* syriace et latine 737. *2* 740. *3* 743 syr. text. rec. post
obitum P. Benedicti Maronitae S. J. Stephanus Evodius *Assemanus.* (T. *1—3* graece et latine 732/46.)
                      M. 150. 160. 180. 240. (voll. 3 syr. M. 70).
Ephraem Syrus († 373).
— S¹ E¹ S¹, Rabulae, Balaei aliorumque opera selecta edidit *J. J.
Overbeck.* Oxon. 65. p. 1—156. 339—351. 355—362.
                                   (sh. 21.) M. 12. 16. 18.
— *Die Gedichte des h. Ephräm gegen Julian den Apostaten,* übersetzt von Professor Dr. *G. Bickell.* ZfkTh. *2,* 335/56.
— carmina nisibena additis prolegomenis et supplemento lexicorum
syriacorum primus edidit, vertit explicavit Dr. *Gust. Bickell,*
Lipsiae 66.   (M. 16.) 8. 8. 50. 10.
— carmina selecta vide *Hahn et Sieffert 1,* 131.
— E¹ S¹ carminis textus syr. sec. cod. bibl. Angel. ed. ac vers. et
annotat. instr. [—?]. Gotting. 1837.   M. 1. 20.
— hymni de paradiso ex opp. 3, 562/73 apud Uhlemann ² 39/53.
— sermones duo ex codicibus syr. romanis edidit. a *P. P. Zingerle.*
Brixiae 68 (69?).   (M. 2. 40.) 1. 50.
— excerpta ex operibus s. Ephr. in Mo *2.* 33/51.
— *Pelt, L.* et *Reinwald, H.,* Homiliarium Patristicum. (Voluminis Primi
Fascic II.) Berolini, Enslin, 1829. 8. etiam sub titulo: Bibliotheca
Concionatoria, Sectionis Primae Vol. *1.* 8. 268/338. (301/28).
— Acta ex anonymo syro excerpta: BO. *1.* 25/6. 26/55 = Uhlem.
¹ 1/23. ₂ 1/27, uberius Opera *3.* *23—63.*
— S¹ E¹ S¹ Hymni et sermones quos e codd. Londiniens., Parisiens.,
et Oxoniens. descripsit, edidit, Latinitate donavit . . . *Thomas
Josephus Lamy.* Mechliniae 1882. 2 voll. 4⁰.   M. 18. 22.
     cf. Nöldeke, GGA. 82. 48. 1505/14.
— de testamento E¹ cf. BO. *1.* 141/6.
— the repentance of Niniveh, a metrical homily. With some smaller
pieces. Translated from the Syriac with notes by *H. Burgess.*
Lond. 1853.   sh. 10½. M. 5.
— *Burgess,* Select metrical Hymns and Homilies of Ephraem Syrus.
Translated from the original Syriac, with an Introduction, and
historical and critical Notes. London 1853. gr. 8? ZDMG. 10,
628. 9, 215 ff.
— Zingerle, P. Pius. Marienrosen aus Damaskus. Gesänge zu Ehren der
allerseligsten Jungfrau. Aus dem Syrischen. Zweite durch vollstän-
dige Uebersetzung der Gebete des heil. Ephraem an die aller-
seligste Jungfrau vermehrte Ausgabe. 12. 1865. Fl. —. 88.
— Hymnen aus dem Zweiströmeland. Dichtungen des hl. Ephrem
des Syrers aus dem syrischen Urtext metrisch ins Deutsche über-

tragen und mit erklärenden Anmerkungen versehen von Carl
Macke. Nebst einem Anhang. Mainz, Kirchheim, 1882. *16.*
270 pp.

Ephraem Syrus († 873).

— P. Martin über Ephräm's Hymnen auf den h. Eremiten Abraham.
ZfkTh. 1880. 3.

— E. des heiligen Kirchenvaters ausgewählte Schriften aus dem
Griechischen und Syrischen übersetzt von *P. Pius Zingerle.*
6 voll. 1845—6.   fl. 8. 40.

    1. Band: Bekenntnisse u. Reden über die vier letzten Dinge.
    2.   „   Sechsundsiebenzig Ermahnungen zur Busse.
    3.   „   Die Tugendschule; eine Sammlung ascetischer
                Schriften.
    4.   „   Die heilige Muse der Syrer.
    5.   „   Gesänge gegen die Grübler über die Geheimnisse
                Gottes.
    6.   „   Reden über die Busse und Zerknirschung sammt
                mehreren anderen verschiedenen Inhalts.

                          Einzeln jeder Band fl. 2. 12.

— Zingerle, Pius. Über sechssylbige Verse bei Ephraem dem Syrer.
ZDMG. *2.* 66/73.

— die Reden des h. E. gegen die Ketzer . . . übers. v. P. P. Z.
Kempten 1850.

— E. des Syrer's Reden über Selbstverleugnung und einsame
Lebensweise. Mit einem Briefe desselben an Einsiedler . . .
übersetzt von P. P. Z. Innsbruck 1871.

— Kayser, C., Ein Brief E.'s des Syrer's an die „Bergbrüder" übersetzt Z. f. kirchl. W. u. k. L. 1884, 5. 251/66.

— Passionspredigten von E. d. S. ibid. 83. 10. 527/41.

— Das Leben des h. E. d. S., als Einleitung zu einer deutschen
und syrischen Ausgabe der Werke Ephraem's übersetzt und mit
erläuternden Anmerkungen versehen. Nebst einer Abhandlung:
„Untersuchungen über die Chronologie Ephraem's" und einem
Anhang „die Werke Ephraems." Berlin 1853. 8. M. 1. 25.

— S^i E^i S^i commentariorum in sacram scripturam textus in codicibus Vaticanis manuscriptis et in editione Romana impressus.
Commentatio critica quam scripsit *Antonius Pohlmann*. Part.
prima Brunsbergae (1863). p. 2. (64).
    cf. Himpel, ThQS. 45, 515/20. ZDMG. 15, 648.

— *Lengerke, C. A.*, commentatio critica de E^o S^o s. script. interprete.
Qua simul versionis syriacae quam Peschito vocant lectiones variae
ex E^i commentariis collectae exhibentur. Halis Sax. 1828. 4°.
                                 M. 1.

— Lengerke, C. A., de E^i S^i arte hermeneutica liber. Regim. 1831.
4. 20.   M. 1. 50.

Ephraem Syrus († 373).

— Gerson, D., Die Commentarien des Ephraem Syrus im Verhältniss zur jüdischen Exegese. 4 Abhandlungen.

— Skat Rördam, T., Zehn Gedichte Afram's des Syrers (Ephraem Syrus) rythmisch übersetzt mit Einleitung Theol. Tidskr. Kjöbh. 1878. 4/5.

— J. D. Michaelis. De Syrorum vocabulis ex Ephraemo. in: Commentationes . . . per annos 1758/62 praelectae oblatae ed. *1.* 4⁰. Bremae 1763. M. 1. 50.

    Ed. *2.* 4⁰. Bremae 1774.

— J. *Fr. Gaab,* Beitrag zur Geschichte der Schrifterklärung aus Ephraem dem Syrer. Paulus Memorabilien 1 (1791) 65 ff.

— — Züge zu einer pragmatischen Biographie von Ephraem dem Syrer. ibid. 2. 136 ff.

— Nilles, J., Dogmatische Stellen aus neuedirten Reden und Hymnen des hl. Ephrem. ZfkTh. *4*, 3. 578/80.

— Lamy, T. J., Studies in oriental patrology. St. Ephrem (Dublin Rev. 1885 July p. 20/44.

Testi orientali inediti sopra i *Sette Dormienti di Efeso* publicati e tradotti del socio *Ignazio Guidi.* Reale Accademia dei Lincei (Anno 282, 1884/5).

    cf. Th. Nöldeke, GGA. 1886. 11. 453/9.

Epiphanius, episcopus Cypri († 403).

    de mensuris ac ponderibus liber nunc primum integer et ipse syriacus. *Paulus de Lagarde* edidit. Gotting. 80. vide II, 126.

— des Epiphanius buch über masse und gewichte zum ersten male vollständig in: P. de Lagarde, Symmicta 2, 149/216.

— [Pseudo-?] Vitae prophetarum (quatuor maiorum) (e tribus codicibus Musei Britannici). Nestle, Gramm. Syr. 53/61.

— I. H. *Hall,* Proc. Am. Or. Soc. *13*, 150.

Esrae apocalypsis de regno islamitico v. *Baethgen, Fr.,* Beschreibung der syrischen Handschrift „Sachau 131" auf der königlichen Bibliothek zu Berlin. ZfdatW. 6 (86) 193/211.

Eusebius Caesareensis († c. 340).

— historia ecclesiast. *1,* 1—4 ed. *Krehl* in Eus. opp. recognovit *Dindorf 4.* 71. p. *18—56.* c. 13 in: Cureton Documents p. 1—5; l. *6.* 16. 17. 25 in: Lagarde, Praetermissa 249/52.

— Hist. eccl. 1—5 descripsit e cod. lond. *Tullberg,* cf. ZDMG. 7, 408.

— on the Theophania or Divine manifestation of Our Lord and Saviour Jesus Christ. a syriac version, edited from an ancient manuscript recently discovered, by *Samuel Lee,* London, printed for the society for the publication of oriental texts. 42.

    M. 15. 5. 12.

— *Eusebius* Bischof of Caesarea on the Theophania or Divine Manifestation of our Lord and Saviour Jesus Christ, translated into

English with Notes, from an ancient Syriac version of the Greek
original now lost; to which is prefixed a vindication of the ortho-
doxy, and prophetical views, of that distinguished writer. In-
scribed by permission to his Grace the Duke of Northumberland,
Chancellor of the University of Cambridge. By Samuel Lee, D. D.
Cambridge 1843. *119.* (1. 1 facs.) 344.

Eusebius Caesareensis († c. 340).
— *Syrisches.* Von Dr. Geiger. ZDMG. 17 (63) 725/9. Emendationes
ad Theophaniam 42, 43.
— History of the Martyrs of Palestine. edited and translated by
W. *Cureton,* London 61. M. 7. 50.
— a panegyric on the christian Martyrs: Journal of sacred literature
4th ser. vol. *5* (64) p. 403; cf. vol. *6,* 129.
— chronicon, operis historici capita ex Eus. chronicis (?) excerpta.
Roediger ² 105/9 et ed. *Schoene 2* (67).
— Eusebii Canonum Epitome ex Dionysii Telmaharensis Chronico
petita sociata opera verterunt notisque illustraverunt Carolus Sieg-
fried et Henricus Gelzer, Lipsiae. In aedibus B. G. Teubner,
1884. 4⁰.
— *H. A. v. Gutschmid,* Untersuchungen über die syrische Epitome der
Eusebischen Canones. Stuttgart 1886. 43 pp. 4. [prog. acad.
Tubingensis.]
— (pseudo-) on the *Star* edited by W. *Wright:* Journ. of sacred
lit. 66. *9,* 117. *10,* 150. M. 1. 50.
— *Merx, A.,* De Eusebianae historiae ecclesiasticae versionibus, syriaca et armeniaca.
    Atti del IV Congresso intern. degli Orientalisti.

Sancti *Eustathii* Antiocheni quae syriace supersunt fragmenta.
Pitra 4, 210/3; lat. 441/3.
I. H. *Hall,* On the Syriac text of the book of the *Extremity* of the
Romans. Am. Or. Soc. Proc. May 1887, 4 f. Journ. *13,* 155 f.

Fragmenta syro-palaestinensia: in *Land,* Anecdota *4* 103/224.
177/233.

Fragmente syrischer und arabischer Historiker, herausgegeben und
übersetzt von *Friedchri Baethgen.* Leipzig 1884. M. 7. 50.
    Abhandlungen für die Kunde des Morgenlandes *8,* 3.
    cf. R. Duval, Rev. crit. 84, 41.

Galenus, ars medica c. 23. 24. 28/31: SI.*) 88/94.
—, de alimentorum facultatibus l. *2* c. 58 fin. — 61: ibid. 94/7.
—, Proben der syrischen Uebersetzung von Galenus' Schrift über die
einfachen Heilmittel. Von A. Merx.
    ZDMG. 39 (1885) 237/305.

---

*) SI. = Sachau, Inedita Syriaca.

Galenus, Löw, Bemerkungen zu *Merx*, Proben der syrischen Uebersetzung von Galenus' Schrift über die einfachen Heilmittel.
ZDMG. 40, 4. 763/5.

Geographica. Ardrijkskundige Fragmenten uit de Syrische Literatur
der zesde en zevende Eeuw. (*Meet en Schetskaartje.*) Mededee-
ling van *J. P. N. Land.* Overgedruckt uit de Verslagen en Mededeelingen der Koninklijke Akademie van Wetenschappen, Afdee-
ling *Letterkunde*, 3de Reeks, Deel *3.* Amsterdam, 1886.

Geoponicon in sermonem syriacum versorum quae supersunt. *P. La-
gardius* edidit. Lips., Lond. exemplaria facta *150.* (M. 12.) 8.

— de Geoponicon versione syriaca scripsit A. P. de Lagarde, Dr.
Berlin 1855. 4⁰. Jahresbericht über die Louisenstädtische Real-
schule. (Repetit. in: *Gesammelte Abhandlungen* 1866).

Georgius Arabum episcopus (c. 714), epistola: LA. 108/34 et *Aphraates* p. 19/37.

— de Sapiente Persa capita tria, ex epistola Georgii episcopi
Arabum excerpta (syr. et lat.) in: *Forget, Juc.*, de vita et scriptis
Aphraatis Sapientis Persae. Lovanii 1882. p. 1—56.

— Ryssel, V., Ein Brief Georgs, Bischofs der Araber, an den Presbyter Jesus, aus dem Syr. übersetzt und erläutert. Mit einer
Einleitung über sein Leben und seine Schriften. Erweiterter
Separatabdruck aus den „Theol. Stud. u. Krit." Gotha 1883. (2.
278/371) 118 pp.

Georgius Arbelensis commentarius de liturgia excerpta in BO.

Georgius Nisibenus hymnus Brev. Moss. p. 54 = Off. Mar. p. 242.

Georgius Patriarcha litania germanice a *Schönfelder.*

Das bald dem Concil von Nicaea, bald einer antiochenischen Synode
zugeschriebene Bekenntniss gegen Paul von Samosata in griechischer und syrischer Sprache: *C. P. Caspari*, alte und neue
quellen zur geschichte des taufsymbols und der glaubensregel
p. 161—175. Christiania 79.

Grabinschriften vid.: Inscriptiones.

Ein *Gregor* von Nazianz († 389/90) beigelegtes Glaubensbekenntniss
in syrischer Sprache aus einer nitrischen Handschrift des British
Museum. ibid. 1—160.

Carmen e carminibus iambicis *Gregorii* (theologi): *Adler*, institutio 62/4.

Gregorius Nyssenus († 394) explicatio exordii orationis dominicae:
Mo *1* 111/6.

Gregorius Abulfarag bar Hebraei (1226 † 30. Juli 1286).

— Chronici excerptum: de rebus gestis Richardi Angliae regis in
Palaestina. Syr. et Lat. ed., not. illustr. P. J. Bruns. Oxon.
1780. 4. 20 (31?) pp.   M. 1. 20. 4.

— cf. Vater, Chrestomathie p. 15—33, inde germanice a *Bruns*,
Repertorium 7, 183/99.

— Chronicon syriacum e codicibus Bodleianis descriptum conjunctim

ediderunt *Paulus Jacobus Bruns* et *Georgius Guilielmus Kirsch.*
Lipsiae 789. 4⁰. 2 voll. [prospectus editionis 1787.]
Gregorius Abulfarag bar Hebraei (1226 † 30. Juli 1286).
— descripsit, maximam partem vertit notisque illustravit Bruns . .
edidit, ex parte vertit notasque adjecit Kirsch. M. 45. 60.
   cf. *Lorsbach* in: Archiv f. d. Morgenl. Lit. *1.* Marburg 1791.
199—301, Paulus Neues Repertorium *3.* Jena 1791. 82—114.
— zur berichtigung der syrischen chronik des BH. von P. J. Bruns
in: Paulus, Memorabilien *3.* Leipzig 792. 196/8.
— Buch der Könige von Barhebräus c. 1—5.
   cf. Hasse. Bibl. orient. Aufsätze. Königsberg 1793. p. 7—17.
— *Arnoldi, A. J.,* Chronici Syriaci Abulpharagiani e scriptoribus Graecis emendati, illustr. specimen. Marp. 1805. 4⁰. M. 1. 1. 50.
— Beyträge zu einer richtigen übersetzung der syrischen chronik
des Gr. BH. oder berichtigung verschiedener stellen der lateini-
schen übersetzung des BH., welche P. J. Br. und G. W. Kirsch
herausgegeben haben. von Ferd. Greg. Mayer. Wien 819. M. 2. 6.
— Nachtrag zu den beyträgen Wien 1820 et in: Wiener Jahrbücher.
Vol. *13,* 1821. Anzeigeblatt p. 39/40.
— append: Rerum seculo quinto decimo in Mesopotamia gestarum
librum e codice bibliothecae bodleianae syriaco edidit et interpretatione latina illustravit Dr. *Ottomar Behnsch.* Vratislaviae 38. 4⁰.
                    M. 2. 50.
— chronici syriaci e codd. mss. passim emendati atque illustrati
specimen primum . . . scripsit Geo. Henr. Bernstein. Lips. 22. 4⁰.
                    M. 1.
— *G. H. Bernstein,* die syrische Chronik des Bar-Hebraeus. 11 pp.
[Sept. 1846]. Druck von Grass, Barth & Comp. in Breslau.
   vide etiam Verhandlungen der DMG. 1845. p. 33.
— ankündigung und probe einer neuen ausgabe und übersetzung
der syrischen chronik des Greg. BH. von *G. H. Bernstein.*
Berlin. 47.
— chronicon ecclesiasticum quod e codice musei britannici descriptum
coniuncta opera ediderunt, latinitate donarunt annotationibusque
theologicis historicis, geographicis et archaeologicis illustrarunt
Joannes Baptista Abbeloos . . . et *Thomas Josephus Lamy.* Lovanii 4. Tomus *1* 72, *2* 74, *3* 77. 2 voll. M. 40. 48. 55. 60.
— extrait de la vie du patriarche Denys de Telmahre qui se trouve
dans la 2ᵉ partie de la chronique de Gr. BH.: Abd - Allatif,
relation de l'Egypte par M. Silv. de Sacy. Paris 810. 4⁰.
p. 501/8. 552/7.
— cf. Kirsch ² 143/5.
— *Origines* ecclesiae Syriacae sive Chronici partis tertiae initium in:
S. Ephraemi Syri . . . opera selecta . . . ed. J. J. Overbeck.
Ox. 1865. 414/423.

Gregorius Abulfarag bar Hebraei (1226 † 30. Juli 1286).
— horreum mysteriorum sive commentarios in testamenti veteris et
  novi libros sacros e codicibus manuscriptis syriacis musei britannici londinensis bibliothecae bodleianae oxoniensis regiae bibliothecae berolinensis primum edidit commentariis instruxit diffici-
  liores locos transtulit atque explanavit *Fridericus Ferdinandus
  Larsow.* [1] Lipsiae 58.   4⁰.   4 8 pp.   [Consociatis Borussorum
  et Britannorum regnis nuptias auspicatissimas felicissimas Friderici
  Guilelmi et Victoriae pia mente congratulatur F. F. L.   Berolini
  die VIII M. Febr. 1858.]   M. 3.
— Scholien zu gen. 49. 50. exod. 14. 15. deut. 32—34 und jud. 5.
  veröffentlicht von Dr. R. Schröter: ZDMG. 24 (70) 495/562.
— scholia in Jobum cf. Kirsch ² 186/210.
— scholia in librum Jobi ex codd. mss. emendata denuo edidit diffi-
  ciliorum locorum interpretatione illustravit notis criticis instruxit
  D. Geo. Henr. Bernstein.   Vratislaviae 58.   fol.   (4) 16 pp|.
  (Academiae Jenensi . . . gratulatur acad. Vratislaviensis.)
                                             M. 1. 20.   1. 50.
— specimen quaestionis de syriaca carminis Deborae jud. V. versione,
  scholiis, quae ad eam a BH. conscripta sunt, integris additis.
  dissert. quam . . . defendet auctor *Joannes Mauritius Winklerus.*
  Vratislaviae 39.   32 pp.
— in librum psalmorum adnotationes e recognitione *Pauli de Lagarde.*   in: Praetermissorum libri duo Gottingae 79, 97/252.
— in psalmos [1. 2. 22. prooem.] scholiorum specimen e codicibus
  mss. syriacis musei brit. lond. et bibl. bodl. oxon. edidit latine
  reddidit et annotationibus illustravit Dr. O. F. Tullberg.   Upsalae
  42.   4⁰.   17. 10 pp.
— scholia in psalmum 5 et 18 e codicibus bibl. bodl. apographo
  Bernsteiniano edita translata et annotationibus prolegomenisque
  instructa. dissert. quam . . . defendet auctor *Joan. Theoph. Guil.
  Henr. Rhode.*   Vratislaviae 32.   5 84 [1. 93]. (1) pp.   M. —. 75.
— Scholien des BH. zu ps. 3. 4. 6. 7. 9—15. 23.⟨53 nebst dessen
  vorrede zum neuen testamente.   veröffentlicht von lic. dr. R.
  Schröter: ZDMG. 29 (75) 247/308.   M. 1.
— scholia in ps. 8. 40. 41. 50 e codice berolinensi primum edita
  cum codicibus bodl. florent. vatic. collata translata et annotationibus instructa. dissert. quam . . . defendet auctor *Rob. Gust. Ferd.
  Schroeter.*   Vratislaviae 57.   (M. 2. 75.)   —. 50.   1. 50.
— scholia in ps. 68 e codicibus mss. syr. bibl. florent. et clement.-
  vatic. et bodl. oxon. primum edita et annotationibus illustrata.
  dissert. quam . . . defendet *Cyrillus Knobloch.*   Vratislaviae 52.
  57. (4) pp.
— Des Gregorius Abulfarag genannt Bar Ebhroyo Anmerkungen zu

den salomonischen Schriften herausgegeben von **Alfred Rahlfs.**
Leipzig 1887. Drugulin. *10.* 29 pp. 8⁰.

cf. ThN. LCBl. 87, 25. *Duval,* Rev. d. Ét· Juives. *15,* 155/8.
Gregorius Abulfarag bar Hebraei (1226 † 30. Juli 1286).
— in *Jesaiam* scholia e codd. mss. syr. musei brit. lond. et bibl. bodl.
oxon. edidit et annotationibus illustravit *Otto Frider. Tullberg.*
Upsalae 42. 4⁰. 22. 36 pp. **M. 2.**
— scholia in *Jeremiam* e codd. mss. syr. edita et annotationibus instructa quae . . . p. p. Mag. *Gust. Freder. Koraen* et *Carolus
Ericus Wennberg.* (p. *1.*) Upsalae 52. 4⁰.
p. *2. Koraen* et *Joh. Aug. Zach. Wittlock.*
p. *3. Koraen* et *Sveno Andr. Gust. Sundberg.*
— in duodecim prophetas minores scholia. ad trium codicum fidem recensuit *Bernh. Morits.* Lipsiae: typis B. G. Teubneri. 1882. 32 pp. **M. 2.**
— in evangelium Matthaei scholia e recognitione *Johannis Spanuth.*
Gottingae 79. 4⁰. [typis Lugd. Bat. Brillianis.] 71 pp. [cap.
1—8, pp. 1—30 separatim prodierunt cf. Cat. ZDMG. 4512.]
M. 2. 2. 50.
— in evangelium Johannis commentarius. e thesauro mysteriorum
desumptum edidit *R. Schwartz* [† 13. Jun. 79, Lagarde, Symm.
2, 98]. Gottingae 78. 28 pp. **M. —. 80. 1.**
— in actus apostolorum et epistulas catholicas adnotationes syriace
e recognitione *Martini Klamroth.* Dissert. inaug. Gottingae 78.
30 pp. **M. 1. 1. 50.**
— opera grammaticalia vide I, 145. 163 et Jacobus Edessenus.
— Berichtigungen und Zusätze zum fünften Kapitel der barhebräi-
schen kleinen Grammatik auf Grund des Textes von Abbé Martin
(Paris 1872) nebst Einleitung. Inaugural-Dissertation zur Erlangung
der Doctorwürde. Eingereicht von Abraham Illch. Leipzig 1885.
Druck von W. Drugulin. 7 29. (1) pp. **M. —. 75. 1. 20.**
— carmina.
— veteris philosophi Syri de sapientia divina poema aenigmaticum
ed. *Gabriel Sionita.* Paris 638.
— Carmen de Divina Sapientia. Auctore celeberrimo Viro Abul-
pharagio Gregorio Filio Haronis Bar-Hebraeo. Accedunt adnotationes et interpretationes P. Joannis Notayn Darauni Libanensis.
Romae: Ex Typographia Polyglotta S. C. de Propaganda Fide. 1880.
48 pp. [cum titulo arabico.] **M. 2. 50. 3. 3. 50. 4. 4. 50.**
— Greg. BH. (aliorumque) carmina syriaca aliquot adhuc inedita
[ed. *Caesar a Lengerke*]. Regiomonti Borussorum, 4⁰. 4 partes
1. 2. 36. 3. 4. 38 (progr. acad.). **M. 1. 75. 2. 50.**
— carmina a patre *Augustino Scebabi* monaco Maronita libanensi
aleppensi correcta ac ab eodem lexicon adjunctum. Rom 77.
L. 12. M. 9. 10. 15.

cf. etiam *Renan,* de philosophia peripatetica apud Syros p. 67.

Gregorius Abulfarag bar Hebraei (1226 † 30. Juli 1286).

— narratiunculae e ܐܟ̣ܬܒ̣ܐ ܕܛܝܳܘܳܬܐ ܡܕܡ: *Adler*, inst. 39/44.
(Kirsch 1·2, Tychsen, Bernstein).
— *L. Morales*, Aus dem Buch der „ergötzenden Erzählungen" des
Bar-Hebräus. ZDMG. 40. 410/456.
— A List of Plants and their Properties, from the M^cnârat^h Kud^hṣê
of Gregorius Bar 'Eb^hrâyâ. Edited by Richard J. H. Gottheil,
B. A. For Private circulation only. [1886.] 8. 26 pp. autogr. 4⁰.
— A Synopsis of Greek Philosophy by Bar 'Ebhrâyâ. By Richard
J. H. Gottheil. Hebraica 3, 4. 249/54.
— (latine tantum) ecclesiae antiochenae Syrorum *nomocanon* a Gr. Ab.
BH. syriace compositus et a *Josepho Aloysio Assemano* in latinam
linguam conversus in: Script. vet. nova collectio X. 2 (38) 1/268. 4⁰.
— vita (ex chron. eccles.) BO. 2, 248/63, Mich. 81/104, Roed. 1 2.
— de morte Gr. a Barsauma fratre, BO. 2, 264/75, Mich. 104/16,
Roed. 1 2.
— Tabulae chronologicae ab orbe condito usque ad excidium Hierosolymitanum in: Chronicon orientale Petri Rahebi (Ibn el Râhib).
2. edit. Ven. 1729, 103 ss. (ab Assemani lat. redditae).
— vide quae *Frick* in Höxter et *Doerwald* in Ohlau promiserunt in
Berl. Phil. Wochenschrift 1886, 22.
— splendidissimus codex historiae Dynastiarum arabicae in collec-
tione Kremeriana; vide Kremer, Acad. Berol. 1885. 109. 1. 156.

Gregorius Thaumaturgus († 270).
— ad Philagrium de homousia: LA. 43/6.
— ad Theopompum de impassibilitate et passibilitate dei: ibid. 46/64.
— fragmenta varia: ibid. 64/7.
— (pseudo = Apollinaris) η κατα μερος πιστις: ib. 31/42.
— Sancti *Gregorii* Thaumaturgi quae syriace supersunt opera et
fragmenta. Pitra 4, 81—133, lat. 345—386.
— *V. Ryssel*, Gregorius Thaumaturgus, Sein Leben u. seine Schriften.
Nebst Uebersetzung zweier bisher unbekannter Schriften Gregors
aus dem Syrischen. Leipzig 1880. 8. 160.　　　M. 3. 50. 5.
cf. E. N., ZDMG. 35, 784/5.
— *C. P. Caspari*, Alte und neue Quellen zur Geschichte des Taufsymbols und der Glaubensregel. 1879. 1 ff.
Dräseke, J., Zu Victor Ryssel's Gregorius Thaumaturgus.
ZfprTh. 83. 4. 634/40.

Hierotheus, liber mysticus vid. Stephanus.

Hippolytus († c. 275) in Danielem, de psalmis, cant. cant.: LA. 79/91
et de Lagarde, anmerkungen zur griechischen übersetzung der
proverbien. Leipz. 63. p. 71.
— Sancti *Hippolyti* quae syriace supersunt fragmenta. Pitra 4, 36—64,
lat. 306—331.

Historia urbis Carcae Beth-Seleuciae et martyrum qui in ea pass
sunt (c. 415): Mo 2, 63/75.
Historia S. Crucis bis inventae (e cod. Londin. add. 12174 anni 1196).
Nestle, Gramm. Syr. 61—78.
(Thomas, Jaballaha, Jacobus et Denha Indiarum episcopi) historia
Indorum bencdictorum deque ipsorum in urbem Gazartae Zebe-
dacae adventu (1509): BO. 3, 1, 589/99.
Historia Syrorum in ripa Malabarica (c. 1730) in: Anecd. 1, 24/30.
123/7. 179/84.
Historia Josephi justi et Asenethae in: Anecd. 3 15/45.
— *Oppenheim, Gust.*, Fabula Josephi et Asenethae apocrypha e libro
Syriaco latine versa. Diss. inaug. Berolini 1886. 50. 2 pp. 8⁰.
  cf. de Lagarde, Mitth. 2, 240.
Hunain Herthensis, medicus et grammaticus († 873).
  cf. Opuscula Nestoriana.
Ein melkitischer *hymnus auf die jungfrau Maria.* veröffentlicht von
Friedrich Baethgen. (mit einer tafel): ZDMG. 33 (79) 666/71.
[I. H.] Hall, On a newly discovered Syriac Manuscript Am. Or. Soc.
Proceed. Oct. 1886. Journ. 13, 126/8. Historia Jabalaha Ca-
tholici et Rabban Sauma visitatoris generalis. (c. 1317).
Jacobus Baradaeus (Burdě'ānā) († 578).
Kleyn, H. G., J. B. de stichter der syrische monophysietische Kerk.
Academisch Proefschrift. Leiden 1882. 210.
Jacobus episcopus Edessenus († 5. Juni 708).
— de versione bibliorum vide 2, 109. Journal des Savants (reim-
press. Amstelod.) Oct. 1765. 1, 67/99.
— Scholia on passages of the old testament by mār Jacob, bish. of
Ed., now first edited in the original syriac, with an english translation and notes by *George Phillips*. Lond. 64. 8 (4) 51. 32 pp.
                                                sh. 2. M. 4. 5.
— specimina exegetica a commentariis J. Ed. e codice syr. vaticano
103: *Adler*, Inst. 50/9.
    cf. etiam *S. Ephraemi* opera syriaca, in quibus haud pauca
Scholiorum Jacobi inveniuntur. BO. 1, 489/93.
— Fragments of the syriac grammar: cf. I. 161.
— a letter by mar J., b. of Ed., on syriac orthography; also a tract
by the same author, and a discourse by Gregory bar Hebraeus
on syriac accents. now edited in the original syriac, from mss.
in the brit. mus., with an engl. translation and notes, by *Geo.
Phillips.* to which are added [3] appendices. Lond. 69. 8. 96.
45 pp.   M. 2. 50. 3. 5. 6. 50.
— epistola ad Georgium episcopum Sarugensem de orthographia
syriaca. textum syr. edidit, latine vertit, notisque instruxit *J. P.
Martin* . . . subsequuntur ciusdem Jacobi nec non Thomae dia-
                                    D*

coni, tractatus de punctis aliaque documenta in eandem materiam.
Paris 69. (autogr.) *12.* 16 pp.   M. 1.50.

Jacobus episcopus Edessenus († 5. Juni 708).
— *P. Martin*, Jacques d'Édesse et les voyelles Syriennes. Paris 69. 36.
  Journal Asiatique Extrait n°. 7. (6. Sér. tom. *13.* 447/82.)
— epistola de antiqua Syrorum liturgia: BO. *1* 479/86.
— two epistles syr. with notes *Wright:* Journal of sacred literature.
  new series vol. *10* (67). p. 430 sqq.   M. 1.25.
— erster brief an Johannes den styliten, veröffentlicht von dr. *Robert
  Schröter:* ZDMG. 24 (70) 261/300.   M. 1. 1.20.
— *canones ecclesiastici: Lamy* dissertatio de Syrorum fide 98/171.
  LR. 117/144. (Mai, Scr. Vet. N. C. *5.*)
— *Kayser*, Die Canones Jacobs von Edessa übersetzt und erläutert,
  zum Theil auch zuerst im Grundtext veröffentlicht. Leipzig 1886.
— (?) Liber generalis ad omnes gentes (s. de causa causarum) herausgegeben von *Pohlmann* ZDMG. 15, 649/63.
— Ex Homiliis *Severi* patriarchae Antiocheni (512—518) secundum
  translationem a Jacobo Edesseno anno 701 confectam et scholiis
  illustratam [Add. MSS. 12159. A. Chr. 868].
  Nestle, Gramm. Syr. 79/83.
— E Jacobi Edesseni epistula de regibus Magis. e cod. Lond. Add.
  12172 (c. 9. saec.). Accedunt nomina corum e Cod. londin. add.
  12143 (anni 1229) et paris. 232 (7. saec.) ibid. 83/85.
— de *Chronico* vide *Baethgen*, Fragmente.
— über den schem hammephorasch und andere gottesnamen. von
  dr. *Eberh. Nestle:* ZDMG. 32 (78) 465/508. 735/7.

Jacobus episcopus Sarugensis (451 † 29. Nov. 521).
— sermo de Thamar ex codice vaticano 117 editus a *Josepho
  Zingerle.* Oeniponte 71, cf. eiusdem Chrest. Syr. p. 360—386.
— *Abbeloos, J. B.*, de vita et scriptis s. J. Batnarum Sarugi in
  Mesopotamia episcopi, cum ejus syriacis carminibus . . . duobus
  integris ac aliorum aliquot fragmentis. Lovan. 67. 106/231.
                                                             M. 5. 6.
— proben syrischer poesie aus J. von Sarug von *Zingerle:* ZDMG.
  12 (58) 117/31. 13 (59) 44/58. 14 (60) 679/91. 15 (61) 629/47.
  20 (66) 511/26.
— gedicht über den palast den der apostel Thomas in Indien baute.
  veröff. von R. Schröter. ibid. 25 (71) 321/77. 28 (74) 584/626.
                                                             M. 1. 50.
— discours sur la chute des idoles par M. *l'abbé Martin.* ib. 29
  (75) 107/47.
— lettres aux moines du couvent de mar Bassus, et à Paul d'Edesse,
  relevées et traduites par M. *l'abbé Martin.* ib. 30 (76) 217/75.
— trostschreiben an die himyaritischen christen. veröff. von R.
  Schröter. ib. 31 (77) 360/405.   M. —.80. 1.

Jacobus episcopus Sarugensis (451 † 29. Nov. 521).
— oratio de Habibo, Guria et Shamuna martyribus, de Edessa in:
Curet. Doc. 86/107.
— de curru Ezechielis etc. in Mo *1* 21/96. *2* 52/63. 76/167. in:
Wenig schola 155/9.
— encomium S. Simeonis stylitae in: Acta Mart. *2* 230/44.
— *preces* quas ipse puer memoriter recitabat in: S¹ E¹ S¹ ... opera
selecta ... edidit *J. J. Overbeck*. 1865. 382 s.
— *homilia* de virginitate, de fornicatione et de conjugio iustorum.
ibidem 384/91. tractatus de Synodo Nicaena ib. 392/408.
— *epistola* ad Stephanum bar Sudaili; vide *Stephen* b. S.
— de *Alexandro* magno (spur?) in: *Knös*, Chrest. (1807) 66, germanice ab A. W[eber], Des Mōr Yakūb Gedicht über den gläubigen
König Alexandrūs. Berlin 1852.
— Frothingham, A. L., l'omelia di Giacomo di Sarûg sul battesimo
di Costantino imperatore, pubblicata, tradotta ed annotata da
A. L. F. 53. 25. 4⁰. Roma 1882. (Atti della r. accad. dei
Lincei. vol. 8.) M. 3. 50. 4.
— *ordo baptizandi* cf. codex liturgicus ecclesiae universalis. 2, 309.
3, 184.
— cf. Officium sanctorum (Rom 666). Breviarum feriale (Rom 787).
— Sechs Homilien des h. J. v. S. Aus syr. Hdschr. übersetzt von
P. P. Zingerle. Bonn 1867. *12.* 107. M. 1.
— Über und aus Reden von zwei syrischen Kirchenvätern über das
Leiden Jesu. Von *P. Pius Zingerle*. ThQS. 1870. 92/114 [Isaac
Ant.] 71. 409/36 [Jac. Sar.]
— *P. P. Zingerle*. Mitteilungen über und aus acht Reden des h. J.
v. S. Bischofs von Batnä in Mesopotamien über das Leiden Christi
oder seine Kreuzigung. ThQS. 53 (76) 465/75.
— vitae compendium ex anonymo syro in: BO. *1* 286/9.
— Saint Jacques de Saroug par Thomas Jos. Lamy. Extrait de la
Revue Catholique. Louvain.
— M. *l'abbé Martin*, un évêque-poète au V⁰ et au VI⁰ siècles ou Jacques
de Saroug, sa vie, son temps, ses oeuvres, ses croyances.
Revue des Sciences Ecclésiastiques. 4⁰ Série, T. *3.* Oct. Nov.
76. 77 pp.
[*Jacobus Tagritensis* † 1241], de la métrique chez les Syriens. par
M. *l'abbé Martin*. Leipz. 79. 71 pp.
Abhandlungen für die kunde des morgenlandes *7,* 2.

Presbyteri *Jesaiae* carmen in Tamerlanum. in: *Knös*, Chrest. 108/19.

de *Jesaja* religioso qui Timothei Aeluri temporibus vixit in: Anecd.
3 346/56.

Jesujab, Adiabenus († 660), epistolae in: BO. *3*, 1. 114/23. 127/37.

Yêšu'yabh (of Gadala) Pseudo-, *R. J. H. Gottheil*, A Syriac Baḥîrâ

Legend. Am. Or. Soc. Proc. May 1887. *27—31* = Journ. *13*,
177/81. from Sachau 10. 87.

Ignatius Antiochenus († 107).
— the ancient syriac version of the epistles of s. J. to st. Polycarp,
  the Ephesians and the Romans: together with extracts from his
  epistles, collected from the writings of Severus of Antioch, Timo-
  theus of Alexandria and others, edited with an engl. transl. and
  notes . . . by *Will. Cureton.* Lond. 45.
— *Corpus Ignatianum:* a complete collection of the Ignatian epistles,
  in syriac, greec and latin. by *W. Cureton.* Lond. 49.　M. 10.
— etiam: Berlin, Asher & Co. Reprinted from the London Edition,
  and authorized by the proprietor for circulation on the continent
  only. 1849.　　　　　　　　　　　　　　　M. 9. 10. 18.
— supplementum Corporis Ignatiani a Giulielmo Curetono editi publici juris factum a dr. *Georgio Moesinger.* Oeniponti 72. cf.
  Anecd. *1*, 32/5.　　　　　　　　　　　　　　　M. 1. 25.
— the Apostolic Fathers. ed. *Lightfoot* Part II. S. Ignatius, S. Polycarp etc. vol. I et vol. II, sect. II. London 1885 [nondum vidi].
— *Cureton, W.,* Vindiciae Ignatianae, or the genuine writings of
  St. Ignatius, as exhibited in the ancient Syriac version, vindicated
  from the charge of heresy. London 846. 8⁰.　　　　M. 3.
— *Lipsius, R. A.,* über das Verhältniss des Textes der 3 syr. Briefe
  des Ignatios zu den übrigen Recensionen der Ignatian. Literatur.
  Leipzig 859. gr. 8. (S. A.) 4½ M.　　　　　　　M. 2. 50.
— Meletemata Ignatiana. critica de epistolarum Ignatianarum versione
  Syriaca commentatio. Diss. inaug. quam. in . . . universitate
  Viadrina . . . *1861* . . . publice defendet auctor *Adalbert Merx*
  Bleicherodensis. Vratislaviae, typis Grassii, Barthii et socii (W.
  Friedrich). *(3).* 82 (1).　　　　　　　　　　　M. 1. 50.

Inedita syriaca. eine sammlung syrischer übersetzungen von schriften
  griechischer profanliteratur. mit einem anhang. aus den handschriften des britt. museums herausgegeben von dr. *Ed. Sachau.*
  Wien 70. [citatur SI.]　　　　　　　　　　(M. 6.) 3.

Inscriptiones.
Merx, A., Bemerkungen über bis jetzt bekannte aramäische In-
  schriften. Leipzig 1868. A.　　　　　　　M. —. 80.
Levy, M. A., Siegel und Gemmen mit aramäischen . . . und alt-
  syrischen Inschriften. Breslau 1869.　　　　　M. 2.
Christlich-palästinische inschriften. von Th. Nöldeke. ZDMG. *32*
  (78) 199/200.
Oratio dominica c. 6. saec. in Deir el-bahari parieti capellae cop-
  ticae inscripta.
  vid. *J. Euting,* Epigraphische Miscellen. Zweite Reihe. Sitz.
  Ber. Akad d. WW. zu Berlin 1887, p. 416, tab. *9*, 114.
Sachau, E., Edessenische Inschriften. ZDMG. 36 (82) 142/67.

Nöldeke, Th., Bemerkungen zu den von Sachau herausgegebenen palmyrenischen und edessenischen Inschriften. ZDMG. 36. (82.) 664/8.

Sachau, eine dreisprachige Inschrift aus Zebed [griech., syr., arab.] Monatsber. d. Akad. zu Berlin. Febr. 1882. S. 169/90 mit Tafel.

Zur Trilinguis Zebedaea. Von *Ed. Sachau.* ZDMG. 36 (82) 345/52 [non 532].

Renan, Deux monuments épigraphiques d'Édesse. Journ. As. 8 sér. février-mars 1883, 246.

cf. *Cl. Ganneau*, mission en Phénicie. Cinquième Rapport. Paris 1884, n. 116 p. 132 s. et pl. *9*.

Pauthier, G., l'inscription syro-chinoise de Si-Ngan-Fou. Monument nestorien, élevé en Chine l'an 781 de notre ère et découvert en 1625. Paris 1856. av. facs. Fl. 2. 50.

I. H. Hall, on the Syriac Part of the Chinese Nestorian Tablet. Am. Or. Soc. Proceed. Oct. 1886. Journ. *13. 124—126.*

Inscriptions Syriaques de *Salamâs*, en Perse, par *M. Rubens Duval*. Extrait du Journal Asiatique. Paris 1885. 28 pp., 3 tabb. (8 Sér. T. 5, Nr. 1. Janv. 1885. 39/62).

Mémoires de l'Acad. Imper. des Sciences de St. Pétersbourg, *7e* Serie. Tome *34*, No. 4.
    Syrische Grabinschriften aus Semirjetschie, herausgegeben und erklärt von D. Chwolson. Mit einer Tafel. Présenté à l'Académie le 1. Avril 1886. St. Pétersbourg, 1886 etc. 4⁰.

Mahler, Ed., Ueber eine in einer syrischen Grabinschrift erwähnte Sonnenfinsterniss. Wien, Gerold. Sitz. Ber. d. k. Acad. d. WW. Wien (1887) 8 pp. M. —. 20.

Johannes bar Abgar patriarcha (c. 900), canones de altari, eucharistia, excerpta; BO. *3*, 238/49.

Johannes Bethrabbanensis. cf. Breviarium Mossul. p. 61.

Johannes Chrysostomus († 407), sermo de divitiis et paupertate. Mo *1*, 117/33.
    cf. *de Lagarde*, Ankündigung einer neuen ausgabe der griechischen übersezung des alten testaments. Göttingen 1882. 51.

Johannes Darensis (soc. *9*.) de sacerdotio 4 libri: exc. in: Ephraemi . . . all. opera selecta (65) p. 409—413 et Mo *1*, 105/10.

— Aus dem handschriftlichen syrischen Werke des Johannes von Dara über das Priesterthum. Von *P. Pius Zingerle*. ThQS. 49 (67) 183/205. 50 (68) 267/285.

Johannes episc. *Ephesi* (*Asiae* † c. 585) monophysita.

— the third part of the ecclesiastical history of John bp. of Eph. now first edited by *Will. Cureton.* Oxford 53. 4⁰.
                                                    (M. 32.) 15. 24.

— the third Part of the Ecclesiastical History of John Bishop of Ephesus. Now first translated from the Original Syriac by R.

Payne Smith, M. A. Sublibrarian of the Bodleian Library. Oxford, at the University Press, 1860. 8⁰.

Johannes episc. *Ephesi* (*Asiae* † c. 585) monophysita.
— Land, J. P. N., cand. theol., Joannes Bischof von Ephesos, der erste syrische Kirchenhistoriker. Einleitende Studien. Mit einer Tafel. Leyden, E. J. Brill 1856. *11*. 200.   M. 4.
— *Die Kirchengeschichte* des *Johannes von Ephesus*. Aus dem Syrischen übersetzt. Mit einer Abhandlung über die *Tritheiten* von Dr. J. M. Schönfelder, Kaplan etc. München 1862. *16*. 311. 8⁰. cf. Hefele, ThQS. 44 (62) 674/84.
— scripta historica quotquot adhuc inedita supererant. syriace edidit *J. P. N. Land.* Anecdotorum syriacorum tomus secundus. Lugd. Bat. 68. 4⁰.
— excerpta apud Dionysium Tellmahr. servata: BO. *1*, 359/86.

Ein glaubensbekenntniss des bischofs *Johannes von Jerusalem* († 417) in syrischer übersetzung aus einer nitrischen handschrift des british museum (sammt allem was uns sonst von Johannes übrig geblieben) in: *Caspari*, quellen zur geschichte des taufsymbols *1* (66) 185 sq.

Johannes metropolita Mardae († 1165) ejus gesta, ejus memoria. BO. *1*, 217/30. ex cod. Syr. 28 (32) fol. 140.

[Johannes Mosulensis] ܝܘܚܢܢ ܡܘܨܠܝܐ ed. [Milos episc. ʿAqrae. Rom 68. 12⁰.

Johannes Saba (6 saec.), sermo et: responsio. Mo *1*, 102/4.

Johannes bar Cursus Tellensis († 538) *canones* in: Lamy, dissertatio 62/97.
— het Leven van Johannes van Tella door Elias. Syrische Tekst en Nederlandsche Vertaling. Academisch Proefschrift, door *H. G. Kleyn.* Leiden, E. J. Brill, 1882. *91* 83 pp. vide *Elias.*

Josephus, Flavius, [† post 100], de bello judaico liber sextus, edere coepit *Ceriani*, in: Monum. sacra et profana. Mediol. 4⁰. t. *5*. fasc. 2. (71?) 181/92; edidit 1883 (supra 2, 9).
— Das sechste Buch des Bellum Judaicum etc. nach der Paschittha-handschrift übersetzt und kritisch bearbeitet von Dr. Heimann Kottek. Berlin 1866. [duo capita tantum; cave lector!] 8⁰.

Josephus Hūzāyā (VI s.) primus Syrorum grammaticus. cf. Opuscula Nestoriana.

[Josephus, Nestorianorum patriarcha † 566.]
    epistola synodica patriarcharum occidentalium ad orientales. BO. *3*, 1. 52/4.

Chronique de *Josué le stylite*, écrite vers l'an 515, texte et traduction par M. *l'abbé Paulin Martin.* Leipz. 76. *86* (1) 82 pp.
    Abhandlungen für die kunde des morgenlandes *6*, 1.   M. 9.
— The chronicle of Joshua the Stylite, composed in Syriac A. D.

507, with a translation into English and notes by *W. Wright*. Cambridge 1882. *10*. 84. 92 pp.

Irenaeus Lugdunensis († c. 190).

fragmenta duo in: Pitra, Spicilegium Solesmense, alia in: Mo *2*, 10/1.

— in: Libri V adv. Haereses ed. W. W. Harley. 2 vol. Cambr. 1857. vol. 2, 431/61.

— Sancti *Irenaei* episcopi Lugdunensis quae syriace supersunt fragmenta. Pitra 4, 17/30; lat. 292/302.

S. Isaaci Antiocheni, doctoris Syrorum († c. 460), opera omnia ex omnibus quotquot exstant codicibus manuscriptis cum varia lectione syriace arabiceque primus edidit, latine vertit, prolegomenis et glossario auxit dr. Gust. Bickell. Gissae pars *1*, 73. *9*, 307. p. *2*, 77. 353 pp. M. 17.

— quae apud *Overbeck*, S¹ E¹ S¹ etc. 379/81 Isaaci esse dicuntur, Cyrillonae esse videntur; cf. Bickell, ZDMG. 27/571 n. 1.

— Mo 1, 13/20, Zingerle, Chrest. Syr. 299. 387, ThQS. 70, 92/114. Cardahi 21/5.

Isaac Ninivita (6 saec.), operis ascetici capita duo in: Mo *1*, 97/101.

— *Bickell, G.*, ausgewählte Schriften der syr. Kirchenväter ... Isaak v. Ninive, zum ersten Male aus dem Syrischen übersetzt. Kempten 1874. p. 273—412. (Thalhofer, Bibliothek).

Isocrates εις Δημονικον in: LA. 167/77.

Julianos der Abtrünnige. Syrische Erzählungen. Herausgegeben von *Johann G. E. Hoffmann*. Leiden, E. J. Brill, 1880. *18*, 250. 4⁰. M. 12. 20.

— Ueber den syrischen roman von Kaiser Julian von *Th. Nöldeke*. ZDMG. *28* (74) 263/92.

— Ein zweiter syrischer Julianusroman. id. ib. 660/74.

Sexti Julii (?) Africani fragmentum. Pitra 4, 71; lat. 337.

— cf. Eusebius, Epitome.

Julius episcopus romanus [† 357 pseudo-] epistolae in: LA. 67/79.

— epistolae nonnullae sub Julii I nomine divulgatae, emendatae, vocalium notis instructae, latine versae. dissert. inaug. quam ... defendet auctor: *Joseph. Franc. Aug. Veith*. Vratislaviae, 62. 27. *20* pp. ex LA. 67/79. M. 1.

— fragmenta septem in: Mo *2*, 1/5.

Justinus Martyr († 166) fragmentum in: Mo *2*, 7/8.

— Sancti *Justini* quae syriace supersunt fragmenta. Pitra 4, 11—16; lat. 287—292.

The book of Kalīlah and Dimnah translated from Arabic into Syriac edited by *W. Wright*, LL. D., Prof. etc. Oxford: at the Clarendon Press. London Trübner 1884. *81*. 406 (1). M. 15.

— conf. Wright, Journ. R. As. Soc. [1874] 7, 1 Appendix. [Spe-

cimen of a syriac version of the Kalilah wa Dimnah with an
engl. transl.]   M. 1. 50.   2.
The book of *Kalilag und Damnag*. alte syrische übersetzung des
indischen fürstenspiegels. text und deutsche übersetzung von
Gust. Bickell. mit einer einleitung von *Theod. Benfey*. Leipzig 76.   M. 18.   24.
— Kalilah and Dimnah: or the fables of Bidpai. Being an account
of their literary history. With an english translation of the later
syriac version of the same and notes by Keith-Falkoner. 8⁰. 406 S.
Cambridge, Warehouse [1884].   sh. 7. 6.
Thomas a *Kempis*, imitatio Christi, a Jos. Guriel, Persa-Chaldaeo,
chaldaice editum [sic?]. Rom. 57.   fr. 6.   M. 6.
Georg. Ebedjesu Khayyath, Syri Orientales, seu Chaldaei, Nestoriani
et Romanorum Pontificum primatus commentatio historico-philo-
logico-theologica . . . accedunt appendices duae . . . Romae,
Propag. 70. 10. 207.   M. 6.
Anecdota syriaca, collegit, edidit, explicuit *J. P. N. Land* Lugd.
Bat. 4⁰. T. *1*. 62. *2*. 68. *3*. 70. *23*. 356. *4*. 75. *15*. 223 (1)
224 tab. 5 [cit: Anecd.]   M. 44.   45.   50.
    de vol. *1* conf. *W. Wright*, Anecdota Syriaca Reprinted from
"The Journal of Sacred Literature and Biblical Record", for
April, 1863. For Private Circulation. London, Mitchell and
Son. 18 pp.
Leges saeculares imperatorum Constantini, Theodosii, Leonis in:
Anecd. *1*, 30/64. 128/55. 184/98.
[Liber chalipharum] opus chronographicum (Thomae presbyteri 7.
sec.?) in: Anecd. *1*, 1/22. 103/21. 165/77.
Liber paradisi sive Vitae patrum aegyptiacorum particula in: codicum
specimina etc.: ed. Tullberg. Ups. 51, 4.   M. 1.50.
Löw, I., Aramäische Pflanzennamen. Mit Unterstützung der k.
Akad. der Wissenschaften in Wien. Leipzig, Engelmann, 1881.
                                                                M. 20.
— Meleagros aus Gadara und die Flora Aramaea. Als Manuscript
gedruckt. Szegedin Mai 1883. 22 SS. [H. Steinthal gewidmet].
Catechesis minor R. P. Martini Lutheri ανευ εκφρασεως Syriasmo
donata. in Orinesius Gymnas. Syr. 1611. Pars altera practica.
Lucianus περι του μη ραδιως πιστευειν διαβολη in: SI. 1/16.
Mara bar Serapion, epistola ad filium: in Ouret. Spic. 43/50.
Marabbas Canones. cf. Ebedjesu, Nomocanon tract. *2* et *9* Brevia-
rium Mossul. p. 46.
— epistolae synodicae fragmentum. BO. *3*, 1, 77/8.
Mares vide Acta S. Mart.
An ancient syriac *martyrology* from a ms. of the year 411. ed. by
W. *Wright* in: Journal of sacred literature 4th. ser. T. *8*. Oct.
65. p. 45 sqq. 423 sqq.   M. 1.

cf. *Bickell*, ThQS. 1866. 466/68. *Nilles*, Calendarium Manuale.
1, 1879. *30*. Acta Sanctorum Oct. *1*. *12*, 183/5; ibidem suppl.
(Oct.) Victor de Buck. *Egli*, *E.*, altchristliche Studien Zürich
1887. 1/58. 103/11. Harnack ThLZ. 87, 13.

Dillmann, *A.*, Ueber die apokryphen Märtyrergeschichten des Cyriacus
mit Julitta und des Georgius. Sitz. Ber. der k. pr. Akad. der
WW. in Berlin 1887. 339/56.

Maruthas episc. Tagritensis (c. 430), acta martyrum persarum in:
Ass. acta mart. *1*.

— scholia duo in Exod. 16, 1. Mt. 26, 6/14 in: Mo *2*, 32.

Melito episcopus Sardum (?), apologia (περι αληϑειας?), fragmenta alia
in: Curet. Spic. 22/3, et Pitra Spic. *2*. *38/66*.

— apologiae ad Marcum Aurelium fragmentum e syriaco vertit
E. Renan. Ex Spic. Solesm. t. 2. seorsim cusum: Paris 55.
19 pp. Fr. 2.

— Th. Nöldeke, über die Apologie unter |Melito's Namen in Cure-
ton's Spicilegium Syriacum. JfprTh. 13, 2.

Menandri sententiae in: Anecd. *1*. 64/73 et: SI. 80.

Sancti *Methodii*, Episcopi et Martyris, quae syriace supersunt fragmenta. Pitra 4, 201/6; lat. 434/9.

Monumenta syriaca ex romanis codicibus collecta. praefatus est
P. Pius Zingerle. Oeniponti. vol. *1*. 69. *6* (2). 44. 123.

— edita a dr. *Georgio Mösinger* vol. 2. ibid. 78. *15* 26. 174.
(M. 8.) 5.

Moses Agellensis (c. 550) vide: *historia Josephi* et Aseneth, quam
transtulit ut et Glaphyra Cyrilli.

Moses bar Cepha († 903) de paradiso transt. A. Masius. Antw.
1569. 4⁰.

Mosis Mardeni theologica de sacrosancta trinitate contemplatio, scripta
ab ipso, anno CIO CI LII. et ex autographo syrico ad verbum
tralata, per eundem Andream Masium. 273/6.

Fidei Professio, quam *Moses Mardenus* Assyrius, Jacobita, Patriarchae
Antiocheni Legatus, suo & Patriarchae sui nomine est Romae
professus Anno CIO CI LII. ex ipso profitentis autographo Syrico
traducta ad verbum, per Andream Masium Bruxellanum p. 257/64.

Andreae Mülleri Greiffenhagii symbolae syriacae sive I. epistolae
duae syriacae amoebaeae *Mosis Mardeni* et *Andreae Masii* cum
versione et notis. ut et 11. dissertationes duae de rebus itidem
syriacis et e reliquis Mardeni epistolis maxime. Berolini 673. 4⁰.
M. 1. 25. 1. 50.

conf. de Andrea Müller ZDMG. 35 p. *13* n. 5.

Mundhir III und die beiden monophysitischen Bischöfe. Von *Ign.*
Guidi. ZDMG. 35. (81). 142/46.

'nanišo' grammaticus (c. 650). cf. Opuscula Nestoriana 2/49.

Narcissi episcopi (a. 350) quae fertur epistola in: Roediger ² 102/4.

Narses († 496). cf. Breviarium Romanum 441 Mossul. 66. editio
praeparata a O. Macke (vide Hymnen aus 'dem Zweiströmeland
p. *13*).

Das *Nicaenum* und *Nicaeno-Constantinopolitanum* in syrischer übersetzung aus einer handschrift des british museum in: Caspari,
quellen zur geschichte des taufsymbols *1.* 100/12.

	vide etiam: *Analecta, concilia.*

Th. Noeldeke, zur geschichte der Araber im 1. jahrh. d. H. aus syrischen quellen in: ZDMG. 29 (75). 76/98.

Opvscvla Nestoriana syriace tradidit Georgivs Hoffmann Professor
Kiliensis.

	'Nânîšô'nis Hdʰaijabʰeni et Hunaini Hêrtʰeni liber canonum de
	aequilitteris.

	'Abʰdîšô'nis Gâzarteni carmen heptasyllabum de aequilitteris.

	Anonymi interpretatio vocum difficilium biblicarum.

	Anonymi scholia biblica.

		Kiliae G. von Maack 1880. Parisiis, Maisonneuve et Soc. *23.*
		163 autogr. 4⁰.								M. 20.

		ed. 2. (novo titulo) 1886.							M. 10.

Otia syriaca = Anecd. T. *4.* 75.

Paulus Persa (c. 570), logica ad regem Chosroem in: Anecd. *4.* 1/32.
1/30. 99/113.

De condemnatione *Pauli Samosateni* quae syriace supersunt fragmenta. Pitra 4, 183/6; lat. 423/5.

Petrus Alexandrinus (a. 306) epistola canonica in: LR.

Sancti *Petri Alexandrini* episcopi et martyris quae syriace supersunt
fragmenta. Pitra 4, 187/94; lat. 425/9.

Philoxenus (Aksĕnâyā) ex Mabbôgh (occisus c. 523) *epistolae* (excerpta in BO. 2, 30/46, Wright, Cat. 1315) v. *Martin*, Gramm.
Syr. p. 71; *Ign. Guidi*, la lettera di Filosseno ai Monaci di
Tell 'Addâ (Teleda) Rome 1886. Reale Accademia dei Lincei
(anno 282 1884/5); *Frothingham*, Stephen bar Sudaili p. 28.

— Philoxenus von Mabug über den Glauben. Von Friedrich Baethgen in Kiel. ZfKG. *5.* 1. 122/38. Translatio 2. homil. ex Add.
MS. 12163 fol. 9.

Philosophorum de anima sententiae in: SI. *5/7.* 76/9.

— consilia: SI. 82/3.

Physiologus syrus seu historia animalium 32 in s. scriptura memora-
torum, ed. O. G. Tychsen. Rostochii 795.				M. 1. 50. 2.

— leydensis: Anecd. *4.* 33/102. 31/98. 115/76.

Plato [pseudo-] consilium ad discipulum: SI. 57/9.

— definitiones (ορα): SI. 56/7. 59.

Plutarchus, περι αοργησιας: LA. 186/95.

—, de exercitatione: LA. 177/86.

Plutarchus, [Ps.-] Plutarchos περι ασκησεωσ. Uebers. a. d. Syr. von Gildemeister & Bücheler. Bonn 72. 8. 8A. M. 1.

Syrische *poesien*, aus zwei handschriften des vatican (Cod. vatican 63 und 64) enthaltend den ehe-ritus der Nestorianer. mitgetheilt von dr. p. Pius Zingerle: ZDMG. 17 (63) 730/5.

Sancti *Polycarpi* quae supersunt syriace et armenice fragmenta. Pitra 4, 5; lat. 282.

— cf. the Apostolic Fathers ed. Lightfoot.

Pythagoras, sententiae: LA. 195/201.

    cf. Gildemeister, Hermes 4, 81 ff. W. Wright, JRAS. 1874, App.; Kalīlah and Dimnah, Praef.; *Schenkl*, Wiener Studien 8, 2, 262/81 Pythagoreersprüche in einer [gr.] Wiener Handschrift.

Probus (5 saec.), translator Aristotelis; v. Hoffmann, de hermeneuticis.

Burton, F., Proverbia communia syriaca. (Journ. of the As. Soc. 1871.) 8⁰. 29 pp. M. 1. 25.

Rabbūlā († Aug. 435). in: S. Ephraemi Syri *Rabulae* episcopi Edesseni Balaei aliorumque opera selecta . . . edidit J. J. Overbeck. Oxonii 1865. p. 159 (210) — 250.

— G. Bickell, ausgewählte Schriften der syrischen Kirchenväter . . . Rabulas . . . zum ersten Male aus dem Syr. übersetzt. Kempten 1874 (Thalhofer, Bibliothek) S. 153—271.

Syrisch-römisches Rechtsbuch aus dem fünften Jahrhundert. Mit Unterstützung der Akademie der Wissenschaften zu Berlin aus den orientalischen Quellen herausgegeben, übersetzt und erläutert von *Karl Georg Bruns* und *Eduard Sachau*. Leipzig, F. A. Brockhaus, 1880. 4⁰. M. 36.

— Bemerkungen zu Bruns-Sachau: „Syrisch-Römisches Rechtsbuch aus dem fünften Jahrhundert." Von Dr. *Perles*, Rabbiner. ZDMG. 1881, 139/41. 725/7.

Reliquiae iuris ecclesiastici antiquissimae. syriace primus edidit *Ant. P. de Lagarde*. [cit: LR.] (Lips.) 56. (M. 13. 50). M. 10. 12.

Sabhrišo' I. [596—604]. Guidi, Ign., die [angebliche] Kirchengeschichte des Catholikos *Sabhrišo'* I. ZDMG. 40. (86) 559/61. [e cod. vat. syr. 183, 367, a].

Salomo Bassorensis (c. 1222). The book of the bee the syriac text edited from the Manuscripts in London, Oxford, and Munich with an English translation by *Ernest A. Wallis Budge* M. A. Oxford 1886. 15 (1). 155 (1). 180. (Anecdota Oxoniensia. Semitic Series. Vol. *1*. Part *2*.) M. 18.

— liber Apis, syriacum arabicumque textum latine vertit J. Schönfelder. Bamberg 66. M. 1. 50.

Schieferdecker, J. D., nativitas Jesu Christi Syro ore depraedic. 4⁰. Cizae 1682. M. —. 75.

 Messias oxinanitus et oxaltatus, stilo Dauidis syre et arabice c. lat.

interpret. Th. Erpenii, Vict. Scialac et Gabr. Sionitae. 4⁰. Cizae
1680.   .   M. —. 75.
Serapionis, Thmuilae episcopi, quae syriace supersunt fragmenta.
Pitra 4, 214/5; lat. 443/4.
Sergius archiater Ras'ainensis (saec. 6.), de effectu lunae: SI. 101/24.
— de motu solis: SI. 125/6.
Severus, Patriarcha Alexandrinus (512/8) homiliae enthronisticae.
vide Jacobus Edessenus.
Sexti Sententiarum recensiones Latinam Graecam Syriacas coniunctim
exhibuit *Joannes Gildemeister* Professor Bonnensis, Bonnae ad
Rhenum apud Adolphum Marcum 1873. 56. 107. cf. Lagarde,
Analecta.
— Charakter und Ursprung der Sprüche des Philosophen *Sextius*
dargestellt von Professor *Meinrad Ott*. Rottweil. Druck von
M. Rothschild 1861. (Progr.) 71 pp. 4⁰.
— Die syrischen „Auserlesenen Sprüche des Herrn Xistus Bischofs
von Rom" — nicht eine Xistusschrift, sondern eine *überarbeitete
Sextiusschrift* nachgewiesen von Prof. M. Ott. ib. 1862 (Progr.)
48 SS. 4⁰.
    Cont. ib. 1863 (Progr.) 1—37 S. 4⁰.
Simeon bar Ṣabbāʿō (filius tinctorum, martyr 339/40).
    hymnus in: Sⁱ Eⁱ Sⁱ ... opera selecta ... ed. J. J. Overbeck
1865. p. 424.
Simeon episcopus Betharsamensis (510/25) epistola de Nestorianismo:
BO. *1.* 346/58, Michaelis 1/15.
— Simeons bref om Nestorianerna. Öfversättning från Syriskan jemte
Kommentarier. Akademisk Afhandling ... af *Axel G. G. Törner*.
Filos Kandidat af Blek. Nationen, Adjunkt vid, Wexioh. Elem.-
Lärovork. Lund, tryckt uti Berlingska Boktryckeriet, 1862. (3) 28.
— ad mar Simeonem Gabulae abbatem de martyrio Homeritarum
BO. *1.* 364/79, Michaelis 22/39.
— *Guidi*, la lettera di Simeone de Vescovo di Bôth-Aršam sopra i
Martiri Omeriti. Reale Accademia dei Lincei. anno 278
Roma 1881.   M. 2. 80.
— Uhlmann, Fr., die Christenverfolgungen in Persien im 4. u. 5. Jahrh.
Aus gleichzeit. syrischen Originalquellen 1861. 8⁰. (A). 162 p.
Harrass. 79, 193.   M. 1. 50.
Simeon Ḳūḳājā (6 s.) 30. hymni. paginae a P. Martin autographicae,
nescio an alicubi publicatae.
Simeon Stylita († c. 459). vita: Assemani, Acta S. mart. 2, 268/77.
Uhlemann ² 53/63.
— Zingerle, Pius, Leben und Wirken des h. Symeon Stylites. Inns-
bruck 1855. 12⁰.
Simon Kephas, praedicatio. cf. Lipsius, Apocryphe Apostelgeschichten.

Sindban oder die sieben weisen Meister. syrisch und deutsch. von
Friedr. Baethgen. Leipz. 79. 38. 26 pp. M. 1. 2. 2.80.
Socrates sive Herostrophus, dialogus de anima: LA. 158/67.
Die Fabeln des *Sophos*, syrisches original der fabeln des Syntipas, in
berichtigtem vocalisirtem texte zum ersten male vollständig mit
einem glossar herausgegeben, nebst literarischen vorbemerkungen
über das vaterland der fabel von dr. *Julius Landsberger*. Posen 59.
M. 3. 3.80. 6.
Spicilegium syriacum: containing remains of Bardesan, Meliton, Am-
brose and Mara bar Serapion. now first edited with an english
translation and notes by the rev. *William Cureton*. London 55.
sh. 9. 20. 36. M. 18. 20. 24. 25.
— Fragmenta e Spicilegio translata in: Clark's Antenicene Library
vol. (21.) 22. 1871 by *William Fletches* D. D. (of 2 & 3 cent.) et
vol. 24. 1872 by *William Macdonald, George Rose Merry*, D. Do-
naldson (Early Liturgics).
Stephen bar Sudaili, the Syrian Mystic and the book of Hierotheos,
by A. L. Frothingham Jr. Brill, Leide 1886. gr. 8⁰. Fl. 2.50.
cf. Baethgen, ThLZ. 87, 10. R. Duval, Rev. Crit. 87, 40.
— On the book of Hierotheus by a Syrian Mystic of the Fifth Century,
by Mr. *A. L. Frothingham*, Jr., of Baltimore, Md. Am. Or. Soc.
Proc. at Balt. Oct. 84. 9/13.
Epistola populi Nestoriani quam anno CIO IO LII. ex Mozal, hoc
est, Seleucia Parthorum scribebat ad Pontificem Romanum pro
Patriarcha initiando, traducta ex autographo Syrico ad verbum,
per *Andream Masium*,
post Mosis BCephae de Paradiso (1569) 264/6.
Epistola Nestorianorum qui electum Patriarcham suum usque ad Jerusalem deduxerant: scripta ex Jerusalem ad Pontificem Romanum
de eadem re, & traducta ex Autographo Syrico ad verbum, per
Andream Masium.
post Mosis BCephae, de Paradiso (1569) 266/9.
Professio fidei, quam *Siud* sive *Sulaka*, electus Patriarcha ab Nestorianis, ore & scripto est professus Romae anno CIO IO LIII. traducta ex Autographo Syrico ad verbum, per Andream Masium.
post Mosis BCephae de Paradiso (1569). 269/72.
Symbolae Syriacae — Anecd. T. *1.* M. 10.
An ancient syriac document purporting to be the record, in its chief
features, of the *second synod of Ephesus*, and disclosing historical
matter "interesting to the church at large"; of which document
an attempt at an entire reproduction in fac-simile characters and
at a translation is now first made by the rev. *S. G. F. Perry*,
M. A. Part I. Oxford 67. 4⁰. privately printed. 23. tab. 20 (1).
(cum tab. photogr.)
— *secundam synodum ephesinam*, necnon excerpta quae praesertim

ad eam pertinent, e codicibus syriacis manuscriptis in museo britanico asservatis primus edidit *Samuel G. F. Perry*, M. A. Oxonii 75. [priv. printed.] 336 pp.

Quo post mortem autoris (Jan. 81) exemplaria impressa pervenerint, nescitur; cf. Wright, Syriac Literature 829, 26.

An ancient syriac document purporting to be the record. The second synod of Ephesus. Acts. English Version with notes, by Rev. S. G. F. Perry, M. A. Cantab. Dartford 1877. *(8)* 387 pp.
M. 6. 10.

— Verhandlungen der Kirchenversammlung zu Ephesus am 22. August 449 aus einer syrischen Handschrift vom Jahre 535 übersetzt von Dr. *Georg Hoffmann*, ordentlichem Professor der morgenländischen Sprachen. Kiel, Mohr 1873. Festschrift Herrn Dr. Justus Olshausen etc. *(7)* 107. 4⁰. M. 2.

— *Actes du Brigandage d'Éphèse.* Traduction faite sur le texte Syriaque contenu dans le manuscrit 14530 du Musée Britannique, par M. *l'Abbé Martin.* Extrait de la Revue des Sciences ecclésiastiques. Amiens 74. 182 (1).

— M. *l'abbé Martin*, le Pseudo-Synode connu dans l'histoire sous le nom de Brigandage d'Éphèse étudié d'après ses actes retrouvés en Syriaque par M. l. M. Paris, Maisonneuve, 75. *21.* 214.

Narratio ex historia *Syntipae* sive de septem sapientibus sumta: Roediger ² 100/1.

— Die Fabeln des Syntipas. Von Dr. *Landsberger.* ZDMG. 12 (58) 149/59.

Das *taufbekenntnis der Nestorianer* aus cod. orient. 147 der königlichen hofbibliothek zu München: *Caspari*, quellen zur geschichte des taufsymbols *1,* 113/42.

Theano, sententiae: SI. 70/5.

Themistius, περι αρετησ: SI. 17/37.

— Themistios περι αρετησ. Nach einer syr. Uebers. bearbeitet v. Gildemeister & Bücheler. Bonn 72. 8⁰. (S. A.) M. 1.

— περι φιλιασ: SI. 38/55.

Theodori Mopsuesteni († 428 [429?]) fragmenta syriaca e codicibus musei britannici nitriacis edidit in latinum sermonem vertit *Ed. Sachau.* Lips. 69. M. 4. 7.

— excerpta: LA. 100/8.

— Der Psalmenkommentar des Th. v. M. in syrischer Bearbeitung. Von Friedrich Baethgen. ZfatW. 5 (85) 53/101.

— Flunk, Theodors v. Mopsuestia Psalmenkommentar. ZfkTh. 87. 1. 181 f.

Les sentences symboliques de *Théodose* patriarche d'Antioche (887/96). text syriac publié et traduit par *H. Zotenberg*: Journal asiatique, sept. ser. tome 8 Nov.-Déc. 76. 425/76.

De *Theodosii* ep. hierosolymitani [post 451] obitu: Anecd. 3. 341/6.

Schaaf, C., relatio historica ad epistolam syriacam a Maha Thome
i. e. *Magno Thoma* ad Ignatium et ipsa illa episcopi Indi epistola
syriaca c. vers. lat. etc. Lugd. Bat. 1714. 4⁰. Fl. —. 75. M. 1. 50.
Thomas Edessenus (hymnus). cf. Breviarium Mossul. p. 59.
Thomas Margensis (9 saec.) historia monasteŕii Beth‘abensis: plurima
excerpta BO. *3.* 1; cf. imprimis 463/501.
Titi Bostreni (post 360) contra Manichaeos libri quatuor syriace.
Paulus Antonius de Lagarde edidit. Berolini 59. exemplaria
facta 160. (4) 186 pp.   (M. 18.) 10.
— cf. *de Lagarde*, Anmerkungen zur griechischen Übersetzung der
Proverbien. 1863. p. 94/5.
Vita Alexandri magni: LA. 205/8.
Vita Secundi philosophi taciturni, fragmentum: SI. 84/8.
Horae syriacae seu commentationes et anecdota res vel litteras syriacas
spectantia. auctore *Nicolao Wiseman.* tomus primus [unicus.]
Rom. 28.   M. 5.
Xysti episcopi romani γνωμαι: LA. 1—31.
Zachariae rhetoris episcopi Melitinensis [Mitylenes Lesbiae c. 518]
historiae ecclesiasticae capita selecta ex codice syriaco vaticano:
A. M[ai], script. vet. nova coll. T. *10* (38). 332/60.   M. 8.
— *Z. episcopi Mitylenes* aliorumque scripta historica graece plerumque
deperdita. syriace edidit *J. P. N. Land.* Lugd. Bat. 70. 4⁰ =
Anecd. tom. *3.*
— J. Guidi, il testo siriaco della descrizione di Roma, nella storia
attribuita a *Zacaria* Retore.
    Bulletino della commissione archeologica communale di Roma.
Ser. 2. Anno XII. Ott-Dic. 1884. [s. Roma 1885] p. 218—239.

APPENDICULA.

Duval, Rubens. Notes sur la Peschitto. *1* Edom et Rome. *2* Le
fils du toit: Revue des Études Juives. Nr. 27. Janv.-Mars 1887.
49—52.
    3 Lo Semadar. ib. 28. Avril-Juin 1887. 277—281. [cf. Nr. 29.
p. 160].
    Recensio, quam suo loco non enumerari, Thesauri Syriaci 1—7.
Journ. Asiat. Extrait Nr. 13. (1887), 8 pp.
Gottheil, Richard J. H. On a Syriac manuscript of the New Testament belonging to the Rev. Mr. Neesan. Am. Or. Soc. Proceed.
May 1887. *31—33* = Vol. *13, 181—183.*
— On the manuscript of a Syriac lexicographical treatise, belonging
to the Union Theological Seminary of New York City; *ibid.*
p. *34* s. = *184* s.
Nestle.

Hall, I. H. On a Syriac Manuscript of the Acts and Epistles. Am. Or. Soc. Proceed. Oct. 1884. p. *18—21* [Williams MS., supra. *2,* 98 b].
— ibid. Proc. May 85 p. *5—8* [de epistola Abgari (v. supra p. 34), nonnullis mss. fragmentis].
— ibid. Proc. Oct. 85 p. *4* [adnotatio de Versione Karkaphensi sec. *P. Martin*].
— On Some Syriac Manuscripts recently acquired by the Union Theological Society.
    Journ. of the Exeget. Soc. (1887) p. 93—100.
— The Lives of the Prophets. ibid. p. 28—30.
— Notes on the "Lives of the Prophets" ibid. p. 97—102.
— ibid. p. 102 et rursus 105 de translatione Apocalypsis *Esrae,* quam Baethgen edidit et vertit (supra p. 44) ab ipso edita in Presbyterian Quarterly about a year ago.
— The Lost Ussher Manuscript ibid. 103—105.
Martin, P. cf. *1,* 165. 191—193 p. 33. 35 ss.
— [quindecim hymni (*madrāšē*) *S. Ephraemi* de Abraham Kidunāyā e cod. lond. 14592: pp. 1—32 autographice redditae, nescio an alicubi publicatae, in quarum ultima hymnos *Simeonis Kukâyâ* e cod. lond. 14520 describere incepit; corrigo supra p. 62.]
 - Introduction à la critique textuelle du Nouveau Testament. Partie théorique. Leçons professées à l'Ecole Supérieure de Théologie de Paris, en 1882—1883. Paris, Lecoffre. *13* 712 pp. autogr. 4⁰. 24 tabb. p. 97—309 des versions syriennes.
— Saint Pierre et le Rationalisme devant les Églises Orientales. Extrait de la Rev. des Sciences ecclésiastiques. Amiens 1876. 58 pp.
— Saint Pierre et Saint Paul dans l'Église Syrienne Monophysite. ibid. [1877?] 115 pp.
    continet translationem officii in honorem S. Pauli et Petri e cod. par. 164.
Phillips, Geo. Syriac Accents. From the Journal of Philology. Vol. *9.* 9 pp.
Ryssel, Victor. Ueber den textkritischen Werth der syrischen Uebersetzungen griechischer Klassiker I. Theil. Leipzig 1880. 48 pp. 4⁰. [Progr. Gymn. Nicol.]
— — II. Theil. [1881] 56 pp. 4 [dissert. eiusdem gymnasii gratulatoria F. A. Eckstein oblata].
— Syrien. PRE ² *15* (1885) 168—192. *18* (1888) 705—718.

CHRESTOMATHIA.

___

I. QUATTUOR PRIMA CAPITA GENESEOS.

CAPUT I.

¹ ܒܪܫܝܬ ܒܪܐ ܐܠܗܐ ܝܬ ܫܡܝܐ ܘܝܬ ܐܪܥܐ. ² ܘܐܪܥܐ
ܗܘܬ ܬܘܗ ܘܒܘܗ: ܘܚܫܘܟܐ ܥܠ ܐܦܝ ܬܗܘܡܐ: ܘܪܘܚܗ
ܕܐܠܗܐ ܡܪܚܦܐ ܥܠ ܐܦܝ ܡܝܐ. ܘܐܡܪ ܐܠܗܐ: ܢܗܘܐ
ܢܘܗܪܐ: ܘܗܘܐ ܢܘܗܪܐ. ³ ܘܚܙܐ ܐܠܗܐ ܠܢܘܗܪܐ ܕܫܦܝܪ.
⁴ ܘܦܪܫ ܐܠܗܐ ܒܝܬ ܢܘܗܪܐ ܠܚܫܘܟܐ. ⁵ ܘܩܪܐ ܐܠܗܐ ܠܢܘܗܪܐ
ܐܝܡܡܐ. ܘܠܚܫܘܟܐ ܩܪܐ ܠܠܝܐ: ܘܗܘܐ ܪܡܫܐ ܘܗܘܐ ܨܦܪܐ
ܝܘܡܐ ܚܕ. ⁶ ܘܐܡܪ ܐܠܗܐ ܢܗܘܐ ܪܩܝܥܐ ܒܡܨܥܬ ܡܝܐ.
ܘܢܗܘܐ ܦܪܫ ܒܝܬ ܡܝܐ ܠܡܝܐ. ⁷ ܘܥܒܕ ܐܠܗܐ ܪܩܝܥܐ:
ܘܦܪܫ ܒܝܬ ܡܝܐ ܕܠܬܚܬ ܡܢ ܪܩܝܥܐ: ܘܒܝܬ ܡܝܐ
ܕܠܥܠ ܡܢ ܪܩܝܥܐ. ⁸ ܘܩܪܐ ܐܠܗܐ ܠܪܩܝܥܐ
ܫܡܝܐ. ܘܗܘܐ ܪܡܫܐ ܘܗܘܐ ܨܦܪܐ ܝܘܡܐ ܕܬܪܝܢ. ⁹ ܘܐܡܪ
ܐܠܗܐ ܢܬܟܢܫܘܢ ܡܝܐ ܕܠܬܚܬ ܡܢ ܫܡܝܐ ܠܐܬܪܐ ܚܕ:

E*

ܘܒܚܣܪܐ ܡܢܝܡܡܬܐ: ܘܗܘܐ ܗܘܟܢܐ . ¹⁰ ܘܩܪܐ ܐܠܗܐ ܠܝܒܝܫܬܐ
ܐܪܥܐ: ܘܠܟܢܝܫܘܬܐ ܕܡܝܐ ܩܪܐ ܝܡܡܐ. ܘܚܙܐ ܐܠܗܐ ܕܫܦܝܪ.
¹¹ ܘܐܡܪ ܐܠܗܐ: ܬܦܩ ܐܪܥܐ ܬܕܐܐ ܒܪܐ ܟܣܒܐ ܕܡܙܪܥ ܙܪܥܐ ܐܝܟܐ
ܠܓܢܣܗ. ܘܐܝܠܢܐ ܕܦܐܪܐ ܕܥܒܕ ܩܐܪܐ ܠܓܢܣܗ:
ܕܢܨܒܬܗ ܒܗ ܟܠ ܐܝܟܐ. ¹² ܘܐܦܩܬ ܐܪܥܐ
ܒܪܐ ܟܣܒܐ ܕܡܙܪܥ ܙܪܥܐ ܐܝܟܐ ܠܓܢܣܗ: ܘܐܝܠܢܐ ܕܥܒܕ ܩܐܪܐ
ܕܢܨܒܬܗ ܒܗ ܠܓܢܣܗ. ܘܚܙܐ ܐܠܗܐ ܕܫܦܝܪ. ¹³ ܘܗܘܐ
ܪܡܫܐ ܘܗܘܐ ܨܦܪܐ. ܝܘܡܐ ܬܠܝܬܝܐ ✦ ¹⁴ ܘܐܡܪ ܐܠܗܐ ܢܗܘܘܢ
ܢܗܝܪܐ ܒܐܪܩܝܥܐ ܕܫܡܝܐ. ܠܡܦܪܫ ܒܝܢܬ ܐܝܡܡܐ
ܠܠܠܝܐ: ܘܢܗܘܘܢ ܠܐܬܘܬܐ ܘܠܙܒܢܐ ܘܠܝܘܡܬܐ ܘܠܫܢܝܐ.
¹⁵ ܘܢܗܘܘܢ ܡܢܗܪܝܢ ܒܐܪܩܝܥܐ ܕܫܡܝܐ ܠܡܢܗܪܘ ܥܠ ܟܠ
ܐܝܟܐ: ܘܗܘܐ ܗܘܟܢܐ. ¹⁶ ܘܥܒܕ ܐܠܗܐ ܒܪܘܡ ܢܗܝܪܐ ܪܘܪܒܐ:
ܢܗܝܪܐ ܪܒܐ ܠܫܘܠܛܢܐ ܕܐܝܡܡܐ: ܘܢܗܝܪܐ ܙܥܘܪܐ
ܠܫܘܠܛܢܐ ܕܠܠܝܐ: ܘܟܘܟܒܐ. ¹⁷ ܘܝܗܒ ܐܢܘܢ ܐܠܗܐ
ܒܐܪܩܝܥܐ ܕܫܡܝܐ. ܠܡܢܗܪܘ ܥܠ ܐܝܟܐ. ¹⁸ ܘܠܡܫܠܛ
ܒܐܝܡܡܐ ܘܒܠܠܝܐ: ܘܠܡܦܪܫ ܒܝܢܬ ܢܘܗܪܐ ܠܚܫܘܟܐ:
ܘܚܙܐ ܐܠܗܐ ܕܫܦܝܪ. ¹⁹ ܘܗܘܐ ܪܡܫܐ ܘܗܘܐ ܨܦܪܐ ܝܘܡܐ ܪܒܝܥܝܐ
ܕܐܪܒܥܐ ✦ ²⁰ ܘܐܡܪ ܐܠܗܐ ܢܪܚܫܘܢ ܡܝܐ ܪܚܫܐ ܢܦܫܐ ܚܝܬܐ
ܘܦܪܚܬܐ ܬܦܪܚ ܥܠ ܐܝܟܐ ܥܠ ܐܦܝ ܐܪܩܝܥܐ ܕܫܡܝܐ.
²¹ ܘܒܪܐ ܐܠܗܐ ܬܢܝܢܐ ܪܘܪܒܐ ܘܟܠ ܢܦܫܐ ܚܝܬܐ ܕܪܚܫܐ

ܕܐܪܚܫܘ ܡ̈ܝܐ ܠܓܢܣܗܘܢ. ܘܟܠ ܦܪܚܬܐ ܕܓܦܐ ܠܓܢܣܗ̇:
ܘܚܙܐ ܐܠܗܐ ܕܫܦܝܪ. [22] ܘܒܪܟ ܐܢܘܢ ܐܠܗܐ ܘܐܡܪ ܠܗܘܢ:
ܦܪܘ ܘܣܓܘ: ܘܡܠܘ ܡ̈ܝܐ ܕܒܝ̈ܡܡܐ: ܘܦܪܚܬܐ ܬܣܓܐ
ܒܐܪܥܐ. [23] ܘܗܘܐ ܪܡܫܐ ܘܗܘܐ ܨܦܪܐ. ܝܘܡܐ ܕܚܡܫܐ܀
[24] ܘܐܡܪ ܐܠܗܐ. ܬܦܩ ܐܪܥܐ ܢܦܫܐ ܚܝܬܐ ܠܓܢܣܗ̇: ܒܥܝܪܐ
ܘܪ̈ܚܫܐ: ܘܚܝܘܬܐ ܕܐܪܥܐ ܠܓܢܣܗ̇: ܘܗܘܐ ܗܟܢܐ. [25] ܘܥܒܕ
ܐܠܗܐ ܚܝܘܬܐ ܕܐܪܥܐ ܠܓܢܣܗ̇: ܘܒܥܝܪܐ ܠܓܢܣܗ̇: ܘܟܠܗ
ܪ̈ܚܫܐ ܕܐܪܥܐ ܠܓܢܣܗܘܢ: ܘܚܙܐ ܐܠܗܐ ܕܫܦܝܪ. [26] ܘܐܡܪ
ܐܠܗܐ: ܢܥܒܕ ܐܢܫܐ ܒܨܠܡܢ ܐܝܟ ܕܡܘܬܢ. ܘܢܫܬܠܛܘܢ
ܒܢܘ̈ܢܝ ܝܡܐ: ܘܒܦܪܚܬܐ ܕܫܡܝܐ. ܘܒܒܥܝܪܐ ܘܒܟܠܗ̇
ܪ̈ܚܫܐ ܕܐܪܥܐ. ܘܒܟܠܗ ܪ̈ܚܫܐ ܕܪܚܫ ܥܠ ܐܪܥܐ. [27] ܘܒܪܐ
ܐܠܗܐ ܠܐܕܡ ܒܨܠܡܗ. ܒܨܠܡ ܐܠܗܐ ܒܪܝܗܝ. ܕܟܪ ܘܢܩܒܐ
ܒܪܐ ܐܢܘܢ. [28] ܘܒܪܟ ܐܢܘܢ ܐܠܗܐ: ܘܐܡܪ ܠܗܘܢ ܐܠܗܐ:
ܦܪܘ ܘܣܓܘ: ܘܡܠܘ ܐܪܥܐ ܘܟܘܒܫܘܗ̇. ܘܐܫܬܠܛܘ ܒܢܘ̈ܢܝ
ܝܡܐ: ܘܒܦܪܚܬܐ ܕܫܡܝܐ: ܘܒܒܥܝܪܐ ܘܒܟܠܗ̇ ܪ̈ܚܫܐ
ܕܪܚܫܐ ܥܠ ܐܪܥܐ. [29] ܘܐܡܪ ܐܠܗܐ: ܗܐ ܝܗܒܬ ܠܟܘܢ
ܟܠܗ ܥܣܒܐ ܕܡܙܕܪܥ ܙܪܥܐ ܕܥܠ ܐܦ̈ܝ ܟܠܗ̇ ܐܪܥܐ.
ܘܟܠ ܐܝܠܢ ܕܐܝܬ ܒܗ ܦܐܪܐ ܐܝܠܢܐ ܕܙܪܥܗ ܡܙܕܪܥ:
ܠܟܘܢ ܢܗܘܐ ܠܡܐܟܘܠܬܐ. ܘܠܟܠܗ̇ ܚܝܘܬܐ ܕܒܪܐ:
[30] ܘܠܟܠܗ̇ ܦܪܚܬܐ ܕܫܡܝܐ: ܘܠܟܠ ܕܪܚܫ ܥܠ ܐܪܥܐ

ܕܐܝܬ ܒܗ ܢܦܫܐ ܚܝܬܐ: ܟܠܗ ܝܘܪܩܐ ܕܥܣܒܐ ܠܡܐܟܘܠܬܐ: ܘܗܘܐ ܗܟܢܐ. [31] ܘܚܙܐ ܐܠܗܐ ܟܠ ܕܥܒܕ: ܘܗܐ ܛܒ ܫܦܝܪ. ܘܗܘܐ ܪܡܫܐ ܘܗܘܐ ܨܦܪܐ ܝܘܡܐ ܕܫܬܐ ܀

CAPUT II.

ܘܫܠܡܘ ܫܡܝܐ ܘܐܪܥܐ: ܘܟܠܗ ܚܝܠܗܘܢ.
[2] ܘܫܠܡ ܐܠܗܐ ܒܝܘܡܐ ܫܒܝܥܝܐ ܥܒܕܘܗܝ ܕܥܒܕ.
ܘܐܬܬܢܝܚ ܒܝܘܡܐ ܫܒܝܥܝܐ ܡܢ ܟܠܗܘܢ ܥܒܕܘܗܝ
ܕܥܒܕ. [3] ܘܒܪܟ ܐܠܗܐ ܠܝܘܡܐ ܫܒܝܥܝܐ ܘܩܕܫܗ.
ܡܛܠ ܕܒܗ ܐܬܬܢܝܚ ܡܢ ܟܠܗܘܢ ܥܒܕܘܗܝ ܕܒܪܐ
ܐܠܗܐ ܠܡܥܒܕ. [4] ܗܠܝܢ ܬܘܠܕܬܐ ܕܫܡܝܐ ܘܕܐܪܥܐ
ܟܕ ܐܬܒܪܝܘ: ܒܝܘܡܐ ܕܥܒܕ ܡܪܝܐ ܐܠܗܐ ܫܡܝܐ
ܘܐܪܥܐ. [5] ܘܟܠܗܘܢ ܐܝܠܢܐ ܕܚܩܠܐ ܥܕܟܝܠ ܠܐ
ܗܘܘ ܒܐܪܥܐ. ܘܟܠܗ ܥܣܒܐ ܕܚܩܠܐ ܥܕܟܝܠ ܠܐ
ܐܢܒܛ: ܡܛܠ ܕܠܐ ܐܡܛܪ ܡܪܝܐ ܐܠܗܐ ܡܛܪܐ
ܥܠ [ܐܪܥܐ] ܐܪܥܐ. ܘܐܢܫ ܠܝܬ ܠܡܦܠܚ ܒܐܪܥܐ ܀

[6] ܘܡܒܘܥܐ ܣܠܩ ܗܘܐ ܡܢ ܐܪܥܐ: ܘܡܫܩܐ
ܗܘܐ [ܠ]ܟܠ ܐܦܝ ܐܪܥܐ. [7] ܘܓܒܠ ܡܪܝܐ ܐܠܗܐ
ܠܐܕܡ ܥܦܪܐ ܡܢ ܐܕܡܬܐ: ܘܢܦܚ ܒܐܦܘܗܝ
ܢܫܡܬܐ ܕܚܝܐ. ܘܗܘܐ ܐܕܡ ܠܢܦܫ ܚܝܐ. [8] ܘܢܨܒ
ܡܪܝܐ ܐܠܗܐ ܦܪܕܝܣܐ ܒܥܕܝܢ ܡܢ ܩܕܝܡ: ܘܣܡ
ܬܡܢ ܠܐܕܡ ܕܓܒܠ. [9] ܘܐܘܥܝ ܡܪܝܐ ܐܠܗܐ ܡܢ
ܐܪܥܐ ܟܠ ܐܝܠܢ ܕܪܓܝܓ ܠܚܙܬܐ: ܘܛܒ
ܠܡܐܟܠ: ܘܐܝܠܢܐ ܕܚܝܐ ܒܡܨܥܬܗ ܕܦܪܕܝܣܐ:
ܘܐܝܠܢܐ ܕܝܕܥܬܐ ܕܛܒܬܐ ܘܕܒܝܫܬܐ. [10] ܘܢܗܪܐ
ܢܦܩ ܗܘܐ ܡܢ ܥܕܝܢ ܠܡܫܩܝܘ ܠܦܪܕܝܣܐ:
ܘܡܢ ܬܡܢ ܦܪܫ ܘܗܘܐ ܠܐܪܒܥܐ ܪܫܝܢ. [11] ܫܡܗ ܕܚܕ
ܦܝܫܘܢ: ܗܘ ܕܡܚܕܪ ܠܟܠܗ ܐܪܥܐ ܕܚܘܝܠܐ: ܕܬܡܢ
ܕܗܒܐ. [12] ܘܕܗܒܗ ܕܐܪܥܐ ܗܝ ܛܒ: ܬܡܢ
ܒܕܘܠܚܐ ܘܟܐܦܐ ܕܒܪܘܠܐ. [13] ܘܫܡܗ ܕܢܗܪܐ
ܬܢܝܢܐ ܓܝܚܘܢ: ܗܘ ܕܡܚܕܪ ܠܟܠܗ ܐܪܥܐ ܕܟܘܫ.

[14] ܦܣܩܗ ܕܢܘܚܐ ܕܬܘܬܐ. ܕܩܛܠܬ: ܗܘ ܕܐܡܪ
ܠܘܩܒܠ ܐܬܬܘܪ. ܘܪܘܚܐ ܕܐܪܥܐ ܗܘ ܚܘܝܐ܀ [15] ܘܐܡܪ
ܡܪܝܐ ܐܠܗܐ ܠܐܕܡ ܘܥܒܕܗ ܒܦܪܫܢܘܬܐ ܕܟܝܢܐ.
ܕܝܠܝܕܘܗܝ ܘܝܠܦܢܘܗܝ. [16] ܘܦܩܕ ܡܪܝܐ ܐܠܗܐ
ܠܐܕܡ ܘܐܡܪ ܠܗ: ܡܢ ܟܠܗܘܢ ܐܝܠܢܐ ܕܦܪܕܝܣܐ
ܡܐܟܠ ܬܐܟܘܠ: [17] ܘܡܢ ܐܝܠܢܐ ܕܝܕܥܬܐ ܕܛܒܬܐ
ܘܕܒܝܫܬܐ ܠܐ ܬܐܟܘܠ ܡܢܗ. ܡܛܠ ܕܒܝܘܡܐ
ܕܬܐܟܘܠ ܡܢܗ ܡܘܬܐ ܬܡܘܬ. [18] ܘܐܡܪ ܡܪܝܐ
ܐܠܗܐ: ܠܐ ܫܦܝܪ ܕܢܗܘܐ ܐܕܡ ܒܠܚܘܕܘܗܝ.
ܐܥܒܕ ܠܗ ܡܥܕܪܢܐ ܐܝܟܘܬܗ. [19] ܘܓܒܠ ܡܪܝܐ
ܐܠܗܐ ܡܢ ܐܪܥܐ ܟܠܗ ܚܝܘܬܐ ܕܕܒܪܐ: ܘܟܠܗ
ܦܪܚܬܐ ܕܫܡܝܐ: ܘܐܝܬܝ ܐܢܘܢ ܠܘܬ ܐܕܡ
ܕܢܚܙܐ ܡܢܐ ܩܪܐ ܠܗܘܢ: ܘܟܠ ܕܩܪܐ ܠܗܘܢ
ܐܕܡ ܢܦܫܐ ܚܝܬܐ ܗܘ ܗܘ ܫܡܗ. [20] ܘܩܪܐ ܐܕܡ
ܫܡܗܐ ܠܟܠܗ ܒܥܝܪܐ: ܘܠܟܠܗ ܦܪܚܬܐ ܕܫܡܝܐ:

ܘܠܟܠܗ ܚܝܘܬܐ ܕܒܪܐ. ܘܠܐܕܡ ܠܐ ܐܫܬܟܚ
[ܠܗ] ܡܥܕܪܢܐ ܐܝܟ ܐܟܘܬܗ. 21 ܘܐܪܡܝ ܡܪܝܐ ܐܠܗܐ
ܫܢܬܐ ܥܠ ܐܕܡ ܘܕܡܟ: ܘܢܣܒ ܚܕܐ ܡܢ
ܐܠܥܘܗܝ: ܘܐܘܥܝ ܒܣܪܐ ܚܠܦܝܗ. 22 ܘܒܢܐ ܡܪܝܐ
ܐܠܗܐ ܐܠܥܐ ܕܢܣܒ ܡܢ ܐܕܡ ܠܐܢܬܬܐ ܘܐܝܬܝܗ
ܠܐܕܡ. 23 ܘܐܡܪ ܐܕܡ. ܗܕܐ ܙܒܢܐ ܓܪܡܐ ܡܢ
ܓܪܡܝ: ܘܒܣܪܐ ܡܢ ܒܣܪܝ: ܗܕܐ ܬܬܩܪܐ ܐܢܬܬܐ
ܡܛܠ ܕܡܢ ܓܒܪܐ ܢܣܝܒܐ. 24 ܡܛܠ ܗܢܐ ܢܫܒܘܩ
ܓܒܪܐ ܠܐܒܘܗܝ ܘܠܐܡܗ: ܘܢܩܦ ܠܐܢܬܬܗ.
ܘܢܗܘܘܢ ܬܪܝܗܘܢ ܚܕ ܒܣܪ. 25 ܘܗܘܘ ܬܪܝܗܘܢ
ܥܪܛܠܝܢ: ܐܕܡ ܘܐܢܬܬܗ ܘܠܐ ܒܗܬܝܢ ܀

CAPUT III.

1 ܘܚܘܝܐ ܥܪܝܡ ܗܘܐ ܡܢ ܟܠܗ ܚܝܘܬܐ ܕܕܒܪܐ ܕܥܒܕ
ܡܪܝܐ ܐܠܗܐ. ܘܐܡܪ ܚܘܝܐ ܠܐܢܬܬܐ. ܫܪܝܪܐܝܬ ܐܡܪ ܐܠܗܐ
ܕܠܐ ܬܐܟܠܘܢ ܡܢ ܟܠ ܐܝܠܢܐ ܕܦܪܕܝܣܐ. 2 ܘܐܡܪܬ ܐܢܬܬܐ

لاحةصًا. وهِجم قَاوْم إمكْنا وهجكْرِومها محهم قَاوْهها.

3 ومَجم قَاوْم إمكْنا وهجحكِحَهو وحرومها اَحْرِ لاحْرِ

ولا كْراجكِم مَحْته هلا محبِجْروهم كَه ولا كْمُحجِم.

4 واهجن سهما للاحْكا لا محُحجه كُمحجِم. 5 مَحْلا وَجِمُو

لاحها. وَجِمُوصحا وُاحكْم إِلاوِن محلِه. مَحجحَحْجي كُملُمحِم

مَهَمحَحِم. إمر لاحها مُبِجْت لهجا وجِمحِها. 6 مَسِرْم

لاهِجا وهحجن امحلا كْهجْاوْها مَهِبَا وِهِنَجْا هو حكْتنا مَرِجِم

امحلا كُهحجن مَه. مَحصحَم جم قَاوَهمم واحكْه.

مُحوصَحَم إم حمححكه حُهحه واهلا. 7 واحجِهَحِم[ا] كْتنا

جُاجَامحِم. مَمجحه وحْتهَحكِيم إنِن. مَرِوَهصه لُمِوْها وَةَاینا.

مَحجحِه كَه فَاوَهحا. 8 مَحجحَحه هُجِم وحرما لاحها

محَهكْر مَحرومها حُهنَهه وهمحا. مَاحَهُحَها[ه] اوِمر

مَانِحَحُا جم حورْمِ محرما لاحها جيْه اححنا وححرومها.

9 مَحَرْا محرما لاحها للاوِمر واحجن حَه. إمحا إِلِم اوِمر.

10 واحجن مُحكر مَحجحِه ححرومها مَسْمِه وحْرهَحُكْم إِنّا

واحنَهحمِه. 11 واحجن حَه محرما مَحُته مَحهم وحْرهَحِجم إِلِم.

مَا جم اححنا وقَحِجحُم. ولا جحاجهها محلِه إَجحها. 12 واحجن

اوِمر. للاحْكا وَمَحوجِه حُهحه جِم مُحوصَحَم حَه جم اححنا

واحجه. واحجن محرما لاحها للاحْكا. 13 مُحته هَانا وحْجحِجِحَه.

واحجُجُه للاحْكا. سهما إِجحهَحمِه واحجه. 14 واحجن محرما

ܐܠܗܐ ܠܚܘܝܐ. ܡܛܠ ܕܥܒܕܬ ܗܕܐ. ܠܝܛ ܐܢܬ ܡܢ ܟܠܗ ܒܥܝܪܐ ܘܡܢ ܟܠܗ ܚܝܘܬܐ ܕܕܒܪܐ. ܘܥܠ ܟܪܣܟ ܬܗܠܟ. ܘܥܦܪܐ ܬܐܟܘܠ ܟܠ ܝܘܡܝ ܚܝܝܟ. [15] ܘܒܥܠܕܒܒܘܬܐ ܐܣܝܡ ܒܝܢܝܟ ܠܐܢܬܬܐ. ܘܒܝܢ ܙܪܥܟ ܠܙܪܥܗ̇. ܗܘ ܢܫܘܦ ܪܫܟ ܘܐܢܬ ܬܡܚܝܘܗܝ ܒܥܩܒܗ܀ [16] ܘܠܐܢܬܬܐ ܐܡܪ ܡܣܓܐܘ ܐܣܓܐ ܟܐܒܝܟܝ ܘܒܛܢܟܝ. ܘܒܟܐܒܐ ܬܐܠܕܝܢ ܒܢܝܐ. ܘܠܘܬ ܒܥܠܟܝ ܬܗܦܘܟܝ. ܘܗܘ ܢܫܬܠܛ ܒܟܝ܀ [17] ܘܠܐܕܡ ܐܡܪ ܡܛܠ ܕܫܡܥܬ ܠܩܠܗ̇ ܕܐܢܬܬܟ. ܘܐܟܠܬ ܡܢ ܐܝܠܢܐ ܕܦܩܕܬܟ ܘܐܡܪܬ ܠܟ ܕܠܐ ܬܐܟܘܠ ܡܢܗ. ܠܝܛܐ ܐܪܥܐ ܡܛܠܬܟ. ܒܥܩܬܐ ܬܐܟܠܝܗ̇ ܟܠ ܝܘܡܝ ܚܝܝܟ. [18] ܟܘܒܐ ܘܕܪܕܪܐ ܬܥܒܕ ܠܟ. ܘܬܐܟܘܠ ܥܣܒܐ ܕܚܩܠܐ. [19] ܘܒܕܘܥܬܐ ܕܐܦܝܟ ܬܐܟܘܠ ܠܚܡܐ. ܥܕܡܐ ܕܬܗܦܘܟ ܠܐܪܥܐ ܕܡܢܗ̇ ܐܬܢܣܒܬ. ܡܛܠ ܕܥܦܪܐ ܐܢܬ ܘܠܥܦܪܐ ܬܗܦܘܟ. [20] ܘܩܪܐ ܐܕܡ ܫܡܗ̇ ܕܐܢܬܬܗ ܚܘܐ. ܡܛܠ ܕܗܝ ܗܘܬ ܐܡܐ ܕܟܠ ܕܚܝ. [21] ܘܥܒܕ ܡܪܝܐ ܐܠܗܐ ܠܐܕܡ ܘܠܐܢܬܬܗ ܟܘܬܝܢܝܬܐ ܕܡܫܟܐ ܘܐܠܒܫ ܐܢܘܢ. [22] ܘܐܡܪ ܡܪܝܐ ܐܠܗܐ. ܗܐ ܐܕܡ ܗܘܐ ܐܝܟ ܚܕ ܡܢܢ. ܠܡܕܥ ܛܒܬܐ ܘܒܝܫܬܐ. ܗܫܐ ܕܠܡܐ ܢܘܫܛ ܐܝܕܗ ܘܢܣܒ ܐܦ ܡܢ ܐܝܠܢܐ ܕܚܝܐ. ܘܢܐܟܘܠ ܘܢܚܐ ܠܥܠܡ. [23] ܘܦܛܪܗ ܡܪܝܐ ܐܠܗܐ ܡܢ ܦܪܕܝܣܐ ܕܥܕܝܢ ܠܡܦܠܚ ܐܪܥܐ ܕܐܬܢܣܒ [ܡܢ ܬܡܢ]. [24] ܘܐܦܩܗ ܡܪܝܐ

CAPUT IV.

(Secundum codicem Ambrosianum seculi fere sexti.)

ܘܩܛܠܗ. [9]ܘܐܡܪ ܡܪܝܐ ܠܩܐܝܢ. ܐܝܟܐ ܗܘ ܗܒܠ ܐܚܘܟ. ܘܐܡܪ ܠܐ ܝܕܥ ܐܢܐ. ܢܛܘܪܗ ܐܢܐ ܒܪ ܕܐܚܝ. [10]ܘܐܡܪ. ܡܢܐ ܥܒܕܬ. ܩܠܐ ܕܕܡܗ ܕܐܚܘܟ ܩܥܐ ܠܘܬܝ ܡܢ ܐܪܥܐ. [11]ܘܗܫܐ ܠܝܛ ܐܢܬ ܡܢ ܐܪܥܐ. ܕܦܬܚܬ ܦܘܡܗ̇ ܘܩܒܠܬ ܕܡܗ ܕܐܚܘܟ ܡܢ ܐ̈ܝܕܝܟ. [12]ܟܕ ܬܦܠܘܚ ܒܐܪܥܐ ܠܐ ܬܘܣܦ ܕܬܬܠ ܠܟ ܚܝܠܗ̇. ܙܝܥ ܘܢܥ ܕܬܗܘܐ ܒܐܪܥܐ. [13]ܘܐܡܪ ܩܐܝܢ ܠܡܪܝܐ. ܪܒܐ ܗܝ ܣܟܠܘܬܝ ܡܢ ܕܠܡܫܒܩ. [14]ܗܐ ܐܦܩܬܢܝ ܝܘܡܢܐ ܡܢ ܐ̈ܦܝ ܐܪܥܐ. ܘܡܢ ܩܕܡܝܟ ܐܬܛܫܐ. ܘܐܗܘܐ ܙܝܥ ܘܢܥ ܒܐܪܥܐ. ܘܟܠ ܡܢ ܕܢܫܟܚܢܝ ܢܩܛܠܢܝ. [15]ܘܐܡܪ ܠܗ ܡܪܝܐ. ܠܐ ܗܟܢܐ ܟܠ ܩܛܘܠܐ. ܩܐܝܢ ܫܒܥܐ ܢܬܦܪܥ. ܘܣܡ ܡܪܝܐ ܐܬܐ ܒܩܐܝܢ ܕܠܐ ܢܩܛܠܝܘܗܝ ܟܠ ܡܢ ܕܡܫܟܚ ܠܗ. [16]ܘܢܦܩ ܩܐܝܢ ܡܢ ܩܕܡ ܡܪܝܐ. ܘܝܬܒ ܒܐܪܥܐ ܕܢܘܕ. ܡܢ ܡܕܢܚܗ ܕܥܕܢ ⁘ [17]ܘܝܕܥ ܩܐܝܢ ܠܐܢܬܬܗ. ܘܒܛܢܬ ܘܝܠܕܬ ܠܚܢܘܟ. ܘܗܘܐ ܒܢܐ ܡܕܝܢܬܐ. ܘܩܪܐ ܫܡܗ̇ ܕܡܕܝܢܬܐ ܥܠ ܫܡ ܒܪܗ ܚܢܘܟ. [18]ܘܐܬܝܠܕ ܠܚܢܘܟ ܥܝܪܕ. ܘܥܝܪܕ ܐܘܠܕ ܠܡܚܘܝܐܝܠ. ܘܡܚܘܝܐܝܠ ܐܘܠܕ ܠܡܬܘܫܐܝܠ.

ܘܡܬܘܫܝܠ ܐܘܠܕ ܠܠܡܟ. [19]ܘܠܡܟ ܢܣܒ ܠܗ ܬܪ̈ܬܝܢ
ܢܫ̈ܝܢ. ܫܡܗ ܕܚܕܐ ܥܕܐ ܘܫܡܗ ܕܐܚܪܬܐ ܨܠܐ[.]
[20]ܘܝܠܕܬ ܥܕܐ ܠܝܒܠ. ܗܘ ܗܘܐ ܐܒܐ ܠܥܡܪ̈ܝ
ܡܫܟܢܐ ܘܩܢ̈ܝܢ ܡܪܥܝܐ. [21]ܘܫܡܐ ܕܐܚܘܗܝ ܝܘܒܠ.
ܗܘ ܗܘܐ ܐܒܐ ܠܟܠ ܕܐܚܝܕ ܩܝܬܪܐ ܘܟܢܪܐ.
[22]ܘܨܠܐ ܐܦ ܗܝ ܝܠܕܬ ܠܬܘܒܠܩܝܢ. ܐܘܡܢ ܟܠ
ܚܪܫ ܕܢܚܫܐ ܘܕܦܪܙܠܐ. ܘܚܬܗ ܕܬܘܒܠܩܝܢ ܢܥܡܐ.
[23]ܘܐܡܪ ܠܡܟ ܠܢܫ̈ܘܗܝ. ܥܕܐ ܘܨܠܐ ܫܡܥܝܢ
ܩܠܝ. ܢܫ̈ܐ ܕܠܡܟ ܨܘܬܝܢ ܠܡܐܡܪܝ. ܡܛܠ ܕܓܒܪܐ
ܩܛܠܬ ܒܡ̈ܚܘܬܝ ܘܛܠܝܐ ܒܫ̈ܘܡܩܝ. [24]ܡܛܠ
ܕܫܒܥܒܥܐ ܢܬܬܒܥ ܩܐܝܢ. ܘܠܡܟ ܫܒܥܝܢ ܘܫܒܥܐ.
[25]ܘܝܕܥ ܐܕܡ ܬܘܒ ܠܚܘܐ ܐܢܬܬܗ. ܘܒܛܢܬ
ܘܝܠܕܬ ܒܪܐ. ܘܩܪܬ ܫܡܗ ܫܝܬ. ܡܛܠ ܕܝܗܒ
ܠܝ ܐܠܗܐ ܙܪܥܐ ܐܚܪܢܐ ܚܠܦ ܗܒܝܠ ܕܩܛܠܗ
ܩܐܝܢ. [26]ܘܠܫܝܬ ܐܦ ܠܗ. ܐܬܝܠܕ ܠܗ ܒܪܐ. ܘܩܪܐ
ܫܡܗ ܐ̱ܢܘܫ. ܗܝܕܝܢ ܫܪܝ ܠܡܩܪܐ ܒܫܡܗ ܕܡܪܝܐ.

II. EVANGELII MATTHAEI CAPUT QUINTUM.

[ex editione Americana, supra nr. 65 c].

1 ܟܕ ܚܙܐ ܕܝܢ ܠܟܢܫܐ ܣܠܩ ܠܛܘܪܐ: ܘܟܕ ܝܬܒ ܩܪܒܘ ܠܘܬܗ ܬܠܡܝܕܘܗܝ܀

2 ܘܦܬܚ ܦܘܡܗ ܘܡܠܦ ܗܘܐ ܠܗܘܢ ܘܐܡܪ܀

3 ܛܘܒܝܗܘܢ ܠܡܣܟܢܐ ܒܪܘܚ ܕܕܝܠܗܘܢ ܗܝ ܡܠܟܘܬܐ ܕܫܡܝܐ܂

4, 5 ܛܘܒܝܗܘܢ ܠܐܒܝܠܐ ܕܗܢܘܢ ܢܬܒܝܐܘܢ܂

5 ܛܘܒܝܗܘܢ ܠܡܟܝܟܐ ܕܗܢܘܢ ܢܐܪܬܘܢ ܠܐܪܥܐ܂

6 ܛܘܒܝܗܘܢ ܠܐܝܠܝܢ ܕܟܦܢܝܢ ܘܨܗܝܢ ܠܟܐܢܘܬܐ ܕܗܢܘܢ ܢܣܒܥܘܢ܂

7 ܛܘܒܝܗܘܢ ܠܡܪܚܡܢܐ ܕܥܠܝܗܘܢ ܢܗܘܘܢ ܪܚܡܐ܂

8 ܛܘܒܝܗܘܢ ܠܐܝܠܝܢ ܕܕܟܝܢ ܒܠܒܗܘܢ ܕܗܢܘܢ ܢܚܙܘܢ ܠܐܠܗܐ܂

10 ܛܘܒܝܗܘܢ ܠܥܒܕܝ ܫܠܡܐ ܕܒܢܘܗܝ ܕܐܠܗܐ ܢܬܩܪܘܢ܂

9, 10 ܛܘܒܝܗܘܢ ܠܐܝܠܝܢ ܕܐܬܪܕܦܘ ܡܛܠ ܟܐܢܘܬܐ ܕܕܝܠܗܘܢ ܗܝ ܡܠܟܘܬܐ ܕܫܡܝܐ܂

11 ܛܘܒܝܟܘܢ ܐܡܬܝ ܕܡܚܣܕܝܢ ܠܟܘܢ ܘܪܕܦܝܢ
ܠܟܘܢ: ܘܐܡܪܝܢ ܥܠܝܟܘܢ ܟܠ ܡܠܐ ܒܝܫܐ
ܡܛܠܬܝ ܒܕܓܠܘܬܐ.܀ 12 ܗܝܕܝܢ ܚܕܘ ܘܪܘܙܘ:
ܕܐܓܪܟܘܢ ܣܓܝ ܒܫܡܝܐ. ܗܟܢܐ ܓܝܪ ܪܕܦܘ
ܠܢܒܝܐ ܕܡܢ ܩܕܡܝܟܘܢ. 13 ܐܢܬܘܢ ܐܝܬܝܟܘܢ
ܡܠܚܗ ܕܐܪܥܐ. ܐܢܗܘ ܕܝܢ ܕܡܠܚܐ ܬܦܟܗ:
ܒܡܢܐ ܬܬܡܠܚ: ܠܡܕܡ ܠܐ ܐܙܠܐ: ܐܠܐ
ܬܫܬܕܐ ܠܒܪ ܘܬܬܕܝܫ ܡܢ ܐܢܫܐ.܀ 14 ܐܢܬܘܢ
ܐܝܬܝܟܘܢ ܢܘܗܪܗ ܕܥܠܡܐ. ܠܐ ܡܫܟܚܐ ܕܬܛܫܐ
ܡܕܝܢܬܐ ܕܥܠ ܛܘܪܐ ܒܢܝܐ.܀ 15 ܘܠܐ ܡܢܗܪܝܢ
ܫܪܓܐ ܘܣܝܡܝܢ ܠܗ ܬܚܝܬ ܣܐܬܐ: ܐܠܐ ܥܠ
ܡܢܪܬܐ: ܘܡܢܗܪ ܠܟܠ ܐܝܠܝܢ ܕܒܒܝܬܐ ܐܝܬܝܗܘܢ.܀
16 ܗܟܢܐ ܢܢܗܪ ܢܘܗܪܟܘܢ ܩܕܡ ܒܢܝܢܫܐ: ܕܢܚܙܘܢ
ܥܒܕܝܟܘܢ ܛܒܐ ܘܢܫܒܚܘܢ ܠܐܒܘܟܘܢ ܕܒܫܡܝܐ.
17 ܠܐ ܬܣܒܪܘܢ ܕܐܬܝܬ ܕܐܫܪܐ ܢܡܘܣܐ ܐܘ

ܢܒܝܐ. ܠܐ ܐܬܝܬ ܕܐܫܪܐ: ܐܠܐ ܕܐܡܠܐ.܀
18 ܐܡܝܢ ܓܝܪ ܐܡܪ ܐܢܐ ܠܟܘܢ: ܕܥܕܡܐ
ܕܢܥܒܪܘܢ ܫܡܝܐ ܘܐܪܥܐ: ܝܘܕ ܚܕܐ ܐܘ ܚܕ
ܣܪܛܐ ܠܐ ܢܥܒܪ ܡܢ ܢܡܘܣܐ ܥܕܡܐ ܕܟܠ
ܢܗܘܐ.܀ 19 ܟܠܡܢ ܕܢܫܪܐ ܗܟܝܠ ܚܕ ܡܢ ܦܘܩܕܢܐ
ܗܠܝܢ ܙܥܘܪܐ: ܘܢܠܦ ܗܟܢܐ ܠܒܢܝܢܫܐ: ܒܨܝܪܐ
ܢܬܩܪܐ ܒܡܠܟܘܬܐ ܕܫܡܝܐ. ܟܠ ܕܝܢ ܕܢܥܒܕ ܘܢܠܦ
ܗܢܐ ܪܒܐ ܢܬܩܪܐ ܒܡܠܟܘܬܐ ܕܫܡܝܐ.܀ 20 ܐܡܪ
ܐܢܐ ܠܟܘܢ ܓܝܪ: ܕܐܢ ܠܐ ܬܬܝܬܪ ܟܐܢܘܬܟܘܢ
ܝܬܝܪ ܡܢ ܕܣܦܪܐ ܘܦܪܝܫܐ: ܠܐ ܬܥܠܘܢ
ܠܡܠܟܘܬܐ ܕܫܡܝܐ. 21 ܫܡܥܬܘܢ ܕܐܬܐܡܪ
ܠܩܕܡܝܐ: ܠܐ ܬܩܛܘܠ: ܘܟܠ ܕܢܩܛܘܠ ܡܚܝܒ
ܗܘ ܠܕܝܢܐ.܀ 22 ܐܢܐ ܕܝܢ ܐܡܪ ܐܢܐ ܠܟܘܢ:
ܕܟܠ ܡܢ ܕܢܪܓܙ ܥܠ ܐܚܘܗܝ ܐܝܩܐ: ܡܚܝܒ ܗܘ
ܠܕܝܢܐ. ܘܟܠ ܕܢܐܡܪ ܠܐܚܘܗܝ ܪܩܐ: ܡܚܝܒ

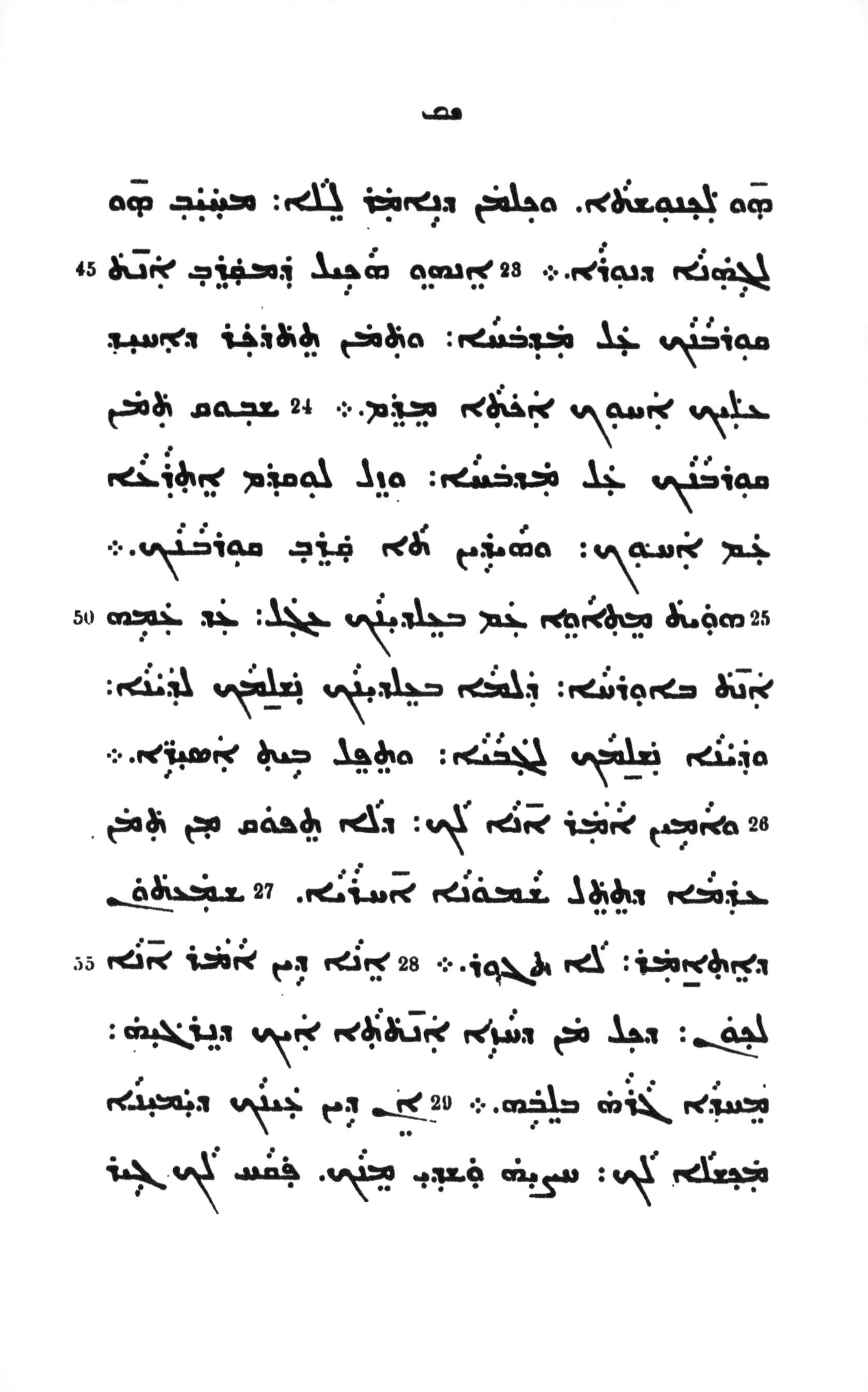

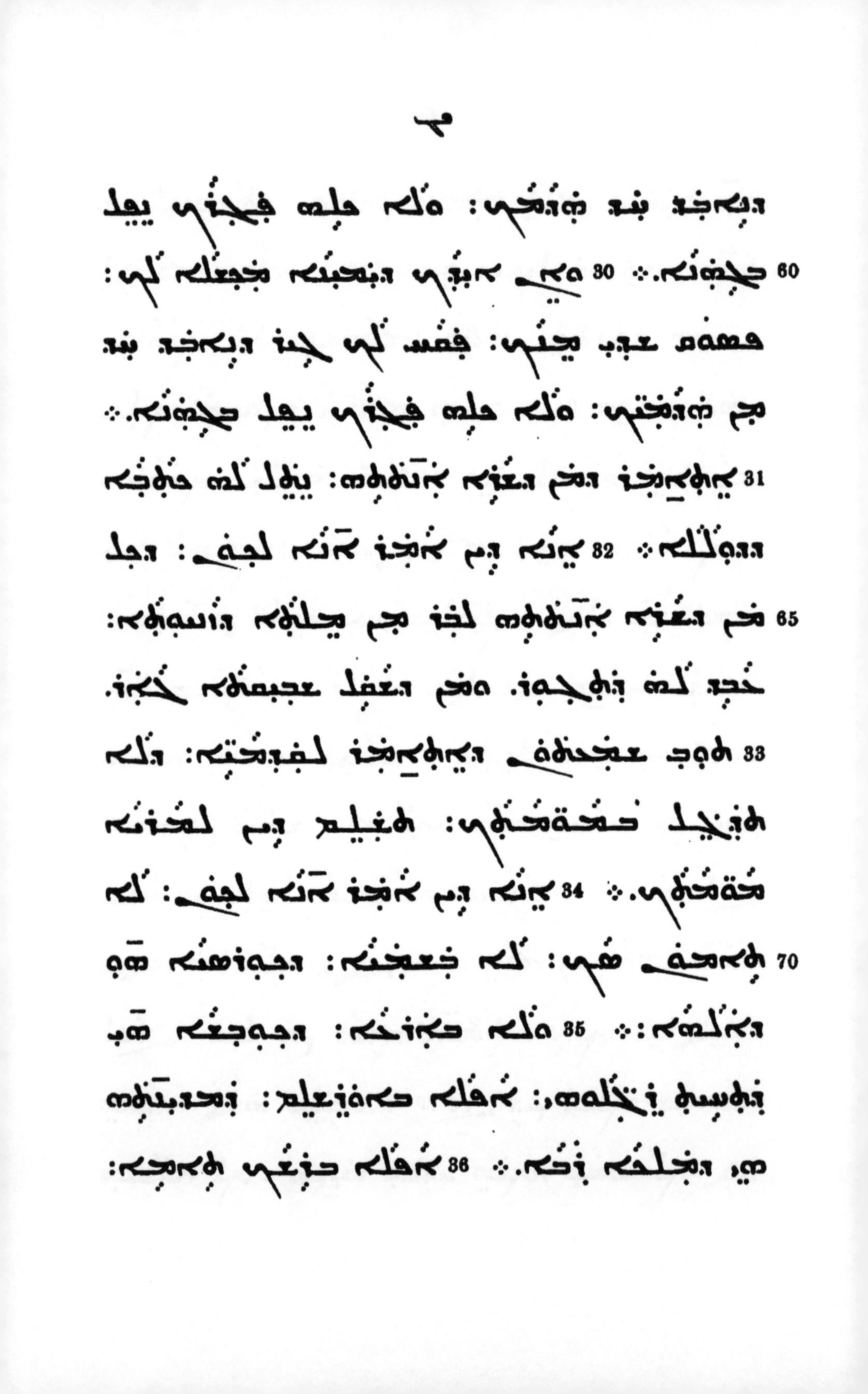

ܕܠܐ ܡܫܟܚ ܐܢ̄ܬ ܠܡܥܒܕ ܒܗ ܡܢܬܐ ܚܕܐ ܕܣܥܪܐ ܐܘܟܡܬܐ ܐܘ ܢܗܘܪܬܐ.܀ 37 ܐܝܠܐ ܕܝܢ ܦܘܣܩܐ ܡܠܬܟܘܢ: ܐܝܢ ܐܝܢ: ܘܠܐ ܠܐ. ܡܝܬܪ ܕܡܢ ܗܠܝܢ ܢܬܒܪ: ܡܢ ܒܝܫܐ ܗ̄ܘ. 38 ܫܡܥܬܘܢ ܕܐܬܐܡܪ: ܕܥܝܢܐ ܚܠܦ ܥܝܢܐ: ܘܫܢܐ ܚܠܦ ܫܢܐ.܀ 39 ܐܢܐ ܕܝܢ ܐܡܪ ܐ̄ܢܐ ܠܟܘܢ: ܕܠܐ ܬܩܘܡܘܢ ܠܘܩܒܠ ܒܝܫܐ: ܐܠܐ ܡܢ ܕܡܚܐ ܠܟ ܥܠ ܦܟܟ ܕܝܡܝܢܐ: ܐܦܢܐ ܠܗ ܐܦ ܐ̄ܚܪܢܐ.܀ 40 ܘܡܢ ܕܨܒܐ ܕܢܕܘܢ ܥܡܟ ܘܢܣܒ ܟܘܬܝܢܟ: ܫܒܘܩ ܠܗ ܐܦ ܡܪܛܘܛܟ.܀ 41 ܡܢ ܕܡܫܚܪ ܠܟ ܡܝܠܐ ܚܕ: ܙܠ ܥܡܗ ܬܪܬܝܢ.܀ 42 ܡܢ ܕܫܐܠ ܠܟ: ܗܒ ܠܗ. ܘܡܢ ܕܨܒܐ ܕܢܐܙܦ ܡܢܟ ܠܐ ܬܟܠܝܘܗܝ.܀ 43 ܫܡܥܬܘܢ ܕܐܬܐܡܪ: ܕܪܚܡ ܠܩܪܝܒܟ: ܘܣܢܝ ܠܒܥܠܕܒܒܟ.܀ 44 ܐܢܐ ܕܝܢ ܐܡܪ ܐ̄ܢܐ ܠܟܘܢ: ܐܚܒܘ ܠܒܥܠܕܒܒܝܟܘܢ: ܘܒܪܟܘ

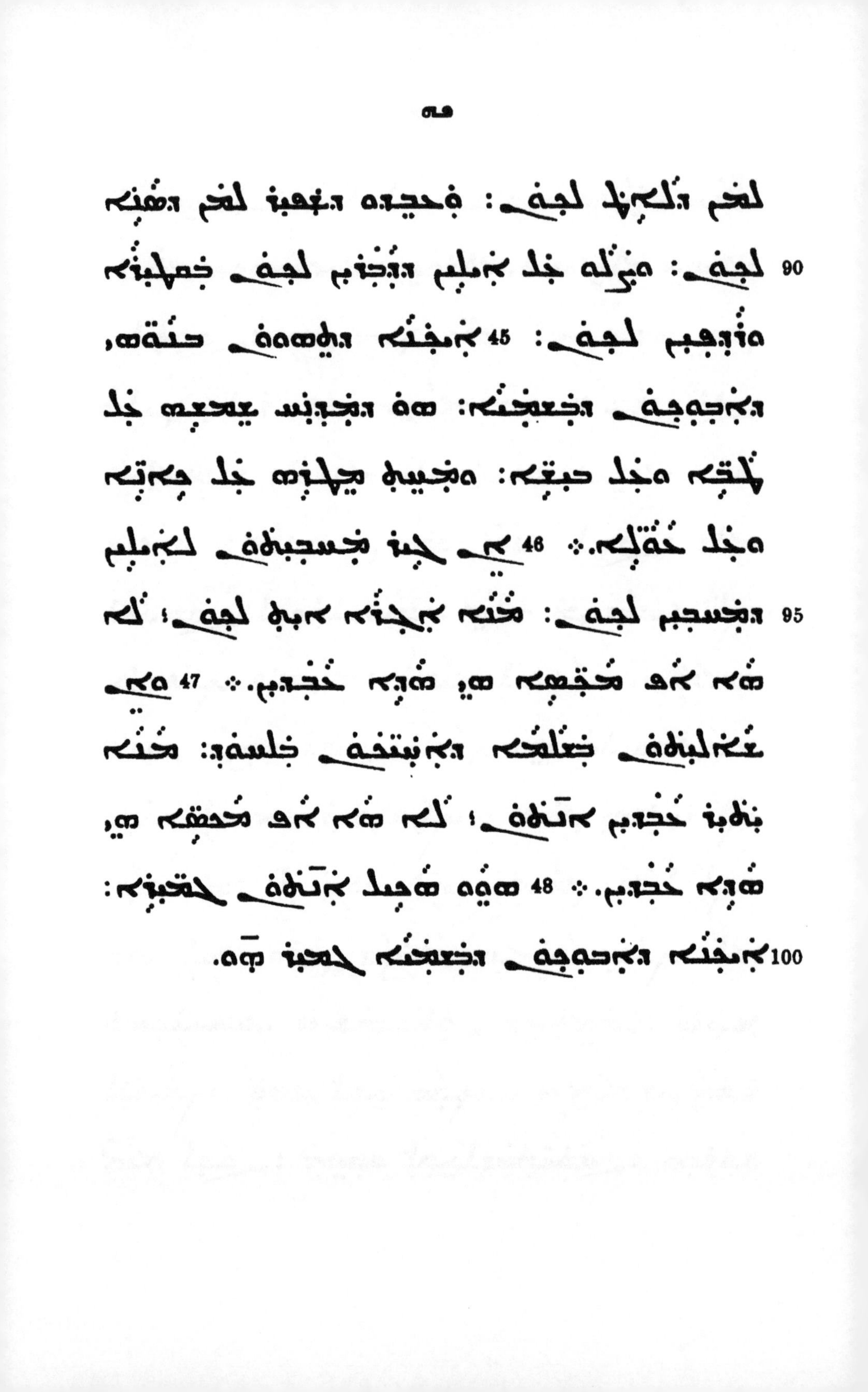

III. VITAE PROPHETARUM.

(E tribus codicibus Musei Britannici.)

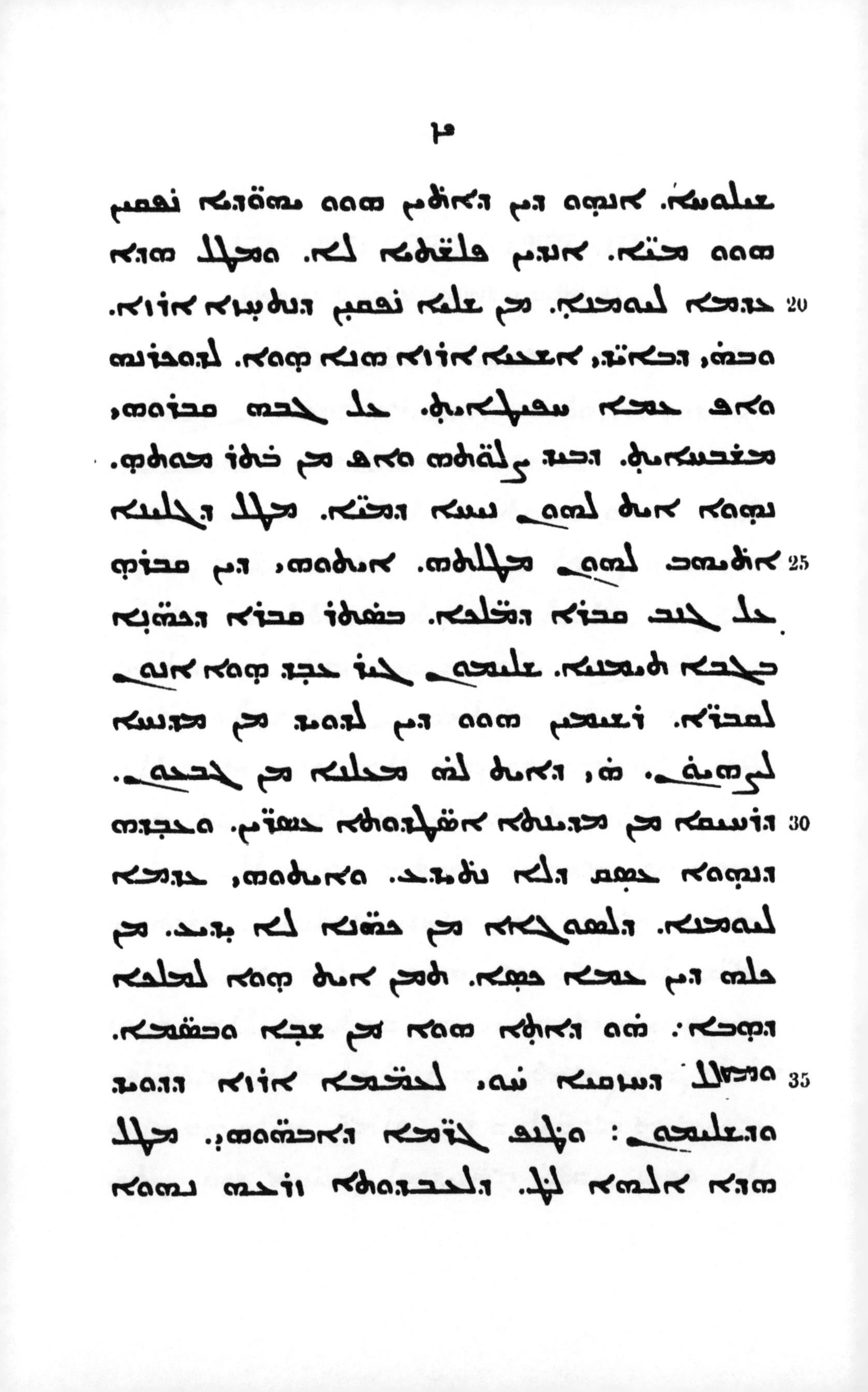

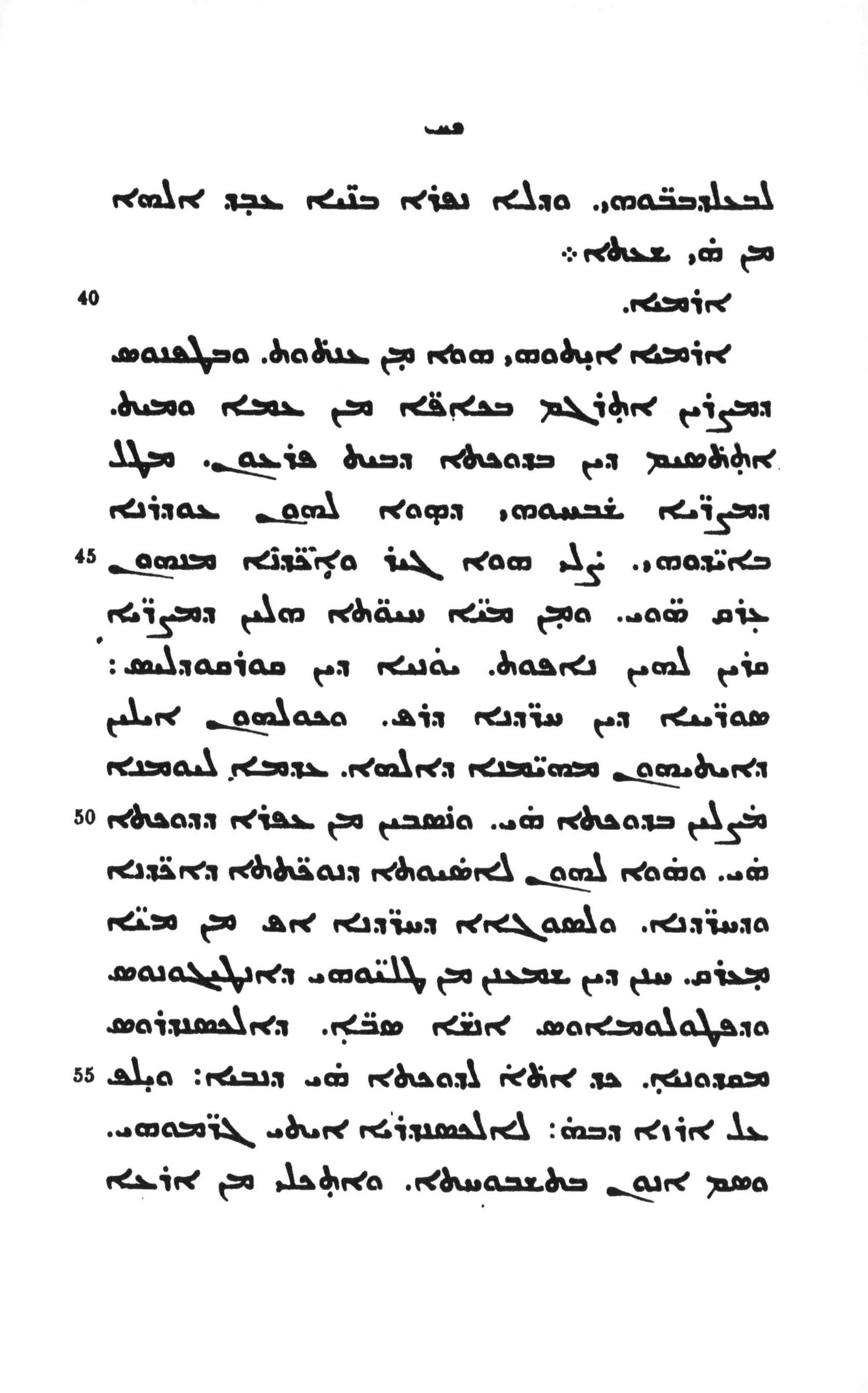

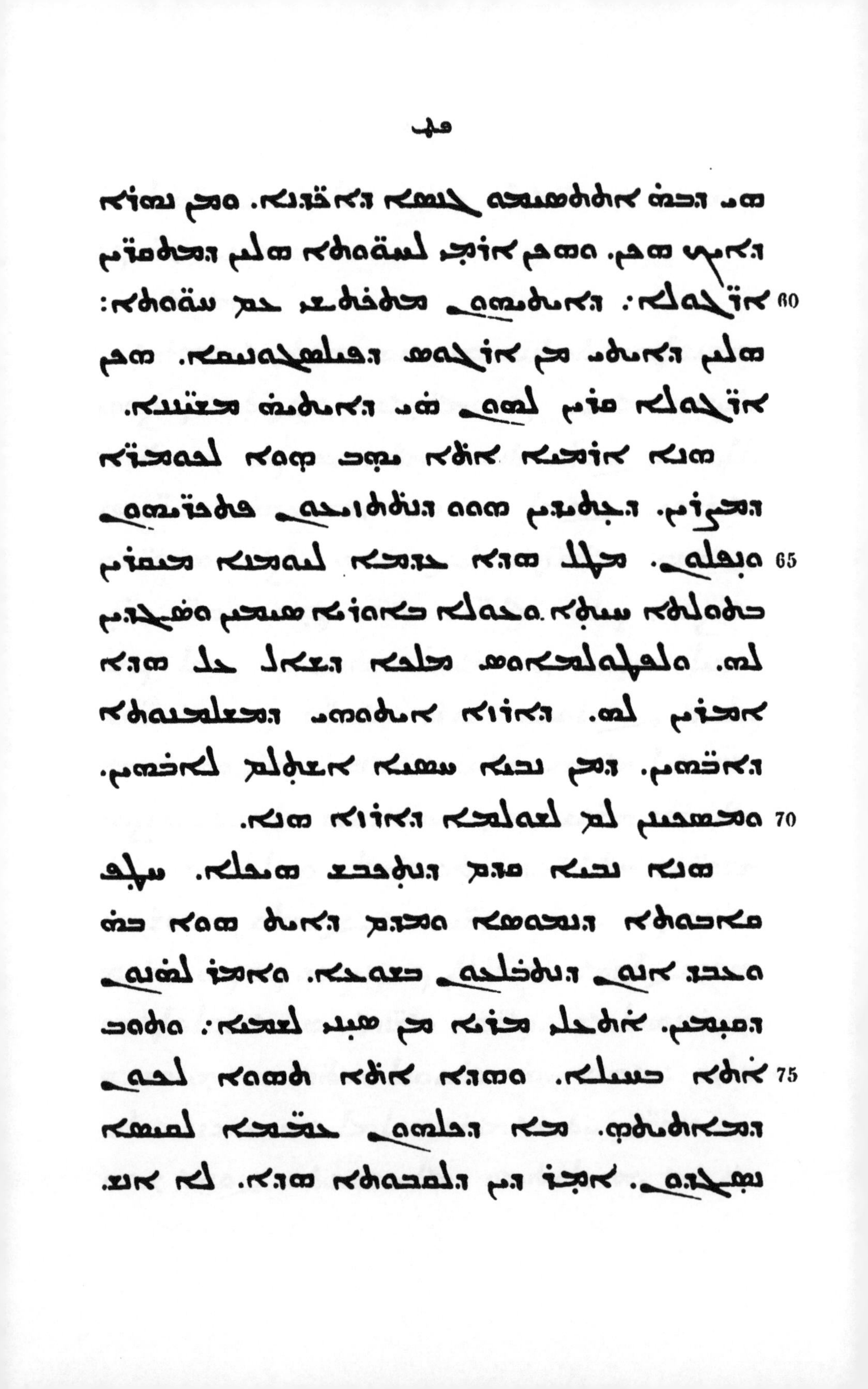

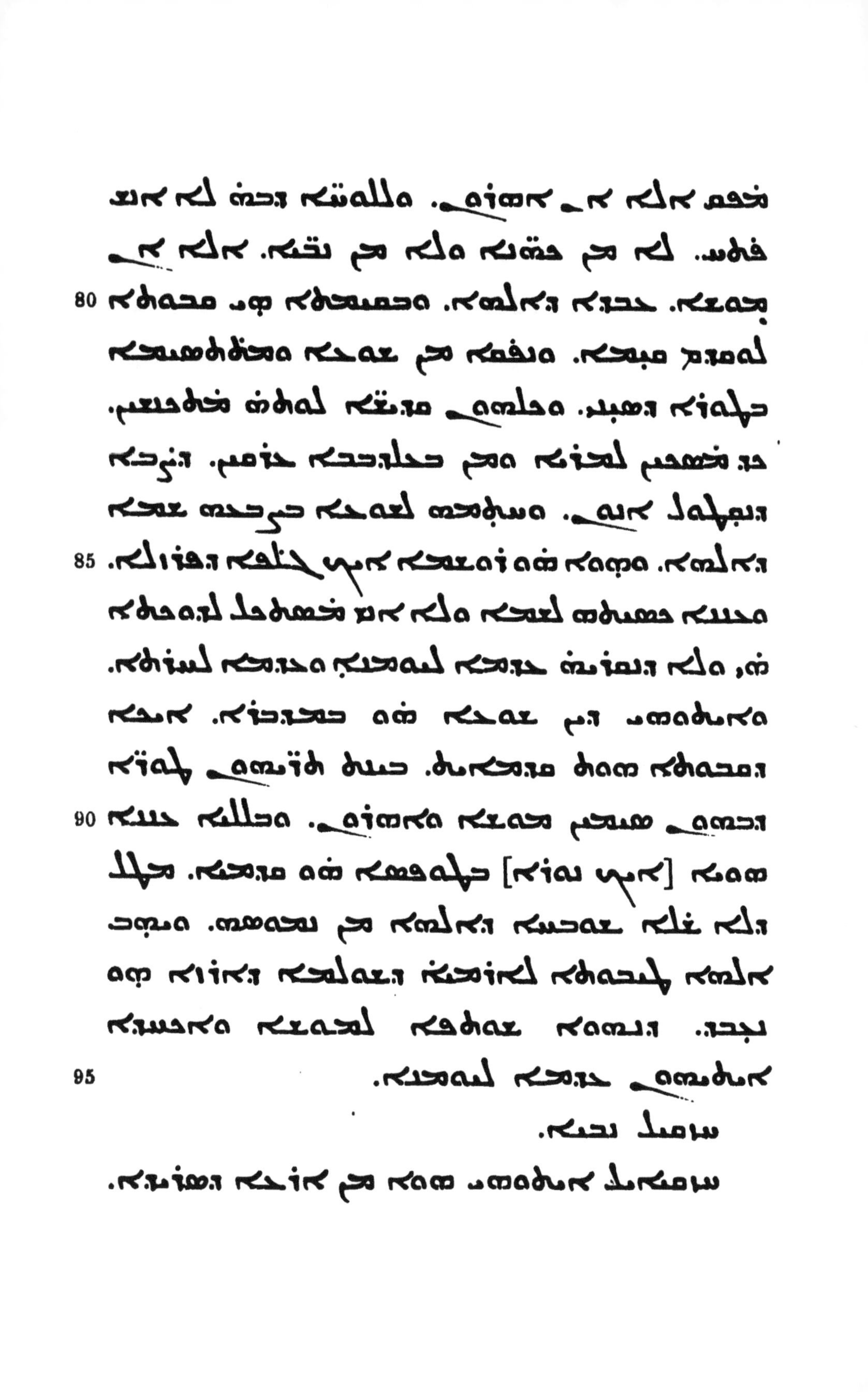

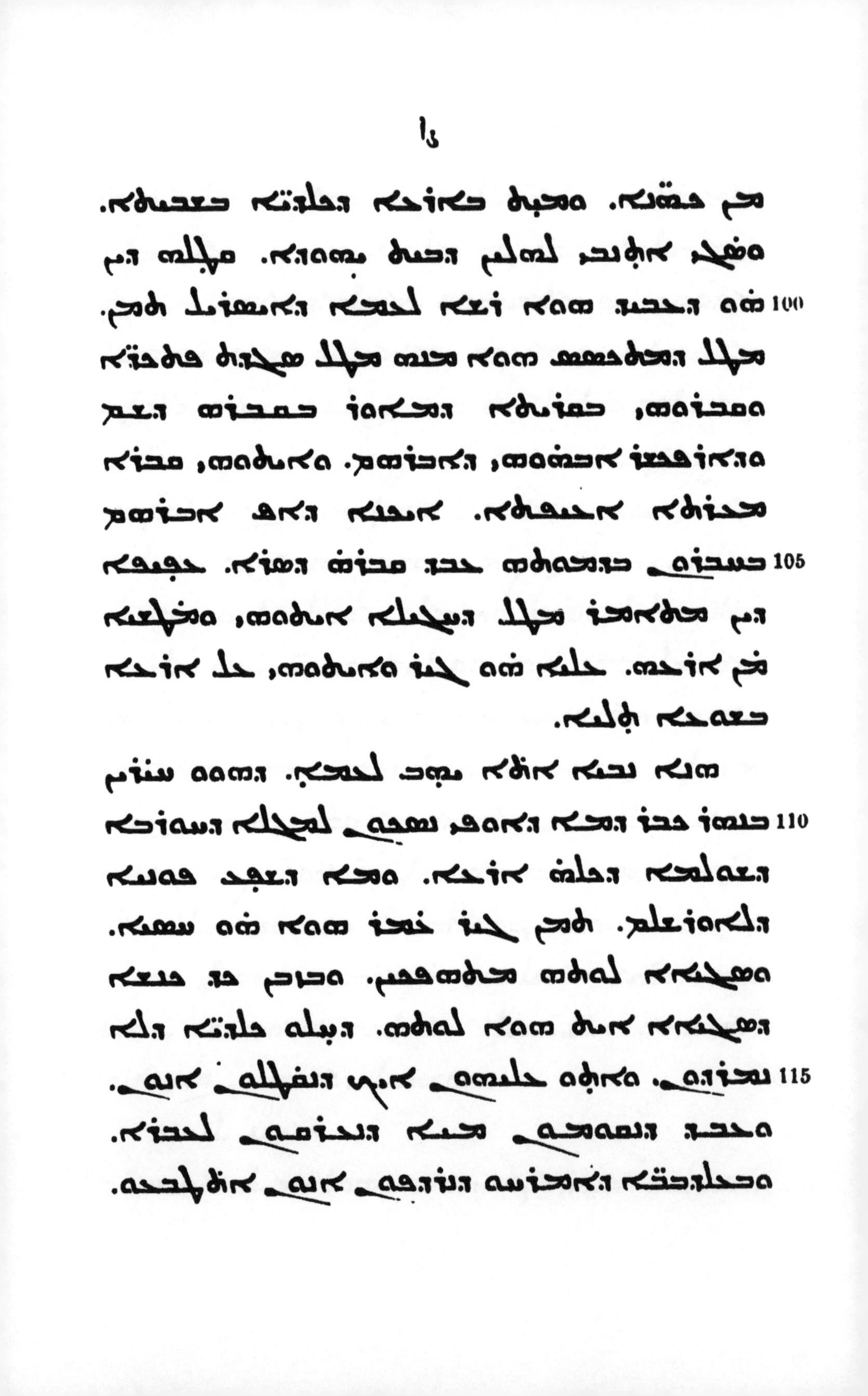

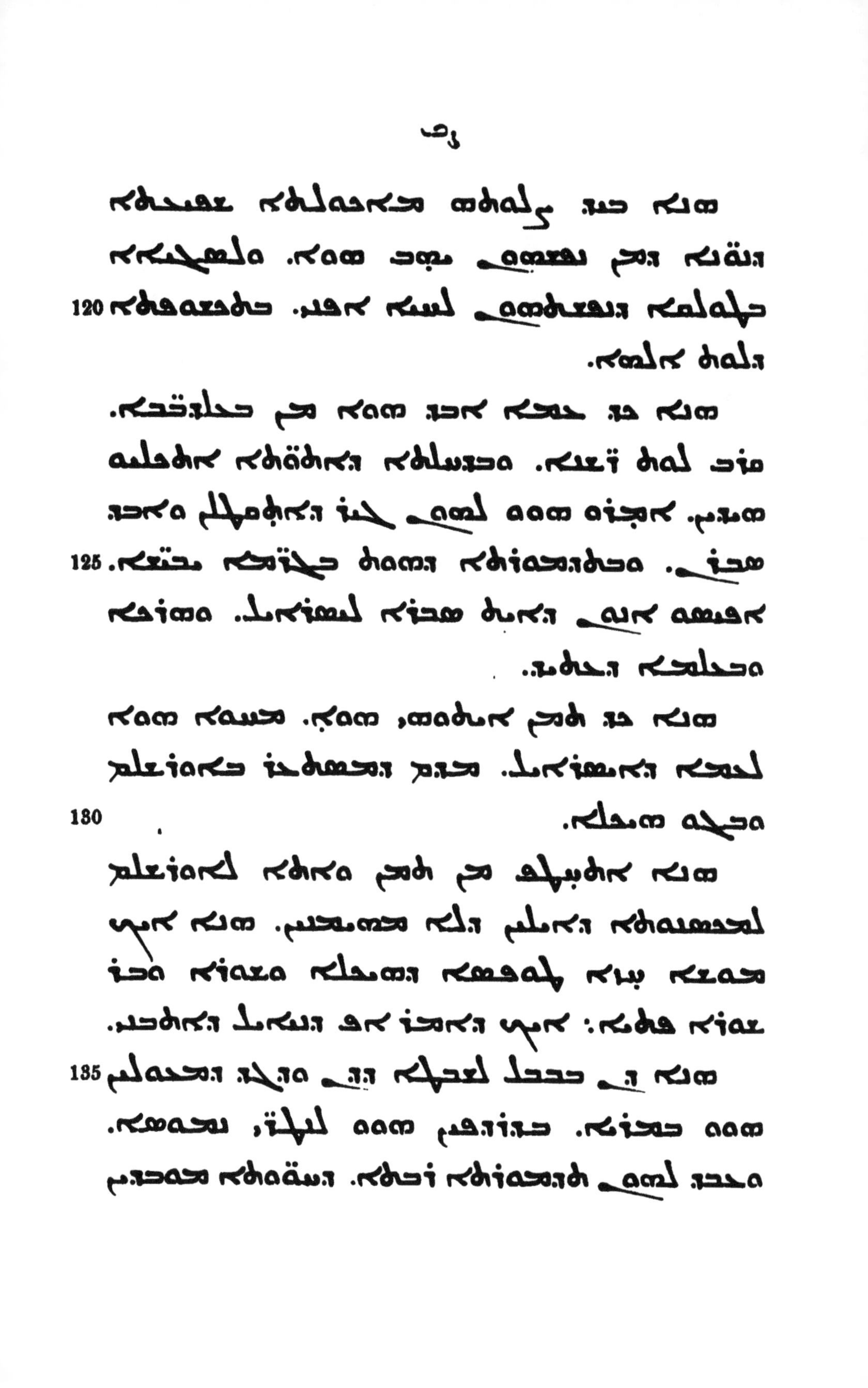

ܗܘܘ ܠܚܒܪ̈ܝܗܘܢ ܘܟܠܗ ܡܫܝܚܘܬܗܘܢ. ܘܦܩܕ ܘܐܡܪ ܕܡܛܠܠܬܗܘܢ ܠܐ ܗܘܝܢ ܚܙܝܐ ܠܐܘܪܚܝܗܘܢ. ܐܠܐ ܒܝܬ ܡܕܝܢܐ ܢܗܘܘܢ. ܚܕܡܐ ܠܫܘܠܡܢܐ ܕܠܚܝܘܬܗܘܢ. ܘܡܚܝܢܘܬܗܘܢ ܐܝܬܘܗܝ، ܗܘܐ ܗ̇ܘ ܕܡܛܠܗ. ܦܐܪܩ ܗܘܐ ܕܝܢ ܠܡܘܒܠܗ ܟܠܗܘܢ ܢܘܟܪ̈ܝܐ ܕܢܦܫܗ.

ܕܢܝܐܝܠ ܢܒܝܐ.

ܕܢܝܐܝܠ ܐܝܬܘܗܝ، ܗܘܐ ܡܢ ܫܪܒܬܐ ܕܝܗܘܕܐ. ܡܢ ܓܢܣܐ ܕܪ̈ܘܪܒܢܐ ܕܡܠܟܘܬܐ: ܘܟܕ ܗܘ ܛܠܝܐ: ܐܬܕܒܪ ܡܢ ܝܗܘܕ ܠܐܬܪܐ ܕܟܠܕ̈ܝܐ. ܗܘܐ ܕܝܢ ܒܐܬܪ ܫܒܝܬܐ: ܘܐܝܬܘܗܝ، ܗܘܐ ܓܒܪܐ ܢܟܦܐ. ܐܝܟ ܕܣܦܪ ܠܝܗܘܕ̈ܝܐ ܘܕܐܘܠܨܢܐ ܐܝܬܘܗܝ، ܘܦܫܩ ܡܬܒܥܠ ܗܘܝܐ ܡܠܠ ܡܕܝܢܬܐ ܘܡܝܘܡܐ ܐܬܟܠܝ ܡܢ ܟܠ ܡܐܟܘܠܬܐ ܪܓܝܓܬܐ. ܘܐܝܬܘܗܝ، ܗܘܐ ܓܒܪܐ ܡܟܝܟܐ ܒܨܘܡܗ ܗܕܪܐ ܕܝܢ ܒܟܢܘܬܐ ܕܩܕܝܫܐ. ܗܢܐ ܦܫܩ ܚܠܡܐ ܕܢܒܘܟܕܢܨܪ. ܟܕ ܡܦܝܣ ܗܘܐ ܠܗ ܒܠܛܫܐܨܪ ܒܪܗ. ܟܕ ܗܘܐ ܫܘܬܐ ܘܒܝܪܐ ܕܠܐ ܢܐܟܪ. ܐܝܬܘܗܝ، ܗܘܐ ܓܒܪ ܡܕܡܝܢ ܘܪܘܫ ܐܝܟ ܕܐܬܪܐ ܘܡܫܘܬܦ ܘܠܗ ܟܡ ܬ̈ܠܬܝܢ، ܐܝܟ ܐܪܝܐ. ܘܐܬܦܠܓ ܠܒܣܝܐ ܟܠ

ܐܪܙܐ ܗܢܐ ܕܟܣܝܐ ܗܘܐ. ܡܛܠ ܡܫܘܬ ܡܕܠܗ
ܘܪܘܚܬ ܐܪ̈ܚܬܐ ܕܦܓܪܗ ܘܐܝܟ ܬܘܪܐ ܗ̇ܘܐ
ܬܘܫܚ ܚܪܐ ܕܗܠܟܐ. ܗܠܝܢ ܐܡܪ ܠܘܬ ܫ̈ܠܝܚܬܐ
ܒܠܠܘܬܗܘܢ. ܐܫܪܬ ܕܝܢ ܒܪܡܫܬ ܫܘ̈ܬܐܬܐ ܗ̈ܘܝܢ:
ܟܕ ܫܠܡܝܢ ܟܕ ܚܕܝܢ ܘܦܚܝܢ ܘܦܠܠܝܢ. ܘܐܬܡܣܟ ܠܗ
ܡܢ ܐܠܗܐ ܠܗ ܠܡܕܝܢܐ. ܕܐܝܟ ܬܘܪܐ ܢܚܠ ܗܘܐ
ܒܡܕܒܪܐ. ܘܗ̇ܘܐ ܗ̣ܘܐ ܠܗ: ܐܝܟ ܡܟܐܒܘܠܬܐ
ܚܝܘܬܐ ܕܒܝܫܬܐ. ܡܛܠ ܗܕܐ ܐܦ ܗ̣ܘ ܢܬܡܕܒܪ.
ܡܢ ܒܬܪ ܕܦܓܪ ܗܘܐ ܘܡܠܟܐ ܕܒܢܝܢܫܐ ܗܘܐ ܗ̣ܘܐ.
ܟܕ ܚܕܐ ܗܘܐ ܘܚܕܐ ܗܘܐ ܡܢ ܡܕ̈ܢܐ ܒܐܡܣܟܐ
ܘܒܠܠܐ: ܐܪ̈ܟܝܢ ܐܟܝܢ ܡܬܦܪܥ ܗܘܐ. ܘܒܕܡܘܬܐ
ܗ̣ܘܐ ܗܘܐ ܕܒܡܘܡܬܐ̇. ܘܦܓܥܐ ܗܘܐ ܕܒܪܢܫܐ
ܐܝܬܘܗܝ، ܘܡܠܘܬܗ̇ ܐܫܬܡܠܬ. ܘܡܟܐ ܕܐܫܬܩܠ
ܡܢܕܐ ܚܕܐ ܗܘܐ. ܘܚ̈ܝܘܗܝ، ܗܘܝܢ ܐܝܟ ܒܣܪܐ
ܡܢ ܫܘܠܛܢܐ ܕܒܒܠܐ. ܫܠܝܛܢܐ ܒܪ ܢܦܫܝܢ ܗܘܘ
ܡܢ ܡܕܝܢܬܐ ܘܫܕܝܢ ܠܗ. ܕܐܟܝܠ ܕܝܢ ܟܠܒܘܗܝ
ܠܐ ܢܓܕܐ ܗܘܐ ܕܢܣܘܒܘܗܝ ܡܛܠ ܕܟܠܗ ܐܟܝܢܐ
ܕܡܬܚܠܦܘܬܗ ܒܝܠܘܬܐ ܐܝܬܘܗܝ، ܗܘܐ ܗܘܐ ܡܛܠܬܗ.
ܐ̇ܡܪ ܗܘܐ ܕܝܢ ܕܬܘܒ ܦܢܐ ܘܗ̇ܘܐ ܒܪܢܫܐ. ܘܠܐ
ܡܬܡܚܝܢ ܗܘܘ ܠܗ. ܗ̣ܘ ܕܝܢ ܕܐܟܝܠ ܗܠܝܢ ܥܒܕ

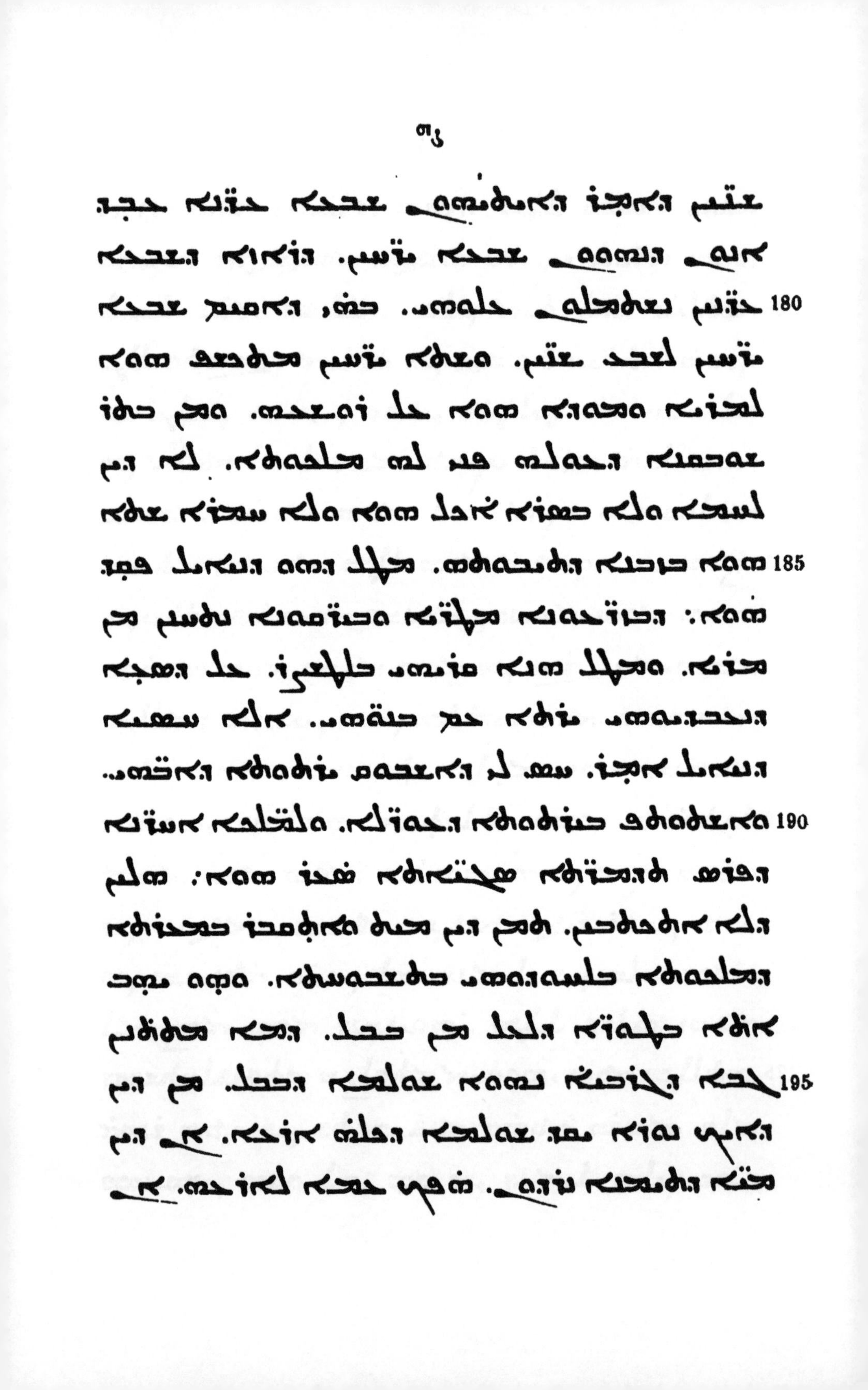

ܕܝܢ ܕܡܚܐ ܢܘܪܐ. ܩܛܠܐ ܢܗܘܐ ܕܩܛܠܐ ܒܒܠܘ ܐܪܒܐ. ܘܡܒܒ ܦܠܚܐ ܗܘ ܣܓܝܐ ܕܢܟܝܠ.

ܬܘܒ ܡܛܠ ܗܘܫܒ.

ܗܘܫܒ ܗܢܐ ܐܝܬܘܗܝ، ܗܘܐ ܡܢ ܒܠܩܘܬ. ܡܢ ܫܒܛܐ ܕܐܝܣܟܪ. ܘܐܬܩܒܪ ܒܐܪܥܗ ܒܫܠܡܐ. ܘܝܗܒ ܐܬܐ ܕܢܬܐ ܡܪܝܐ ܥܠ ܐܪܥܐ. ܐܢ ܗܘ ܕܒܠܘܛܐ ܕܐܝܬ ܒܫܝܠܘ ܡܬܦܠܓܐ ܠܬܪܬܥܣܪ ܡܢ ܢܦܫܬ ܢܗܘܘܢ ܘܗܘܝܐ ܬܪܬܥܣܪ ܦܠܓܝܢ.

ܡܝܟܐ.

ܡܝܟܐ ܐܝܬܘܗܝ، ܗܘܐ ܡܢ ܬܘܡܒ ܘܐܡܘܪܝܐ ܕܝ ܒܒܠ ܚܙ ܐܠܝ ܗܘܐ ܠܗ. ܠܚܪܬܐ ܐܦ ܩܛܠܗ ܒܪܗ. ܒܡܫܘܬܐ ܕܒܠ ܢܕܒܗ ܒܒܘܠܫܐ ܘܒܕ. ܒܕܒܠ ܐܝܬ ܒܗ ܢܦܫ ܐܬܩܐ ܠܐܪܒܗ ܘܡܢ ܒܬܪ ܩܠܝܠܐ ܡܝܬ ܘܐܬܩܒܪ.

ܝܘܐܝܠ.

ܝܘܐܝܠ ܐܝܬܘܗܝ، ܗܘܐ ܡܢ ܐܪܥܐ ܕܪܘܒܝܠ. ܡܢ ܐܓܪܘܣܐ ܕܒܝܬ ܡܪܘܢ. ܒܫܠܡܐ ܡܝܬ ܘܐܬܩܒܪ ܬܡܢ.

ܥܒܕܝܐ.

ܥܒܕܝܐ ܗܘ ܡܐܪܥܐ ܐܝܬܘܗܝ، ܗܘܐ ܡܢ

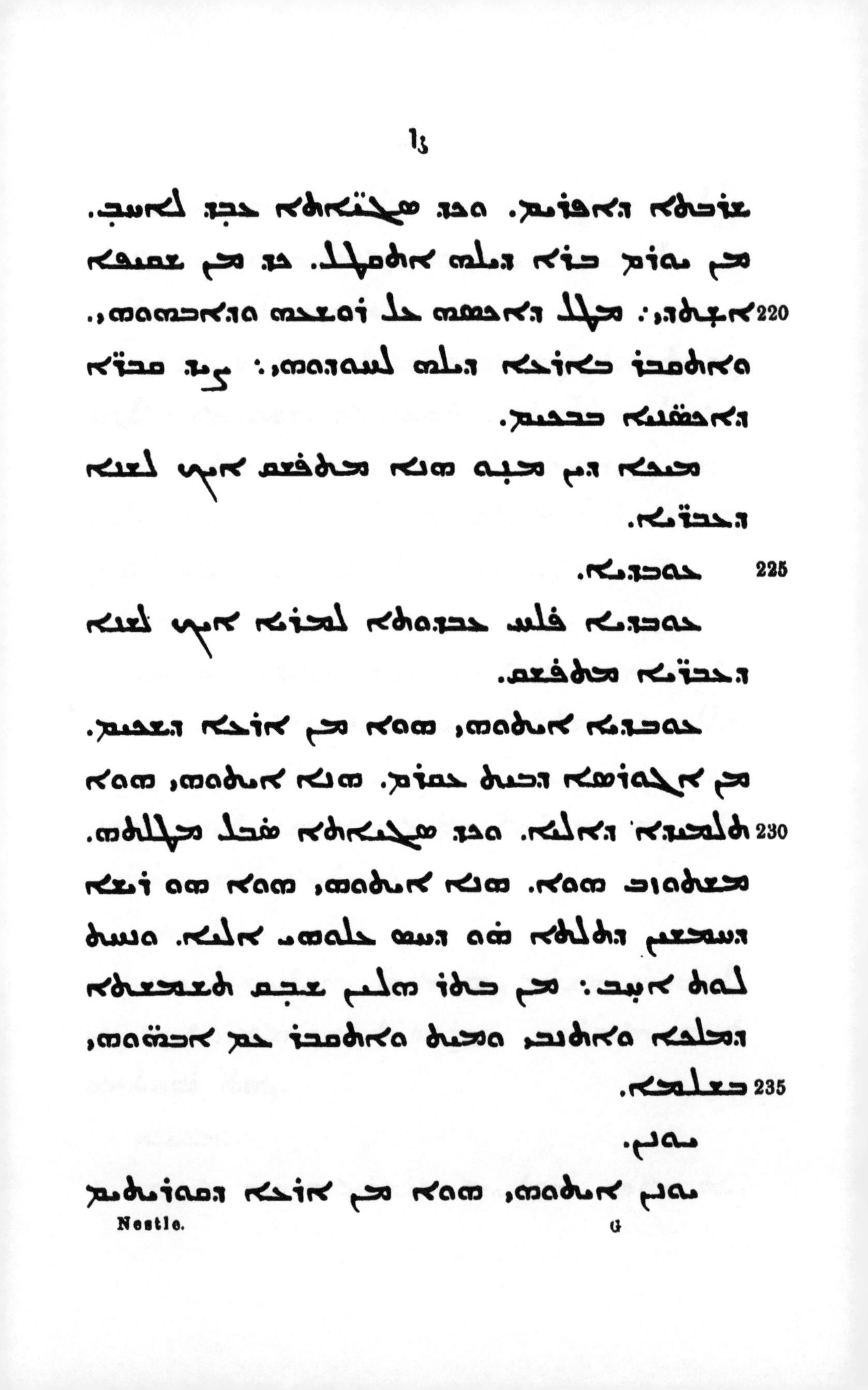

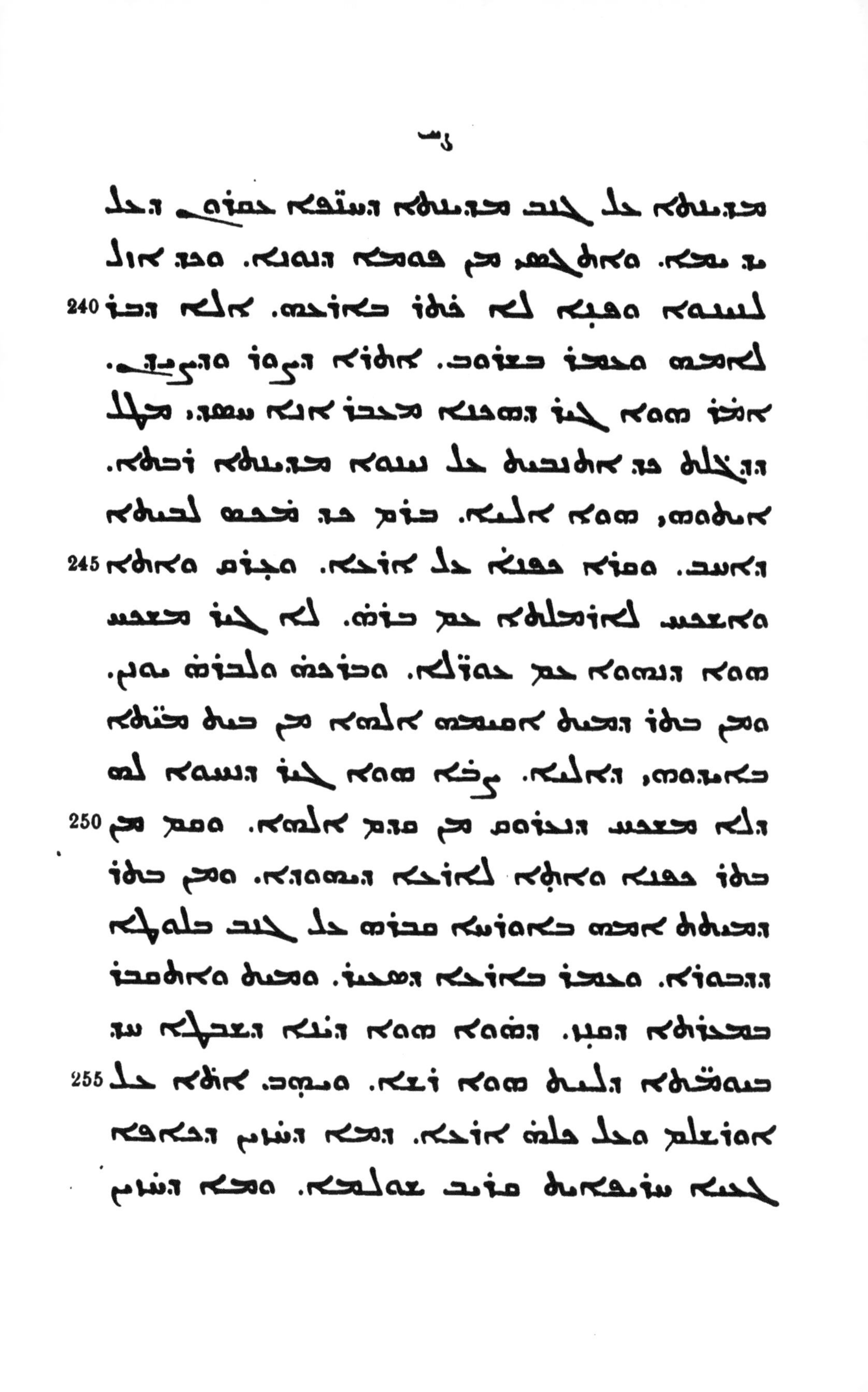

ܒܐܘܪܫܠܡ ܠܗܘܢ ܒܩ̈ܘܡܐ ܕܗܘ̇ ܡܕܝܢܬܐ ܒܕܡܐ ܠܐܪܥܐ ܡܬܢܒܠܐ ܒܠܗ̇.

ܢܚܘܡ.

ܢܚܘܡ ܐܝܬܘܗܝ ܗܘܐ ܡܢ ܐܠܩܘܫ. ܡܢ ܥܒܪܐ ܕܒܝܬ ܓܘܒܪܝܢ. ܡܢ ܫܒܛܐ ܕܫܡܥܘܢ. ܗܢܐ ܡܢ ܒܬܪ ܝܘܢܢ ܐܬܬܐ ܢܒܝ ܠܢܝܢܘܐ. ܕܡܢ ܡܝ̈ܐ ܚ̈ܠܝܐ: ܘܡܢ ܢܘܪܐ ܕܠܬܚܬ ܡܢ ܐܪܥܐ ܐܚܪ̈ܢܐ. ܘܗ̇ܝ ܗܕܐ ܗܘܬ. ܘܐܚܪܬܐ ܓܝܪ ܕܒܪܝܬܐ ܠܗ̇ ܐܬܚܦܟܬܗ ܒܡܒܘܥܐ ܕܗܘܐ. ܘܢܘܪܐ ܐܚܪܬ ܡܢ ܡܕܒܪܐ. ܘܐܓܒܐ ܕܐܝܬ ܗܘܐ ܒܗ̇ ܕܘܩ ܐܘܩܕܬ. ܡܝܬ ܕܝܢ ܒܫܠܡܐ ܘܐܬܩܒܪ ܒܐܪܥܗ.

ܚܒܩܘܩ ܢܒܝܐ.

ܚܒܩܘܩ ܐܝܬܘܗܝ ܗܘܐ ܡܢ ܫܒܛܐ ܕܫܡܥܘܢ. ܡܢ ܐܓܪܘܣܐ ܕܒܝܬ ܙܘܟܪ. ܗܢܐ ܚܙܐ ܡܢ ܩܕܡ ܫܒܝܬܐ ܥܠ ܡܬܟܒܫܢܘܬܐ ܕܐܘܪܫܠܡ ܘܐܬܐܒܠ ܣܓܝܐܐ. ܘܟܕ ܐܬܐ ܢܒܘܟܕܢܨܪ ܠܐܘܪܫܠܡ. ܥܪܩ ܠܒܝܬ ܦܣܪܐ. ܘܐܬܬܘܬܒ ܗܘܐ ܬܘܬܒܐ ܒܐܪܥܐ ܕܐܝܫܡܥܝܠ. ܟܕ ܕܝܢ ܗܦܟܘ ܟܠܕ̈ܝܐ: ܘܫܪܟܐ ܗܠܝܢ ܕܦܫܘ ܒܐܘܪܫܠܡ ܢܚܬܘ ܠܡܨܪܝܢ. ܦܠܚ ܗܘܐ ܕܝܢ ܒܐܪܥܗ: ܘܡܫܡܫ ܗܘܐ ܠܚܨܕܐ ܕܐܓܘܪܗ.

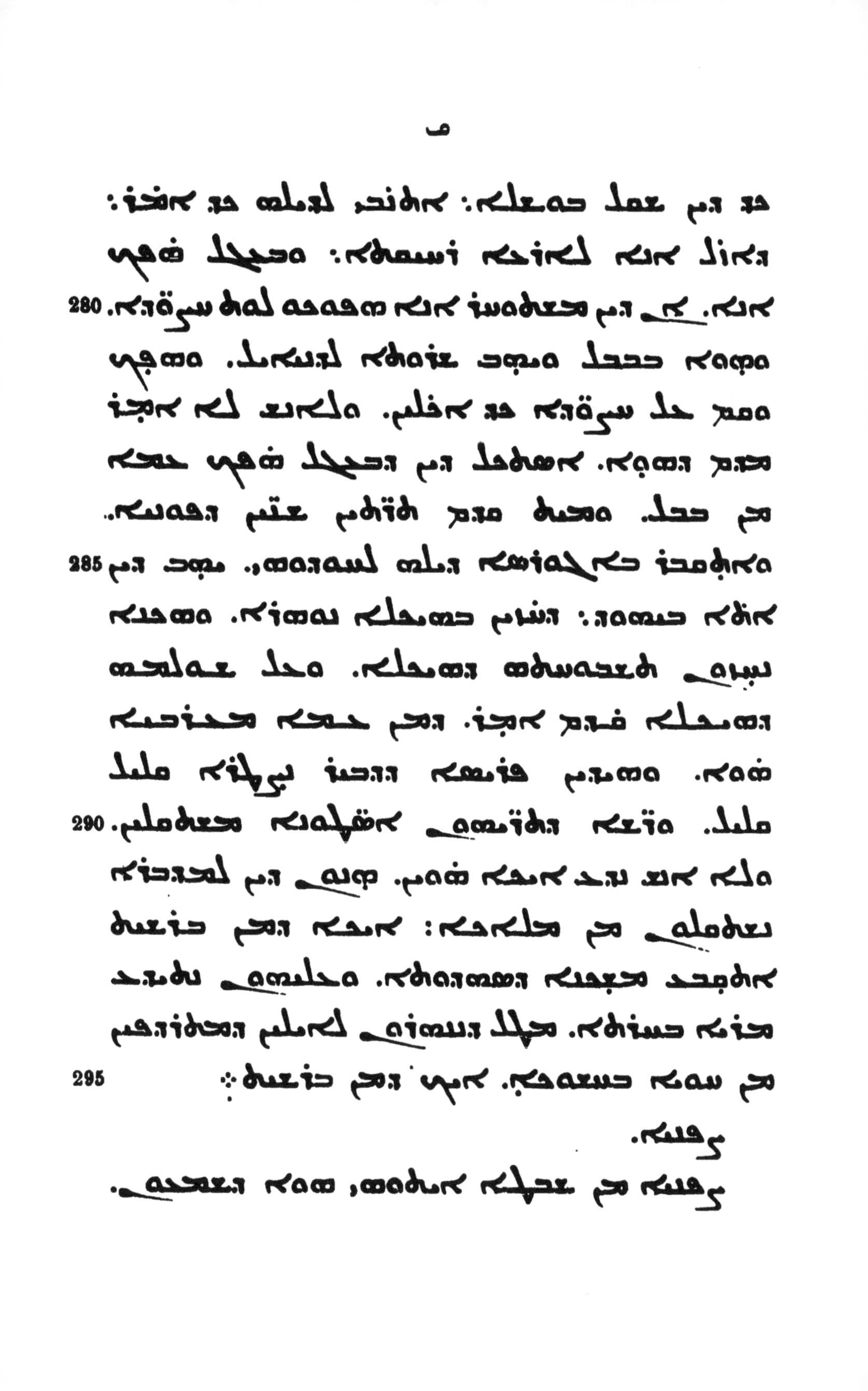

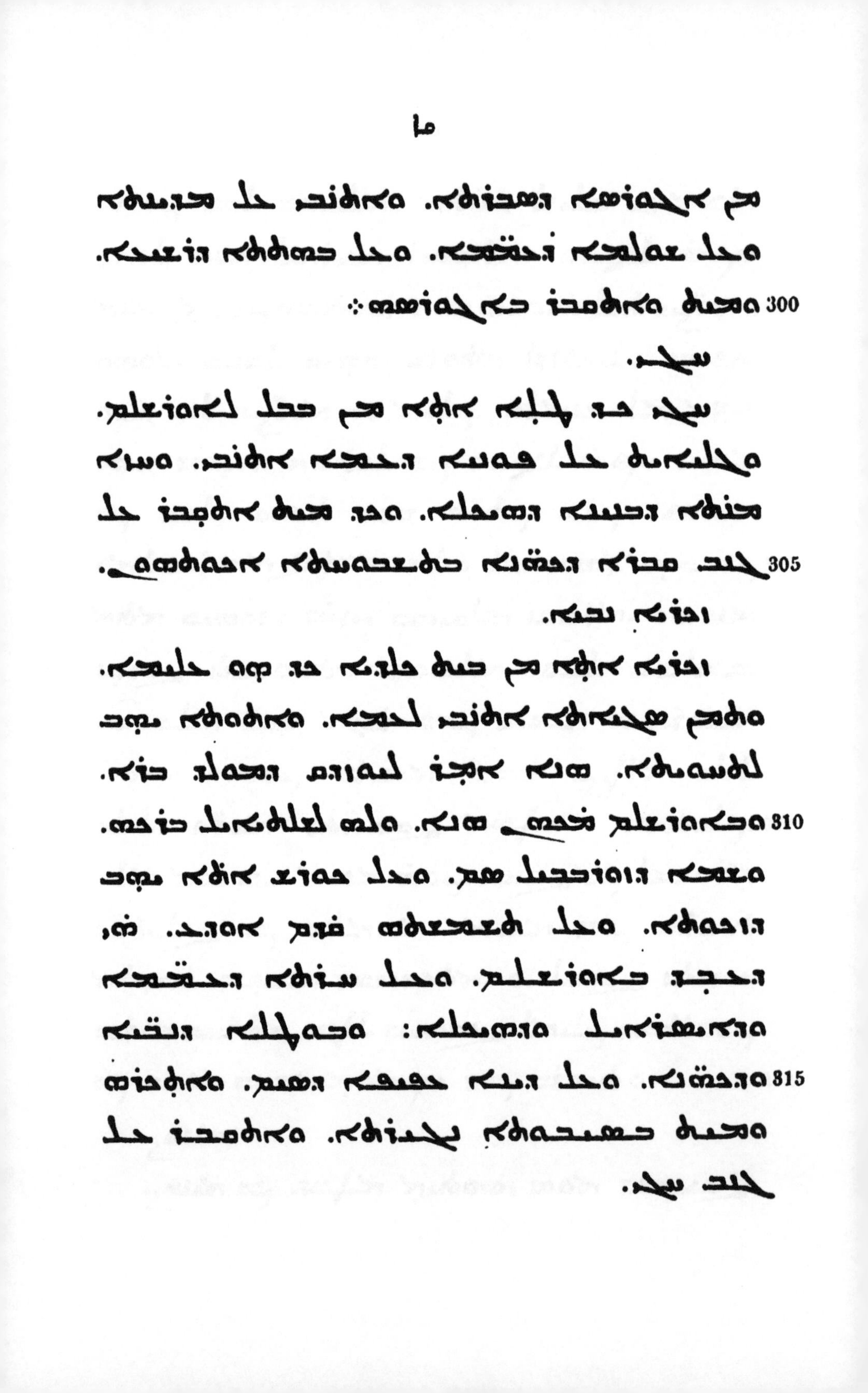

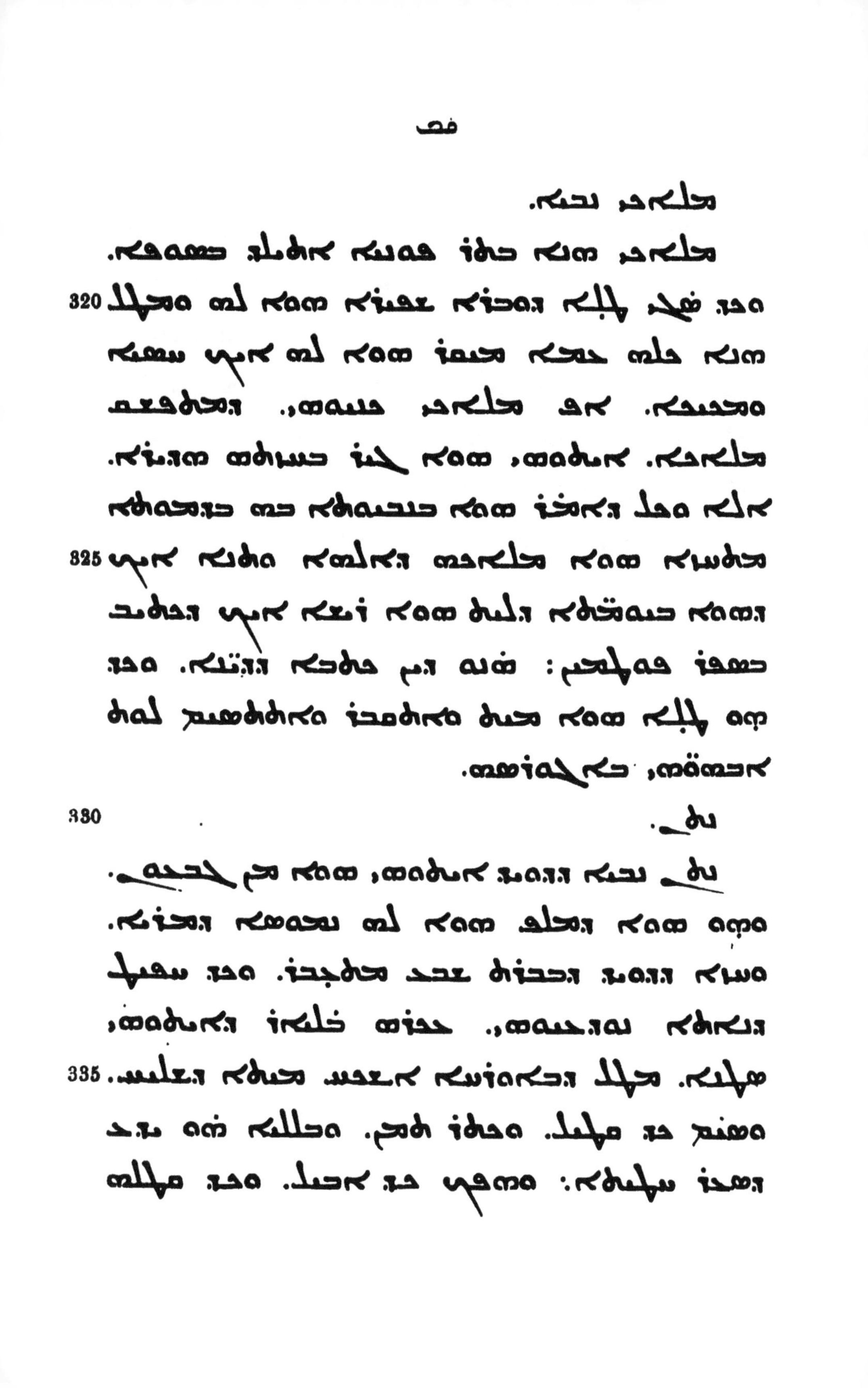

ܠܚܪܢܐ. ܫܪܘ ܡܢܐ ܕܢܦܫܗܘܢ، ܘܟܕ ܦܫܛ ܠܟ ܡܝܬ ܘܐܬܩܒܪ ܒܐܪܥܗ.

ܐܚܝܐ.

ܐܚܝܐ ܡܢ ܫܝܠܘ ܐܝܬܘܗܝ، ܗܘܐ: ܐܬܪܐ ܕܐܝܬܘܗܝ، ܗܘܐ ܡܫܟܢܐ ܡܢ ܩܕܡ ܒܝܘܡܬܗ ܕܥܠܝ. ܗܢܐ ܐܡܪ ܥܠ ܫܠܝܡܘܢ ܕܢܚܛܐ ܠܡܪܝܐ. ܘܚܙܐ ܙܘܓܐ ܕܬܘܪ̈ܐ ܕܕܝܫܝܢ ܠܥܡܐ ܕܡܪܝܐ. ܘܥܠ ܟܗ̈ܢܐ ܪܗܛܝܢ. ܘܩܕܡ ܐܡܪ ܠܫܠܝܡܘܢ. ܕܢܫ̈ܐ ܡܫܚܠܦܢ ܠܗ ܘܠܟܠܗ ܓܢܣܗ. ܘܡܝܬ ܘܐܬܩܒܪ ܥܠ ܓܢܒ ܒܠܘܛܐ ܕܫܝܠܘ.

ܥܘܕܡ.

ܥܘܕܡ ܡܢ ܐܪܥܐ ܗܘܐ ܕܫܡܪܝܢ. ܗܢܐ ܐܝܬܘܗܝ، ܗܘ ܕܢܟܬܗ ܐܪܝܐ ܘܡܝܬ. ܟܕ ܐܟܣܗ ܠܝܘܪܒܥܡ ܥܠ ܥܓ̈ܠܐ ܕܕܗܒܐ. ܘܐܬܩܒܪ ܒܒܝܬ ܐܝܠ ܥܠ ܓܢܒ ܐܚܘܗ̱ܝ ܢܒܝܐ ܕܓܠܐ ܕܛܥܝ ܗܘ.

ܥܙܪܐ.

ܥܙܪܐ ܐܝܬܘܗܝ، ܡܢ ܣܘܒܬܐ. ܗܘ ܕܐܗܦܟ ܡܢ ܐܝܣܪܝܠ ܠܫܒܝܬܐ ܕܝܗܘܕܐ. ܘܟܕ ܡܝܬ ܐܬܩܒܪ ܒܐܓܘܪܗ.

ܐܠܝܐ ܢܒܝܐ.

ܐܠܝܐ ܡܢ ܬܫܒܝ ܗܘܐ ܡܢ ܐܪܥܐ ܕܓܠܥܕ. ܡܢ ܫܒܛܐ ܕܐܗܪܘܢ. ܘܥܡܪ ܗܘܐ ܒܐܪܥܐ ܕܓܠܥܕ. ܡܛܠ ܕܬܫܒܝ ܡܬܩܪܝܐ ܗܘܬ ܕܟܗܢ̈ܐ. ܘܟܕ ܐܬܐ ܗܘܐ ܕܢܬܝܠܕ. ܚܙܐ ܫܘܒܟܝ ܐܒܘܗܝ ܕܓܒܪ̈ܐ ܚܘ̈ܪܐ, ܒܚܙܘܐ ܫܐܠܝܢ ܗܘܘ ܒܫܠܡܗ. ܘܒܢܘܪ̈ܐ ܕܢܘܪܐ ܡܚܪܟܝܢ ܗܘܘ ܠܗ. ܘܫܠܗܒܝܬܐ ܡܘܟܠܝܢ ܗܘܘ ܠܗ ܕܢܐܟܘܠ. ܘܐܬܐ ܘܐܘܕܥ ܒܐܘܪܫܠܡ. ܘܐܬܐܡܪ ܠܗ ܒܚܠܡܐ ܕܠܐ ܬܕܚܠ. ܢܗܘܐ ܓܝܪ ܒܝܬ ܢܘܗܪܐ ܘܡܠܬܗ ܕܝܢܘܬܐ. ܘܢܕܘܢ ܠܐܝܣܪܝܠ ܒܚܪܒܐ ܘܒܢܘܪܐ ✣

ܐܠܝܫܥ.

ܐܠܝܫܥ ܡܢ ܐܒܠ ܡܚܘܠܐ ܗܘܐ. ܡܢ ܐܪܥܐ ܕܪܘܒܝܠ. ܘܟܕ ܝܠܕܐ ܗܘܬ ܐܬܐ ܟܕ ܐܬܝܠܕ. ܒܓܠܓܠܐ ܥܓܠܬܐ ܡܬܦܠܚܬܐ ܚܢܦܐܝܬ ܓܥܬ. ܐܝܟ ܕܬܬܥܩܪ ܒܐܘܪܫܠܡ. ܗܘ ܕܦܣܩ ܠܦܠܚܘܗ̈ܝ ܘܠܦܬܟܪ̈ܐ. ܘܡܢܗ ܘܐܬܡܪ ܒܥܒܪܝܢ.

ܝܘܢܐ.

ܝܘܢܐ ܡܢ ܐܘܪܫܠܡ ܐܝܬܘܗܝ, ܗܘܐ ܒܪܗ ܕܐܡܬܝ ܒܥܘܠܐ. ܗܘ ܕܡܛܠ ܢܦܩ ܡܠܟܐ ܕܢܝܢܘܐ

ܥܠ ܝܕܝ ܡܕܒܪܢܐ. ܘܐܫܬܕܘ ܕܡܢܗ ܕܒܝܬ ܕܘܝܕ. ܒܝܬ ܡܠܟܘܬܐ. ܘܫܠܛܘ ܒܥܡ̈ܐ ܘܡܕܪ̈ܘ. ܥܡ ܐܒܗ̈ܬܗܘܢ. ܡܢ ܗܕ̈ܡܝ ܗܘ̈ܝ ܐܬܘ̈ܬܐ ܒܡܫܠܡܐ ܕܩܝܛܝܗ. ܘܠܐ ܡܫܬܡܫ ܗܘܐ ܒܥܡ̈ܐ ܕܢܒܝܘ̈ܗܝ ܣܘܦܐ ܕܡܠܐܟ̈ܐ ܕܐܠܗܐ. ܘܠܐ ܕܢܬܠܘܢ ܚܝܠܐ ܡܢ ܕܒܝܬ. ܘܠܐ ܕܢܫܐܠܘܢ ܒܐܦܘܕܐ ܘܠܐ ܒܕܢ̈ܚܐ ܕܢܚܘܢܘܢ ܠܗܢܐ ܐܝܟ ܕܡܢ ܩܕܝܡ.

ܐܡܪ.

ܐܡܪ ܗܢܐ ܐܝܬܘܗܝ ܗܘܐ ܡܢ ܐܪܥܐ ܕܒܒܠ. ܗܒܝܠܐ ܒܪ ܡܬܬܪܝܢ ܡܢ ܒܬܠܐ ܐܪ̈ܥܐ. ܘܒܐܪܥܐ ܕܒܒܠ ܚܙܐ ܚܙܘܐ ܗܢܐ. ܥܠ ܬܫܘܡܬܐ ܕܐܬܘܬ ܡܕܝܢܬܐ. ܘܫܡܗ ܡܢ ܩܕܝܡ ܗܘܒܒ. ܘܫܡܠ ܐܬܢܬܬܐ ܡܢ ܐܪ̈ܥܐ. ܘܠܒܬ ܒܪܐ ܘܫܡܗ ܫܠܘ. ܘܫܡܗ ܕܝ ܕܐܒܘܗܝ ܙܪܚ ܕܡܢ ܒܝܬ ܒܗܘ. ܡܢ ܒܢܝ ܒܢܘܗܝ. ܘܐܡܗ ܒܝܪܘܬܐ. ܘܐܬܘܬܗܘܢ ܡܢ ܙܪܥܗ ܕܐܒܪܗܡ ܢܒܝܝܐ. ܘܗܠܝܢ ܟ̈ܠܗܘܢ ܕܐܡܠܟܘ ܒܐܪܥܗܘܢ. ܐܡܝܢܐ ܕܐܦ ܗܘ ܐܫܬܠܛ ܥܠ ܐܬܪܐ. ܡܕܝܢܬܐ ܟܠܗ ܒܪ ܚܘܪ. ܘܫܡܗ ܕܝ ܕܡܕܝܢܬܐ ܕܬܒܐ. ܘܡܢ ܟܠܗ ܗܟܢ. ܕܡܬܘܪܐ ܐܡܪ. ܡܢ ܒܬܪܗ ܐܚܝܡ. ܕܐܬܘܬܗܘܢ ܟܠܗܘܢ ܡܢ ܐܬܪܐ

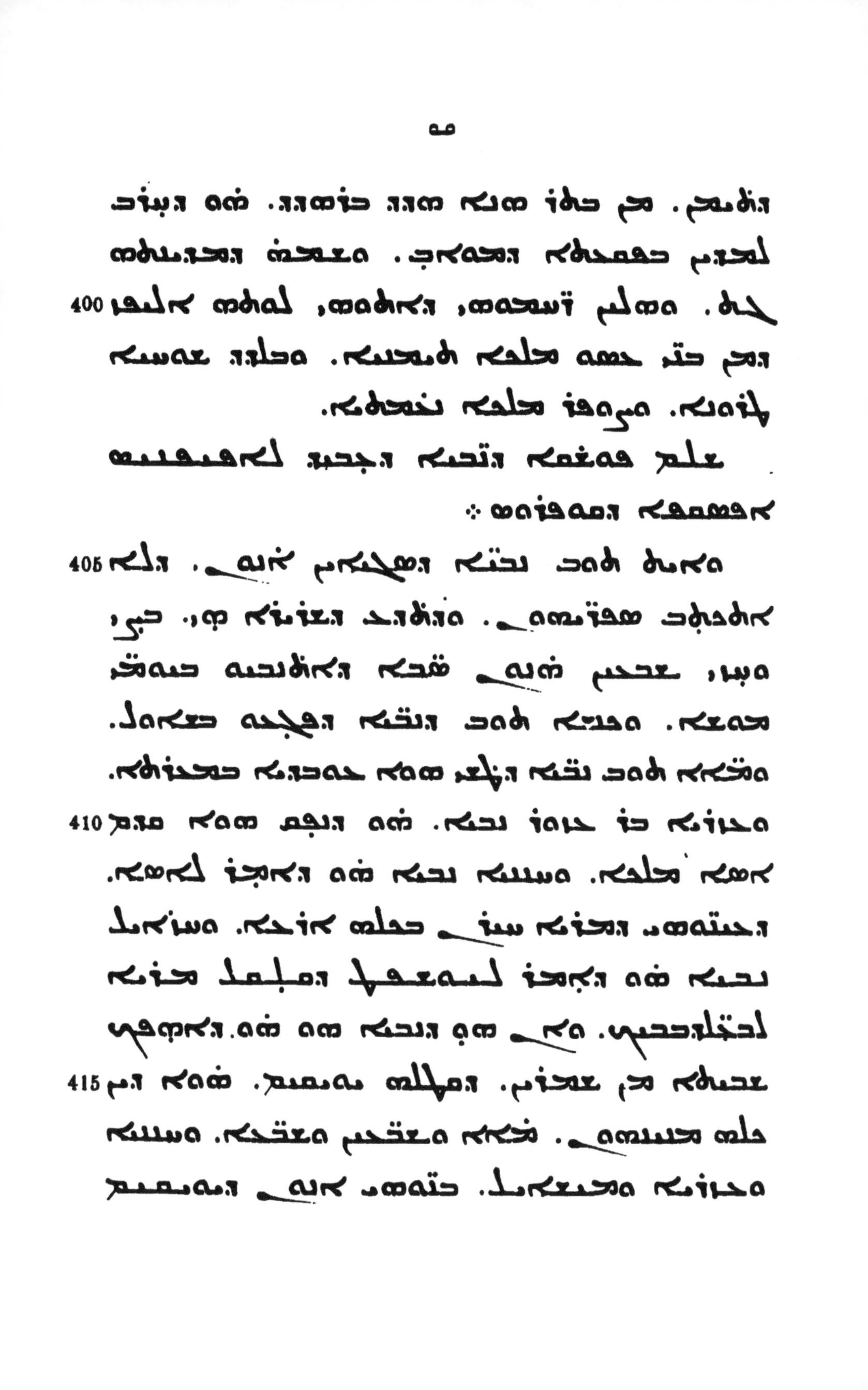

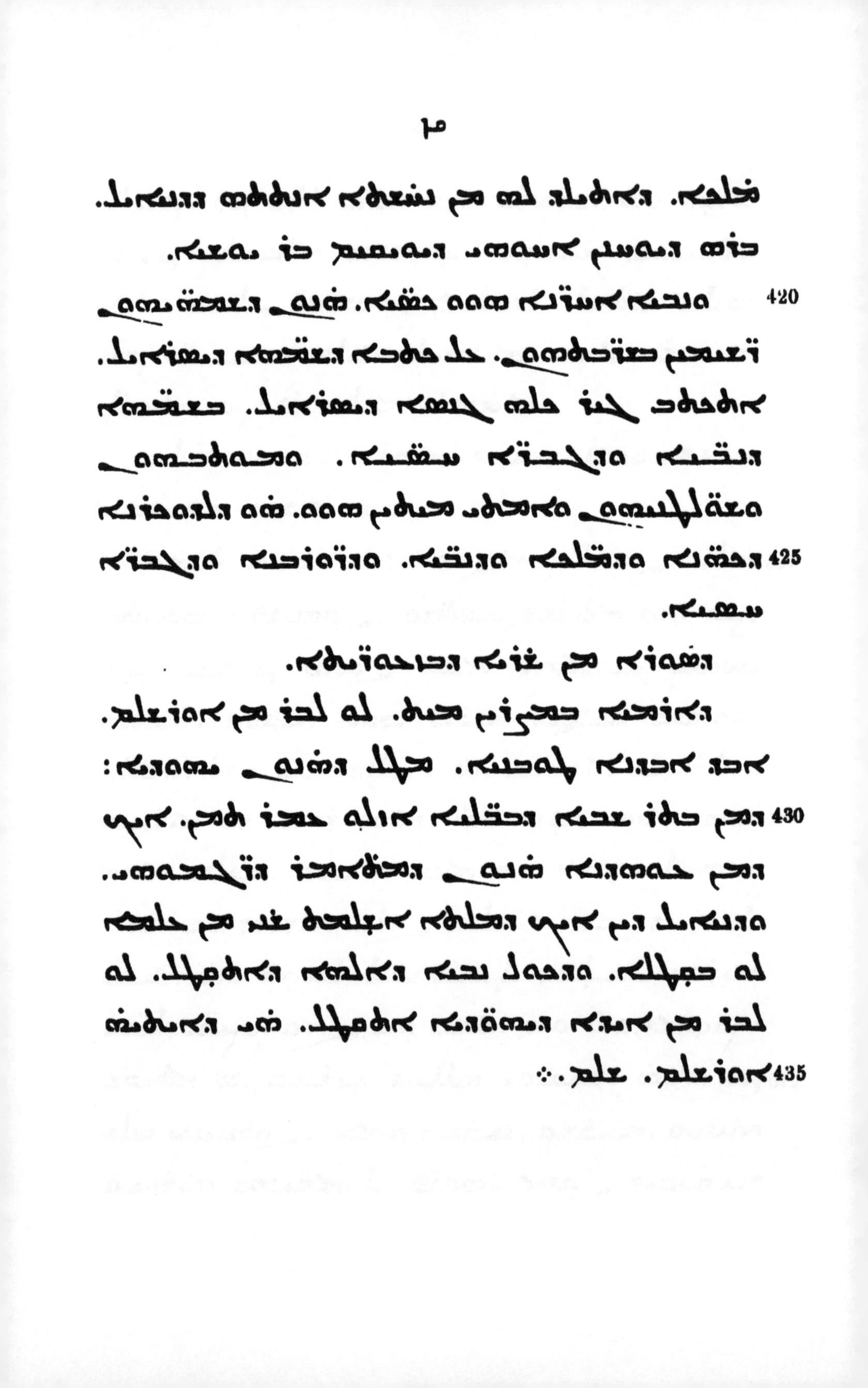

IV. HISTORIA INVENTIONIS SANCTAE CRUCIS.

1) e cod. paris. 234.

 (fol. 293, *recto*, col. 1.)

 (a, col. 2.)

 (b, col. 1)
: (b, col. 2)

(f. 294, a, 1)
. (a, 2.)

 (b, col. 1.)

80 (b, col. 2.)

 (fol. 295, a, col. 1.)

2) e codice Mus. Brit. Add. 14,644.

1 (18 r.)

15 محكك ححك اللهومحمحكلا ٮم جٮ .محمحجٮ لحٮٯ .اٯه
ٮحمحكٮ احٮللهمٯ .اجٮ احمصٯ احٮٯ لحٮهٮحكٯلل
احٯٯٮٮ محٮ ٯحملٮٯ ٯٯمكملٮٯ محٮٯٯحٮٮ محٯ .امٮ سٮمٮٯ
ٯٮٯٯ ٯٯ .حٮحٮ احٮٮ محمحملٯ (f. 18 vers.) حٮحٮ
.ٯللحٮ جحٮٯ محمٮ اٮ حٮ اٮ للا .ٯحمحٮ احملٯٯحٯ

20 ٮحٮ محمحٯٯٯٮ .حٮحٯ محملٯٯٮٯ احٯٯحٮٯ احٮٯٯٯمحٮٯ
احمٮحٮ ٯحٮ ٯللٯٯ .احٯٯ احٮٯحٮ احٮٯ ٯٯمٮ احمٯ احٯ ٯٯٯ
.حٯمٮحٮ محٯ .ٯٯ ٯمحٯحٯ احٯٯٯٯٯحٮ احٯٯ حٮحٮ احٯحٮٯ
.احٮٮٯٯ احٯٯ محٮ حجحٮ اٮٯ .احٯٯحٯ حٯٯ حٮٯٮٯ
محلحٯٯٯ .حٮٯٮ محٮ احٯحٯ ٯٯٯمٯٯ احٯحٮٮٮٯ

25 ٯٯٯحٮحٯٯٯحٮ اٯٯ احٯٯ محٯحٮ .احٯٯٯ احٯٯٮٮ ٯٯٯ
حٯحٮ ٯٯمٯ جٮمٮ ٯحٯٯ .حٯٯٯٯٯ احٯٯٯحمحٮ احٯٮٯ ٯٯٯ
احمٮٮ احٯٯمٯ .ٯٯٮٮٯ احٯمٯ احٯمٯٯ احٯحٮٯ
ٯحٯٯ حٯٯححٮ احٮٯ ٯٯٯ احمٯٯٯ .ٯٯمٯٯٯٯ احٯحمٯٯ احٮٮحٯٯٯ
احٮٯٯ احٯمٯٯ ٯٯ محمٯ .ٯحٯٯٯٯٯحٮ حٯمٯٯ احٯٯحٮ

30 ٯٯٯٯ .احٯٯٯمٯٮ احٯٯحٮ حٯٮٯٯ احٮحٮ ٯٯمٯحٮ
جٮ ٯٯٯٯ .حٯٯ اٮٯ احٯمحٯٯ حٯ حٮٮٯٯٯٯٯٮٯ
احٮحٮ ٯٯٮحٯ ٯٯٯحٮ ٯٯٯٯ .احٯٮٯ احٯٯٯٯٮٮ ٯٮحٯٯٯٯ محٮ ٯٯٮٯ
ٯٯٯ محٮ احٮٯ احٯٯٯٯٯٯ .حٮٯ احٯٯ احمٯٯٯٯ احٯٯٯٯحٮ حٯٯحٮ
حٮحٮ ٯٯٯٯٯ .ٯٯٯٯ ٯٯٮٯٯ احٯٯحٯ محٯٯٯ .احٯٯٯٯ

 (fol. 19 rect.)

 (fol. 19 vers.)

75 ...

80 ...

85 ...

90 ... (f. 20 rect.) ...

ةمس

 (f. 20 vers.)

 (fol. 21 rect.)

(fol. 21 vers.)

| 180
| 185
(f. 22 rect.)

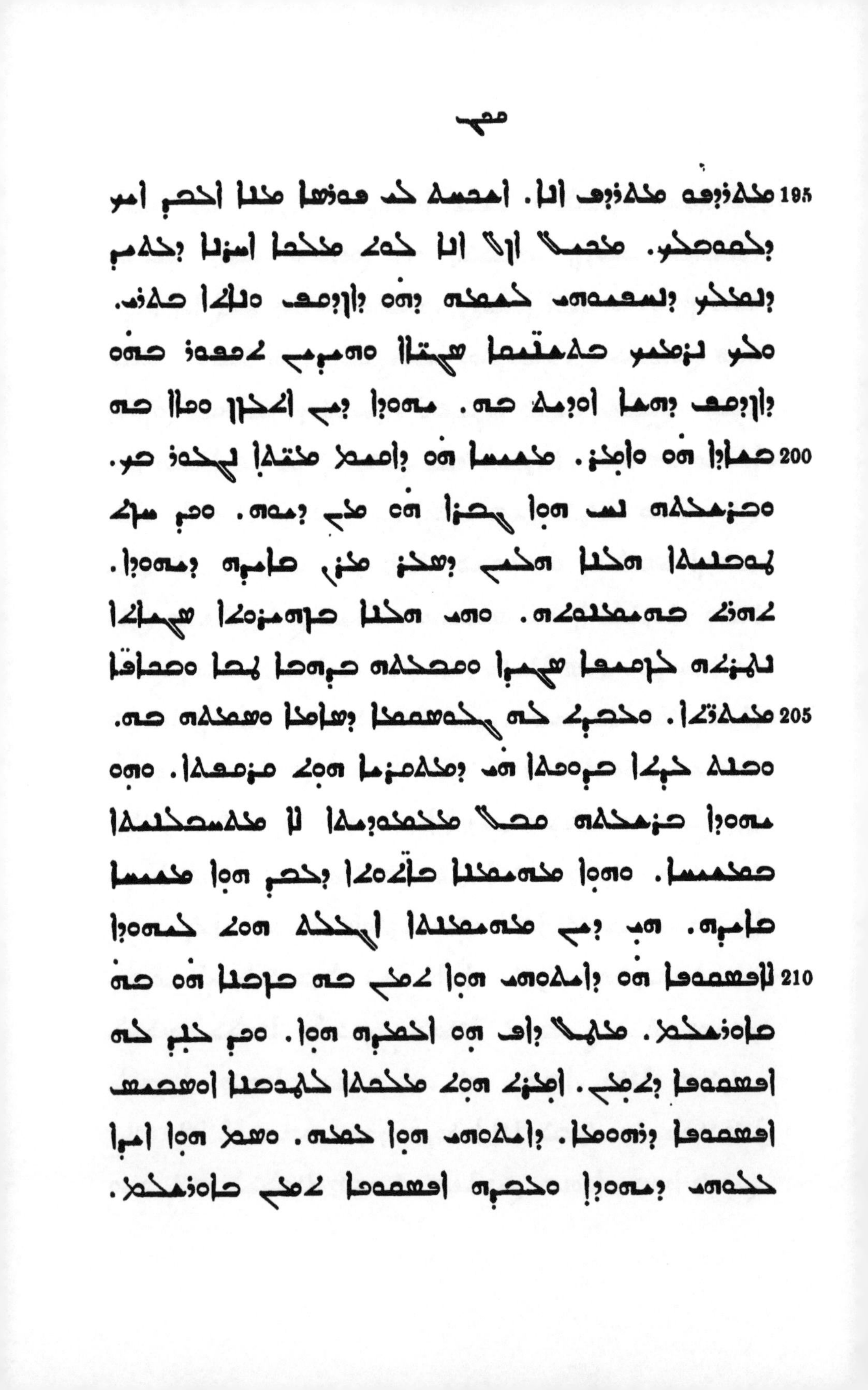

(fol. 22 vers.)

 (fol. 23 rect.) .

 (f. 23 vers.)

3) e Cod. Vat. syr. 148 (a. Chr. 1267).

[ex explanatione officiorum ecclesiasticorum a Georgio Arbelensi
conscripta.] (I, 24.)

 .corr) .

───────────

ª inclusa a secunda manu.

45 .[a]

(؟).[b]

(o)[b]

---

[a] erasum.

[b] inclusa a secunda manu.

)[b]

---

[a] primo .
[b] a secunda manu.

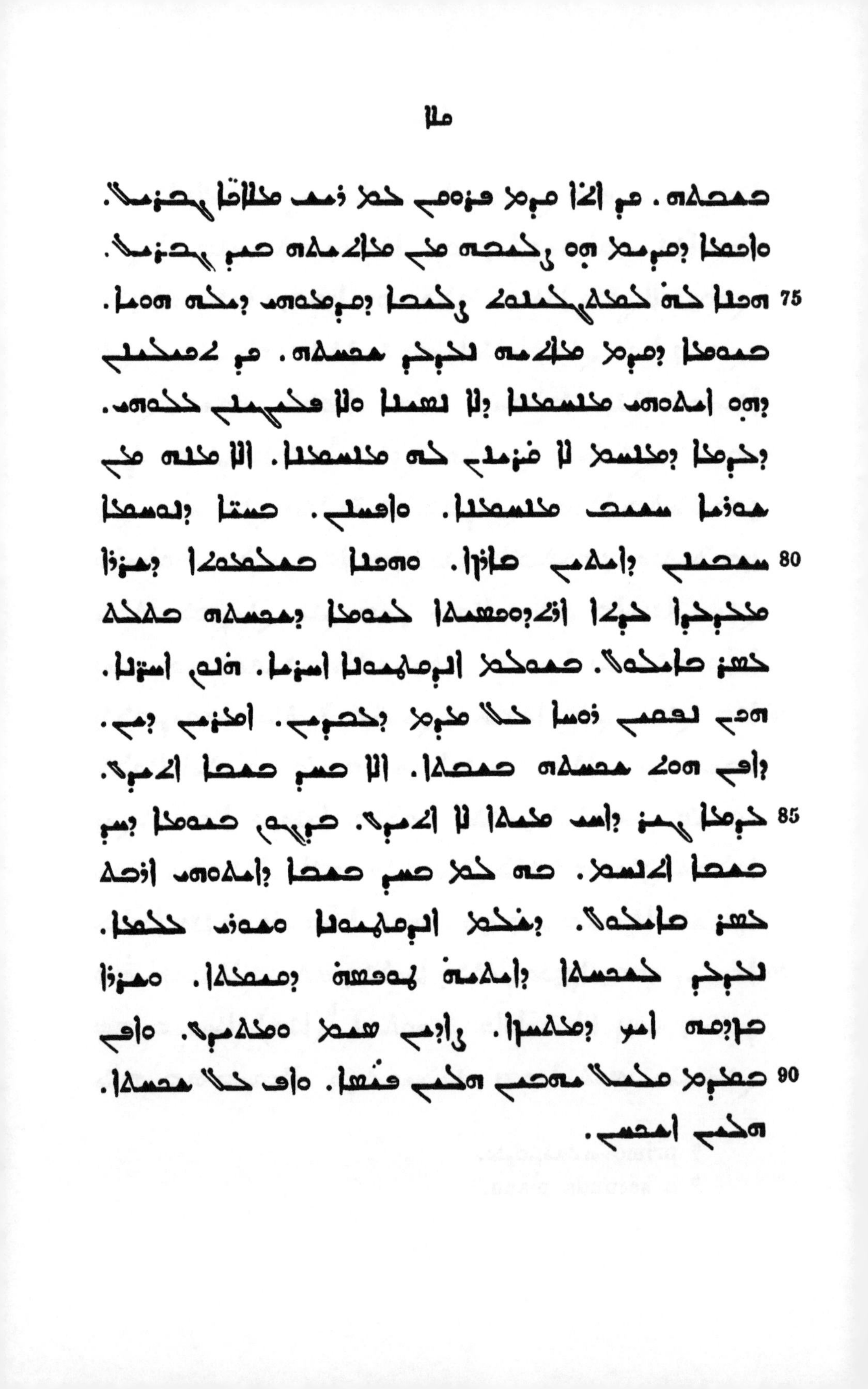

MENSES ANNI SYRIACI

INCIPIENTIS AB INTERLUNIO SEPTEMBRIS.

1. ܬܫܪܝ[ܢ] ܩܕ[ܝ]ܡ Oct. 2. ܬܫܪܝ[ܢ] ܐܚܪܝ Nov
3. ܟܢܘܢ ܩܕ[ܝ]ܡ Dec. 4. ܟܢܘܢ ܐܚܪܝ Jan. 5. ܫܒܛ Febr
6. ܐܕܪ Mart. 7. ܢܝܣܢ Apr. 8. ܐܝܪ Maj. 9. ܚܙܝܪܢ Jun
10. ܬܡܘܙ Jul. 11. ܐܒ Aug. 12. ܐܝܠܘܠ Sept.

DIES SEPTIMANÆ.

ܚܕܒܫܒܐ dies solis, dominica, ܬܪܝܢ ܒܫܒܐ, ܬܠܬܒܫܒܐ, ܐܪܒܥܒܫܒܐ (ܐܪܒܥܐ), ܚܡܫܒܫܒܐ, ܥܪܘܒܬܐ, ܫܒܬܐ [ܫܒܬ].

GLOSSARIUM.

I

ﺍﺍ̈ﺭ c., *plerumque m., pl.* ﺍﺍ̈ﺭ̈ﻮﺱ ἀήρ, aer.

ﺍ̇ﺑﺎ § 33 Vater | father.

ﺍ̇ﺑﺮ *impf. a* verloren gehen, untergehen | go astray, perish. *Aph.* verderben | destroy. ‖ ﺍ̇ﺑﺮﻮ, ﺍ̇ﺑﺮﻮﻧﺎ Untergang, Verderben | destruction, decline. ‖ ﻣﺒﺪﺑﺮﻧﺪ verderblich | pernicious.

[ﺍﺣﻞ] *part. pass.* ﺍ̇ﺻﻞ traurig | mournful. *Ethpe.* trauern, betrübt sein | mourn, be sad.

ﺍﺑﺪﻟ ﻣﺸﺪﻧﻞ ﺍ̇ﺻﻞ = h. אָבֵל מְחֹלָה *n. l.*

ﺍ̇ﻣﺪﻭ, ﺍ̇ﺟﻮﻧﺎ *m.* ἀγών.

ﺍ̇ﺟﻮﺭﺳﺎ *m.* ἀγρός; *pl.* ﺍ̇ﺟﻮﺭﺷﺎ Dörfer | villages.

ﺍ̇ﺟﺮ *u,* § 41 mieten | hire. ‖ ﺍ̇ﺟﺮﺍ, ﺍ̇ﺟﺮﺍ *m.* Lohn | wages.

ﺍ̇ﺟﺮﺍ (*sic,* § 3, *V* ﺟﺮﻝ) Dach | roof.

ﺍ̇ﺩﻣﺘﺎ, nest. ﺍ̇ﺩﻣﺜﺎ *f.,* h. אֲדָמָה Boden | soil.

ﺍ̇ﺩﻧﺎ *f.,* h. אֹזֶן Ohr | ear.

ﺍ̇ﺩﺷﺎ *m.,* εἶδος (G. Hoffmann, ZDMG, 32, 748 n.), Gestalt, Art, Aussehen | form, species, appearance.

ܐܗܐ § 3 *interjectio irridentis, ehe,* εὖγε.

ܐܘ oder | or. ‖ ܐܘܟܝܬ (cf. ܟܝܬ) oder, das heisst | or, i. e.

ܐܘܐ, *Ethpa.* sich vereinigen, versöhnen | be reconciled, be at peace. ‖ ܐܬܐ *f., pl.* ܐܬܘܬܐ Zeichen, Wunderzeichen, Buchstabe | sign, token, miracle, letter.

ܐܘܗ oh! Wehe! | oh! woe! *cum* ܠܝ, ܠ, ܥܠ.

ܐܘܢܓܠܝܘܢ (ܐܘܢܓܠܝܘܢ, ܐܘܢܓܠܝܘܢ) εὐαγγέλιον.

ܐܘܢܘܟܐ εὐνοῦχος.

ܗܘܦܘܡܢܡܛܐ, "ܗܘܦܘܡ[illegible], "ܗܘܦ ὑπομνήματα.

ܐܘܪܕܥܐ § 14 Frosch | frog.

ܐܘܪܝܐ *m., pl.* ܐܘܪܘܝܢ, ܐܘܪܘܝܬܐ (√ ܐܪܐ?) Krippe | manger.

ܐܘܪܫܠܡ (*vel* ܐܘܪܝܫܠܡ), Jerusalem.

ܐܙܠ § 48, g, 1 gehen | go. *Part.* nützlich sein | serve.

ܐܚܐ § 32, *m.* Bruder | brother. ‖ ܚܬܐ *f.* Schwester | sister ‖ ܐܚܘܬܐ *f.* brüderliche Liebe, bes. als Anrede | brotherly, love, "brethren".

ܐܚܕ, *impf. u,* nehmen, annehmen, halten | take, accept, hold. *Ethp.* festgehalten werden | be retained. *Aph.* ergreifen lassen | cause to seize. ‖ ܐܚܝܕ *pass. et act.* ‖ ܐܘܚܕܢܐ Besitz, Gewalt | possession, power.

[ܐܚܪ] ܐܬܐܚܪ zurückgelassen, übrig sein | be left. ‖ ܐܬܘܚܪ verweilen | remain. ‖ ܐܚܪܝ, ܐܚܪܝܐ, *f.* ܐܚܪܝܬܐ; *pl.* ܐܚܪܝܐ, ܐܚܪܝܬܐ der letzte | last. ‖ ܐܚܪܝܬ *st. const.* (*sc.* ܚܪܬܐ) = *adverb.* ‖ ܐܚܪܢ, ܐܚܪܢܐ, *f.* ܐܚܪܬܐ; *pl.* ܐܚܪܢܝܢ, ܐܚܪܢܐ, ܐܚܪܢܝܢ, ܐܚܪܢܝܬܐ, *etiam sine* ܐ *et in Sing. sine* ܐ *scribitur* ܚܪܢܐ, ein anderer | an other. *Adv.* ܐܚܪܢܝܬ

et ܐܚܪܢܐܝܬ im Gegenteil | on the contrary. || ܚܪܬܐ *f., st. cstr.* ܚܪܬ das Ende | end. || ܥܕܡܐ ܠܚܪܬܐ bis zuletzt | up to the last moment.

ܐܝܬܐ *v.* ܐܬܐ; ܐܝܬܐ *v.* ܐܝܬܝܐ.

ܐܝܙܓܕܐ, *etiam sine* ܝ, pers., Bote | messenger.

ܐܝܟ (āχ) wie, gemäss | as, according to. || ܐܝܟ ܕ, ܐܝܟ ܡܢ ܕ *conj.* wie | as. || ܐܝܟ ܗܢܐ, wie dieser, ein solcher | such. || ܐܝܟ ܗܟܢ, auf solche Weise | in such a way. || ܐܝܟܘܬ, *cum Suff.*, wie | like. (Cf. G. Hoffmann, ZDMG 32, 753.) ܐܟܙܢܐ auf solche Weise, z. B. | in such a way, *e.g.* || ܐܟܚܕܐ zugleich | together. || ܐܟܡܐ nachdem, entsprechend | according to, corresponding to.

ܐܝܟܐ wo? | where? || ܐܝܟܘ = ܐܝܟܐ ܗܘ wo ist (er)? | where is (he)? || ܡܢ ܐܝܟܐ woher? | whence? || ܐܝܟܢ, ܐܝܟܢܐ auf welche Weise? | in what way? *cum.* ܕ *relative.*

ܐܝܠܢ v. ܐܝܠܢܐ. ܐܝܠ h. אֵל § 3.

ܐܝܠܢ, ܐܝܠܢܐ *m.* Baum | tree.

ܐܝܢ, ܐܝܢ wahrhaftig, gewiss | truly, certainly.

ܐܝܢܐ § 21 wer? | who? || ܐܝܢܐ ܕ § 22.

ܐܝܩܐ *etiam* ܐܝܩܝ, εἰχῆ.

ܐܝܪܣ v. ܗܪܣ.

ܐܝܬ es ist, sind | there is, are; hebr. יֵשׁ. || ܐܝܬ ܗܘܐ es war | there was. || ܐܝܬ ܠܝ ich habe | I have. || ܐܝܬܝ etc. ich bin | I am. || ܠܝܬ = ܐܝܬܝܗ ܠܐ es ist nicht | it is not. || ܐܝܬܘܬܐ *f.* das Wesen | being, existence.

ܐܟܕܢܐ *f., pl.* ܐܟܕܢ̈ܐ ἔχιδνα.

ܐܡܪ .v ܐܡܪܟ, ܐܡܪܢܟ, ܐܡܪ.

ܐܟܠ *impf. u,* § 41 essen| eat. || ܐܘܟܠܬܐ § 19, a. || ܡܐܟܘܠܬܐ
f. Speise, Lebensunterhalt | food, victuals.

ܐܟܡ *impf. u,* schwarz sein | be black. *Aph.* schwärzen |
make black. *Part. pass.* ܡܘܟܡ geschwärzt | blackened.
ܐܘܟܡܐ, ܐܘܟܡܬܐ schwarz | black.

ܐܡܟܐ ܐܡܪ .v .: ܐܟܣܢܝܐ, ܐܟܣܢܝܐ ξένος.

ܐܟܦ, *a,* § 41 sorgen | attend to.

ܐܟܪܐ § 25 Bauer | peasant.

ܐܟܬܐ *m.* Zorn, Ärger | wrath, vexation.

ܐܢ—ܐܠܐ wenn, ܐ nicht; aber, sondern | if not, but. (Cf.
ἀλλά.) || ܐܢ ܠܐ wenn nicht, nach einer Negation | if
not (after a negation) ܐܠܐ *v.* ܐܢ.

ܐܠܗ, ܐܠܗܐ *m.* Gott| God. || ܐܠܗܝ göttlich | divine. || ܐܠܗܘܬܐ
f. Gottheit | divinity.

ܐܠܡ § 41 Zorn halten | keep his anger.

ܐܠܥܐ *f., pl.* ܐܠܥܐ, ܐܠܥܐ h. אֵלָע § 14, b Rippe | rib.

ܐܠܦ, ܝܠܦ et ܐܠܦ ܝܠܦ, *impf.* ܢܐܠܦ lernen | learn. *Pael.*
lehren|teach. || ܝܠܝܦ gelehrt | learned. ܡܠܦܢܐ Lehrer |
teacher. || ܡܠܦܢܘܬܐ Gelehrsamkeit | learning. || ܝܘܠܦܢܐ
§ 25, 4, b 1 Lehre | doctrine.

ܐܠܦ 1000, § 33, d. *St. emph. sg. scribit* Nöld. ܐܠܦܐ (k.);
pro ܐܠܦܐ *editio americana* Apoc. 6, 11; 7, 1—4;
14, 1 (19, 18) ܐܠܦܝܐ.

ܐܠܦܐ *f.* § 17 *b* Schiff | ship.

ܐܠܨ, *impf.* *u*, drängen, drücken | press, oppress. || ܗܘܐ ܠܨ es war nötig | it was necessary. || ܐܘܠܨܢܐ *m.* Bedrängnis, Not | oppression, calamity.

ܐܡܐ *f.* Mutter | mother. § 32.

ܐܡܝܢ (ܐܡܢ) beständig | constant. (*Etiam* = ἀμήν.) *Adv.* ܐܡܝܢܐܝܬ. || ܐܘܡܢܐ Handwerker | artisan. || ܐܘܡܢܘܬܐ Handwerk, Kunst | trade, art. *Aph.* ܐܗܡܢ, הֶאֱמִין glauben | believe. || ܗܝܡܢܘܬܐ Glaube | faith. || ܡܗܝܡܢܐ, *f.* ܡܗܝܡܢܬܐ gläubig, treu | faithful, true.

ܐܡܪ, *impf.* *a*, sprechen | speak. || ܡܐܡܪܐ, *pl.* ܡܐܡܪܐ *m.* Wort, Predigt, Abhandlung | word, sermon, treatise.

ܐܡܪܐ *m.* Lamm | lamb.

ܐܡܬܝ wann? | when?

ܐܢ wenn | if. || ܐܢ ܗܘ ?, ܐܢ ܕܝܢ ? wenn aber | but if. || ܐܠܘ häufig in nicht erfüllten Bedingungssätzen (often for conditions not likely to be fulfilled).

ܐܢܐ, ܐܢܐ ich | I. *Pl.* ܚܢܢ wir | we. § 19.

ܐܢܕܝܩܛܝܘܢܐ *f.* ἰνδικτιῶνα, indictio.

ܐܢܫ, ܐܢܫ v. ܗܘ, ܗܘ.

ܐܢܫ, ܐܢܫܐ *m.* Mensch, ursprünglich kollektiv Menschheit | man, originally mankind || der einzelne | the single. ܐܢܫܐ, ܐܢܫܝܢ, *pl.* ܐܢܫܘܬܐ; *pl.* ܐܢܫܝ einige | some. || ܐܢܫܝ menschlich | human. || ܐܢܫܘܬܐ Menschennatur | human nature. || ܬܩܢ v. ܐܬܩܢ.

ܐܢܬ *m.*; ܐܢܬܝ *f.* du | thou. || ܐܢܬܘܢ *m.* ܐܢܬܝܢ ihr | ye. § 19.

ܐܢܬܬܐ *f.* Frau | woman. § 32.

ܐܣܝ, *Pael.* ܐܣܝ heilen | cure. || ܐܣܝܘܬܐ Heilkunst, Arzenei |
medicine. *Pl. plerumque* ܐܣܘܬܐ.

ܐܣܛܕܝܘܢ *m.*, *pl*, ܐܣܛܕܝܘ̈, ܐܣܛܕܝܘܬܐ τὸ στάδιον.

ܐܣܛܘܢ, ܐܣܛܘܢܐ *m.* στύλος.

ܐܣܛܪܛܝܘܛܐ ὁ στρατιώτης.

ܐܣܦܝܪܐ *f.*, *pl.* ܐܣܦܩܐ ἡ σφαῖρα.

ܐܣܪ *impf.* *u* binden | bind. || ܐܣܝܪܐ ܒܝܬ Gefängnis | prison. ||
ܐܣܪܐ *m.* § 25 Band | bond.

ܐܟܣܦ doppelt | double; v. ܟܣܦ.

ܐܦ auch, sogar | too, even. || ܐܦܠܐ auch nicht, und nicht |
neither.

ܐܦܐ, ܐܦܐ *f.*, *pl. tant.* Gesicht, Oberfläche, Gestalt | face,
surface, figure.

ܐܦܪܢ (*pers.*) *plerumque Plur.* Schloss, Burg | castle,
fortress, tower.

ܐܦܣܩܘܦܐ, ܐܦܣܩܦܐ *m.* ὁ ἐπίσκοπος. || ܐܦܣܩܘܦܘܬܐ Bischofs-
würde | bishopric.

ܐܦܪܣܢܐ Hinterhalt | ambush v. ܨܪܒ.

ܐܨܪܐ v. ܨܪܝ.

ܐܨܐ, ܐܨܝ v. ܝܨܐ.

ܐܘܪܚܐ, ܐܘܪܚܐ *f.*, *pl.* ܐܘܪܚܬܐ Weg | way.

ܐܘܪܚܐ v. ܐܘ.

ܐܪܝܐ *m. pl.* ܐܪܝܘܬܐ Löwe | lion.

ܐܪܡܠܬܐ *f.* Witwe | widow.

ܐܪܥܐ, ܐܪܥܐ *f.*, *pl.* ܐܪܥܬܐ Erde, Land | earth, country. ||
ܐܪܥܢܝ irdisch | earthly.

ܐܪܥ *impf. u* (Lag. Semit. 1, 26) begegnen | meet. ‖ ܐܘܪܥ, *cum* ܠ *et Suff.* entgegen | to meet.

ܐܪܬܡܚܐ *v.* ܪܬܡ; ܐܘܪܚܐ *v.* ܪܚܩ.

ܐܪܬܘܕܘܟܣܐ, *f.* ܐܪܬܘܕܘܟܣܝܬܐ ὀρθόδοξος.

ܐܫܕ, *impf. u*, ausgiessen, vergiessen | pour out, shed.

ܐܫܬܡ *v.* ܫܡܥ.

ܐܬܐ, § 48 *d* 2 kommen, ankommen | come, arrive. *Aph.* bringen, führen | bring, lead. ‖ ܡܬܝܬܐ, ܡܐܬܝܬܐ Ankunft | arrival.

ܐܬܐ Zeichen | sign, token s. p. 134.

ܐܬܪܐ, ܐܬܪܐ *m.* Ort, Gegend | place, region. *Pl.* ܐܬܪܘܬܐ. ‖ ܒܬܪ *praep.* nach | after (§ 49, *h*) ܡܢ ܒܬܪ ܒܬܪ *et* ܡܢ ܒܬܪ; ܒܬܪܟܢ später | later. Cf. de Lag. Mitth. 1, 77.

ܒ *bith.*

ܒ *praep. in*, von Ort, Zeit, Zustand, Ursache, Instrument | in (*prepos.* denoting place, time, circumstance, reason, instrument).

ܒܐܪܐ, ܒܐܪܐ *h.* בְּאֵר, φρέαρ (?) Brunnen, Cisterne | well, cistern.

ܒܐܫ, *impf.* ܢܒܐܫ schlecht sein | be bad. *Ethpe.* ܐܬܒܐܫ, (ܐܬܒܐܫ) *nestor.* ܒܐܫ ܠܝ, *cum* ܠ es missfiel ihm | it displeased him. ‖ ܒܝܫ böse | bad, wrong. ‖ ܡܒܐܫ etwas Schlechtes | something wrong. ‖ ܒܝܫܬܐ Verbrechen, Unheil | crime, mischief. ‖ ܒܝܫܘܬܐ *f.* Schlechtigkeit | wickedness. ‖ ܒܝܫܐ § 6 arm | poor.

ܚܨܦܐ p. 27 *puerulus; pupilla.*

ܨܡܪ (*u*) suchen, untersuchen | seek, investigate. *Pa.* be-
zeichnen | mean.

ܨܪ (*u*) *pa.* zerstreuen | disperse. *Ethpa.* zerstreut werden |
be dispersed.

ܨܡܘܬܐ h. בַּהֲמוֹת.

ܒܗܬ *impf. a* sich schämen | be ashamed. ‖ ܒܗܬܬܐ *f.*
Schande | disgrace.

ܒܗܘ h. בָּהוּ.

(ܨܚ *vel* ܨܚܝ) *pa.* ܨܚ erklären | explain. *Ethpa.* ver-
stehen | understand. ‖ ܨܘܚܐ Erklärung | explanation.

ܥܬܟ, ܨܝܬ, *contr.* ܨܝܕ zwischen | between. *Plerumque
sequente* ܠ.

ܩܘܒܠܣܐ, *alter cod.* ܩܘܒܠܣܐ, Scholion ܪܘܦܐ, = ῥόπαλός,
ܨܘܒܐ, βάκλος, baculus.

ܒܙ *impf. u* plündern | plunder. *Ethpe.* geplündert, in die
Gefangenschaft geführt werden | be robbed, be led
into captivity. ‖ ܒܙܬܐ *f.* Beute | prey.

ܒܛܠ *impf. a,* müssig sein, Zeit haben | be idle, have
time. *Ethpe. cum* ܠ eifrig sein | be busy. *Pa.* auf-
hören machen, abschaffen | stop, abolish. ‖ ܒܛܝܠܐ
ἀργία, Trägheit | idleness. ‖ ܡܒܛܠܢܟ verhindernd |
being a hindrance.

ܒܛܡܬܐ *f.* Terebinthus. *Pl.* ܒܛܡܐ die Frucht derselben |
its fruit.

ܒܛܢ *impf. a* empfangen, schwanger werden | conceive,

be pregnant. *Ethpe.* empfangen werden | be conceived. || ܒܛܢܐ Empfängnis | conception.

ܒܝܐ § 40*b*. 47, 5 trösten | comfort.

ܒܝ̈ܢܬ, ܒܝܢܬ v. ܒܝܢ.

ܒܝܥܬܐ *pl.* ܒܝ̈ܥܐ *et* ܒܝ̈ܥܬܐ Ei u. Eiförmiges, z. B. (Hirn-) Schädel | egg, and what looks like an egg, *e.g.* skull. (Bar Ali ܒܪ̈ܥܬܐ *cum* R).

ܒܝܬ v. ܒܘܬ.

ܒܝܬܐ cf. § 32, Haus, Ort, Stätte | house, place. || ܒܝܬ ܦܚܪ̈ܐ Töpferwerkstätte | pottery. || ܒܝܬ ܩܒܘܪܐ u. ܒ' ܩܒܘܪܐ Grabstätte | cemetery.

ܒܟܐ weinen | weep. || ܒܟܝܬܐ das Weinen | weeping.

ܒܟܝܪܐ, *f.* ܒܟܝܪܬܐ frühreif | premature. || ܒܟܝܪܬ ܦܐܪ̈ܐ zuerst reif | what ripens first. || ܒܘܟܪܐ, *pl.* ܒܘ̈ܟܪܐ Erstling | firstling.

ܒܠܥ *impf. a*, verschlingen, (Schläge) erleiden | swallow, suffer (blows). *Ethpa.* verzehrt werden | be devoured.

ܒܢܐ bauen | build. *Ethpe.* errichtet werden | be constructed. || ܒܢܝܢܐ *m.* Gebäude | building.

ܒܢܝܐ, ܒܢ̈ܝܐ v. ܒܪ.

ܒܣܡ *impf. a,* süss sein, sich ergötzen | be sweet, rejoice. || ܒܣܡܐ Wohlgeruch, Salbe | perfume, ointment (*st. abs. et. cstr. ap. PSm. bis* ܒܣܡ). || ܒܣܝܡ süss, wohlwollend | sweet, benevolent. || ܒܣܝܡܘܬܐ Annehmlichkeit | agreeableness.

ܒܣܪ, ܒܣܪܐ, *pl.* ܒܣܪ̈ܐ *et* ܒܣܪ̈ܘܬܐ Fleisch | meat.

ܒܣܬܪ v. ܣܬܪ.

ܒܥܐ suchen, fordern, bitten | seek, demand, request.‖ ܒܥܬܐ, ܒܥܘܬܐ *f.* Bitte | request. ‖ ܒܥܬܐ *f.* das Suchen, die Frage | petition, question.

ܒܥܠ, ܒܥܠܐ Herr, Besitzer | lord, owner. ‖ ܒܥܠܕܒܒܐ, *pl.* ܒܥܠܕܒܒܐ Feind | enemy.‖ ܒܥܠܕܒܒܘܬܐ Feindschaft | enmity.‖ ܒܥܠܕܝܢܐ Gegner vor Gericht | opponent (in court).

ܒܥܝܪܐ *coll.*, h. בְּעִיר *plerumque f.*, das Vieh | cattle.

ܒܨܐ suchen, fragen | investigate, ask.

ܒܨܪ vermindern | diminish.‖ ܒܨܝܪ *adj. et adv.* abnehmend, weniger | diminishing, less. ‖ ܒܨܝܪ ܩܠܝܠ beinahe | about.

ܒܪܐ *v.* ܒܪܝ.

ܒܪ, ܒܪܐ *m.* das unbebaute Feld | uncultivated field. ‖ ܠܒܪ draussen | out of doors. ‖ ܡܢ ܠܒܪ ausser | without.

ܒܪ, ܒܪ § 32. Der Sohn | son. In Zusammensetzungen (in composition) ܒܪܢܫܐ *v.* ܐܢܫ Mensch | man.‖ ܒܪ ܬܘܪܐ Glacis (ob zum vorhergehenden ܒܪ? if it does not belong to the preceding ܒܪ).‖ ܒܪ ܫܥܬܐ zur Stunde, sogleich | at once. ‖ ܒܪܬܐ Tochter | daughter. § 32. ‖ ܒܪܬ ܩܠܐ, בַּת קוֹל Wort | voice.‖ *Pl.* ܒܪܬ ܩܠܐ Worte, Rede | words, speech.

ܒܪܐ schaffen, machen | create, make. *Ethpe.* geschaffen werden | be created.‖ ܒܪܝܬܐ *f.* Schöpfung | creation. *Pl.* ܒܪܝܬܐ Creaturen | creatures. ‖ ܒܪܘܝܐ § 25. Schöpfer | creator.

ܒܪܒܪܝܐ βάρβαρος.

ܒܪܘܠܐ m., in pl. plerumque f. beryllus. ‖ ܒܪܘܠܚܐ, h. בְּדֹלַח Perle | pearl.

ܒܪܟ impf. u, sich beugen, niederknien | bow down, kneel. ‖ܒܪܝܟ gesegnet | blessed. Pa. segnen | bless. Part. pass. ܡܒܪܟ gesegnet | blessed. ‖ ܒܘܪܟܬܐ f. Segen | blessing.

ܒܪܡ aber, im Gegenteil | but, on the contrary.

ܒܪܩ (impf. u) blitzen | lighten. Aph. strahlen | radiate.‖ ܒܪܩܐ m. Blitz | lightning.

ܒܪܬܐ v. ܒܪ.

ܒܫܠ reifen, kochen | ripen, boil. ‖ ܒܫܝܠܐ gekochte Speise | meat, ἔδεσμα.

ܒܬܐ v. ܒܝܬܐ sub ܒܬ.

ܒܬܘܠܬܐ f. Jungfrau | virgin. ‖ ܒܬܘܠܘܬܐ Jungfräulichkeit| virginity.

ܒܬܪ v. ܐܬܪ.

ܓ ܓܡܠ

ܐܝܐ, ܐܝܐ glänzend, herrlich | splendid, glorious.

ܓܐܪܐ § 3, m. Pfeil | arrow (V ܓܪ).

ܓܒ v. ܓܒܐ.

ܓܙܒܪܐ m. Gerichtsdiener | officer.

ܓܒܠ impf. u bilden, formen | form, shape. Ethpe. pass.

ܓܒܪ, ܓܒܪܐ Mann | man, v. ܣܠܡ. ܐܬܓܒܪ § 38 (BH. Gr. 1, 48).

ܓܓܘܠܬܐ Γολγοθã.

ܓܕܦ Pa. schmähen, lästern|revile, blaspheme.Ethpa.pass.

ܓ݂ܕ݂ܰܫ *impf. a,* sich treffen, ereignen (unpersönl.) | chance, happen.

ܓܺܗܰܢܳܐ *et* ܓܺܗܰܢܳܐ *f.* γέεννα.

ܓܰܘ, ܓܰܘܳܐ Mitte, das Innere | middle, interior. ‖ ܒܓܰܘ inner-halb | within. ‖ ܠܓܰܘ hinein | in, inwards.

(ܓܘܒ) *Aph.* antworten | answer; ἀποκριθῆναι.

ܓܽܘܒܳܐ *m. et* ܓܽܘܒܳܐ *f.* Cisterne | cistern. Cf. de Lagarde, Mittheilungen 2, 354 A. 2.

ܓܰܝܳܣܳܐ Räuber, Dieb | robber, thief.

ܓܳܪ ehebrechen | commit adultery, *c. acc.* ‖ ܓܰܘܪܳܐ Ehe-bruch | adultery.

ܓܙܽܘܪܬܳܐ *f.* Entscheidung | decision, ἀπόφασις.

ܓܶܝܪ γάρ nemlich | namely, for. (Arab. جَيْرِ ?).

ܓܺܝܓܠܳܐ Kreis, Rad | circle, wheel.

ܓܠܳܐ offenbaren, entdecken | reveal, discover. *Ethpe. pass.* *Pa.* aufdecken | uncover. ‖ ܓܶܠܝܳܢܳܐ (ܓܶܠܝܳܢܳܐ § 25) Offenbarung | revelation. ‖ ܓܰܠܝܳܐܝܺܬ öffentlich | pub-licly. ‖ ܡܶܬ݂ܓܰܠܝܳܢܽܘܬ݂ܳܐ Offenbarung | revelation.

ܓܠܽܘܣܩܡܳܐ τὸ γλωσσόκομον (*PSm.* ܩܽܘܡܳܐ—).

ܓܠܰܙ *impf. u,* wegnehmen, berauben | take away, rob. ‖ ܓܠܺܝܙܽܘܬ݂ܳܐ Beraubung | robbery.

ܓܠܰܦ, *impf. u,* aushauen | hew out, carve. ‖ ܓܠܺܝܦܳܐ γλυπτά. ‖ ܓܠܳܦܳܐ Bildhauerkunst | sculpture.

ܓܡܰܪ *impf. u,* vollenden | finish. *Impf. a,* vollendet sein | be complete. ‖ ܥܳܒ݂ܕܰܝ̈ ܨܶܒ݂ܝܳܢܳܐ die den Willen thun | who

do the will. || ܚܡܝܠ völlig, vollständig | completely.||
ܚܡܝܡ vollkommen | perfect.

ܓܒܢ et ܓܒܒ st. abs. et cstr., ܓܢܒܐ, pl. ܓܢ̈ܒܐ die Seite|
side. || ܓܢܒ ܥܠ neben | by the side of.

ܓܢܒܪܐ (ܓܒܘܪ); ܓܢܒܪ̈ܐ kräftig | strong.

(ܓܢܙ) ܓܢܝܙ verborgen, geheim | hidden, secret.

ܓܢܣ, ܓܢܣܐ τὸ γένος.

ܓܥܐ ausspeien | spit out. Ethpe. pass.

ܓܥܐ schreien | cry. || ܓܥܬܐ, f. Geschrei | cry.

ܓܥܠ Af. zuteilen, anvertrauen | commit to, entrust.

ܓܥܪ, impf. u, schelten | scold.

ܓܪܡܐ, pl. ܓܪ̈ܡ Ellen | cubits (= ܓܪ̈ܡ ?).

ܓܪܒܐ § 8, m. Aussatz | leprosy || ܓܪܒ, ܓܪܒܐ aussätzig|
leprous.

ܓܪܒܝܐ, ܓܪܒܝܐ Nord (Wind u. Gegend) | North (of wind &
region). ||ܓܪܒܝܝܐ nördlich | northern. | Pro ܓܪܒܝ أخذ?
leg. vid. ܪܓܒ?.

ܓܪܡܐ, ܓܪ̈ܡܐ m. Knochen | bone.

ܓܫܡܐ, ܓܫ̈ܡܐ m. Leib, Körper | body.

ܓܫܦ, impf. u, berühren, betrachten | touch, consider.

ܕ (ܕ?) Particula relationis, genitivi; Conjunctio weil |
because.

ܕܐܒܐ؟ h. זְאֵב § 25 Wolf | wolf.

Nestle.

ܕܒܚ, *impf. u,* opfern | sacrifice. || ܕܒܚܐ *m.* Opfer | sacrifice. ||
ܡܕܒܚܐ *m.* Altar | altar.

ܕܒܩ anhäugen | cleave to. *Pa.* verbinden | join.

ܕܒܪ, *impf. a,* führen, leiten | lead, guide. *Ethpe. pass.;*
Pa. leiten, regieren | guide, rule. || ܕܒܪܐ Feld | field. ||
ܡܕܒܪܐ Wüste | desert. || ܕܘܒܪܐ Lebensführung | way
of living. || ܡܕܒܪܢܐ Leiter, Vorsteher | leader, ruler. |
ܡܕܒܪܢܘܬܐ die (Heils-)Ökonomie | economy, plan (of
salvation). || ܕܒܝܪ (ܕܒܝܪ ?) = h. דְּבִיר Allerheiligstes |
the holy of holies. || ܕܒܘܪܝܬܐ *f.* Biene | bee.

ܕܓܠ *Pa.* lügen | lie || ܕܓܠ lügnerisch | lying, false. ||
ܕܓܠܘܬܐ Lüge | falsehood.

ܕܗܒ, ܕܗܒܐ *m.* Gold | gold. || ܡܕܗܒ *vel* ܡܕܗܒ *part.*
pass. pa. vel af. vergoldet | gilt.

ܕܘܟ, ܕܘܟܐ, *st. cstr.* ܕܘܟܬ, *emph.* ܕܘܟܬܐ Ort | place (δοχεῖον?
vel ܕܘ ?) *pl.* ܕܘܟܝܬܐ, ܕܘܟܬܐ.

ܕܢ, *impf.* ܢܕܘܢ, richten | judge. || ܕܝܢܐ Gericht | court. ||
ܕܝܢܐ Richter | judge. || ܡܕܝܢܬܐ, ܡܕܝܢܬܐ, *st. cstr.* ܡܕܝܢܬ
Stadt | town.

ܕܘܨ; *part.* ܕܐܨ, *f.* ܕܝܨܐ jubeln | rejoice.

ܕܪ, ܕܪܐ *m.* = h. דּוֹר Generation | generation.

ܕܫ mit Füssen treten | tread down. *Ethpe. pass.*

ܕܚܠ, *impf. a,* fürchten | fear. || ܕܚܝܠ fürchtend u. zu
fürchten | fearing & formidable. || ܕܚܠܐ, ܕܚܠܬܐ *f.*
Furcht, Verehrung, Gegenstand der Verehrung |
fear, devotion, object of worship. *Pl.* ܕܚܠܬܐ.

ܕܝ݂ܘ݂ܐ *m. pers.* Dämon | demon, *pl.* ܕܝ݂ܘ݂ܐ.

ܕܝ݂ *c. suff. ex* ܝ *et* ܠ § 23.

ܕܶܝܢ δὲ, aber, nämlich | but, for.

ܕܝ݂ܬܩ̈ܣ *una formarum pluralis vocis* ܕܝ݂ܬܩ̈ܣ διαϑηκη.

ܕܟܐ, ܕܟ݂ܐ rein sein | be pure. || *Part. pass.* ܕܟ݂ܐ rein | pure.

ܕܟ݂ܪ *Ethpe.* gedenken | remember. || ܕܘ݂ܟ݂ܪܢܐ Gedächtnis | memory. || ܕܟ݂ܪܐ, ܕܶܟ݂ܪܐ Männchen | male.

ܕܘ݂ܟ݂ܠܐ *m.* Scheidung | divorce.

ܕܟ݂ܡܐ *v.* ܕܡܟ݂.

ܕܡܐ, ܕܡܐ *m.* Blut | blood (*pl.* ܕܡܐ̈).

ܕܡܐ ähnlich sein | be like. *Ethpe.* ähnlich gemacht werden | be made alike. *Pa.* vergleichen, phantasiren | compare, rave. || ܕܡܘ݂ܬܐ Bild | likeness. || ܗܟܢ ܒܗ ܒܕܡܘ݂ܬܐ in eben dieser Weise | in the very same way.

ܕܡܟ݂, *impf. a,* schlafen | sleep.

ܕܡܥܬܐ *f. pl.* ܕܡ̈ܥܐ Thränen | tears.

ܕܡܪ *Ethpa.* sich wundern | wonder. || ܬܕܡܘ݂ܪܬܐ2 *f. pl.* ܬܕܡ̈ܪܬܐ2 Wunder | miracle.

ܕܢܚ, *impf. a,* aufgehen | rise. *Af.* aufgehen lassen | cause to rise, raise. || ܕܢ̣ܚܐ *m.* Osten, Licht, Erscheinung | east, light, epiphany. || ܕܢ̣ܚܐ, ܕܡܕܢ̣ܚܐ *m.* Osten | east.

ܕܘ݂ܥܬܐ *m.* Schweiss | sweat.

ܕܪ̈ܕܪܐ *pl.* ܕܪ̈ܕܪܐ Diesteln | thistles

ܕܪ݂ܟ, *impf. u,* eintreten | enter. *Ethpe.* begriffen werden | be understood. || ܡܬܕܪ̈ܟܢܘ݂ܬܐ Begreifbarkeit | comprehension. || ܕܪܘ݂ܟܬܐ *f.* παλλακή.

ܟ*

ܐܠܦ *impf. u,* üben, lehren | practice, teach. *Part. pass.*
Pa. ܡܐܠܦ geübt, erfahren | practised, experienced.

--

ܗܐ *particula demonstrativa,* siehe, hier | lo, here. || ܗܘ *m.,*
ܗܝ *f., pl. m.* ܗܢܘܢ, ܗܢܝܢ *Pron.* § 20. || ܗܝܕܝܢ damals |
then. || ܗܟܘܬ ebenso, ähnlich | likewise, similarly. ||
ܗܟܢܐ daher, nun | therefore. || ܗܟܢ, ܗܟܢܐ auf diese
Weise, so | in this way, thus. || ܗܢ, ܗܢܐ *m.* dieser | this.
ܗܕܐ *f., pl.* ܗܠܝܢ § 20. || ܗܪܟܐ hier | here. || ܗܫܐ (v. ܫܥܐ)
zu dieser Zeit | at this time.

(ܗܓܐ) ܗܓܝܢܐ *m.* Betrachtung | consideration.

ܗܓܓܐ *m.* Erscheinung, Phantasie | apparition, fancy.
ܗܓܓܝ phantastisch | fantastical.

ܗܕܝ *Pa.* führen, leiten | guide, lead.

ܗܕܝܘܛܐ ἰδιώτης, Laie | layman.

ܗܕܡܐ *m.* Glied | member.

ܗܕܝܪ glänzend, herrlich | splendid, glorious.

ܗܘ, ܗܝ v. ܗܐ.

ܗܘ, ܗܝ; ܗܢܘܢ, ܗܢܝܢ v. § 19.

ܗܘܐ sein, werden | be, become. § 48 b.

ܗܘܢ, ܗܘܢܐ *m.* Verstand, Einsicht | understanding, in-
telligence. *denom. Pa. part. pass.* einsichtig | in-
telligent, judicious.

ܗܘܦܬܣܣ ὑπόθεσις, *sg. & pl.*

ܗܘܦܘܡܢܡܛܐ ὑπομνήματα; *vid.* ܐܘܦ.

ܗܝ v. ܗܘ; ܗܝ, ܗܝܡܢ v. ܐܗ.

ܗܝܟܠ, ܗܝܟܠܐ *m.* Tempel | temple.

ܗܝܡܢ, ܗܝܡܢܘܬܐ v. ܐܡܢ.

ܗܟܢܐ, ܗܟܢܐ, ܗܟܢ v. ܐܗ.

ܗܠܠ, h. הִלֵּל *Pa.* loben | praise. || *Aph.* ܐܗܠ verspotten, verlachen | deride, mock.

ܗܠܟ *Pa.* gehen | go.

(ܗܡܐ) *Aph.* abwenden (die Augen) | turn away (the eyes).

ܗܢ, ܗܢܐ; ܗܢܘܢ, ܗܢܝܢ v. ܐܗ; ܗܢܘܢ, ܗܢܝܢ v. ܗܘ.

ܗܦܟ, *impf.* *u,* wenden, häufiger *intrans.* sich wenden | turn, more frequently *intrans.* *Ethpe.* gewendet werden | be turned. *Ethpa.* umhergetrieben sein | be driven about, be agitated.

ܗܪܘܡܐ, *pl.* ܗܪܘܡܐ τὸ ἄρωμα.

ܗܪܛܝܩܘ, *et* ܗܪܛܝܩܘ αἱρετικοί.

ܗܪܟܐ, ܗܪܟܐ v. ܐܗ.

ܘ wau

ܘ *copula* und, sogar | and, even. § 49 b.

ܙܘܕ *Pa.* versammeln, zusammenkommen | assemble, meet. § 44 a. || ܥܕܬܐ, *st. c.* ܥܕܬ, *pl.* ܥܕܬܐ h. עֵדָה Versammlung, Kirche | congregation, church.

ܙ zain

ܙܒܢ, ܙܒܢܐ *m.* Zeit | time. || ܙܒܢܬܐ einmal | once. || ܙܒܢܝܢ... ܙܒܢܝܢ bald ... bald | sometimes ... sometimes. || *Pl.*

ܙܒ̈ܢܝܢ Fälle | cases. || *F.* ܙܒܢܐ, ܙܒܢܬܐ Zeit | time. || *Pl.* ܙܒ̈ܢܐ.

ܙܓ klingeln | ring the bell.

(ܙܕܩ) *Part.* ܙܕܩ *et f.* ܙܕܩܐ es geziemt sich | it is becoming. || ܙܕܩܐ ܗܘܬ es hätte sich geziemt | it would have been becoming. || ܙܕܩܐ *m.* Gerechtigkeit | justice. || ܙܕܩܬܐ *f.* Almosen | alms. || ܙܕܝܩ gerecht | just.

ܙܗܐ lauter, trefflich | pure, excellent. || *Adv.* ܙܗܝܐܝܬ trefflich, züchtig | *adv.* in a pure and modest way.

ܙܗܪ *Pa.* ermahnen, warnen | advise, warn. || ܙܗܝܪܘܬܐ *f.* Vorsicht, Sorgfalt | prudence, care.

ܙܘܓܐ Joch, Paar | yoke, pair; ζυγόν, ζεῦγος. || *denom.* *Pa.* vereinigen | unite. || ܙܘܘܓܐ *m.* Verehlichung | marriage.

ܙܘܚܐ *m.* Prunk, Pomp | show, state.

ܙܥ bewegt werden | be moved. || *Ethpe.* erschüttert werden | be shaken. || ܙܘܥܐ *m.* Bewegung, Erdbeben | motion, earthquake.

ܙܘܦܐ § 3 h. אֵזוֹב, ὕσσωπος.

ܙܘܪܐ *m.* Faust | fist. || *Pl.* ܙܘܪ̈ܐ *et rarius* ܙܘܪ̈ܬܐ.

ܙܝܢܐ *m.* Waffen, Schmuck | arms, attire.

ܙܟܐ siegen, gerechtfertigt werden | conquer, be justified. || ܙܟܘܬܐ *f.* Sieg | victory. || ܙܟܝ, ܙܟܝܐ Sieger | conqueror. || ܙܟܝ *n. pr.* Zacchaeus.

(ܙܠܓ) *Aph.* glänzen, strahlen lassen | shine, radiate. || ܙܠܓܐ *m.* Strahl | ray.

ܙܘܡܐ *m.* ἦχος, Geräusch, Klingeln | noise, ringing. || ܡܙܡܙܡܐ (*deest apud* PSm) *et* ܡܙܡܙܡܢܘܬܐ *idem.*

ܙܡܢ *Pa.* einladen | invite. || ܙܡܝܢ eingeladen, bereitet | invited, prepared.

ܙܡܪ *impf. a et Pa.* singen, spielen | sing, play. || ܡܙܡܪܢܐ Psalmist | psalmist. || ܡܙܡܘܪܐ Psalm | psalm.

ܙܢ, ܙܢܐ *m.* Art, Weise | manner, way. *Pl.* ܙܢܝܢ, ܙܢ̈ܐ.

ܙܢܐ huren | commit fornication. || ܙܢܝܘܬܐ *f.* Hurerei | fornication.

ܙܥܩ, *impf. a.* schreien | cry. || ܡܙܥܩܢܘܬܐ *f.* Geschrei cry.

ܙܥܪ, *impf. a,* vermindert, klein sein | be small, diminished. || ܙܥܘܪ *m.*, ܙܥܘܪܐ, ܙܥܘܪܬܐ *f.* klein | small. || *Pl.* ܙܥܘܪܝܢ, ܙܥܘܪ̈ܢ, ܙܥܘܪ̈ܬܐ; ܡܙܥܘܪ̈ܬܐ in Kürze | briefly.

ܙܩܦ, *impf. u,* aufrichten, kreuzigen | erect, crucify. || *Ethpe.* gekreuzigt werden | be crucified. || ܙܩܝܦ 1. *part. pass.* gekreuzigt | crucified. || 2. *subst.* Kreuz | cross. || ܙܩܝܦܘܬܐ Kreuzigung | crucifixion. || ܙܩܘܦܐ Kreuziger | he who crucifies.

ܙܪܥ, *impf. u,* säen | sow. *Ethpe.* pass. || ܙܪܥ, ܙܪܥܐ *m.* Same | seed. || *Pl.* ܙܪ̈ܥܐ, ܙܪܥܘܢܐ Gemüse | seeds, vegetables.

ܙܩܬ, ܙܩܬܐ *f.* Faust | fist. *Pl.* ܙܩܝܢ; cf. ܙܘܪܐ.

ܚ

ܚܡܬܐ, *pl.* ܚܡ̈ܬܐ *m.* Glut, Gewalt, Angriff | violence, attack.

ܚܒܝܒ Geliebter, Freund | beloved, friend. || ܚܘܒܐ *m.* Liebe | love.

ܚܒܠ *Pa.* verderben | destroy. *Ethpa.* pass. ‖ ܡܬܚܒܠܢܐ, *f.*
ܠܐ ܡܬܚܒܠܢܘܬܐ verweslich | corruptible. ‖ ܠܐ ܡܬܚܒܠܢܘܬܐ
Unverweslichkeit | incorruption.

ܚܒܪ, ‖ ܚܒܪܐ Genosse | comrade. ‖ ܚܒܪܬܐ Gefährtin | com-
panion *f.*

ܚܒܫ, *impf.* u, einschliessen, zusammenhalten | enclose,
block up. ‖ ܚܒܘܫܝܐ Einschliessung, Belagerung | siege.

ܚܒܝܟܐ ἑλικτός, εἱλικιώδης.

ܚܕ *f.* ܚܕܐ 1, § 33. ܚܕ ܫܒܥܐ 7mal | seven times. ‖ ܐܟܚܕܐ
zusammen | together. ‖ ܡܚܕܐ (*rarius scribitur* ܡܢ
ܚܕܐ) sogleich | at once.

ܚܕܝ sich freuen | be glad. ‖ ܚܕܘܬܐ, ܚܕܘܬܐ *f.* Freude | joy.

ܚܕܝܐ *m.* Brust | breast. *Pl.* ܚܕܘܬܐ *et* ܚܕ̈ܝܬܐ.

ܚܕܪ, *impf.* u et a, umgeben | surround. ‖ ܚܕܪ̈ܝ *st. cstr. pl.*
praep. ringsum | round about. ‖ ܚܕܪܐ Umkreis,
Zirkel | circuit, circle.

ܚܕܬ *Pa.* erneuern | renew.

ܚܘܐ *Pa.* zeigen, beweisen | show, prove. ‖ ܬܚܘܝܬܐ *f.*
Beweis | argument. ‖ ܡܚܘܝܢܘܬܐ Beweiskraft, Beweis-
barkeit | force of argument.

ܚܘܝܐ *m., pl.* ܚܘܘܬܐ Schlange | serpent.

ܚܨ unterliegen | succumb. ‖ *Pa.* besiegen, verurteilen |
conquer, condemn.

ܚܕܝܐܝܬ heiter, freudig | gay, joyous *adv.*

ܚܤ sich erbarmen, schonen | have pity, spare. ‖ ܚܤ ܠܝ
ferne sei es von mir | far be it from me.

ܚܳܪ ansehen | look at.

ܚܶܘܳܪ weiss | white. *f.* ܚܶܘܳܪܬܳܐ ; ܚܶܘܳܪ̈ܝ ܦܰܪ̈ܨܘܦܳܐ λευκοφανεῖς.

ܚܙܳܐ sehen | see. ‖ *Ethpe.* erscheinen | appear. ‖ ܚܶܙܘܳܐ *m.* Ansehen, Gesicht, Erscheinung | look, face, appearance. ‖ ܚܙܳܝܳܐ *m.* Gesicht | sight. ‖ ܚܶܙܬܳܐ *f.* Erscheinung | apparition.

ܚܛܳܐ sündigen | sin. ‖ ܚܛܳܗܳܐ *m., pl.* ܚܛܳܗ̈ܶܐ Sünden | sins. ‖ ܚܛܺܝܬܳܐ *f. idem.* ohne Plural (no plur.).

ܚܛܰܦ, *impf. u,* wegraffen, berauben | take away, rob. *Ethpe.* pass. ܚܛܘܦܝܳܐ *Infinitiv.*

ܚܝܳܐ (§ 48 c.) leben | live. ‖ ܚܰܝ, ܚܰܝܳܐ, *f.* ܚܰܝܬܳܐ lebendig | living. ‖ *Subst.* ܚܰܝܬܳܐ *pl.* ܚܰܝ̈ܳܬܳܐ *f.* die Hebamme | midwife. ‖ ܚܰܝ̈ܶܝܢ, ܚܰܝ̈ܶܐ das Leben | life. (ܚܰܝ̈ܶܐ ܢܽܘܨܳܐ ܘܚܣܝܢܐ ?). ‖ ܚܰܝܘܬܳܐ *f.* 1) Lebenskraft | vigour. 2) Tier | animal. *St. cstr.* ܚܰܝܘܰܬ. *Pl.* ܚܰܝ̈ܘܳܬܳܐ (p. 32, n. 1). ‖ ܡܚܰܝܳܢܳܐ Erlöser | saviour. *f.* ܡܰܚܝܳܢܺܝܬܳܐ lebengebend | life-giving.

ܚܰܝܶܠ *Pa.* stärken | strengthen. *Ethpa.* pass. ‖ ܚܰܝܠ, ܚܰܝܠܳܐ *m.* Kraft | strength, force. *Pl.* ܚܰܝ̈ܠܶܐ *et saepius* ܚܰܝ̈ܠܘܳܬܳܐ Truppen | troops. ‖ ܚܰܝܠܬܳܢ stark, mächtig | strong, mighty (Zebaoth). ‖ ܡܚܺܝܠܘܬܳܐ *f.* Schwäche | weakness.

ܚܟܰܡ, *impf. a,* erkennen | recognise. ‖ ܚܶܟܡܬܳܐ, *st. cstr.* ܚܶܟܡܰܬ *f.* Weisheit, Erkenntnis | wisdom, knowledge. ‖ ܚܰܟܺܝܡ weis | wisc. ܚܰܟܺܝܡܳܐܺܝܬ *adv.*

ܚܠܳܒܳܐ (ܚܰܠܒ) *m.* Milch | milk.

ܚܠܐ, ܚܰܠܝܳܐ *f. emph.* ܚܰܠܺܝܬܳܐ; *pl.* ܚܰܠܝܺܢ, ܚܰܠ̈ܝܶܐ; ܚܰܠ̈ܝܳܢ, ܚܰܠ̈ܝܳܬܳܐ süss | sweet.

ܚܠܛ, *impf. u*, mischen | mix. *Pa.* einfügen | insert. ܚܠܝܛ vermischt, zusammenhängend | mixed, coherent.

ܚܠܝܡ gesund, kräftig, ganz | sound, vigorous, whole.

ܚܠܦ, *impf. u*, verändern | change. || ܚܠܦ *praep.* anstatt | instead. || ܐܫܬܚܠܦ verändern | change. || *Part. pass.* ܡܫܚܠܦ verschieden | various. || ܡܫܬܚܠܦܢܘܬܐ *f.* ἀλλοίωσις.

ܚܣܢ (*a* ܚܣܢ stark sein | be strong) stark machen, aushalten | strengthen, endure.

ܚܡܪܐ *m.* Wein | wine.

ܚܡܫ etc. 5, § 33.

ܚܢ, *impf.* ܢܚܘܢ, sich erbarmen | have mercy. *Ethpe.* ἐξιλεοῦσθαι, Barmherzigkeit erlangen | find mercy.

ܚܢܢ v. ܐܢܐ § 19.

ܚܢܦܐ *m.* unrein, Heide | unclean, heathen. || ܚܢܦܘܬܐ *f.* Unreinheit, Heidentum | uncleanness, heathendom.

ܚܣܝܐ, ܚܣܝܐ heilig | holy; ὅσιος; Bischof | bishop. *Pl.* ܚܣܝܐ.

ܚܣܕ *Pa.* beschimpfen | revile. || ܚܣܕܐ *m.* Schande, Schimpf | disgrace, insult. || (ܚܣܕܐ Gnade | grace.)

ܚܣܡ, *impf. u*, beneiden | envy (*c.* ܒ). || ܚܣܡܐ *m.* Neid | envy.

ܚܣܝܪ entbehrend | deficient. || ܚܣܝܪ ܝܬܝܪ mehr oder weniger, ungefähr | more or less, about.

ܚܦܐ *Pa.* verbergen, bedecken | conceal, cover. || ܬܚܦܝܬܐ *f.* Bedeckung | veil. || ܬܚܦܝܬܐ ܕܠܐ offen | openly.

ܚܦܛ *Pa.* den Eifer locken, ermahnen | exhort, admonish. ||

ܚܦܝܛ eifrig | diligent. *Adv.* ܚܦܝܛܐܝܬ. || ܚܦܝܛܘܬܐ *f.* Eifer | zeal. || ܡܚܦܛܢܘܬܐ *f.* Ermahnung | advice.

ܚܦܪ, *impf.* *u*, graben | dig.

ܚܨܐ spalten, abhauen, herausreissen | split, cut off, pluck out.

ܚܕܝ, ܚܕܝܐ *pl.* ܚܕܝܢ (חדין) *m.* Brust | breast.

ܚܨܘܕܐ *m.* Schnitter | reaper.

ܚܩܠ, ܚܩܠܐ *f.*, *pl.* ܚܩܠܬܐ Acker | field.

ܚܪܝܢܐ *m.* Streit | dispute, contest.

ܚܪܒ, *impf.* *u*, verwüsten | waste. || ܚܪܒ, *impf.* *a*, zerstört sein | be destroyed. || ܚܪܒܐ *f.* Schwert | sword. || ܚܘܪܒܐ *m.* Wüste, Zerstörung | wilderness, destruction.

ܚܪܕܘܢܐ *m.* Eidechse, Krokodil | lizard, crocodile.

ܚܪܝܐ, ܚܪܬܐ v. ܐܚܪ.

ܚܪܝܦܐܝܬ scharf, schnell | *adv.* sharp, swift.

ܚܫܐ *m.*, *pl.* ܚܫܐ Leiden | passion; πάθος.

ܚܫܒ, *impf.* *u*, denken, berechnen, schätzen | think, count, estimate. *Ethpe.* bei sich überlegen | deliberate. || ܚܫܝܒ bestimmt zu | appointed for. || ܚܘܫܒܐ Gedanke | thought. || ܡܚܫܒܬܐ, *pl.* ܡܚܫܒܬܐ *idem.*

ܚܘܫܚܐ *m.* Gebrauch | use.

ܚܫܘܟ, ܚܫܘܟܐ 1. *adj.* dunkel | dark. 2. *subst.* Finsternis | darkness.

ܡܚܫܘܠܐ *m.* Sturm, Wellen | tempest, waves.

ܚܬܝܬܐܝܬ sorgfältig, genau | *adv.* carefully, accurately.

ܚܬܐ v. ܐܚܐ.

ܚܬܡ, *impf.* u, versiegeln | seal. || ܚܵܬ݂ܡܵܐ *m.* Siegel, Zeichen | seal, token.

ܛ

ܛܸܒ݁ܵܐ, ܛܸܒ݂ܵܐ *m.* Gerücht, Sage | rumour, tradition.

ܛܒܲܥ, *impf.* u, untertauchen (*intr.*) | immerse. *Ethpe.* untergetaucht werden | be immersed.

ܛܵܒ݂ gut | good. || *F.* ܛܵܒ݂ܬ݂ܵܐ; ܛܵܒ݂ *adv.* wohl | well. || ܛܘܼܒ݂ܵܐ *m.* Seligkeit | blessedness. || ܛܘܼܒ݂ܰܝܗܘܿܢ selig die — | blessed are —. || ܛܘܼܒ݂ܵܢܵܐ, ܛܘܼܒ݂ܵܢܵܐ selig | blessed. || ܛܘܼܝܵܒ݂ܵܐ (ܛܲ ܛܲܝܸܒ݂ bereiten | prepare) Bereitung | preparation. ܛܘܼܝܵܒ݂ ܡܸܠܬ݂ܵܐ ἐτοιμολογία = ἐτυμολογία. || ܛܲܝܒ݁ܘܼܬ݂ܵܐ *f.* Gnade | mercy.

ܛܵܣ fliegen | fly.

ܛܵܦ überströmen | overflow. *Aph.* anschwellen | increase.

ܛܘܼܦ݂ܣܵܐ *m.* ὁ τύπος. ܛܲܦܸܣ *Pa.* bilden | form.

ܛܘܼܪܵܐ *m.* Berg | mount.

ܛܘܼܪܵܐ *m.* Zeitraum, Distanz | space of time, distance.

ܛܲܝ bestreichen | besmear. *Pa.* verunreinigen | defile.

ܛܲܟ݂ܣܵܐ *m.* ἡ τάξις. ܛܲܟܸܣ *Pa.* ordnen, an— | order, arrange.

ܛܠܵܐ, ܛܲܠܝܵܐ *m.* Knabe | boy. *Pl.* ܛܠܵܝܹ̈ܐ & ܛܠܵܝܹ̈ܐ.

ܛܠܲܡ auflösen, verschmähen, zerstören | dissolve, repudiate, destroy. || ܛܘܼܠܵܡܵܐ Verderben, Untergang | dissolution, destruction.

ܛܲܡܐܘܼܬ݂ܵܐ, ܛܲܡܐܘܼܬ݂ܵܐ *f.* Unreinigkeit | uncleanness.

ܛܡܲܪ, *impf.* u, graben, vergraben | dig, conceal.

ܛܢܦ *Pa.* verunreinigen | defile.

ܛܥܐ irren, vergessen | err, forget. *Aph.* vergessen machen | cause to forget. || ܛܘܥܝܝܬܐ *f.* Irrtum | error.

ܛܥܢ, *impf. a,* beladen sein, tragen | be laden, bear. || ܛܥܝܢ tragend u. getragen | bearing and borne. || ܛܥܢ, ܛܥܢܐ Last | load. *Cum* ܢܦܫܐ, ܒܨܦܐ Sorge (tragen) | take care, see to it that —.

ܛܦܣ v. ܛܘܦܣܐ.

ܛܘܪܢܘܣ τύραννος.

ܛܪܦ, *impf. u,* schlagen, treffen | beat, hit. || ܡܛܪܦ ܥܝܢܐ, Augenaufschlag, Augenblick | cast of the eye, moment. || ܛܪܦܐ *m.* Blatt | leaf.

ܛܫܐ verborgen sein | be hidden. *Pa.* verbergen | hide. *Ethpe.* sich verbergen | hide one's self. || ܛܫܝܐ, *f., pl.* ܛܫܝܬܐ Dunkles | hidden things. || ܡܛܫܐ *Infinitiv.* || ܡܛܫܝܬܐ *f., pl. a* ܡܛܫܝܢ Schlupfwinkel | hole, ambush.

ܝ

ܝܐܐ sich geziemen | become, be seemly.

ܝܒܠ *Pa.* führen, herleiten | lead, derive. || ܝܘܒܠܐ Herleitung, Abstammung | extraction, descent. *Aph.* wegführen | carry away.

ܝܒܝܫ trocken | dry. || ܝܒܝܫܬܐ *f.* das Trockene | the dry land. || ܝܒܫܐ *m.* das Festland | continent.

ܐܝܕ, ܐܝܕܐ *f., pl.* ܐܝܕܝܢ, ܐܝܕܝܐ, trop. ܐܝܕܝܬܐ Hand | hand. || ܐܝܕܐ ܒܐܝܕܐ allmählich | by degrees. || ܠܝܕ ܐܝܕ zur Seite, neben | at hand, beside. || ܐܘܪܝ § 48 d. *Af.* bekennen, preisen | confess, praise. || ܬܘܪܝܬܐ *f.* Bekenntnis, Danksagung | confession, thanksgiving. || ܬܘܪܥܬܐ § 12 *protasis.*

ܝܕܥ § 44 d, wissen | know. *Ethpe.* bekannt werden | become known. *Aph.* kund thun | make known. || ܝܕܝܥ bekannt | known. *Pl.* οἱ δῆλοι = Orakel | oracle. || ܝܕܥܬܐ *f.* Kenntnis | knowledge. || ܡܕܥܐ *m.* Verstand | mind. || ܝܕܘܥܐ Kenner | connoisseur. || ܡܬܝܕܥܢܐ νοη-τός, geistig | intelligent. || ܡܫܘܕܥܢܐ bezeichnend | marking, denoting.

ܝܗܒ § 48 g, 5, geben | give. || ܝܗܒ ܛܘܒܐ selig preisen | bless. *Ethpe.* gestattet sein | be allowed. || ܡܘܗܒܬܐ *f.* Gabe, Geschenk | gift, present.

ܝܘܕ *f. decima littera alfabeti.*

ܝܘܡ, ܝܘܡܐ *m.* Tag | day. *Pl.* ܝܘܡܬܐ *et* ܝܘܡܬܐ. || ܝܘܡܢ heutig | of to-day. || ܝܘܡܐ ܚܡܝܡܐ ܗܢܐ bis auf diesen Tag | till this day. || ܐܝܡܡܐ, ܐܝܡܡܐ *m.* Tag, im Gegensatz zur Nacht | day, in opp. to night.

ܝܩܕ herausreissen, erretten | pull out, save. || ܐܬܝܩܕ gerettet werden | be delivered.

ܝܙܦ, *imp* a, entlehnen | borrow.

ܝܚܝܕ einzig | unique. || ܝܚܝܕܝܐ Einsiedler | hermit. || ܝܚܝܕܐܝܬ, ܒܠܚܘܕܘܗܝ allein, einzig | alone, only. *Cum suff. pl.*

[ܝܠܠ] *Af.* ܐܝܠܠ § 44 heulen | howl, moan.

ܝܠܕ, *impf.* a, gebären | bear, to give birth. *Ethpe.* pass.

Aph. erzeugen, hervorbringen | beget, bring forth. ||

ܝܠܶܕ, ܝܰܠܕܳܐ Kind | child. || ܝܳܠܕܰܬ ܐܰܠܳܗܳܐ, Θεοτόχος. ||

ܝܰܠܕܳܐ (*pass.*) Kind | infant. || ܝܳܠܘܕܳܐ (*act*) *genitor.*

ܡܰܘܠܕܳܢܳܐ *m.* Erzeugung | begetting. || ܡܰܘܠܳܕܬܳܐ *pl.* ܡܰܘܠܳܕܳܬܳܐ

f., h. תּוֹלְדוֹת.

ܝܰܡ V. ܝܰܡ.

ܝܰܡܳܐ *m.* Meer | sea. *Pl.* ܝܰܡܡܳܬܳܐ || ܝܰܡܬܳܐ *f.* Teich | lake. *Pl.*

ܝܰܡܳܬܳܐ. || ܝܰܡܝܢܳܐ *f.* die rechte Seite | the right hand. ||

ܝܰܡܝܢܳܐ *f.* die südliche Gegend | the south country.

Etiam ܝܰܡܝܢܳܐ. || ܝܰܡܝܢܳܝ südlich | southern.

ܝܺܡܳܐ § 48e, schwören | swear. || ܡܰܘܡܳܬܳܐ *f.* (*sg. et pl.*, cf.

de Lagarde, Orientalia 2, 9; Hoffmann, ZDMG.

32, 572) Eid | oath.

ܝܢܶܩ § 44 saugen | suck. || *Af.* (*etiam* ܐܰܘܢܶܩ) säugen |

suckle.

(ܝܣܦ) ܐܰܘܣܶܦ *Aph.* hinzufügen | add. || ܬܰܘܣܶܦܬܳܐ *f.* Hinzu-

fügung | addition.

ܝܥܳܐ § 49, רָצָא wachsen | grow. *Aph.* hervorbringen |

bring forth.

ܐܰܘܦܺܝ *Aph.* verzehren, aufhören, verschwinden | consume,

cease, disappear.

ܝܰܨܝܦܘܬܳܐ *f.* Sorgfalt, Fleiss | care, diligence.

ܝܩܶܕ, *impf.* *a*, anbrennen | catch fire. *Aph.* anzünden |

kindle. || ܝܩܶܕܬܳܐ Feuersbrunst | fire.

ܝܩܰܪ schwer, teuer sein | be heavy, dear. *Pa.* ehren |

honour. || ܐܝܩܪܐ *m.* Ehre | honour. || ܐܝܩܪܬܐ *f.* Last, Tross | burden, baggage.

ܝܪܒ grösser werden | grow. *Af.* mehren, verherrlichen | increase, glorify.

ܝܪܚ (ܐܝܪܚ), ܝܪܚܐ *m.* Monat | month. *Pl.* ܝܪ̈ܚܝܢ.

ܝܘܪܩܐ grün | green. || ܝܘܪܩܬܐ *f.* das Grüne | green. || ܝܪ̈ܩܘܢܐ Kräuter | green herbs.

ܝܪܬ erben | inherit. || ܝܪܬܐ Erbe | heir. || ܝܪܬܘܬܐ *f.* Erbschaft, Besitz | inheritance, possession.

(ܝܫܛ) *Aph.* ausstrecken, darreichen | stretch out, tender.

(ܝܫܢ) ܫܢܬܐ, ܫܢ̇ܬܐ *f.*, *st. cstr.* ܫܢܬ Schlaf | sleep.

ܝܬ, ch. יַת, h. אֶת.

ܝܬܒ § 44 d, sitzen | sit. || ܡܘܬܒܐ *m.* Sitz | seat. || ܬܘܬܒܐ *m.* Beisitzer | assessor.

ܝܬܪ übrig, besser sein | be left over, be better. || ܝܬܝܪ übrig | left. || ܝܬܝܪ ܡܢ mehr als | more than. | ܡܝܬܪ vorzüglich, ausgezeichnet | excellent, distinguished.

ܟ

ܟܐܐ § 48 f., beschuldigen, beschimpfen | find fault with, scold. *Cum* ܒ.

ܟܐܒ § 45, Schmerzen, Sorge haben | have pains, sorrow. || ܟܐܒ, ܟܐܒܐ Schmerz | pain, sorrow.

ܟܐܡܬ nemlich, versteht sich, d. h. | namely, scil., i. e.

ܟܐܢܐܝܬ billig, mit Recht | justly, with reason. || ܟܐܢܘܬܐ *f.* Gerechtigkeit | justice.

ܩܐܦ, ܩܐܘܦܐ *f.* Fels | rock.

ܡܨܪ vielleicht, möglicherweise, nur | perhaps, possibly, only.

ܟܒܫ *impf.* u, unterdrücken | oppress, subdue. *Ethpc.* pass. || ܟܘܒܫܐ *m.*, ὑποπόδιον, Schemel | footstool. || ܡܟܒܫܬܢܘܬܐ *f.* ἅλωσις.

ܟܕ wenn, da, während (*c. partic.*) | when, as, while. || ܗܘ ܟܕ ܗܘ ebenderselbe | he himself.|| ܟܕܘ es genügt | it suffices. || ܟܕ ܟܕܘ schon | already.

ܟܗܢ, ܟܗܢܐ *m.* Priester | priest. || ܟܗܢ *Pa.* ἱερατεύειν.

ܟܘܒܐ *m.* Dorn | thorn.

ܟܘܟܒ, ܟܘܟܒܐ *m. et f.* ܟܘܟܒܬܐ Stern | star.

(ܟܠ) ܐܟܝܠ *Aph.* messen | measure.

ܟܝܢ, ܟܝܢܐ *m.* Natur | nature. || ܟܝܢܐ natürlich | natural.

ܟܝ *particula enclitica optandi, interrogandi, dubitandi.*

ܟܝܬ *particula explanandi,* nemlich | namely. || ܐܘܟܝܬ oder, d. h. | or, i. e.

ܟܠ, ܟܠܐ, *rarius* ܟܘܠ ganz, all, jeder | whole, all, every. || ܟܠܢܫ, ܟܠܢܫ jedermann | everyone.

ܟܠܐ verhindern, zurückhalten | hinder, keep back. *Ethpe.* pass. || ܟܘܠܝܬܐ *f., pl.* ܟܘܠܝܬܐ Nieren | reins.

ܟܡܢ *impf.* a, nachstellen | lay snares. || ܟܡܐܢܐ *m.* Hinterhalt | ambush.

ܟܡܪ *Ethpe.* traurig sein | mourn. || ܟܘܡܪܐ *m.* Priester | priest.

N e s t l e.

ܟ݂ܢܬ *Pa.* benennen | name, designate. ‖ ܟ݂ܘܢܳܝܳܐ *m.* Benennung, Beinamen | name, surname.

ܩܝܬܳܪܳܐ *m.* Zither | guitar.

ܟ݂ܢܫ, *impf. u, Pa.* versammeln | assemble. *Ethpa.* versammelt werden | be assembled. ‖ ܟ݂ܶܢܫܳܐ *m.* Versammlung, Haufe | assembly, troop. ‖ ܟ݂ܢܽܘܫܝܳܐ *m.* Versammlung | assembly. ‖ ܟ݂ܢܽܘܫܬܳܐ, *pl.* ܟ݂ܢܽܘܫܳܬ݂ܳܐ *f.* Synagoge | synagogue.

(ܟܣ) ܐܰܟ݂ܶܣ *Aph.* ermahnen, tadeln | reprove, rebuke. *Ethpa. pass.* ‖ ܡܰܟ݂ܣܳܢܽܘܬ݂ܳܐ *f.* Tadel | rebuke.

(ܟܣܐ) *part. pass.* ܟܣܶܐ verborgen | concealed. ‖ ܟ݂ܣܝܳܐܝܬ heimlich | secretly. *Pa.* verbergen, verhüllen | cover, hide, conceal. ‖ ܟ݂ܽܘܪܣܝܳܐ, ܟ݂ܽܘܪܣܝܳܐ, *pl.* ܟ݂ܽܘܪܣܰܘܳܬ݂ܳܐ *m.* Thron | throne.

ܟ݂ܦ § 42 beugen | bend.

ܟ݂ܰܦ, *pl.* ܟ݂ܰܦܳܐ *pl.* ܟ݂ܰܦܳܐ *f.* (hohle) Hand | palm, hand.

ܟ݂ܦܶܢ, ܟ݂ܰܦܢܳܐ 1) *subst. m.* Hunger | hunger. 2) *adj. verb.* hungrig | hungry.

ܟ݂ܦܰܪ, *impf. u,* leugnen, verleugnen, abfallen | deny, apostatise, revolt.

ܟ݂ܰܪܘܳܒ݂ܳܐ, *pl.* ܟ݂ܪܽܘܒ݂ܶܐ *m.* h. כְּרוּב.

(ܟܪܗ) *Ethpe.* ܐܶܬ݂ܟ݁ܪܰܗ krank sein | be ill ‖ ܟ݂ܽܘܪܗܳܢܳܐ *m.* Krankheit | illness.

(ܟܪܙ) ܐܰܟ݂ܪܶܙ *Aph.* verkündigen, predigen | announce, preach, χηρύσσειν. ‖ ܟ݂ܳܪܽܘܙܳܐ χήρυξ, Herold | herald. ‖ ܟ݂ܪܺܝܙ v. ܣܰܠܺܝܟ݂ܳܐ *et PSm. col.* 1818 ܟ݂ܪܺܝܙ.

ܟ݂ܪܰܟ݂, *impf. u et a,* herumgehen | go about. ‖ ܟ݂ܪܶܟ݂ eingewickelt | wrapped. *Ethpe.* umgeben werden, herumgehen | be surrounded, go round. *Aph.* herumführen | lead about.

ܟܪܣ, ܟܪܣܐ *f.*, *pl.* ܟܪ̈ܣܬܐ Bauch | belly.

ܟܘܪܣܝܢ v. ܟܣܐ.

(ܟܫܠ) *Aph.* ärgern | anger, offend.

(ܟܫܦ) *Ethpa.* anflehen | entreat. ‖ ܬܟܫܦܬܐ (Nestor. ܬܟܫܦܬܐ, *codex meus* ܬܟܫܘܫܦܬܐ) *f.* Bitte | prayer.

ܟܬܒ, *impf. u,* schreiben | write. *Ethpe. pass.*; *Aph.* verfassen | compose. ‖ ܟܬܒܐ *m.* Buch, Schrift | book, writing. ‖ ܟܬܝܒܬܐ *f.* Geschriebenes, Buchstabe | letter. ‖ ܡܟܬܒܢܘܬܐ Schrift | book.

ܟܘܬܝܢ *et* ܟܘܬܝܢܬܐ, *pl.* ܟܘܬܝ̈ܢܐ *et* ܟܘܬܝ̈ܢܬܐ, χιτών, Kleid | dress, garment.

ܟܬܦ, ܟܬܦܐ *f.*, *Pl.* ܟܬ̈ܦܬܐ Schulter | shoulder.

ܟܬܪ *Pa.* bleiben, warten, aushalten | remain, wait, hold out.

(ܟܬܫ) *Ethpa.* kämpfen, ringen | fight, wrestle, exert one's self. ‖ ܬܟܬܘܫܐ *m.* Kampf | fight.

ܠ Lamadh

ܠ *praepositio directionis, dativi, accusativi.*

ܠܐ *particula negationis:* nicht | not. ‖ ܒܠܐ, ܕܠܐ ohne | without.

ܠܐܝ § 48, f. müde sein, leiden | be tired, suffer.

ܡܠܐܟ, ܡܠܐܟܐ, h. מַלְאָךְ, ἄγγελος.

ܠܒܐ *m.* Herz | heart. *pl.* ܠܒ̈ܐ *et* ܠܒܘ̈ܬܐ.

ܠܒܟ (*sic, corrige* p. 43, g) verdichten | condense.

ܠܒܰܟ݂, *impf. u*, ergreifen | seize hold. || ܠܳܒܶܟ݂ haltend | holding.

ܠܒܽܘܢܬܳܐ *f.* Weihrauch | incense. || ܠܒܶܢܬܳܐ § 25 Ziegel | brick. [ܠܒܶܢ v. ܡܶܢ.]

ܠܒܶܫ, *impf. a*, anziehen | put on. *Aph. cum dupp. Acc.* einen mit etwas bekleiden | dress (act.).

ܠܰܓܠܶܓ stammeln | stammer, prattle.

(ܠܗܶܒ) ܡܰܠܗܶܒ anzünden | light. || ܡܰܠܗܰܒܬܳܐ *f.*; *pl.* ܡܰܠܗܒܳܝܳܬܳܐ Flamme | flame.

ܠܳܐ *particula negationis:* nicht, nein | not, no.

ܠܽܘܚܳܐ *f.*; *pl.* ܠܽܘܚܶܐ Tafel | table.

ܠܛܰܛ verfluchen | curse. *p. pass.* ܠܺܝܛ verflucht | cursed.

ܠܘܳܬ *praep.* bei, zu | to, with (cf. Hoffmann ZDMG 32, 753, de Lagarde, Orientalia 2, 20).

ܠܽܘܚܛܳܝܳܐ *m.* σκηνοποιός.

ܠܦܘܣܛ v. ܦܘܣܛ.

ܠܚܳܐ auslöschen, austilgen | rub out, efface.

ܠܚܘܕܐ v. ܚܕ.

ܠܚܶܡ, ܠܰܚܡܳܐ *m.* Brot | bread.

ܠܰܚܡܳܐܺܝܬ *adv.* geziemend, passend | becoming, fitting.

ܠܚܰܫ, *impf. u et a*, beschwören | conjure. *Pa.* beschmeicheln | flatter.

ܠܟ thöricht | silly, foolish.

ܠܺܠܝܳܐ *m.*, *pl.* ܠܺܠܰܘܳܬܳܐ Nacht | night. *St. abs.* ܠܺܠܶܐ *et* ܠܺܠܝܳܐ (opp. ܐܺܝܡܳܡ).

ܠܰܝܬ *ex* ܐܺܝܬ *et* ܠܳܐ es ist, war nicht | there is (was) not.

[ܚܒܘܟܐ *m.* Verwirrung | confusion. ?]

ܟܒܪ *particula assertionis,* gewiss, wahrhaftig | certainly, truly.

ܬܠܡܝܕܐ *m.* Schüler, Jünger | disciple.

ܠܫܢܐ, ܠܫܢܐ *m.* Zunge | tongue.

ܡ ܡ

ܡܐ *interrog.* (§ 21) was? wie? | what? how? ܡܐ ܕ das, was, als | that which, when. ܠܡܢ wozu? | whereto? ܠܡܢܐ warum? sollte wohl? | why? might it be that? ܠܡܟܐ v. ܡܟܐ; ܡܛܠ wozu das? warum? | wherefore? why? ܡܐܐ 100, § 33, ܡܐܬܝܢ 200.

ܡܐܢ § 45, Ekel haben | be disgusted with.

ܡܪܥܐ v. ܡܪܚܠ, ܡܪܚܐ v. ܪܚܠ.

ܡܕܡ irgend etwas, τι, ein Teil | anything, a part.

ܡܗܝܪ gewandt, geschickt, klug | instructed, skilled, clever.

ܡܘܚܐ *m.* Mark, Hirn | marrow, brain.

ܡܘܕܥ v. ܝܕܥ.

ܡܘܪܐ *m.* Myrrhe | myrrh.

ܡܘܬ § 46, b, 1 sterben | die. ‖ ܡܘܬܐ *m.,* *st. cstr.* ܡܘܬ Tod | death. ‖ ܡܝܘܬܐ sterblich | mortal.

ܡܚܐ schlagen | beat. ‖ ܡܚܘܬܐ, ܡܚܘܬܐ *f.;* *pl.* ܡܚܘܬܐ Schlag | stroke, blow.

ܡܚܣܐ v. ܚܣܐ; ܡܚܠܡ v. ܚܠܡ.

ܡܛܐ erreichen, kommen | reach, come. *Pa.* erlangen | reach (cf. Hoffmann, ZDMG 32, 757).

ܡܛܠ *Praep.* wegen | on account of. ‖ ܡܛܠܗܕܐ deswegen | on that account, therefore. ‖ ܡܛܠܕ weil | because.

ܡܛܪܐ *m.* Regen | rain. ‖ ܡܛܪܝ vom Himmelsregen bewässert | watered by the rain from heaven.

ܡܝܐ § 33, Wasser | water.

ܐܬܡܛܪܦܠܛ *metropolitanus factus est* (BH. Gr. 1, 48).

ܡܝܠܐ *m.* μίλιον.

ܡܟܝܟ demütig | humble. ‖ ܡܟܝܟܐܝܬ *adv.*

ܡܟܝܠ schon, jetzt, hierauf | already, now, then.

ܡܟܣܐ *m.* Zöllner | Publican.

ܡܟܪ *impf.* u, (eine Frau) gewinnen | get (a wife), (cf. G. Hoffmann, ZDMG 32, 751 n. 2). ‖ ܡܟܝܪܐ ܚܬܐ verheiratet | married.

ܡܠܠ *Pa.* sprechen | speak. *Ethpa.* gesagt werden | be said. ‖ ܡܠܐ, ܡܠܬܐ, *st. c.* ܡܠܬ *f.* Wort | word. *Pl.* ܡܠܐ. ‖ ܡܠܟܬܢܐ Verkleinerungswörter | diminutives (*PSm.* ܡܠܬܐܬܐ). ‖ ܝܠܦ ܡܠܟܬܐ ܡܠܦܢܘܬܐ (*melius* ܡܠܟܘܬܐ) Theologie | theology.

ܡܠܐ 1) füllen | fill. 2) voll sein | be full. *Pa.* erfüllen | fulfill. *Ethpa. pass.* ܐܬܡܠܝ es ist vollbracht | it is finished. ‖ ܡܠܐ (ܡܠܐܐ) ܐܪ *m.* Fülle, Materie | quantity, matter. ‖ ܡܡܠܝܐ voll, vollkommen | full, perfect. ‖ ܠܐ ܡܡܠܝܢܘܬܐ Unvollkommenheit | imperfection.

ܡܠܐܛܐ *v.* ܦܠ.

ܡܠܚ *impf.* u, salzen | salt. *Ethpe. pass.* ‖ ܡܠܚܐ, ܡܠܚܐ *f.* Salz | salt.

ܡܠܟ *impf.* *u,* raten | counsel. *Ethpa.* Rat halten, über-
legen | deliberate. *Aph.* 1) an die Spitze stellen | set
at the head. 2) die Herrschaft übernehmen | take
the government. || ܡܠܟ, ܡܠܟܐ *m.* König | king. ||
ܡܠܟܘܢܐ *diminut.,* ܡܠܟܝܐ *adj.* || ܡܠܟ, ܡܠܟܐ *m.* Rat |
counsel. || ܡܠܟܘܬܐ *f.* Herrschaft, königliche Majestät |
kingdom, majesty.

ܡܢ *Praep.* von | from, by. || ܡܢܫܘܡ v. ܫܘܡ.

ܡܢ μέν, zwar | indeed.

ܡܢ wer? | who? ܡܢܘ wer ist? | who is? || ܡܢ, ܡܢܐ was? |
what? ܡܢܘ was ist? | what is? ܡܢ, ܡܢܐ wozu?
warum? | wherefore? why?

ܡܢܐ zählen | count. *Ethpe. pass.* || ܡܢܝܢܐ *m.* Zahl | number. ||
ܡܢܬܐ *f.* Teil | part. *Pl.* ܡܢܘܢ, ܡܢܘܬܐ. || ܡܢܬܐ teilweise |
partially. | ܡܢܬܐ, ܡܢܬܐ *f.* Haar, Saite | hair, string. *Pl.*
ܡܢܐ.

ܡܢܝܢܝܐ Manichäer | a Manichee.

ܡܢܥ *Pa.* 1) hinkommen | arrive. 2) hinführen | bring, adduce.

ܡܢܣܡ v. ܣܡ; ܡܢܠܐ v. ܢܠܐ.

(ܡܨܝ) *part. pass.* ܡܨܐ, ܡܨܝܐ im stande | able. || ܠܐ ܡܨܝܐ
es ist unmöglich | it is impossible. || ܡܨܝܢ wir können |
we can.

ܡܨܥܬܐ *f.* Mitte | middle (*cum suffix.* ܡܨܥܬܟܘܢ *et* ܡܨܥܗܘܢ,
μεσσότης? G. Hoffmann ZDMG. 32, 752).

ܡܨܪܝܢ *f.* Egypten | Egypt.

ܡܪܝܪ bitter | bitter.

ܡܳܪܶܐ, ܡܳܪܝܳܐ ܡܳܪܶܐ § 33 Herr | Lord.

ܡܰܪܓܳܐ § 8 Wiese | meadow.

ܡܪܰܕ, *impf. a,* widerspenstig sein, abfallen | resist, desert, revolt; *cum* ܥܰܠ.

ܡܳܪܳܕܳܐ frech, übermütig | insolent, proud.

ܡܰܪܛܽܘܛܳܐ *m.* Obergewand | coat, cloak.

ܡܪܰܩ, *impf. u,* abreiben, polieren | rup up, polish. ‖ ܡܡܰܪܩܳܐ gebildet | refined.

ܡܫܰܚ, *impf. u,* 1) salben | anoint. 2) messen | measure. ‖ ܡܫܺܝܚܳܐ Christus | Christ. ‖ ܡܫܽܘܚܬܳܐ *f.* Mass | measure.

ܡܶܫܟܳܐ *m.* Fell, Haut, Schlauch | hide, skin, wine-skin.

ܡܬܽܘܡ zu irgend einer Zeit, einmal | at any time, once. ‖ ܡܶܢ ܡܬܽܘܡ, ܡܶܢ ܡܬܽܘܡ von jeher | at all times, always. *Cum* ܠܳܐ nie | at no time, never.

ܢ

ܢܳܐ § 3 = h. ܢܳܐ.

ܢܰܚܒܳܐ = äg. νεφώϑ = gr. χροχόδειλος.

ܢܒܺܝܳܐ *m.* Prophet | prophet. ‖ ܐܶܬܢܰܒܺܝ *Ethpa.* weissageu | prophesy. ‖ ܢܒܺܝܽܘܬܳܐ Weissagung | prophecy.

ܢܶܒܥܳܐ *m.* Quelle | spring, well.

ܢܓܰܕ § 42 ziehen, führen | pull, draw.

ܢܓܰܪ lang sein | be long. *Aph.* in die Länge ziehen, warten | put off, wait. ‖ ܢܰܓܺܝܪ lang | long. ‖ ܢܰܓܳܪܳܐ *m.* Zimmermann | carpenter.

ܢܕܰܡ verabscheuungswürdig | detestable.

ܢܒܰܚ brüllen, heulen | roar, howl.

ܢܗܰܪ, *impf.* ܢܶܢܗܰܪ, hell werden | grow bright. *Aph.* leuchten lassen, anzünden | cause to shine, kindle. *Ethpa.* erleuchtet werden | be illuminated. || ܢܰܗܺܝܪ, *Adj. et Subst.* Licht, Leuchter | light, candlestick. || ܢܘܗܪܐ *m.* Licht | light (*st. cstr.* ܢܘܗܰܪ?). || ܢܰܗܪܐ *m.* Fluss | river. *Pl.* ܢܰܗܪܰܘ̈ܬܐ.

ܢܘܕ umhergetrieben werden | be driven about (a vagabond).

ܢܳܚ Ruhe haben | have rest. *Ethpe.* sich der Ruhe hingeben | enjoy rest. *Aph.* ausruhen u. ausruhen lassen | rest (trans. and intr.). || ܢܝܳܚܐ *m.* Ruhe, Erholung | rest, recreation. || ܢܝܳܚܬܐ *f.* Ruhe | rest. || ܡܢܳܚ *part. pass. Aph.* ausruhend, verstorben | at rest, deceased.

ܢܘܢܐ *m.* Fisch | fish.

ܢܘܪܐ *f.* Feuer | fire. *Pl.* ܢܘܪܰܘ̈ܬܐ. || ܡܢܰܪܬܐ *f.* Leuchter | candlestick.

ܢܙܰܪ *Ethpe.* Nasiräer werden | become a Nazarite.

ܢܰܚܠܐ *m.* Thal | valley.

ܢܚܶܡ *Pa.* erwecken | raise. *Ethpa. pass.* || ܡܢܰܚܡܳܢܐ Erwecker | he who resuscitates. || ܢܘܚܳܡܐ *f.* Auferweckung | raising (of the dead).

ܢܚܳܫܐ *m.* Kupfer, Erz | copper, bronze.

ܢܚܶܬ, *impf. u,* hinabsteigen | descend. *Aph.* hinabbringen | bring down.

ܢܛܰܪ, *impf. a et u,* bewachen | watch. *Ethpe.* bewacht

werden ‖ be watched. ‖ ܢܳܛܽܘܪܳܐ *m.* Wächter │ watchman. │
ܡܢܰܛܪܳܢܳܐ *m.* Verteidiger │ defender.

ܢܺܝܪܳܐ *m.* Joch │ yoke.

ܢܶܟܠܳܐ *m.* Hinterlist, Betrug │ fraud, deceit.

ܢܶܟܣܬܳܐ *f.* Schlachtung │ slaughter. *Pl.* ܢܶܟܣܳܬܳܐ.

ܢܟܶܦ, ܢܟܰܦ züchtig, keusch, ehrwürdig │ modest, pure,
reverend.

ܢܶܟܬܳܐ (*m.? potius pro*) ܢܶܟܬܬܳܐ *f.* Biss │ bite.

ܢܰܡܘܣܳܐ *m.* ὁ νόμος (cf. de Lagarde, Mittheilungen 2, 358 n).

(ܢܣܐ) *Pa.* versuchen │ try, tempt. ‖ ܢܶܣܝܳܢܳܐ *m.* Versuchung │
temptation. ‖ ܡܢܰܣܝܳܢܳܐ *m.* Versucher │ tempter. ‖ ܢܶܣܝܳܢܳܐ
m. Probe, Erfahrung │ trial, experience.

ܢܣܰܒ nehmen, erhalten │ take, receive. ‖ ܢܣܰܒ ܡܶܠܟܳܐ sich
beraten │ take counsel. *Ethpe.* genommen, gewählt
werden │ be accepted, elected. ‖ ܢܣܺܝܒ genommen,
hergeleitet │ taken, derived.

ܢܣܰܟ gegossen │ molten. ܢܶܣܟܬܳܐ χωνευτά.

ܢܣܰܩ *v.* ܣܠܩ.

ܢܣܰܪ *impf. u,* zersägen │ saw. *Ethpe. pass.* ‖ ܡܰܣܳܪܳܐ *m.*
Säge │ saw.

ܢܦܰܚ, *impf. u,* blasen, anhauchen │ blow, breathe on.

ܢܦܰܠ *impf.* ܢܶܦܶܠ fallen, sinken │ fall, sink.

ܢܦܰܩ, *impf. u,* herausgehen, herauskommen │ go out,
come out. *Aph.* herausbringen (beim Rechnen, Sub-
trahieren u. Dividieren) │ bring out (in reckoning). ‖
ܡܰܦܩܳܢܳܐ *m.* Ausgang │ departure, issue.

ܢܩܦ, ܢܥܡܐ *f.*, *Pl.* ܢܩܡܬܐ Seele, Person | soul, person. *C. suff.* = selbst | self.

ܢܨܐ streiten | contest.

ܢܨܒ, *impf. u,* pflanzen | plant. || ܢܨܒܬܐ *f., pl.* ܢܨܒܬܐ Pflanze | plant.

ܢܨܚ, *Ethpa.* triumphieren | triumph. || ܢܨܝܚܐ Triumphator, glänzend, herrlich | triumphant, splendid, glorious.

ܢܨܪ, *impf. a,* singen | sing. *Pa.* die Stimme modulieren | modulate the voice. || ܢܨܪܬܐ Lispeln, Lallen, Schmeicheln | whispering, lisping, flattery.

ܢܩܒܐ, ܢܩܒܬܐ *f.* weiblich, Weib | female, wife.

ܢܩܕ, ܢܩܕܐ rein, fein, kostbar | pure, fine, costly.

ܢܩܦ, *impf. a,* anhängen, sich anschliessen, folgen | adhere, cleave to, follow.

ܢܩܫ, *impf. u.* schlagen (die Hände zusammen) | clasp (the hands together).

ܢܪܓܐ *m.* Beil | axe (ostsyr. ܟ K., westsyr. R.)

ܢܫܒ, *impf. a,* wehen | blow. || ܢܫܒܐ *m.* Strick, Netz | rope, net.

ܢܫܡܬܐ, ܢܫܡܬܐ *f.*, *st. cstr.* ܢܫܡܬ Wehen, Atem | breath.

ܢܬܠ, *impf.*, § 48, g, 6, geben | give.

ܢܬܦ, *impf. u,* an sich ziehen | attract.

ܣ Semkath

ܣܐܐ, ܣܐܬܐ *f.* dualis ܣܐܬܝܢ, *pl.* ܣܐܝܢ h. סְאָה.

ܣܒ, ܣܒܐ *m.* Ältester, Greis | elder, old man. *Rarius* ܣܐܒ *part.* || ܣܝܒܘܬܐ *f.* das Alter | old age.

ܣܐܡܐ *m.* ἀσήμιον, Silber | silver.

ܣܒܠ, *impf. u,* tragen | bear.

ܣܒܝܣ dicht, häufig, verschieden | dense, frequent, various.

ܣܒܥ, *impf. a,* satt werden | be satiated.

ܣܒܪ, *impf. a,* glauben, urteilen | believe, judge. *Ethpe.* gehalten werden, gelten | be estimated, pass for. || ܣܒܪܐ *m.* Hoffnung | hope. || ܡܣܒܪܢܘܬܐ *f.* Meinung | meaning. || ܡܣܒܪܢܐ Evangelist | evangelist. || ܣܝܒܪܬܐ *f.* Unterhalt, Nahrung | food, means of subsistence.

ܣܓܐ, wachsen, viel sein | grow, increase in number. *Aph.* wachsen machen, vermehren | increase, multiply. || ܣܓܝ *adj.* viel, häufig | much, many, frequent. ܣܓܝܐܐ; *f. st. cstr.* ܣܓܝܐܬ, ܣܓܝܐܬܐ; ܣܓܝ *adv.* sehr | very. || ܣܓܝܐܘܬܐ *f.* Menge | multitude. || ܣܘܓܐܐ, *st. cstr.* ܣܘܓܐܬ Menge | multitude.

ܣܓܕ, *impf. u,* προσκυνεῖν, anbeten, grüssen, verehren | worship, greet, revere. || ܣܓܘܕܐ Gottesverehrer | he who reveres God. || ܣܓܝܕ verehrenswert | worthy of adoration. || ܣܓܕܬܐ *f.* Anbetung, Verehrung | worship, adoration.

ܣܗܕ, *impf. a,* zeugen, be- | witness. *Aph.* do. || ܣܗܕܘܬܐ *f.* Zeugnis | witness.

ܣܗܪܐ *c.* Mond | moon.

ܣܝܓ umzäunen | make a hedge.

ܣܟ beendigen | finish. *Ethpa.* begrenzt, beendigt, ent-
halten sein | be bounded, finished, contained. ‖ ܣܟ
adv. gänzlich, überhaupt | totally, in general.

ܣܡ *impf.* *i,* legen, setzen, bestimmen | lay, put, order.
Ethpe. bestimmt sein | be appointed. ‖ ܣܝܡܬܐ *f.* Schatz |
treasure. ‖ ܡܣܡ ܒܪܝܫܐ Züchtigung, Strafe | chastise-
ment, punishment.

ܣܘܣܝܐ *m.* Pferd | horse. *Pl.* ܣܘܣܝܢ *et* ܣܘܣܘܬܐ.

ܣܚܦ, *impf.* *u,* wegwerfen, zerstören | cast away,
destroy.

(ܣܟܐ) *Pa.* erwarten | await.

ܣܟܠ *Ethpa.* vernünftig werden, einsehen | become wise,
understand. ‖ ܣܟܠ, ܣܟܠܐ *m.* Thor | fool. ‖ ܣܟܠܘܬܐ *f.*
Thorheit, Sünde | foolishness, offence. ‖ ܣܘܟܠܐ *m.*
Einsicht, Sinn, Verständnis | intelligence, sense,
understanding.

ܡܣܟܢ, ܡܣܟܢܐ arm | poor; *f.* ܡܣܟܢܬܐ.

ܣܟܪ, *impf.* *u,* schliessen, hemmen | close, hinder. *Ethpe.*
pass., verstummen | be silent.

(ܣܠܐ) *Aph.* verwerfen | refuse, reject.

ܣܠܩ § 48, g, 2, hinaufsteigen | mount, ascend. *Aph.*
herausführen | bring out. ‖ ܣܘܠܩܐ Auferstehung
(Christi) | resurrection.

ܣܡ, ܣܡܐ *m.* Gift | poison. *Pl.* ܣܡܡܢܐ Heilmittel, Farben, bes. rote | medicines, colours, especially red.

ܣܡܝܐ, ܣܡܝܐ blind | blind. || ܣܡܝܘܬܐ *f.* Blindheit | blindness.

ܣܢܐ hassen, verabscheuen | hate, abhor. || ܣܢܐܐ *pl.* ܣܢܐܐ Hasser, Gegner | hater, enemy.

ܣܥܐ laufen, angreifen, wagen | run, attack, dare.

ܣܥܪ, *impf.* *u*, besuchen, mustern, handeln | visit, inspect, act. *Ethpe.* vollbracht werden | be completed. || ܣܘܥܪܢܐ *m.* Werk, Sache, That | work, thing, fact.

ܣܥܪܐ *m.* Haar | hair. *Pl.* ܣܥܪܐ. || ܣܥܪܬܐ das einzelne Haar | a single hair.

ܣܦܩ *part.* ܣܦܩ *et* ܣܦܩܐ es genügt | it suffices.

ܣܦܪ, ܣܦܪܐ *m.* Schrift, Buch | writing, book. || ܣܦܪܐ *m.* Schreiber, Schriftgelehrter | writer, Scribe. || ܣܦܝܪܐ *m.* Gelehrter, Grammatiker | a scholar, grammatician.

ܣܘܩܘܒܠܐ v. ܩܒܠ.

ܣܘܪܐ *m.* Feind, Gegner | foe, enemy.

ܣܘܪܕܐ *m.* Schrecken | fear, terror.

ܣܪܛܐ *m.* κεραία, Schrift, Linie | writing, line.

ܣܪܝܩܐܝܬ *adv.* leer, umsonst | in vain, for nothing.

ܣܬܪ, *impf.* *u*, zerstören | destroy. *Pa.* decken, bedecken | cover. || ܣܬܪܐ *m.* das Geheime | the secret. || ܒܣܬܪ, ܒܣܬܪܐ *adv.* hinter | behind.

ܥ

ܥܒܰܕ *impf.* e, machen, thun | make, do. || ܥܒܶܕ, ܥܰܒܕܳܐ *m.* Knecht | servant. || ܥܒܳܕ, ܥܒܳܕܳܐ *m.* Arbeit, Werk | labour, work. || ܥܰܒܕܽܘܬܳܐ *f.* Knechtschaft | servitude. || ܥܳܒܽܘܕܳܐ *m.* Schöpfer, Künstler | creator, artist. || ܡܰܥܒܕܳܢܽܘܬܳܐ *f.* Wirksamkeit | efficacy. || ܫܽܘܥܒܳܕܳܐ (ܫܽܘܒܳܕܳܐ) *m.* Unterwerfung | submission.

ܥܒܺܝܛ dicht, dick | dense, thick.

ܥܒܰܪ, *impf.* a, überschreiten | transgress. *Aph.* entfernen | remove. *Ethpe.* (Gesetz) übertreten | transgress (the law). || ܥܒܳܪ, ܥܰܒܪܳܐ *m.* Übergang, Ufer | bank, shore. || ܠܥܶܒܪܳܐ hinüber | across. || ܡܶܢ ܥܶܒܪܳܐ von drüben | from the other side.

ܥܶܓܠ *m.* Eile | haste. *Adv.* ܒܥܶܓܠ eilends | in haste.

ܥܶܓܠܳܐ *m.* Kalb | calf. *Pl.* ܥܶܓܠܶܐ; *f.* ܥܶܓܠܬܳܐ.

ܥܕܰܡ *Praep.* bis | unto. || ܥܕܰܠܳܐ solang nicht, ehe | before. || ܥܕܰܡܳܟܺܝܠ bisher | hitherto. || ܥܕܰܡܳܐ bis dahin, so sehr | to such a degree.

ܥܺܐܕܳܐ *m.* Fest | feast. || ܥܰܐܕܺܝ Fest feiern | keep festivals. || ܥܺܕܬܳܐ v. ܥܕܐ.

ܥܕܰܠ, *impf.* u, tadeln | rebuke. *Ethpe pass.*

ܥܶܕܳܢܳܐ *m.* Zeit, Zeitpunkt | time, moment.

ܥܽܘܕܪܳܢܳܐ *m.* Hilfe | help. || ܡܥܰܕܪܳܢܳܐ Helfer | helper.

ܥܗܰܕ, *impf.* a, sich erinnern | remember (ܒ = ܐ) || ܥܽܘܗܕܳܢܳܐ *m.* Gedächtnis | memory.

ܥܰܝܶܕ *Pa.* gewöhnen | accustom. *Aph.* do. || ܡܥܰܝܰܕ gewöhnt | accustomed. || ܥܝܳܕܳܐ *m.* Gewohnheit, Sitte | custom, use. || ܥܝܳܕܽܘ § 3 *particula,* scilicet.

ܐܰܥܘܶܠ *Aph.* ungerecht handeln | deal unjustly. || ܥܰܘܠܳܐ *m.* Unrecht, Frevel | injustice, crime. || ܥܰܘܳܠ, ܥܰܘܳܠܳܐ *m.* ungerecht; Frevler | wicked, transgressor.

ܥܝܰܪ *Pa. et Aph.* aufwecken | awaken. *Ethpe.* aufgeweckt werden | be awakened.

ܥܘܺܝܪܽܘܬܳܐ *f.* Blindheit | blindness.

ܥܙܰܙ *Ethpa.* sich kräftig zeigen | be strong. || ܥܰܙܺܝܙ gewaltig | valid.

ܥܶܙܩܬܳܐ *f.* Ring | ring (Lag., Or. 2, 55).

ܥܙܳܪܽܘܪ̈ܶܐ Windeln | swaddling-clothes (de Lagarde, Orientalia 2, 47).

ܥܶܛܪܳܐ *m.* Weihrauch, Dampf | incense, vapour.

ܥܰܝܢ, ܥܰܝܢܳܐ *f.* Auge | eye.

ܥܰܘܶܩ *Pa.* hemmen, hindern | hinder, stop.

ܥܰܠ *impf. u,* eintreten | enter. || ܥܶܠܬܳܐ *f.* Sache, Ursache | cause, reason. || ܡܰܥܰܠܬܳܐ *f.* Eintreten | entering. || ܡܰܥܠܳܐ, ܡܥܰܠܳܐ *et* ܡܰܥܠܢܳܐ *m.* Eingang | entrance. || ܡܰܥܠܢܳܝܳܐ zum Eingang gehörig | belonging to the entrance.

(ܥܠܳܐ) *Aph.* in die Höhe heben | raise; *cum* ܒ abfallen von | revolt, rise against. *Ethpe.* hervorragen | be prominent. || ܥܰܠ *Praep.* über | over. || ܥܰܠ ܓܢܒ, ܥܰܠ ܝܰܕ zur Seite | at the side of. || ܥܰܠ ܕ weil | because. ||

ܚܠܐ, ܠܚܠܐ in die Höhe | upwards. ‖ ܠܥܠܝܐ der oberste | the Most High.

ܚܠܡܨܐ *m.* Jüngling | young man (p. 31 b).

ܚܠܕܐ *m.* Welt, Zeit, Ewigkeit | world, time, eternity.

ܥܡܐ *m.* Volk | people. *Pl.* ܥܡܝܡܬܐ.

ܥܡ *Praep.* mit | with.

ܥܡܕ, *impf.* *a*, eingetaucht, getauft werden | be immersed, baptised. *Aph.* taufen | baptise. ‖ ܥܡܕܐ *m.* *et* ܡܥܡܘܕܝܬܐ (K. ?) *f.* Taufe | baptism. ‖ ܥܡܘܕܐ h. עמוד.

ܥܡܠܐ *m.* Mühe | labour.

ܥܘܡܩܐ *m.* Tiefe | depth.

ܥܡܪ, *impf.* *a*, wohnen | dwell, inhabit. ‖ ܥܡܘܪܐ *m.* Bewohner | inhabitant.

ܥܢܐ antworten, sich unterhalten, sich aufhalten | answer, converse, stay. ‖ ܥܢܝܢܐ *m.* Orakel | oracle. ‖ ܥܢܘܝܐ *m.* Mönch | monk.

ܥܢܐ *f. coll.* Schafherde | sheep (coll.)

ܥܢܒܬܐ *f., pl.* ܥܢܒܐ Traube | grape.

ܥܢܕ, *impf.* *a*, scheiden, sterben | depart, die.

ܥܢܢܐ *f.* Wolke | cloud.

ܥܣܒܐ *m.* Kraut, Gras | herb, grass (*Pl. sec. BA.* ܥܣܒܐ).

ܥܫܢ, ܥܫܝܢ *m.* schwer | heavy.

ܥܣܪ 10. § 33.

ܚܩܦܐ διπλοῦς; varia lectio ܐܚܣܦ = ضعيف de Lagarde, Semitica 1, 25.

ܥܦܰܪ, ܥܰܦܪܳܐ *m.* Staub, Erde | dust, earth.

ܥܨܳܐ bekämpfen, bedrücken | compel, oppress.

ܥܨܰܒ verbinden, herstellen | dress (a wound), restore.

ܥܩܰܒ, *impf. u*, mit der Ferse treten, folgen | tread on (with the heels), follow. *Pa.* untersuchen, erforschen | investigate, examine. || ܥܶܩܒܳܐ, *pl.* ܥܶܩ̈ܒܶܐ et ܥܶܩ̈ܒܳܬܳܐ Ferse | heel.

ܡܥܰܪܬܳܐ *f. pl.* ܡܥܰܪ̈ܶܐ Höhle | cave.

ܡܰܥܪܒܳܐ et ܡܥܰܪܒܳܐ Westen | west || ܡܰܥܪܒܳܝ *adj.*

ܥܰܪܛܶܠܳܝ nackt | naked.

ܥܰܪܠ, ܥܘܪܠܳܐ unbeschnitten | uncircumcised.

ܥܰܪܺܝܡ schlau | subtil, cunning.

ܥܰܪܣܳܐ *f.* Bett | bed. *Pl.* ܥܰܪ̈ܣܳܬܳܐ.

ܥܪܰܩ, *impf. u*, fliehen | flee. *Aph.* in die Flucht treiben | put to flight.

ܥܰܪܩܶܠ zu Falle bringen, verwickeln | entangle, turn down.

ܥܫܶܢ, *impf. a*, stark sein, siegen | be strong, gain. *Ethpa.* gekräftigt werden | be strengthened.

ܥܬܺܝܕ bereit | ready; *sequente* ܠ *vel* ܕ *futuro significando inservit.*

ܥܰܬܺܝܩ alt | old.

ܦ

ܦܓܽܘܕܬܳܐ *f.* Zaum | bridle. *Pl.* ܦܓܽܘ̈ܕܶܐ.

ܦܓܰܥ, *impf. a*, begegnen | meet.

ܦܓܪ, ܦܓܪܐ *m.* Leib | body. || ܦܓܪܢܘܬܐ *f.* Leiblichkeit | the flesh, man's carnal nature. || ܦܓܪܢܝܐ *BH. Gr.* 1, 48.

ܦܕ § 43 irren | err.

ܦܕܢܐ, *pl.* ܦܕܢܐ ζεῦγος, Joch | yoke, pair.

ܦܘܠܚܡܝ = h. שְׁפַטִּים.

ܦܘܚ blasen, hauchen | blow, breathe.

ܦܘܠܟܘܢܝ palatium.

ܦܘܡܐ, ܦܘܡܐ *m.* Mund | mouth (*cf.* ܦܘܡܐ, *Pl.* ܐܦܐ).

(ܦܘܣ) *Aph.* ܐܦܣ (πεῖσαι) raten, bestimmen | counsel, advise (*Ethpe.* ܐܬܦܝܣ). || ܡܦܣ überzeugt, entschlossen | persuaded, resolved.

ܦܘܣܩܡܢܘܣ piscinae.

ܦܘܪܣ, ܦܘܪܣܐ *m.* πόρος. ܦܘܪܣ ܡܢ ܟܠ ܒܝ durchaus | at all hazards, come what may.

ܦܫ ausruhen, bleiben, übrig sein | rest, remain, be left.

ܠܦܘܬ *adv.* entsprechend | according, corresponding (h. לְפִי).

ܦܚܐ *m.* Strick | snare.

ܦܚܪܐ *m.* Töpfer | potter. || ܟܣܐ ܦܚܪܐ ὀστρακίνη.

ܦܚܬ *Pa.* graben, ausgraben | dig, excavate. || ܦܚܬܐ *m.* Graben | ditch.

ܦܟ zerbrechen | break. || ܦܟܐ *m.* Backen | cheek.

ܦܟܗ, *impf. a,* kraftlos, dumm werden | become insipid, lose the savour.

ܦܠܓ, *impf. u,* teilen | divide. *Ethpe.* sich teilen | be divided. || ܦܠܓ, ܦܠܓܐ *m.* Hälfte | half, middle.

ܝ*

ܦܠܓܗ ܦܠܓܗ ܘܦܠܓܗ Mitternacht | midnight. || ܝܪܚܐ ܦܠܓ
Mitte des Monats | middle of the month. || ܡܬܦܠܓ
zweifelnd an | doubtful as to.

ܦܠܚ, *impf. u,* arbeiten | labor.

ܦܢܐ sich wenden, zurückkehren | turn, return. *Ethpe.* do.
Pa. zurückgeben, antworten | give back, answer
(*cum vel sine* ܦܬܓܡܐ). *Aph.* zuwenden | turn towards. ||
ܦܢܝܬܐ *f., st. c.* ܦܢܝܬ Gegend | country. || ܦܢܝܐ Be-
kehrung, Neigung | conversion, inclination. || ܦܘܢܝܐ
Rückkehr, Antwort | return, answer.

ܦܢܛܣܝܐܣ φαντασίαι.

ܦܨܚܐ τὸ πάσχα.

ܦܣܩ *impf. u,* abschneiden | cut off. *Pa.* verstümmeln |
mutilate.

ܦܩ zerreiben, verkleinern | grind, crumble.

ܦܚܙܐ Schlucht | gulf, ravine.

ܦܨܝ *Pa.* erretten, befreien | save, deliver.

(ܦܨܚ) *Ethpe.* heiter sein | be cheerful. || ܦܨܚܐ Passah |
Passover.

ܦܩܕ, *impf. u et Pa.* befehlen | command. || ܦܩܘܕܐ *m.*
Anordner | commander. || ܦܘܩܕܢܐ *m.* Befehl | com-
mand.

ܦܩܚ nützlich, gut | useful, good.

ܦܩܥܬܐ *f.* Ebene | plain.

ܦܪܐ fruchtbar sein | be fruitful. *Aph.* hervorbringen |
bring forth. || ܦܐܪܐ *m.* Frucht | fruit. *Pl.* ܦܐܪ̈ܐ.

ܡܙܪܝܐ *f.*, *pl.* ܡܙܪ̈ܐ Korn | grain.

ܡܙܪܘܦܐ Umwurf, Mantel | cloak, mantle.

ܦܪܙܠܐ *m.* Eisen | iron.

ܨܦܪܐ *f.* Vogel | fowl. *Pl.* ܨܦܖ̈ܐ.

(ܡܛܐ) *Ethpa.* einen Weg suchen, überlegen | seek a way, deliberate. ‖ ܐܬܡܛܠܐ Rat, List | counsel, device. ‖ ܡܬܛܠܝܐ Versorgung | management, provision.

ܡܛܪܐ ἁπλωμα.

ܡܪܐ, *impf. u,* wiederherstellen, ersetzen, leisten | restore, replace, accomplish. *Ethpe. pass.*

ܡܪܘܩܐ *m.* Befreier, Erlöser | deliverer, saviour.

ܡܪܩ, *impf. u,* trennen, weggehen | separate, remove from, depart.

ܡܫܩ, *impf. u,* ausbreiten | spread, extend.

ܩܡܫ *Pa.* erwärmen | warm.

ܩܦܫ *Pa.* erklären | expound. *Ethpa. pass.* ܩܘܦܫܐ Erklärung, Deutung | exposition, interpretation.

ܩܡܪ, *impf. a,* schmelzen, kochen | melt, boil, πέπτω.

ܩܕܐ, ܩܕܐ *m.* Seite | side.

ܩܕܡܠܐ Wort, Ausspruch | word, sentence.

ܩܫܡ, *impf. a,* öffnen, erobern | open, conquer. *Ethpe.* geöffnet, aufgedeckt werden | be opened, uncovered.

ܩܡܪܐ (πάταχρα) Götzenbild | idol; de Lagarde, Mittheilungen 2, 354 n.

ܨ

ܨܒܐ wollen | wish, will. *Ethpe.* eifrig, begierig sein, begünstigen | be busy, anxious, favor. || ܨܒܘܬܐ *f.* Eifer, Ding, Sache | zeal, thing, cause. ܡܢ ܨܒܘܬ ܢܦܫܗ ἀφ᾽ ἑαυτῆς. || ܨܒܝܢܐ *m.* Wille | will.

ܨܒܥ, ܨܒܥܐ *f.* Finger | finger. *Pl.* ܨܒܥܐ et ܨܒܥܬܐ.

ܬܨܒܝܬܐ *m.* Schmuck | ornament.

ܨܕܥܐ Schläfe | temple; χρόταφος.

ܨܗܐ dürsten | be thirsty. || ܨܗܐ durstig | thirsty. || ܨܗܝܐ *m.* Durst | thirst.

ܨܘܒܐ Ankunft | arrival. || ܒܝܬ ܨܘܒܐ Versammlungsort | meeting-house.

ܨܕ jagen | hunt.

ܨܘܡܐ *m.* Fasten | fast.

ܨܪ malen | paint. || ܨܝܪܐ *m.* Maler | painter.

ܨܬ ausrufen, aufmerken | cry out, attend. || ܨܘܬܐ *m.* Geschrei | cry.

ܨܚܝ *Pa.* schmähen | revile.

ܨܝܕ *Praep.* bei, nach | at, with, up to. § 49 h.

ܨܠܐ neigen | incline. *Pa.* beten | pray. || ܨܠܘܬܐ *f.* Gebet | prayer.

ܨܠܒ, *impf.* *u,* aufhängen, kreuzigen | hang, crucify. *Ethpe. pass.* || ܨܠܝܒܐ 1) *adj.* der Gekreuzigte | crucified. 2) *subst.* Kreuz | cross. || ܨܠܘܒܐ Kreuziger | he who crucifies.

ܨܠܡ, ܨܠܡܐ *m.* Bild | likeness.

ܨܘܠܥܬܐ *f.* Wunde | wound. *Pl.* ܨܘܠܥܬܐ.

ܨܡܚܐ *m.* Glanz, Strahl | splendour, ray.

ܨܥܪ *Pa.* schmähen, Unrecht thun | despise, injure. || ܨܥܪܐ *m.* Verachtung | contempt.

ܨܦܪ, ܨܦܪܐ *m.* Morgendämmerung | dawn.

ܨܦܪ, ܨܦܪܐ *f.* Vogel | bird. *Pl.* ܨܦܪܐ.

ܨܨܐ *m.* Nagel | nail. *Pl.* ܨܨܐ.

ܨܪܐ spalten | rend asunder. *Ethpe.* gespalten werden | be rent.

ܩ

ܐܩܒܘܬܐ, ܩܒܘܬܐ ἡ κιβωτός (G. Hoffmann, ZDMG 32, 748 n. 1.)

ܩܒܠ, *impf. u,* entgegengehen | go to meet. *Pa.* annehmen, empfangen | receive, accept. (ܩܘܒܠ, ܩܘܒܠܐ Gegenseite | opposite side.) ܠܩܘܒܠܐ, *st. c.* ܠܩܘܒܠ gegenüber | over against. ܕܠܩܘܒܠܐ *et* ܩܘܒܠܝܐ, ܩܘܒܠܢܝܐ Gegner | opposed, hostile, enemy. || ܡܬܩܒܠܢܐ annehmbar | acceptable.

ܩܒܥ, *impf. u,* befestigen, fassen | fix, mount (with gold). *Ethpe. pass.*

ܩܒܪ, *impf. u,* begraben | bury. *Ethpe. pass.* || ܩܒܪܐ *m.*, ܩܒܪܬܐ *f.* Grab | tomb. || ܩܒܘܪܐ Begräbnis | burial. Cf. ܩܒܥ.

ܩܽܘܡ *m.* Scheitel | back of the head, top.

ܩܰܕܶܡ *Pa.* vorsetzen, zuvorkommen (*reddit* πρό *Graecorum*) | place at the head, prevent, anticipate. || ܡܶܢ ܩܕܺܝܡ von vorn, längst | from before, long ago. || ܩܕܳܡ *Praep.* vor | before. || ܩܕܳܡ ܕ ; ܡܶܢ ܩܕܳܡ ehe | before (*conj.*). || ܩܰܕܡܳܝܳܐ der frühere, erste | former, first. || ܩܕܳܡܳܝܳܐ der erste | the first. *Pl.* die Früheren und Oberen | those anterior and superior to us. || ܩܰܕܡܳܐܺܝܬ zuerst, zum erstenmal | at first, for the first time. || (ܩܕܳܡܘܳܬ) *cum* ܠ *adverb.* ܠܩܘܳܡܰܝ (cf. ܠܩܘܕܡ) zuerst | at first. ܡܶܢ ܠܩܘܕܡܰܝ vor langer Zeit | long ago.

ܩܰܕܶܫ *Pa.* heiligen | hallow. || ܩܰܕܺܝܫ heilig | holy. || ܩܽܘܕܫܳܐ, *abs. et cstr.* ܩܘܕܫ Heiligkeit | holiness.

ܩܰܘܺܝ *Pa.* bleiben, bestehen, dauern | abide, remain, last.

ܩܳܠܳܐ *m.* Stimme | voice. ܩܳܠܳܐ ܪܳܡܳܐ mit lauter Stimme | with a loud voice. ܩܳܠܳܐ ܨܰܝ v. ܨܝ.

ܩܡ aufstehen, bestehen | stand up. *Aph.* aufrichten, bestimmen | set up, appoint. || ܩܰܘܡܬܳܐ *f.* Statur, Stufe, Elle | stature, degree, cubit. || ܡܩܰܝܡܳܐ *m.* Vorstand | prefect. || ܩܝܳܡܬܳܐ *f.* Auferstehung | resurrection. || ܡܩܳܡܳܐ *m.*, Standort | stand, station.

ܩܶܡܛܪܳܐ *m.* Kanal, Teich | canal, channel, pond.

ܩܘܪܩܘܕܳܝܠܘܣ χορχόδειλος.

ܩܛܰܠ, *impf. u,* töten | kill. *Ethpe. pass. Pa.* morden | murder. || ܩܛܳܠܳܐ *m.* Morden | murder. || ܩܳܛܘܠܳܐ Mörder | murderer.

ܩܰܛܺܝܢ klein | thin, small.

ܡܚܐ, *impf. u et Pa.* abhauen, abschneiden | cut off.

ܩܛܝܪܐ *m. subst.* Gewalt | force. ܩܛܝܪ ܡܢ, ܒܩܛܝܪܐ mit
Gewalt | forcibly.

ܩܝܣܐ, ܩܝܣܐ *m.* Holz | wood.

ܩܝܬܪܐ κιϑάρα.

ܩܠܝܠ wenig, leicht, schnell | little, light, swift. *Etiam*
adv. ܩܠܝܠ ܩܠܝܠ εἰς μικρά.

ܩܠܛ verdrehen, verkehren | distort, pervert.

ܩܢܐ erwerben, besitzen | acquire, possess. ܩܢܐ begabt
mit | gifted with. ‖ ܩܢܝܢܐ *m.* Besitz, bes. an Vieh |
property, espec. cattle.

ܩܢܝܐ, ܩܢܝܐ *m.* Rohr | reed.

ܩܣܡܛܘܪܐ = αἰλάμ.

ܩܣܪ Caesar.

ܩܥܐ ausrufen | cry out. Cf. ܩܠܐ. ‖ ܩܥܬܐ *f.* Geschrei | cry.

ܡܩܦܣ zusammengezogen | restrained, drawn together.

ܩܦܝ verabreden | agree upon; *Ethpa. pass.*

ܩܪܐ rufen, nennen, lesen | call, name, read. *Ethpe.* ge-
nannt werden | be called.

ܩܪܝܐ cf. § 33, Dorf | village.

ܩܪܒ *impf. u,* sich nähern, streiten | come near, fight.
Pa. herbeibringen, darbringen | bring near, offer.
Ethpa. herbeikommen | approach. ‖ ܩܪܒܐ *m.* Streit,
Krieg | fight, war. ‖ ܩܘܪܒܢܐ *m.* Darbringung, Gabe |
offering, gift. ‖ ܩܪܝܒ nahe, benachbart | near, neigh-
bouring.

ܩܘܛܵܦܵܐ Unterbrechung der Rede | interruption of the speech.

ܩܲܪܢܵܐ, ܩܪܸܢ f. Horn | horn.

ܩܲܪܩܲܦܬܵܐ f. Schädel | scull.

ܩܫܹܐ schwer | hard. ܩܲܫܝܵܐܝܼܬ adv. hart, rauh, heftig | roughly, harshly. || ܩܲܫܝܘܼܬܵܐ f. Härte | harshness, cruelty.

ܩܲܫܝܼܫܵܐ alt, Presbyter | old, presbyter.

ܪ

ܐܪܵܙ, ܐܪܵܙܵܐ m. Geheimnis | mystery. Pl. ܐܪ̈ܵܙܹܐ (cf. de Lagarde, Agathangelus 138, 139). ܠܵܐ ܡܸܬܪܲܙܙܵܢܵܐ ἀμυσταγώγητος. F. pl. ܡܪ̈ܲܙܙܵܢ angedeutet | signified.

ܪܲܒ, ܐܪܲܒ gross | great. Pl. ܪܵܘܪ̈ܒܹܐ; ܪܵܘܪ̈ܒܵܢܹܐ Magnaten | the peers, grandees.

ܪܲܒ lärmen | make a noise. || ܪܵܘܒܵܐ Laut | sound. ܪܵܘܒ̇ܬܵܐ f. Lärm, Geräusch | noise, sound.

ܪܲܒܝ Pa. wachsen lassen, ernähren | cause to grow, nurse. || ܡܪ̈ܲܒܝܵܢܝܵܬܵܐ f. pl. Amme, Wärterinnen | nurse, attendant.

ܪܒܲܥ sich hinlegen | lie down. || ܡܲܪܒܥܵܐ f. Platz | place. || ܐܲܪܒܲܥ 4 § 33. || ܪܘܼܒܥܵܐ ein Viertel | a quarter.

ܪܵܓ wünschen | wish; impers. ܠܝܼ ܪܵܓ mir ist erwünscht | it is my wish. Ethpa. ܐܸܬܪܲܓܪܲܓ bestürzt sein | be confounded. || ܪܓܝܼܓ erwünscht, wünschenswert | desired, desirable. || ܪ̈ܓܝܼܓܵܬܵܐ f. pl. Vergnügungen | pleasures. || ܪܸܓܬܵܐ f. Begierde | desire.

ܪܓܙ zürnen | be angry. *Aph.* zum Zorn reizen | provoke to anger. ‖ ܪܓܝܙܐ zornig | angry.

ܪܓܠ, ܪܓܠܐ *f.* Fuss | foot.

ܪܓܡ steinigen | stone. *Ethpe. pass.* v. ܪܓܡ.

ܪܗܛ laufen, fliessen | run, flow.

ܪܕܦ, *impf. u,* verfolgen | pursue. *Ethpe. pass.*‖ ܪܕܘܦܝܐ *m.* Verfolgung | pursuit, persecution.

ܪܗܛ laufen | run. § 48 g, 7.

ܪܘܙ jubeln | rejoice. ‖ ܪܘܙܐ Jubel | joy.

ܪܘܚ, ܪܘܚܐ *c.* Wind, Geist | wind, spirit. ‖ ܪܝܚܐ *m.* Ausdünstung, Geruch | scent, smell.

ܪܡ hoch sein | be high. ‖ ܐܪܝܡ erhöhen | elevate. *Aph.* aufheben, erheben | lift up. *Ethpe.* erhaben werden | be lofty. ‖ ܪܡ *adj.* hoch | high. ‖ ܪܘܡܐ *f.* Höhe | height. ‖ ܡܪܝܡܐ der höchste | the highest.

ܪܘܩܐ Speichel | spittle.

ܪܚܡ lieben | love. ‖ ܪܚܡ ܟܚܗܐ gottliebend | loving God. ‖ ܪܚܡܐ *m.* Freund | friend. ‖ ܪܚܡܐ *pl.* Barmherzigkeit | mercy.‖ ܡܪܚܡܢܘܬܐ do. ‖ ܡܪܚܡܢ barmherzig | merciful. ‖ ܪܚܡܐ *f.* Liebe, Wohlwollen | love, kindness. ‖ ܪܚܡܐ freundlich | friendly. ‖ ܪܚܝܡܐ *act.;* ܪܚܝܡܐ *pass.*

ܪܦܫ *Pa.* die Flügel ausbreiten, brüten | spread the wing, brood.

ܪܚܩ ferne, abwesend | far away, absent. ‖ ܪܘܚܩܐ *m.* Entfernung | distance.

ܪܫ kriechen | creep. *Aph.* hervorbringen | bring forth. ‖ ܪܚܫܐ *coll.* kriechendes Getier | every creeping thing.

ܪܫ, ܪܫܐ *m.* Kopf, Kapitel | head, chapter. ܡܫܚܪ ܪܝܫܐ v. ܡܫܚ. ‖ ܪܝܫܝܐ erst, best | first, best. ‖ ܪܝܫܢܐ *m.* Vor-steher | head of an institution. ‖ ܪܝܫܢܘܬܐ *f.* Führerschaft | leadership. ‖ ܪܫܝܐ, Nestor. ܪܫܝܬܐ (Ge, 1, 1. Joh. 1, 1) Anfang | beginning. ܡܢ ܒܪܫܝܬ von Anfang (der Welt) an | from the beginning (of the world).

ܪܩܝܩ sanft, weich | smooth, tender. ‖ ܪܩܝܩܐܝܬ *adv.* all-mählich | by degrees.

ܪܩܩ *Pa.* mischen | mingle, mix. ‖ ܪܘܩܩܐ Mischung | mix-ture. ‖ ܪܩܘܒܬܐ *f.* Wagen | chariot.

ܪܡܐ werfen | throw. *Part. pass.* ܪܡܐ hingestreckt | stretched out. *Aph.* hinwerfen | throw down.

ܪܡܙܐ *m.* Wink, Anzeichen | hint, sign. ‖ ܪܡܙܢܝܐ anzeigend | signifying.

ܪܢܐ denken | think. *Ethpe.* überlegen, besorgt sein | consider, be anxious.

ܪܥܐ weiden | feed. ‖ ܪܥܝܐ, ܪܥܝܐ *pl.* ܪܥܘܬܐ Hirte | shepherd. ‖ ܪܥܝܢܐ *m.* Sinn | meaning. ‖ ܬܪܥܝܬܐ *f.* Meinung, Ge-danke | opinion, thought.

ܪܥܡ *et Ethpe.* donnern | thunder. ‖ ܪܥܡܐ donner | thunder.

ܪܦܐ, ܪܦܦ ܪܘܦܐ ‗ Krokodil | crocodile.

ܪܩܝܥܐ, ܪܩܝܥܐ *m.* Firmament | firmament.

ܪܫܐ tadeln, vorwerfen | blame, accuse.

ܪܫܡ, *impf.* u, zeichnen, bezeichnen | mark, indicate. ‖
ܪܘܫܡܐ *m.* Zeichen | mark.

ܪܫܥ *Aph.* freveln | be wicked. ‖ ܪܫܝܥܐ Frevler | wicked
person. ‖ ܪܘܫܥܐ *m.* Frevel | offence, wickedness.

ܪܕܐ *Aph.* den Weg zeigen, ermahnen | show the way,
exhort. ܡܪܕܝܢܐ χατηχήτης. ‖ ܡܪܕܝܢܘܬܐ *f.* χατήχησις. ‖
ܡܬܪܕܝܢܐ χατηχούμενος.

ܪܬܡ stottern | stammer.

ܫ · ...

ܫܐܕܐ *m.* Teufel | demon, devil.

ܫܐܠ fragen, bitten | ask, request. ‖ ܫܠܡܐ ܫܐܠ grüssen |
greet. *Pa.* sich erkundigen | inquire. *Ethpa.* er-
forscht werden | be examined. ‖ ܫܐܠܬܐ *f.* Frage,
Wunsch | question, wish.

ܫܝܢ *Pa.* Friede schaffen | make peace. ‖ ܫܝܢܐ, ܫܝܢܐ *m.*
Friede, Ruhe | peace, quietness. ‖ ܡܫܝܢܢܐ Friede
schaffend | peace-making; λαιός.

ܫܒܝܐ *m. et* ܫܒܝܬܐ *f.* Gefangenschaft | exile.

ܫܒܚ *Pa.* loben | praise. *Ethpa. pass.* (v. de Lagarde,
novae psalterii graeci editionis specimen, p. 35, ult.). ‖
ܫܒܝܚ rühmenswert | worthy of praise. ‖ ܫܘܒܚܐ *m.*
Lob, Ehre | praise, glory; δόξα. (v. ܐܝܩܪ). ‖ ܬܫܒܘܚܬܐ *f.*
Lob, Ehre, Hymnus | praise, glory, hymn. ‖ ܡܫܒܚܐܝܬ
adv. herrlich | gloriously. ‖ ܡܫܒܚܐܝܬ do.

ܫܰܒܛܳܐ *m.* Stock, Scepter, Stamm | rod, sceptre, tribe.

ܫܒܰܥ 7, § 33. || ܫܒܘܽܥܬܳܐ *f., pl.* ܫܒܘܽܥܶܐ Woche | week.

ܫܒܰܩ, *impf.* u, verlassen, nachlassen | leave, desert, pardon. || ܫܒܺܝܩܬܳܐ *f.* die Geschiedene | she that is divorced. || ܫܘܽܒܩܳܢܳܐ *m.* Verzeihung | pardon.

ܫܰܒܪܳܐ *m.* Kind | child. || ܫܰܒܪܬܳܐ *f.* Mädchen | girl.

ܫܰܒܶܬ *Aph.* Sabbat feiern | keep sabbath. || ܫܰܒܬܳܐ *f., pl.* ܫܰܒܶܐ Sabbat, Woche | sabbath, week. *Etiam* ܫܰܒܳܐ *m. sg.*

ܫܓܰܫ, *impf.* u, stören, verwirren | trouble, disturb. *Ethpe. pass. Pa.* erregen | excite.

ܫܕܳܐ werfen | throw. *Ethpe. pass.*

ܫܕܰܪ *Pa.* schicken | send. *Ethpa. pass.* || ܡܫܰܕܪܳܢܳܐ *m.* Gesandter | messenger.

ܫܘܳܐ (ܗܘܐ) gleich, würdig sein | be equal, worthy. *Ethpe.* für würdig gehalten werden | be found worthy. *Aph.* für würdig halten | find worthy. || ܫܰܘܝܳܐܝܬ *adv.* gleichmässig, zugleich | equally, likewise.

ܫܘܳܐ *v.* ܫܘܳܐ.

ܫܘܽܥܳܐ *m.* Fels | rock.

ܫܘܽܪܳܐ *m.* Mauer | wall. || ܫܳܪ ܫܳܪ *v.* ܫܘܽܪ.

ܫܘܫܶܦ *v.* ܫܘܫܶܦ. || ܫܰܚܠܶܦ *v.* ܚܠܰܦ.

ܫܘܽܢܩܳܐ *m.* Druck, Qual, Folter | pressure, torment, torture.

ܫܰܚܰܪ *Pa.* zum Botendienst nötigen | compel to go (as messenger). | *v.* ܐܚܰܪ.

ܫܚܺܝܢ *Aph.* täuschen | deceive.

ܫܰܚܶܢ *v.* ܚܶܡ, ܫܝܘܽܠܬܳܐ *v.* ܫܝܘܽܠܬܳܐ.

ܐܫܟܚ finden, auffinden, können | find, find out, be able. *Ethpe.* gefunden werden | be found. || ܡܫܟܚ gefunden | found. || ܡܫܟܚܬܐ *f.* Auffindung | invention.

ܡܫܟܢ, ܡܫܟܢܐ *m.* Wohnung | habitation, dwelling.

ܫܟܒ ruhen | rest.

ܫܠܐ aufhören, ausruhen | cease, rest. || ܫܠܝܐ, ܫܠܝܐ Ruhe | rest. ܡܢ ܫܠܝ, ܡܢ ܫܠܝܐ *et* ܡܢܬܫܠܝ plötzlich | suddenly. || ܕܠܐ ܫܠܝ ohne Aufhören | without ceasing. (de Lagarde, Symmicta 2, 100.)

ܫܠܕܐ (σκελετόν?) Leichnam | dead body, corpse.

ܫܠܡܘܢܐ v. ܫܠܡ.

ܫܠܝܚ ausgezogen, nackt | bare, naked. || ܫܠܝܚܐ *m.* *subst.* Apostel | apostle.

ܫܠܛ, *impf.* u, herrschen | rule. *Ethpa.* Herr werden, siegen | become master, overcome. || ܫܘܠܛܢܐ *m.* Herrschaft | dominion.

ܫܠܡ, *impf.* a, vollständig sein, zusammenstimmen | be complete, agree; *explicit.* *Ethpe.* überliefert werden | be delivered. *Pa.* vollenden, erfüllen | finish, fulfill. *Aph.* überliefern | deliver, hand down. ||

ܫܠܡܐ *m.* Friede | peace. || ܫܘܠܡܐ *m.* Vollendung, Ende | completion, end. || ܠܫܘܠܡܐ für immer | for ever. || ܡܫܠܡܢܘܬܐ *f.* Verrat, Überlieferung | treachery, tradition.

ܫܡ, ܫܡܐ *m.*, *pl.* ܫܡܗܐ Name | name. || ܫܡܗ nennen |

call. *Ethpe.* genannt werden | be called. ‖ ܡܶܫܬ̇ܡܰܗ berühmt | famous.

ܫܡܰܝܳܐ Himmel | heaven. § 28 c.

ܫܳܡܽܘܢܳܐ Heller | farthing.

ܫܰܡܺܝܢ fett | fat.

ܫܡܰܥ, *impf.* a, hören | hear. *Ethpe. pass.* ‖ ܫܳܡܽܘܥܳܐ *m.* Hörer | hearer. ‖ ܫܶܡܥܬ̇ܳܐ *et* ܫܶܡܥܳܐ das Hören | the hearing.

ܫܰܡܰܥ *Pa.* hineinlassen, hineinschicken | let in, send in.

ܫܰܡܶܫ *Pa.* dienen | serve. ‖ ܬܶܫܡܶܫܬܳܐ *f.* Dienst | service.

ܫܶܡܫܳܐ Sonne | sun.

ܫܶܢ, ܫܶܢܳܐ *f.*, *Pl.* ܫܶܢ̈ܐ Zahn | tooth. ‖ ܫܶܢܳܐ *m.* Schärfe | sharpness.

ܫܶܢܬܳܐ, ܫܶܢ̈ܳܬ̣ܳܐ, *f.*, *st. cstr.* ܫܶܢܰܬ Schlaf | sleep. (*V* ܫܶܢ.)

ܫܰܢܺܝ *Pa.* bewegen, entfernen, (aus dem Leben) scheiden | move, remove, depart (this life).

ܫܰܢܬܳܐ, ܫܰܢܬܳܐ *f.* Jahr | year. ‖ *Pl.* ܫܢ̈ܝܢ, ܫܢ̈ܝܳܐ.

(ܫܢܩ) *Ethpa.* gefoltert werden (foltern) | be tortured (torture). ‖ ܫܽܘܢܳܩܳܐ *m.* Folter | torture.

ܫܰܢܶܩ *Pa.* foltern | torture. ‖ ܫܽܘܢܳܩܳܐ *et* ܬܶܫܢܺܝܩܳܐ Würgen, Erdrosseln, Foltern | strangling, torture.

(ܫܥܐ) *Ethpa.* durch Reden erfreuen, erzählen | gladden, recite. ‖ ܬܶܫܥܺܝܬ̣ܳܐ *f.* Geschichte | history.

ܫܳܥܬܳܐ, ܫܳܥܬ̣ܳܐ *f.* Stunde | hour. ‖ *Pl.* ܫܳܥ̈ܐ; ܫܥܳܐ *v.* ܫܥܐ.

ܚܨ *v.* ܡܚܨܡ

ܥܡܠ arbeiten | labour.

ܕܟܝܘܬܐ f. Reinheit, Lauterkeit | purity.

ܥܩܠ Pa. drücken, demütigen | oppress, humble.

ܫܦܪ schön sein, gut machen | be beautiful, do well. ||
ܫܦܝܪ schön | beautiful.

(ܫܩܐ) Aph. tränken, bewässern | give to drink, irrigate.

ܫܩܠ, impf. u, (weg-)tragen | bear (away). || ܫܩܠ ܝܨܦܐ
Sorgo tragen | take care, see to it that. || ܫܩܠܐ
tragend | bearing. Ethpe. weggetragen, weggeführt
werden | be carried off.

ܣܘܩܦܐ Ohrfeige | box on the ear, chastisement.

ܫܪ Ethpa. versichert sein | be assured. || ܫܪܪܐ m. Wahr-
heit | truth. || ܫܪܝܪ wahr, fest | true, firm. || ܫܪܝܪܐܝܬ
adv. sicher | certainly.

ܫܪܐ auflösen, entlassen, weilen, wohnen | loosen, dis-
miss, abide, stay. Ethpe. befreit werden | be de-
livered. Pa. anfangen | begin. || ܫܪܝܐ m. Auflösung |
solution. || ܫܘܪܝܐ m. Anfang | beginning. || ܫܪܘܬܐ f.
Essen | meal. || ܡܫܪܝܐ Lager | camp. || ܫܝܦܘܪܐ Trom-
peten | trumpets.

ܫܪܒܬܐ f. Stamm, Familie | tribe, family.

ܫܪܓܐ Licht | light.

ܫܪܟܐ m. Rest | rest; "ܣܘ etc.

ܫܝܫܠܬܐ et "ܫܫܠܬܐ f., pl. ܫܫܠܬܐ Kette | chain.

ܫܬ 6 § 33.

Nestle.

ܐܫܬܝ, *impf.* ܢܫܬܐ trinken | drink. ‖ ܡܫܬܝܐ, ܡܫܬܝܢ *m.*
Gelage | banquet.

ܫܬܐܣܬܐ *pl.* ܫܬܐܣܐ Fundament | foundation.

ܫܘܬܦ mitteilen | communicate. ‖ ܐܫܬܘܬܦ teilhaben |
participate. ‖ ܫܘܬܦܐ *m.* Genosse | companion. ‖ ܫܘܬܦܘܬܐ
Gemeinschaft | communion, fellowship.

ܫܬܩ *impf.* u schweigen | be silent.

—

ܬ

ܬܐܢܬܐ, ܬܬܐ Feigenbaum | figtree. *Pl.* ܬܐܢܐ, de Lagarde,
Mittheilungen 1, 58.

ܬܒܥ, *impf.* u, suchen | seek. ‖ *Ethpe pass.* ܬܒܥܬܐ *f.*
Untersuchung, Frage | investigation, question.

ܬܪܐ, ܬܪܐ *m.* Kraut | green herbs (דֶּשֶׁא).

ܬܗܘܡܐ *m.* Tiefe | depth.

ܬܗܪ sich wundern | wonder.

ܬܘܒ *adv.* wiederum | again. ‖ ܬܝܒܘܬܐ *f.* Bekehrung.
Reue | conversion, penitence.

ܬܘܗ h. תוח.

ܬܘܪܐ *m.* Stier | bull. ‖ ܬܘܪܬܐ *f.* Kuh | cow.

ܬܚܘܡܐ *m.* Grenze | border, frontier.

ܬܚܝܬ, ܬܚܘܬ et ܬܚܬ *Praep.* unter | under (§ 49h).
ܬܚܬ ܡܢ. ‖ ܬܚܬܝܐ der untere | the lower.

ܬܟܣ v. ܟܣܐ.

ܬܟܝܠ vertrauend | trusting.

ܥܕܠ Vorwürfe machen | rebuke.

ܬܠܐ aufhängen | hang. *Ethpe. pass.*

ܚܣܡ v. ܥܬܚܣܡܐ.

ܬܠܬ 3 § 33. || ܬܠܝܬܝܘܬܐ *f.* Dreiheit, Dreieinigkeit | trinity.

ܬܡܗܐ *m.* Bewunderung | admiration. || ܬܡܝܗ bewundernswert | admirable.

ܬܡܢ *adv.* dort | there.

ܬܡܢܝܐ 8 § 33.

ܬܡܪܐ Augenbrauen | eye-brow; v. ܚܕܦ.

ܬܢ *et Ethpe.* rauchen | smoke.

ܬܢܝܢ *m.* Seeungeheuer | sea-monster; χῆτος.

ܬܢܐ wiederholen | repeat. *Pa.* erzählen | narrate. || ܬܢܝܢܐ zweit | second.

ܬܘܩܠܬܐ *f.* Fallstrick | snare.

ܬܩܢ, *impf.* a, stehen, fest sein | stand,. be firm. *Pa.* feststellen, ordnen | fix, order.

ܬܩܝܢ 2 § 33.

ܬܪܓܡ erklären, übersetzen | expound, translate. *Ethpa. pass.*

ܬܪܥ, ܬܪܥܐ *m.* Thüre | door.

ܬܪܝܨ gerade, recht | upright, straight. || ܬܪܝܨܐܝܬ *adv.* recht | right. || ܬܪܝܨ ܫܘܒܚܐ ὀρθόδοξος.

ܬܫܥ 9 § 33.

Printed by W. Drugulin, Leipzig.